Concerning Architecture

Concerning Architecture

H · R · HITCHCOCK

PHOEBE STANTON ✳ MARK GIROUARD

FRANK JENKINS Essays on MAURICE CRAIG

J · M · RICHARDS Architectural JOHN FLEMING

HUGH CASSON Writers and Writing JOHN PIPER

J · MORDAUNT CROOK presented to ALEC CLIFTON-TAYLOR

H · M · COLVIN Nikolaus Pevsner JOHN HARRIS

R · D · MIDDLETON edited by BASIL F · L · CLARKE

P · FERRIDAY John Summerson S · LANG

KERRY DOWNES ✳ PAUL THOMPSON

REYNER BANHAM

PENGUIN BOOKS · BALTIMORE

PENGUIN BOOKS INC., 7110 AMBASSADOR ROAD,
BALTIMORE, MARYLAND 21207
THIS EDITION FIRST PUBLISHED IN THE U.S.A.
BY PENGUIN BOOKS INC. IN 1968
COPYRIGHT © ALLEN LANE THE PENGUIN PRESS 1968
LIBRARY OF CONGRESS CATALOGUE CARD
NUMBER 68-55287

PRINTED IN GREAT BRITAIN
THE TEXT BY THE CAMBRIDGE UNIVERSITY PRESS
THE PLATES BY W. S. COWELL, IPSWICH
BOUND BY MANSELL, LONDON N I
DESIGNED BY HANS SCHMOLLER

THE EDITOR TO NIKOLAUS PEVSNER

My dear Nikolaus,

Here, for your birthday, is a collection of essays composed for you by some of your friends. All are about writers and writings concerned with architecture, across three hundred years. The collection has, therefore, something of the character of a family album – the family of writers, past and present, who have been and are dedicated and industrious observers of architectural fabrics, inquiring into the how, why, and when of fabrics; the art, philosophy, and craft of fabrics; and the mystery of fabrics considered in the mesh of time. We, members of that family, salute you as a very excellent brother. We honour you for what you have achieved among us and in the world at large and wish you all happiness.

Yours ever,
JOHN

London, January 1967

List of Contents

LIST OF CONTENTS

Aubrey's *Chronologia Architectonica*

BY H. M. COLVIN

W<small>HEN</small> Eastlake set out to write the history of the Gothic Revival, he began, quite rightly, by devoting a good deal of space to the historians and antiquaries of the seventeenth and eighteenth centuries. For it was they who created that awareness of the medieval past without which no revival of its architecture would have been possible, and it was they too who provided illustrations of abbeys, castles, and funeral monuments for Georgian architects to translate into churches, villas, and chimney-pieces. But, as Eastlake noted, 'an interval occurred between the works of Dugdale and Dodsworth, of Herbert and Wood, on the one side, and those of Grose, Bentham, Hearne, and Gough, on the other – between the men who recorded the history of Mediaeval buildings in England, and the men who attempted to illustrate them'.[1] Dugdale's works were, of course, embellished by Hollar's engravings, but these were for the most part views of a general kind, often unreliable in matters of detail, and well over a century elapsed before men like Carter, Capon, Pugin, and Blore began making measured drawings of specific architectural features which could serve as exemplars for the Gothic Revivalists. The gap was filled, after a fashion, by the views of the brothers Buck, whose amateurish engravings constituted – then as now – the only record of many a ruined castle or mouldering abbey. But neither Buck's views, nor those of other Georgian topographers such as Stukeley, provided an adequate basis for the serious study of Gothic architecture, nor was there, as yet, much interest in Gothic as a style of architecture with its own historical evolution. For most educated men it was, in the words of Roger North, 'a mode introduct by a barbarous sort of people, that first distrest then dissolved the Roman Empire'.[2] 'The Goths', wrote Sir John Clerk of Penicuik,

were those barbarous nations from the north of Europe, who overspread Italy and ruin'd the Roman Empire. They likewise broke and destroyd all monuments of antiquity, statues

1. C. L. Eastlake, *A History of the Gothic Revival* (1872), p. 42.
2. Roger North, 'Of Building' (B.M., Add. MS. 32540), f. 31.

I

& ornaments of all kinds which fell in their way. They introduced a bad manner not only in Architectory but in all other arts & sciences. We have been for upwards of 200 years endeavouring to recover ourselves from this Gothicism. Yet there still are too many amongst us whose bad taste neither example nor precept will ever rectify & therefore are to be left to themselves. For Goths will always have a Gothic taste.[1]

There could be no point in studying the architecture of such barbarians. Clerk, like Horace Walpole, had 'no curiosity to know how awkward and clumsy men have been in the dawn of arts, or in their decay'.[2] For him the only past that was worth investigating was that of the ancient world, and he was (in the words of his friend Sandy Gordon) all out for the 'Extirpation of *Gothicism*, Ignorance and a bad Taste'.[3]

Despite the stigma of barbarism which thus attached to it, Gothic architecture drew reluctant admiration from those who could appreciate its technical daring. 'To do those good men who built our churches right', says Roger North,

I must . . . profess that in the ordinance of walls and abbutment they have done as much as is possible, to make the stone & lime work its utmost, and that now we have not any that will venture to set such weight upon so small support, and I question whether they are able, or have the skill they had to calculate those propositions. To give one instance, there is the cathedrall of Salisbury . . . There is nothing in appearance to support the tower but 4 uprights, and the weight is prodigious. But observing it with some curiosity, I found abbutments wrought very cunningly in the walls and severall ways by 2 half arches, the uppermost resting upon the 2d pillar from the tower, and the undermost upon the next to it. These two arching abuttments appear in crossing the windoes next to the tower, so that at seting on the tower hath a very broad support otherwise it were impossible it should stand.

He also found much to admire in King's College Chapel, a building 'wonderfully thought & executed, the abuttment being small, & the roof broad & massy', while at Gloucester he 'never saw anything neater then some of their monachal cloysters'. What attracted him particularly at Gloucester was the fan-vaulting, which he thought 'admirably pretty' and even superior, for its purpose, to 'Regular' (i.e. classical) vaulting.

Having got so far, North found it 'no unpleasant thing to observe the cours of proceeding in that sort of building which prevailed in our nation, till almost King James the first' – in other words to trace the history of English Gothic. 'Now [he continues] I give three periods, exemplified in the building of the respective times.' The first, 'seen in the church of Durham', he attributed to the period before the Danish invasions.

1. The passage forms one of the notes to Clerk's unpublished poem, 'The Country Seat' (1727), the MS. of which is among the Clerk of Penicuik papers deposited in the Register House, Edinburgh.
2. *Letters of Horace Walpole*, ed. Toynbee, x (1904), p. 313 (to Wm. Cole, 1 September 1778).
3. Quoted by Stuart Piggott, 'The Ancestors of Jonathan Oldbuck', *Antiquity*, XXIX (1955), p. 152. Cf. the well-known remarks of Evelyn in his *Account of Architects and Architecture* (1706), p. 9.

2

The order is round upright lumps for columnes, with perfect semi-circular arches . . . derived from the Greek & Roman Regular columnes, but for want of art, and learning . . . so rudely executd as we see. But devious from the right as it is, none can deny but it bears not onely an air of grandeur, but hath a strength and reasonableness . . . such as an extraordinary high spirited judicious Barbarian, might be supposed originally to invent . . . This Round work lastd to the inroads of the Danes, the next order was the birdsey arch & diagonall columne[1] which I propose lasted to the Edwards' time, and then a still finer sort of building came in, which is exemplified in the cathedrall of New Sarum, which church for the area of it, I believ stands upon the least support of any in the world. It is all of one order, and instead of the diagonall thredded columns it is composed of rounds, whereof one is the midle, and four about it much smaller, upon which the thredds of the arches fall, & are therefore diagonall to the rang. This conceipt is taken from the Temple Church in London, which is more ancient, but its columnes are four rounds consolidated . . . There are the 3 periods of the Gothick building, which is now expired in the world, & the Regular taken from old ruins, & books succeeds it.[2]

Despite the acuteness of some of his observations, Roger North was, of course, as wrong in his dating as he was confused in his attempt at stylistic analysis. In a letter to the Dean of Westminster his contemporary, Nicholas Hawksmoor, came somewhat nearer the mark in distinguishing between the round-arched Romanesque, which he recognized as 'the most Antient style in the Gothick or Monastick manner', the pointed Gothic of Henry III's time (exemplified in the Abbey), and the later manner 'which is what the ingenious Masons call Tracery'.[3] But his chronology was vague (he thought St Albans Abbey Church was the work of King Offa), and it was not until 1763 that anything like a correct historical analysis of English Gothic appeared in print as part of Thomas Warton's *Observations on Spenser's Faerie Queene*. Fifty years of antiquarian investigation followed before in 1817 Rickman produced the definitive classification of styles which remained in use throughout the nineteenth century. The importance of Rickman's work was to propound an evolutionary sequence of forms whose logic was so compelling that there could be no doubt as to its essential correctness. Much remained to be done before the history of medieval English architecture was fully understood (especially in its relationship to French prototypes), but Rickman's *Attempt* provided the basic stylistic chronology without which no medieval church could make historical sense.

A century and a half before Rickman, a hundred years before Warton, another treatise on English Gothic had been written by a man whose contribution to the

---

1. In another passage North indicates that this was the style in which Westminster Abbey was built.

2. 'Of Building', op. cit., ff. 31–5, 70–1.

3. K. Downes, *Hawksmoor* (1959), Appendix A, No. 147. Compare Wren's observations on the same subject in *Parentalia*, ed. S. Wren (1750), pp. 297, 306–7.

subject has never been generally recognized.[1] The name of John Aubrey (d. 1697) is well known to prehistorians for his *Natural History of Wiltshire* and for his un-published *Monumenta Britannica*, works in which he laid the foundations of British field-archaeology. Less well known is the original manuscript of the *Monumenta*, now in the Bodleian Library.[2] It is divided into four parts, the first (*Templa Druidum*) dealing with prehistoric monuments, especially Avebury and Stonehenge, the second with Roman remains, the third with barrows, pottery, earthworks, and burials, and the fourth with a variety of antiquarian topics including heraldry, paleography, the history of prices, and the history of dress. It is in this fourth section that we find the *Chronologia Architectonica*, a treatise of some fifty pages written, it appears, chiefly in the 1670s.[3] Like all Aubrey's works, it is half a collection of notes, half a connected essay. On the title-page there is a direction to the printer to 'begin to print this Treatise at page 31', and here we find some cursory remarks about Roman archi-tecture in Britain, followed by an account of its degeneration 'into what we call Gothick, by the inundation of the Goths'. This 'barbarous fashion [he goes on] continued till Henry 7th of England about which time the old Roman Architecture began to be revived in Italie, by Palladio'.

'Twas first revived in England, in the time of King Edward the sixth. Seymour Duke of Somerset Ld Protector of England, sent for Architects & workmen out of Italie who built Somerset House in the Strand, and that august House of Longleate in Wiltshire, which is great enough to receive the King's Court: it is 3 stories high (above the stately vaults under ground) adorned with Doriq, Ioniq and Corinthian pillars, leaded on the top. The first Tombe that I have seen of Roman Architecture is Bishop Gardiner's in the Cathedral Church at Winchester: and at this time the Clavies, or mantle-pieces of Chimneys were Ioniq, or Corinthian Cornices, which about that time generally came in vouge. In Queen Elizabeth's time Architecture made no growth: but rather went backwards: great wide win-dows which were not only cold, but weakned the Fabriq. Burleigh-House and Audeley-end were the two best piles of her raigne. Earl of Salisbury's [at] Hatfield was built *tempore* Jac. I.

The next step of Roman Architecture was the New Exchange in the Strand, which was surveyed by Mr. Inigo Jones, and after that, A° Dni 16   [4] was that magnificent building

1. It was, however, appreciated by John Britton (see his *Memoir of John Aubrey*, 1845, p. 3), and more recently Professor Stuart Piggott has briefly indicated the significance of Aubrey's work on Gothic architecture in his essay on 'Antiquarian Thought' in *English Historical Scholarship in the Sixteenth and Seventeenth Centuries*, ed. L. Fox (1956), p. 109.

2. MS. Top. Gen. c. 25, ff. 152–79. I am indebted to Professor R. J. C. Atkinson for his kindness in lending me a photostat of the MS. Professor Atkinson has in preparation a critical edition of the *Monumenta*.

3. The date 1671 appears on the intended title-page, but passages in the text bear various dates from 1656 (f. 153^v) to 1672 (f. 156), and on the first page there is a reference to Wood's *Antiquities of Oxford*, which was not published until 1674. On f. 166 there are notes, obviously added later, about architectural changes under James II and William III. It is clear, therefore, that the MS. is a composite work of various dates.

4. This and the next date are left incomplete in the MS.

4

of the Banquetting House at White-Hall, built by King James I with the £10,000 which the City of London was fined, for the Prentices killing Dr. Lamb in the streetes for a conjurer, which was donne by Mr. Inigo Jones his Majestie's surveyor and is so exquisite a piece, that if all the Books of Architecture were lost, the true art of Building might be retrived thence. The Hall and Staire-cases of Greenwich &c. there, were also of Mr. Inigo Jones surveying. But the stateley new Building by the Thames side there, was donne by Mr. Webb surveyor to King Charles II, Aº Dni 166 and since that, the old Roman fashion is become the common mode.

As a brief history of the progress of English classical architecture during the previous century this is by no means bad. Almost every significant building is mentioned and the perspicacity of the remark about Elizabethan architecture going backwards will not be lost on those who have read Dr Mark Girouard's paper on 'Elizabethan Architecture and the Gothic Tradition'.[1] Elsewhere we find further scattered notes about Elizabethan and Jacobean architecture, including a sketch of two sorts of sixteenth-century window-mouldings, an anecdote about Queen Elizabeth at Burghley ('Will,' she said to Lord Treasurer Burghley, 'thy witt and my money have made a stately House'), and an interesting characterization of the architecture of Northumberland House as 'Ditterling (as they call it)'.[2] John Evelyn (to whom the manuscript was evidently lent) initials various additional observations of his own, including an aside about the Queen's House at Greenwich being built 'like a pair of panniers for the sake of the high way very foolishly'. None of this – least of all the conventional remarks about the Goths – prepares us for the main body of the treatise, which is nothing less than an attempt to establish the chronology of English medieval architecture. The enterprise was one in which (remembering that Aubrey was a Fellow of the Royal Society) we can recognize the influence of contemporary scientific thought. For its purpose was to classify and to compare, and classification and comparison were both features of the new 'experimental philosophy' to which the Royal Society was dedicated. The method was to find examples of window-tracery and other characteristic details to which a date could be attached, if possible by documentary evidence, to sketch them in diagrammatic fashion, and then to arrange the sketches in chronological order so as to establish a continuous sequence. For information about buildings and documents Aubrey was able to turn to his many learned and antiquarian friends. On the very first page we find a memorandum of a conversation about freemasons which Aubrey had had with Wren and Dugdale and a note that Bishop Seth Ward had told him that 'the Bull for the building our Ladies church at Salisbury is (or was) in the Archives of that church'.

1. *Architectural History*, VI (1963). See also Dr Girouard's essay in the present volume, p. 14.

2. In his *Natural History of Surrey* Aubrey mentions 'a handsome Ditterling gate' at Byfleet (*Surrey Archaeological Collections*, L, 1946–7, p. 102). He was, of course, referring to the style of the German Wendel Dietterlin.

Elsewhere Dr Plot informs him that at Dover there is 'a good deale of Roman build-ing', while Sir Thomas Browne 'affirmes to me, that the Cathedrall Church at Norwich, was built tempore Willelmi Rufi; the arches there are semi-circular, and so at the Castle'. Sir Thomas Browne is also the source of information about tombs of Saxon kings supposed to be at Blythburgh in Suffolk. 'I wish', Aubrey writes, 'I could have had the leisure to have gone thither, quaere somebody, what kind of architecture there.'

Luckily one rich source of information was easily available in Wood's recently published *Antiquities of Oxford*. Here Aubrey 'found in what King's reigne & yeare of the Lord such or such part of a College was built'. It was at Oxford that the main body of the manuscript was written,[1] and Oxford buildings figure prominently among the drawings. First we have a two-light Romanesque window 'at the Checquer-Inne in Oxford, heretofore Kempe-hall', and an early Gothic one in the tower of St Giles's church, supposed by Aubrey to have been built *tempore regis Stephani* [2] (Plate 1). Then there is a fully developed Gothic window in the chapel at Wood-stock Manor, rightly compared with Henry III's work at Westminster Abbey, another with intersecting tracery from St Mary's tower, and a third, with reticulated tracery, from St Aldate's church (Plate 2). The second is wrongly ascribed to the late fifteenth century (the date, as Aubrey knew, when the body of the church was rebuilt), the last correctly to the year 1335, when it was commissioned by Sir John of Ducklington.[3] Merton, Magdalen, All Souls, Corpus, and Christ Church all contribute dated examples to Aubrey's *corpus*, and there is a valuable sketch of the moulded plinth of 'the magnificent chapelle or cathedral intended by Cardinal Wolsey, which did runne from the College to the Blew-bore-Inne; and was pulled downe by Bishop Fell, about 1671' (Plate 4). Other examples were derived from London (Westminster Abbey, Westminster Hall, Old St Paul's, St Bartholomew Smithfield, Clifford's Inn), from his native Wiltshire (Kington St Michael, Bishop's Lavington, Devizes), from Herefordshire, the county from which the Aubreys sprang (Abbey Dore, Wigmore, Goodrich and Penyard Castles, Hereford Cathedral), from Somer-set (Wells), Sussex (Battle Abbey), Winchester, and Norwich. But in almost every case he went on to note the existence of similar windows elsewhere. 'The arches of this church of St. Marie's [at Devizes] are of the fashion in the margent: and likewise some of the windowes of the Tower' we read on folio 154. A memorandum then draws our attention to the east window of Wimborne Minster, which is 'like those of Sarum Castle, but ha[s] a great deal of moulding. The west end of Hereford Minster is just such work as at Winburne...The other windowes of that church are of later

---

1. 'I writt this at Oxford & left it with Mr. Anth. Wood.' The introductory essay was written 'at London, not having the other part by me'.
2. This was the date, recorded by Dugdale, when the church was given to the nuns of Godstow.
3. Cf. J. Peshall, *City of Oxford* (1773), p. 146 (based on Wood's Collections).

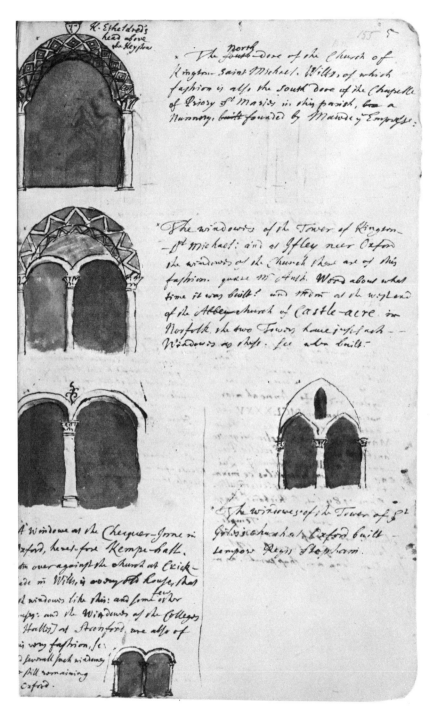

1. Sketches by John Aubrey of Romanesque and early Gothic windows from Kington St Michael church, Wiltshire, Kemp Hall, Oxford, and St Giles church, Oxford (Bodleian Library, MS. Top. Gen. c. 25, f. 155)

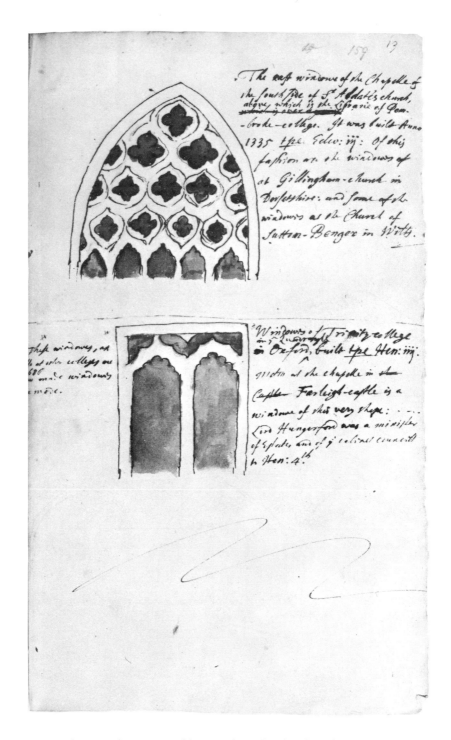

2. Sketches by John Aubrey of fourteenth- and early-fifteenth-century tracery from St Aldate's church, Oxford, and Trinity College, Oxford (Bodleian Library, MS. Top. Gen. c. 25, f. 159)

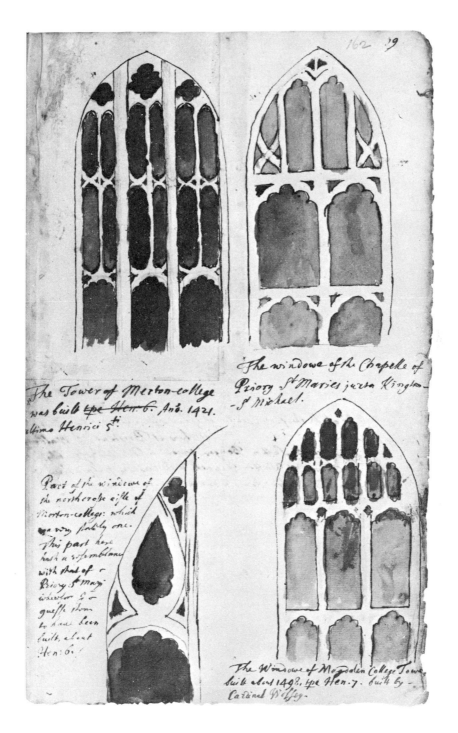

The Tower of Merton-college was built *ype Henr. 6.* Anô. 1421. ultimo Henrici 5ti

The windowe of the Chapelle of Priory St Maries juxta Kington-St Michael.

Part of the windowe of the north crosse aisle of Merton-college: which was a very stately one. This part here hath a resemblance with that of r Priory St Mary: wherefore I doe guesse them to have been built, about Hen: 6:

The Windowe of Magdalen College Tower built about 1498, *ype Hen. 7.* built by Cardinal Wolsey.

3. Sketches by John Aubrey of Perpendicular tracery from Merton and Magdalen Colleges, Oxford, and Kington Priory, Wiltshire (Bodleian Library, MS. Top. Gen. c. 25, f. 162)

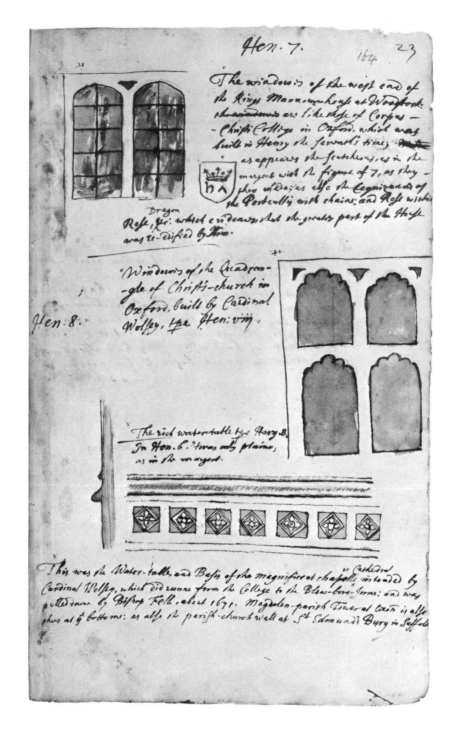

4. Sketches by John Aubrey of Tudor windows from Woodstock Manor and Christ Church, Oxford, and of the plinth of Cardinal Wolsey's unfinished chapel at Christ Church (Bodleian Library, MS. Top. Gen. c. 25, f. 164)

structure, as will hereafter appear'. Altogether there are over fifty drawings, and at least eighty buildings are either illustrated or mentioned.

Though the facts were not invariably correct, the method was sound, and the arrangement of the drawings shows that Aubrey was feeling towards a typological sequence which would serve to date other buildings for which no documentary evidence was available. 'The fashions of building', he noted, 'do last about 100 years, or less; the windows the most remarqueable, hence one may give a guess about what Time the Building was.' He made no attempt to give his examples stylistic labels, but anyone who turns over the pages of the manuscript can see at a glance the development of Romanesque into what Rickman was to call 'Early English', of 'Early English' into 'Decorated', and of 'Decorated' into 'Perpendicular'. Thanks to Aubrey's careful delineation of the Oxford examples, one can even trace some of the changes in 'Perpendicular' window-tracery recently analysed by Mr R. H. C. Davis[1] (Plate 3).

To John Aubrey, therefore, must go the credit for being the first to think historically about medieval English architecture. As a child, Aubrey's 'greatest delight' had been 'to be continually with the artificers (e.g. Joyners, carpenters, coupers, masons)' who came to his father's house at Easton Piers, and thus to 'understand their trades'. 'At 8', he tells us, 'I was a kind of Engineer; and I fell then to drawing, beginning first with plaine outlines, e.g. in draughts of curtaines.'[2] He was, therefore, predisposed to look at buildings with an eye for significant details such as mouldings, and he had the skill to sketch what he saw in a manner that, if not very elegant, was adequate to his purpose. What, unfortunately, he lacked was the ability to get his work into print. The archaeological part of the *Monumenta Britannica* had had its origin in a command given by Charles II to publish an account of Avebury, which Aubrey assured the King 'did as much excell of Stoneheng as a Cathedral does a Parish Church'. But, as Mr Oliver Lawson Dick tells us, 'Aubrey had proceeded so slowly with the work and had added so many facts about other antiquities that five separate dedications of the book were made, as death took away one hoped-for patron after another, before it even got near the press'.[3] The direction to the printer on the first page of the *Chronologia Architectonica* seems to imply that its author regarded the manuscript as ready for publication, but no compositor would have been able to make sense of it as it stood. And so, like the rest of his written work, it remained unpublished and unknown except to the small circle of learned friends with whom Aubrey discoursed of antiquities. At the time of his death in 1697 all four parts of the *Monumenta* were in the hands of a bookseller named Awnsham Churchill, who

1. R. H. C. Davis, 'The Chronology of Perpendicular Architecture in Oxford', *Oxoniensia*, XI–XII (1946–7).

2. *Aubrey's Brief Lives*, ed. O. Lawson Dick (1962), pp. 11, 13.

3. ibid., pp. 94–5.

had borrowed the manuscript to help in the preparation of a new edition of Camden's *Britannia*, and it was not until 1836 that they joined the rest of Aubrey's collections in the Bodleian.[1] While it was in private hands, Hutchins, the historian of Dorset, made a copy of the manuscript from which some 'rude etchings' illustrating the 'Fashion of Windows in Civil and Ecclesiastical Buildings' were made by Francis Perry as a supplement to his *Series of English Medals*, published in 1762. Perry's book did not, however, have a very wide circulation, and the supplementary plates seem to have attracted little notice in the antiquarian world. By the time Britton drew attention to them in the preface to his *Architectural Antiquities of Great Britain* (1826) Rickman's book had reached its third edition, and Aubrey's work had been superseded. Now its only value is as a partial record of some buildings, such as Woodstock Manor, that have long since disappeared. But in a volume written to honour the author of *The Buildings of England* it may not be inappropriate to pay a belated tribute to one who deserves recognition, not only as our first archaeologist, but also as our earliest architectural historian.

1. R. Gough, *British Topography*, II (1780), p. 369, n. g.

Attitudes to Elizabethan Architecture, 1600–1900

BY MARK GIROUARD

WHEN George Chapman dedicated his masque *Musaeus* to Inigo Jones in 1616, he commended him for his appreciation of 'Ancient Poesie, and ancient Architecture, requiring to their excellence a like creating and proportionable Rapture, and being alike over-topt by the monstruous Babels of our Moderne Barbarisme'. This scornful attitude to contemporary buildings is what one would expect from the Inigo Jones circle. But for at least half a century it was to be confined to a small handful of connoisseurs. Among ordinary educated people the slide out of fashion of Elizabethan and Jacobean architecture was a gentle one. The diaries and writings of John Evelyn enable one to plot fairly accurately the course of a representative gentleman of culture. In his early days Evelyn's comments on Elizabethan buildings were far from derogatory. In 1642 Hatfield was 'inferior to few for its architecture then in England'. In 1654 Worksop was 'a faire house' and Littlecote 'a noble seate'. His comments on Audley End, on 1 September 1654, are full of enthusiasm:

that goodly Palace . . . It is a mixt fabric, 'twixt antique & modern, but observable for its being compleately finish'd, & without comparison one of the statliest Palaces of the Kingdome. . . The Gallery is the most cherefull, & I thinke one of the best in England . . . for the rest a perfectly uniforme structure, & shewes without like a diademe, by the decorations of the Cupolas & other ornaments on the Pavilions.

Evelyn returned to Audley End on 22 July 1670. After a sixteen years' interval his comment is superficially the same, but it is possible to detect a change of attitude: a touch of patronage has crept in. Audley End is now 'that fine Palace: It is indeede a cherefull piece of Gotic-building, or rather *antico-moderno* but placed in an obscure bottome'. A rather similar waning of enthusiasm is to be found if one moves, culturally speaking, a storey lower, and consults the diary of Pepys. On 27 February 1660 Audley End is a 'house, in which the stateliness of the ceilings, chimney-pieces, and form of the whole was exceedingly worth seeing'. But by 8 October 1667,

The house indeed do appear very fine, but not so fine as it hath heretofore to me; particularly the ceilings are not so good as I always took them to be, being nothing so well wrought as my Lord Chancellor's one; and though the figure of the house without be very extraordinary good, yet the stayre-case is exceeding poor.

The Lord Chancellor Clarendon's house, by its brief but brilliant appearance in Piccadilly, launched a new image for English domestic architecture, after fifty years of comparative uncertainty. The old prodigy houses at once seemed out of date by comparison. At the same time, as the language of classical ornament became more familiar, the Elizabethans' lack of proficiency in it and their fondness for a mixture ''twixt antique & modern' seemed increasingly less pardonable. Evelyn's translation of Fréart's *Parallel of the Orders* in 1664 inevitably led him to a more censorious attitude. And in 1671 another educated gentleman, John Aubrey, in the course of making the first known attempt at a historical analysis of English architecture in his *Chronologia Architectonica*,[1] stated a point of view about the Elizabethans that was to remain the dominant one for the next hundred years. 'In Queen Elizabeth's time', he wrote, 'architecture made no growth but rather went backwards.' He grouped Somerset House and Longleat together and contrasted their relative correctness with the lack of scholarship of later Elizabethan buildings. As long as architecture was seen primarily as a correct disposition of the orders and of classical ornament, this was a perfectly reasonable and accurate analysis.

Even so, it would be possible to exaggerate the completeness of change in opinion. As late as the reign of James II Henry Winstanley produced his sumptuous folio of views of Audley End – 'I think it ought to be esteemed, not inferiour to any in this kingdom but equall to any in Europe' – with a dedication to Christopher Wren.[2] Celia Fiennes, probably typical of the average middle-brow, is always civil about Elizabethan houses, though obviously far more interested in new ones. Even Evelyn remained for a long time lukewarm rather than hostile. It was not until 1697 that he inserted into his *Account of Architects and Architecture* (published as an appendix to his translation of Fréart) his well-known and vitriolic attack on Gothic architecture. Elizabethan architecture was included in this by insinuation, for the Schools at Oxford was among the buildings singled out for comment, and unfavourable comparison with the Sheldonian.

Even in the eighteenth century there were considerable variations of opinion within the classical framework. Elizabethan architecture contained elements which appealed both to the Baroque and Rococo spirit. When Hawksmoor visited Wollaton in 1733 he deplored its infection with 'ye style of John Ditterlin of Strasburgh' but at the same time found that it contained 'some true stroaks of architecture'.[3] It was

1. *Chronologia Architectonica* is discussed in the preceding essay by Mr Howard Colvin.
2. Winstanley's book is not dated, but James II is mentioned as the reigning monarch in the text.
3. 'Letters and Drawings of Nicholas Hawksmoor relating to the Building of the Mausoleum at Castle Howard 1726–1742', ed. G. Webb, *Walpole Society*, XIX (1931), p. 126.

not surprising that the bold groupings and striking skylines of the Elizabethan prodigy houses should appeal to the Hawksmoor–Vanbrugh circle. Vanbrugh was influenced by Elizabethan plans, and defended the Holbein gate in Whitehall as 'one of the greatest curiositys there is in London'.[1] The Palladians, as one would expect, were much less sympathetic. Longleat was allowed a certain measure of approval, as a prophecy of better things to come. As such it appears in the second volume of *Vitruvius Britannicus* (Plate 5), with the comment 'of this Date . . . esteemed to be the most regular building in the kingdom . . . The proportions of each Order, their intercolumnation and gradual Diminution is duely observed'. Palladian comment on other Elizabethan buildings is hard to find; they were simply ignored. Pope, for instance, thought that Walter Ralegh's lodge at Sherborne was something over which, literally, a veil should be drawn. He wrote to Martha Blount, probably in 1724, that the Ralegh centre 'has the wings of a newer Architecture with beautiful Italian Window-frames done by the first Earl of Bristol, which, if they were joined in the middle by a Portico covering the Old Building, would be a noble front'.[2]

But when Richard Pococke was travelling through England in the mid eighteenth century,[3] he was far from unsympathetic to Elizabethan buildings. As was to be expected, he admired Longleat, but his appreciation ranged wider. The Greenwich Charlton was 'a good old house', the Wiltshire one 'a fine regular old house', Knole was an 'exceeding good old house', and Cranborne a 'good old seat'. At Worksop the turrets 'give it a grand look like a castle'. Wootton Lodge was 'a very romantick place'. At Cardiff, in 1756, he noticed 'a very fine old house in ruins, built with beautiful bow windows of the architecture of Queen Elizabeth's time'. It would be a mistake to exaggerate the significance of these rather perfunctory comments, which bulk very small in contrast to the long description of 'improvements', the new landscapes with their temples, follies, and grottoes which were what Pococke really enjoyed. Even so this modest measure of curiosity about Elizabethan buildings was perhaps typical of what can, with qualification, be called the rococo spirit. It was a spirit that was intrigued by the old or the exotic, and that was prepared to experiment and take liberties with the classical tradition. Pococke's admiration of Elizabethan bay-windows is significant; the reintroduction of the curved or canted bay into architecture was one of the main innovations of the mid eighteenth century. And in the same period occurs the first important example of neo-Elizabethan architectural work. This was the enlargement of Burton Constable, Yorkshire, in the 1750s, which gave it a new façade in the Elizabethan manner of the original house, and a new long gallery complete with neo-Elizabethan plasterwork.

But the first eighteenth-century writer to treat Elizabethan architecture to more

1. L. Whistler, *Sir John Vanbrugh* (1938), p. 151.
2. Pope, *Correspondence*, ed. George Sherburn (1956), pp. 236–7.
3. Richard Pococke, *Travels through England*, ed. Camden Society (1887–8).

than passing mention regarded it with nothing but dislike. In his *Anecdotes of Painting* Horace Walpole pays it a certain amount of attention, almost always unfavourable. The Grecian style, he says, was introduced towards the end of the reign of Henry VIII:

It was plaistered upon Gothic, and made a barbarous mixture. Regular columns, with ornaments neither Grecian nor Gothic and half embroidered with foliage, were crammed over frontispieces, facades and chimnies, and lost all grace by wanting simplicity. This mongrel species lasted till late in the reign of James I.[1]

Elsewhere he talks of 'barbarous and ungraceful ornaments' and 'that barbarous style which one calls *King James's Gothic*'.[2]

Walpole's most revealing comment comes not in the *Anecdotes* but in a letter. He wrote to Cole on 12 August 1769: 'In Queen Elizabeth's reign there was scarce any architecture at all: I mean no pillars or seldom; buildings then became quite plain. Under James a barbarous composition succeeded.'[3] The remark shows an appreciation of the difference between Elizabethan and Jacobean architecture that was an advance on the undiscriminating approach of earlier critics, and indeed of Walpole himself in the *Anecdotes*. At the same time it makes clear how exclusively Walpole, like most of his age, regarded architecture in terms of ornament; where there was no ornament there was no architecture. Moreover, Walpole was a purist. He widened the frontiers of taste by maintaining that there was correct Gothic ornament as well as correct classical ornament, and that the former was also worth study and imitation. But judged from his standpoint the vagaries of both Elizabethan and Rococo ornament were equally worthy of condemnation.

In the posthumous history of Elizabethan architecture Walpole is important. No one had written before – and published what he had written – at such length about it. Although there was nothing especially original about his derogatory point of view, the fact that someone of his standing had expressed it in print, and in lively language, probably did a good deal to delay the restoration of the style into favour. Yet, however unfriendly he may have been, Walpole deserves to be called the father of Elizabethan architectural history. He publicized the names – though in most cases little more than the names – of John Shute, Stickles, Robert Adams, Ralph Simons, Theodore Haveus, Bernard Jansen, Gerard Christmas, John Smythson, and Stephen Harrison as Elizabethan and Jacobean architects. Above all he was the discoverer of John Thorpe's book of architecture, which he introduced in a 'supplement' to the third edition of his *Anecdotes* in 1782. Launched by Walpole, Thorpe set out on his exaggerated career as the master Elizabethan architect, with a reputation that was not to be reduced to scale until this century.

1. Walpole, *Anecdotes of Painting*, ed. Wornum (1888), I, p. 128.
2. ibid., I, pp. 201–2; II, p. 54.
3. *Letters of Horace Walpole*, ed. Toynbee (1904), VII, p. 304.

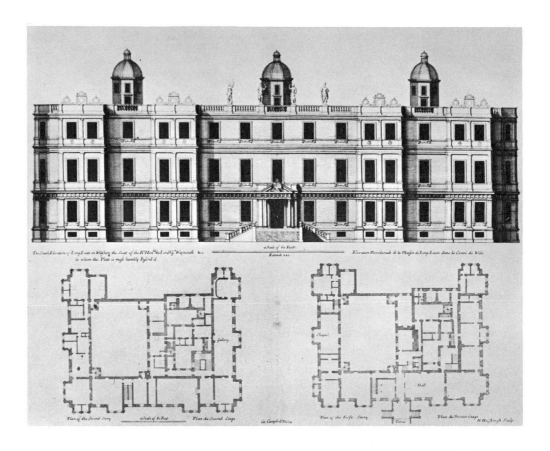

5. ELIZABETHAN ARCHITECTURE AND THE PALLADIANS: Longleat (here shown as illustrated in *Vitruvius Britannicus*) was one of the very few Elizabethan buildings which the Palladians regarded with respect

In spite of Walpole, the standing of Elizabethan architecture slowly but steadily improved in the second half of the eighteenth century. In the first place with each decade it could benefit increasingly from the period's growing antiquarian and archaeological sense. Buildings were now felt to have a historical as well as an architectural value, and the older Elizabethan buildings grew, the more they were appreciated as the product of a past age and the evidence of a vanished way of life. This kind of archaeological appreciation could quickly turn into romantic sentiment, to admiration of buildings that were reminiscent of the 'good old days' and the 'old English hospitality'. In the second place the growth of the cult of the Picturesque resulted in new standards of aesthetic criticism, judged by which Elizabethan buildings made a much better showing than when considered in their relationship to the classical tradition.

It is instructive to compare three reactions to Hardwick (Plate 6). Walpole thoroughly disliked it. He was there in August 1760, and wrote to Lord Strafford on 4 September that 'there is no grace, no ornament, no Gothic, in it'.[1] He had described it at greater length to George Montagu on 1 September: 'Never was I less charmed in my life. The house is not Gothic, but of that betweenity, that intervened when Gothic declined and Palladian was creeping in – rather, this is totally naked of either ... The gallery is sixty yards long, covered with bad tapestry and wretched pictures.'[2] But Walpole's contemporary and friend Thomas Gray, who visited it in December 1762, was much intrigued by it from an antiquarian point of view.[3] Twenty years or so later, when he saw it on its hill-top 'looking like a great old castle of romance', John Byng was more than intrigued, he was enthusiastic: 'Such lofty magnificence! And built with stone, upon a hill! One of the proudest piles I ever beheld.'[4]

There is a reasonable sprinkling of Elizabethan and Jacobean houses in the volumes of *Seats of the Nobility and Gentry* published by W. Watts in 1779 and W. Angus in 1787. The descriptions, though perfunctory, are invariably favourable – perhaps a shade warmer and fuller in Angus than in Watts. But a generation later, in Neale's long series of views of seats, a respectful attitude has been replaced by an enthusiastic one. The entrance door of Blickling, for instance, appears as the title-page of the second volume (1819) and is described as 'the beautiful entrance ... an admirable example of the characteristic ornament used at that period'. Blickling is given three views, in addition to the title-page, and a room-by-room description. Neale is equally enthusiastic about Bramshill, illustrated in the same volume: 'It is built in the very splendid style, peculiar to the period; and having been preserved with care from modern attempts at alteration, it remains a curious example of the prevailing national taste in Architecture in the time of its erection, when much of our old

1. ibid., IV, p. 426.   2. ibid., IV, p. 423.
3. *Correspondence of Thomas Gray*, ed. Toynbee and Whitley (1935), p. 787.
4. *Torrington Diaries*, ed. C. Bruyn Andrews (1934–8), II, p. 30 (13 June 1789).

6. ELIZABETHAN ARCHITECTURE AND THE ROMANTICS: Hardwick Hall by torchlight from Joseph Nash's *Mansions of England in the Olden Time*

Gothic manner was retained with some Italian improvements then newly introduced.' In volume III next year the Jacobean porch of Ingestre is on the title-page, and among the houses described is Burghley: 'a fantastic combination, but on the whole producing an effect of the most splendid character, which will bear a comparison with the advanced state of architectural science, even in the present time'.

This steady growth of sympathy towards Elizabethan architecture was generated far more by topographers, antiquarians, novelists (*Kenilworth* was published in 1821), and landscape theorists than by architects, who continued to find its stylistic impurities hard to stomach. Soane, for example, stigmatized it in his lectures as a 'licentious, whimsical and capricious mode', though he was intrigued by some of the geometrically ingenious plans in Thorpe's book (which he had acquired in 1810).[1] But it was the landscapists who were responsible more than anyone else for the return of the style to favour, and its ultimate adoption as a permissible style for revival. As early as 1794 Richard Payne Knight, in his poem *The Landscape*, had quietly slipped a gabled Elizabethan house into the background of the first of his two contrasted plates, 'A brook flowing in its natural banks' and 'The same brook, with its banks dressed by an improver'. In the second plate (Knight, of course, favoured the 'natural' landscape) the Elizabethan house has been replaced by a square Georgian block. In his *Essays on the Picturesque* (1810) Uvedale Price makes a comparison between Wollaton and Nottingham Castle which clearly shows the particular qualities in Elizabethan architecture that appealed to Picturesque theorists. Wollaton is 'a house, which for the richness of its ornaments in the near view, and the grandeur of its masses from every point, yields to few, if any, in the kingdom'. By comparison Nottingham is

a long square house of the Italian style ... Such a building, on such high ground, and its outline always distinctly opposed to the sky, gives an impression of ridicule and disgust. The hills and town are absolutely flattened by it; while the comparatively low situation of Wollaton is so elevated by the form of the house, that it seems to command the whole country round it.[2]

Humphry Repton, however much he might scrap with Price about niceties of theory, was equally sympathetic to the Elizabethan period. 'There is something so venerable and picturesque in many houses of this date', he wrote in his *Fragments on the Theory and Practice of Landscape Gardening* (1816), 'that I have always endeavoured to preserve as much of them as could be adapted to modern uses; and even in some cases advised new houses in that style of architecture' (p. 29). His son and architectural partner, John Adey Repton, made Elizabethan architecture his speciality, and in collaboration with his father designed substantial alterations or additions to existing Elizabethan houses at Barningham Hall, Norfolk (1805),

1. Soane, *Lectures on Architecture*, ed. Bolton (1929), pp. 88 and 131.
2. op. cit., II, p. 210 n.

Cobham Hall, Kent, and Bourn House, Cambridgeshire (*c.* 1815). Bourn is illustrated by Neale (first series, VI, 1823), with a compliment to J. A. Repton's 'usual ability and good taste'. But a closer examination of the Reptons in connexion with Elizabethan architecture shows how far the style still was from unqualified acceptance. Earlier on in the passage quoted above Humphry Repton remarks that 'the style of the early Gothic of Elizabeth, when not disfigured by an unseemly mixture of bad Grecian, seems better adapted to habitation than the castle, abbey or collegiate Gothic'. At Corsham, where he remodelled the Georgian front with the architectural collaboration of John Nash, 'the Grecian mouldings are omitted, which the corrupt taste of King James's time had introduced, and the true Gothic mouldings of Elizabeth's reign are introduced'.[1] These remarks show how very hazy knowledge of Elizabethan architecture still was; at Corsham the result was scarcely distinguishable from 'abbey or collegiate Gothic', and in J. A. Repton's designs the removal of 'bad Grecian' and the infiltration of 'modern improvements' produced results that were only very dimly neo-Elizabethan. Moreover, although it was by now generally accepted that additions to an Elizabethan house should be in a similar style, it was still rare to find a patron brave enough to use the style for a completely new house. The earliest examples I can trace are, curiously enough, in Ireland, three rather watery designs by Richard and William Morrison – Miltown (1818), Borris (illustrated 1819), and Glenarm ('lately built' in 1825), all illustrated and described by Neale.[2] Then comes Eshton Hall, Yorkshire (1825–7), by Webster of Kendal, described by Neale (second series, V) as 'a faithful composition from some of the finest specimens of our old domestic architecture'. Webster, unlike the Reptons, had no scruples about introducing 'bad Grecian' details and his design is recognizably Elizabethan. But most architects were more cautious, and if they went to the sixteenth century for inspiration kept to the Tudor end of it.

The real break-through for Elizabethan architecture came in the 1830s and can be dated almost exactly to 1833. In that year T. H. Clarke produced his *Domestic Architecture of the Reigns of Queen Elizabeth and James I* – as far as I know the first publication to deal exclusively with Elizabethan and Jacobean architecture. The Rev. James Dallaway devoted a sixth discourse of sixty pages to the Tudor and Elizabethan styles in his *A Series of Discourses upon Architecture in England*. Two-thirds of P. F. Robinson's abortive attempt to launch a new *Vitruvius Britannicus* was given over to detailed description and illustration of Hatfield and Hardwick. And J. C. Loudon, in his *Encyclopaedia of Cottage, Farm and Villa Architecture*, chose an Elizabethan design for his 'Beau Idéal of an English Villa'. In 1835, the year in which Elizabethan was selected with Gothic as one of the two eligible styles in the competition for the new Houses of Parliament, J. Hakewill published his *Attempt to*

1. *Observations on the Theory and Practice of Landscape Gardening* (1805), p. 191.
2. Miltown, first series, III (1820); Borris, first series, II (1819); Glenarm, second series, II (1825)·

Determine the Exact Character of Elizabethan Architecture. In 1837 Soane's pupil, C. J. Richardson, produced his *Observations on the Architecture of England during the Reigns of Queen Elizabeth and James I*. Richardson was one of the best informed and most enthusiastic advocates of the style, and continued with *Architectural Remains of the Reigns of Elizabeth and James I* volume I in 1840,[1] and *Studies from Old English Mansions* in four folio volumes in 1841. Meanwhile in 1839 Henry Shaw had published *Details of Elizabethan Architecture* (including some plates engraved as early as 1834) and Joseph Nash launched the first volume of his famous series *The Mansions of England in the Olden Time* (Plate 6). Three more volumes followed it, the last in 1849. Nash's luscious lithographs, in which figures in the dress of the time disport themselves in medieval or Elizabethan settings, proved enormously influential in popularizing the period. The rather feebler lithographs in Hall's *Baronial Halls* (1845–8) were an obvious attempt to jump on the same bandwagon. E. B. Lamb's *Studies of Ancient Domestic Architecture* and John Clayton's *Ancient Timbered Edifices of England* followed in 1846.

In 1835 the choice of Elizabethan as a possible style for the Houses of Parliament had not received a very good press. John Britton, writing to the *Morning Chronicle* on 10 June, stigmatized it as 'a debased and capricious sort of architecture which I am persuaded the Committee cannot recommend, and would never approve' and A. W. Hakewill called it 'that *truly electrifying* style – that startling assembly of incongruities, Elizabethan architecture'.[2] By 1839, however, Henry Shaw could claim that the style 'had survived the prejudices which at first embarrassed its revival' and that 'it is no longer necessary to apologize for a zealous attachment to the pursuit of its characteristic features'.[3] By then numerous neo-Elizabethan houses had been built, and more followed in a rising flood during the 1840s. The growing number of publications on the style made its more obvious features increasingly familiar. In 1834 Francis Goodwin, in the second series of his *Domestic Architecture*, had included a 'villa in the Elizabethan style' which could not conceivably be recognized as what it claimed to be. By 1840 such ignorance would not have been possible.

In no sense, however, could the revival be called a learned one. Most of the publications were essentially scrapbooks of disconnected pictures and details, from which architects could concoct their designs. The only writer who made a serious attempt to give some kind of coherent account was the Rev. James Dallaway, in his *Discourses upon Architecture in England* (1844) already mentioned. Dallaway, as the editor of Walpole's *Anecdotes*, had inherited his master's lukewarmness about the style but also his historical approach to it. He made a sporting, if not very impressive effort

1. Vol. II never appeared.

2. A. W. Hakewill, *Thoughts upon the Style of Architecture to be adopted in Rebuilding the Houses of Parliament* (1835), p. 18.

3. Introduction to *Details of Elizabethan Architecture*.

to describe its development, and gave a list of the eleven principal architects and the eighteen most important houses. If he has to bear the responsibility of crediting John of Padua with Somerset House and Longleat, he also publicized, for example, Peake's translation of Serlio and Haydock's of Lomazzo, and quoted from the Parliamentary survey of Wimbledon House. C. J. Richardson, though much more enthusiastic than Dallaway, was even more haphazard as a historian. He deserves the credit, however, for having attempted to publish John Thorpe's drawings, of which he issued a prospectus around 1837. The scheme never came to anything, and its failure emphasizes the lack of any real scholarly background to the revival.[1]

In the various publications already listed numerous different reasons are given as to why the style deserved a return to favour. They can be grouped under three main headings, of picturesqueness, convenience, and association. Its picturesqueness was generally agreed on. As Richardson wrote,

for the parsonage-house, the rural and sequestered villa, amidst coppices and garden grounds, the Elizabethan style is not only admissible but in accordance with the *genius loci*: its quaint gables, fantastic pinnacles and pendants; its intricate parapets and grotesque carvings connect themselves intimately with the surrounding scenery, and form a picture far more readily and agreeably than uniform symmetrical objects.[2]

This passage is in the same vein as Price's comparison of Wollaton and Nottingham Castle made twenty-seven years earlier. But by now it was a slightly different kind of picture that was admired, richer in texture, crowded with incident, and with a touch of the bizarre – a shift in taste from which the more fanciful Jacobean houses, in particular, could benefit.

The convenience of Elizabethan houses was considered to derive partly from their 'windows admitting an abundance of light and air',[3] and partly from what was considered (quite wrongly) the typical irregularity of their plan, so much easier to adapt for the increasingly complex needs of a country house than a symmetrical classical one. But perhaps the main source of attraction of Elizabethan architecture is revealed in the name frequently given to it at this period: 'the Old English Style'. Loudon wrote that 'as a British domestic style, it has more interesting associations connected with it than any other';[4] Richardson thought that 'an age and a country that could produce a Bacon and a Shakespeare was not like to prove contemptible in architecture'.[5] Elizabethan architecture appealed both to patriotic and to romantic sentiments.

1. *The Book of Architecture of John Thorpe*, ed. Summerson, *Walpole Society*, XL (1964–6), pp. 15–16. Some of the Thorpe drawings were reproduced in Richardson's *Architectural Remains* (1840).
2. C. J. Richardson, *Observations* (1837), p. 8.
3. T. H. Clarke, *Domestic Architecture* (1833), Preface.
4. J. C. Loudon, *Encyclopaedia* (new edn, 1835), p. 1124.
5. C. J. Richardson, *Observations*, p. 7.

In an age which was increasingly interested in the associational rather than the formal values of architecture, this gave it a tremendous advantage.

It was still readily agreed that, judged by standards of classical correctness, Elizabethan architecture left much to be desired. But by the 1830s the country land-owners, who were the principal patrons of the style, were no longer sensitive about this kind of correctness. As the Grand Tour went out of fashion, and the amateur architect almost entirely disappeared, the average patron increasingly lost his ear for the inflections of classical architecture. The ideal of the man of taste was re-replaced by the ideal of the English gentleman, for whom a neo-Elizabethan house, with its suggestion of 'the old English hospitality' (not to mention its convenience and relative cheapness), seemed an ideally appropriate setting. On the other hand one gets the impression that architects, all of whom had had a conventional classical training, were somewhat apologetic about advocating the style, and were almost surprised at the enthusiasm with which their clients accepted it. It was a committee of peers and Members of Parliament, not of architects, that chose Elizabethan as one of the two required styles for the Houses of Parliament competition. Even Richardson, in his first book, spoke of its 'extraordinary incongruities' and said, 'I do not desire that it should become extensively adopted'.[1] But architects were less squeamish than they had been. Looking back in the perspective of time one can see how easily the Elizabethan Revival could grow and flourish, at a period when the classical tradition was on the decline and the serious Gothic Revival was only just beginning.

In fact Victorian Gothic, although it by no means killed neo-Elizabethan, certainly put it in the shade. Large Elizabethan houses continued to be built in consider-able numbers. In 1865 Robert Kerr, who himself built the biggest and brassiest of them (for the owner of *The Times*), spoke up for the style in language not so very different from that used thirty years previously.[2] It was English and convenient – 'The native English model of three hundred years seems as fit as ever for English uses now' – and it was inexpensive – 'Although no style carries ornament better, none can more easily dispense with it ... Cheap Elizabethan however, as such, is only fit for a Workhouse' – a sentiment with which many Poor Law Boards found themselves in complete agreement. But although still found suitable both for the very rich and the very poor, its publicity value had gone, and in the fifties, sixties, and seventies the earlier stream of books about it almost completely dried up. When C. J. Richardson, the bright boy of an earlier generation, produced his appalling *Picturesque Designs in Architecture* in 1870, he seemed like a greasy remittance man, forced to go through his out-of-date society patter to saloon-bar audiences. The kick was all with the Gothicists, where puritanical devotion to their own style left little room for tolerance of anything else. The Palladians had despised the Eliza-

1. ibid.
2. Robert Kerr, *The Gentleman's House* (1865), pp. 350, 356.

bethans for being ignorant classicists; the Gothic Revivalists despised them for being degenerate Goths. Ruskin, except in his juvenile writings, ignored Elizabethan architecture altogether, while Eastlake commented that 'it requires no great discernment on the part of modern critics to perceive both in the Tudor and Elizabethan styles abundant evidence of a fallen art'.[1]

Throughout the mid-Victorian years, however, a rather lonely interest in Elizabethan architecture was maintained by Wyatt Papworth. The six volumes of the *Architectural Publications Society Dictionary*, produced, edited, and largely written by him in instalments between 1853 and 1892, gave the style a reasonable coverage, with a general and numerous particular articles. Papworth was interested in Elizabethan architecture as a historian rather than a practising architect, and deserves to be ranked with Walpole and Dallaway as one of the founders of Elizabethan architectural history. But, although he was less superficial than his predecessors, he himself would have been the first to admit that his researches were only of a preliminary nature. In his entry on 'Elizabethan Architecture' he complains that 'there is no work which can be said to give a satisfactory history or practical synopsis or analysis of it'. There was still no satisfactory history when he produced his *Renaissance and Italian Styles of Architecture in Great Britain* in 1883. This was little more than a pamphlet, a series of notes for further study. It consisted of a bibliography, old and new, a list of architects (which brought Dallaway's ten up to the respectable total of seventy), and a list of principal houses, with brief comments on each of them. The bibliography can produce virtually nothing published between 1852 and 1883. But the one entry under the latter year introduces a new name and a new era in Elizabethan architectural history, for it is *The Buildings erected in Northamptonshire by Sir Thomas Tresham* by J. Alfred Gotch.

In fact the tide had already turned some years previously. It was, for instance, in 1876 that Thomas Jackson had won the competition for the Examination Schools in Oxford with a design derived from the Elizabethan courtyard at Kirby. The younger generation of Gothicists had got bored with their self-imposed boundaries, and among the new pastures they selected, Elizabethan was to prove one of the most remunerative.

The revival of interest produced a series of new publications at the end of the nineteenth and beginning of the twentieth centuries. But it was Gotch who wrote most prolifically and frequently on the style, besides conducting a flourishing neo-Elizabethan architectural practice from his home town of Kettering. His two massive volumes *Architecture of the Renaissance in England* appeared in 1891–4, followed by *Early Renaissance Architecture in England* in 1901. A steady output of other books and articles gained him a secure reputation as the leading expert on Elizabethan architecture.

1. *History of the Gothic Revival* (1872).

Gotch's point of view is noticeably different from that of earlier generations. It comes out very clearly in his comments on the orders in the courtyard at Kirby. These

are handled in a manner so free from conventional restraint as to be very pleasing, though opposed to those strict rules of propriety which are rightly held up as examples to the student. Our best friends, however, do not all possess features of classic regularity, yet we love no less to look upon them for all that.[1]

The happy-go-lucky Elizabethan approach to classical detail, which even in the revival of the 1830s and 40s was something to be apologized for, appeared to Gotch to be an actual virtue, leading to 'that piquant flavour which renders the work of the early Renaissance so delightful a study'.[2] It was 'piquant' detail that caught his eye, not the bold compositions that had appealed to Hawksmoor or the devotees of the Picturesque, or the all-over richness that had charmed the early Victorians. For him Hardwick was 'an example of the less interesting houses of the period, large, symmetrical, tame, and without any piquant detail'.[3] At Hatfield he commented that 'there are not many piquant features about the house. It is a large and stately building, and depends for its effect rather upon size and symmetry than upon varied and charming detail'.[4] In his *Early Renaissance Architecture*, although, unlike *Architecture of the Renaissance* (which was primarily an unrelated collection of individual examples), it claimed 'to trace in a systematic manner the development of style', the emphasis is noticeably on smaller houses, or on details and corners of the bigger ones.

Gotch's use of the word 'Renaissance' also helps to pinpoint his attitude towards Elizabethan architecture. He was writing at a period of renewed interest in the Italian Renaissance. But for most people in the eighties and nineties, this meant primarily the Quattrocento. 'Italian art of this Golden Age', T. G. Jackson wrote,

...has a charm that is all its own; a charm that gradually dwindled away as it fell under the spell of convention and pedantry, till at last it was lost in the cold shadow of an unnatural formality...Never was there a time when art was more free, more natural, more joyous.[5]

Jackson had his reservations about the quality of Elizabethan detail; but for Gotch English architecture seemed to have been going, a hundred years later, through a parallel development to that of the early Italian Renaissance. It produced

work which exhibits a vitality, a fancy, and a sense of romance for which we look in vain in the more correct architecture of the eighteenth century ... And just as the literature of the period, as it became more in accordance with rule, lost half its originality and more

1. *Architecture of the Renaissance in England*, I, p. 34.
2. ibid., Introduction.　　　3. ibid., p. 3.　　　4. ibid., II, p. 40.
5. Sir Thomas Graham Jackson, *The Renaissance of Roman Architecture*, part II, *England* (1922), p. 139. Jackson's view in the 1890s would have been much the same.

than half its fascination, so Renaissance Architecture, as it passed from the Elizabethan to the Jacobean, and so to the succeeding phases, became more homogeneous, more scholarly, more true to its classical origin, and yet withal lost vitality in the process.[1]

Although *Early Renaissance Architecture* is still the best available monograph on its period, by present-day standards it is a far from satisfactory production. It is primarily a series of descriptions and illustrations of individual aspects, with sections devoted to plans, gables, chimneys, ceilings, long galleries, market houses, gardens, and so on. Any attempt at a description of the historical development of Elizabethan architecture is of a rudimentary nature. Little use is made of original manuscript sources, although the labours of antiquaries and historians were making these increasingly available. The Palladians had been well aware of the importance of the Protector Somerset, and the connexions between Somerset House and Longleat; but for Gotch Longleat is a house of no especial significance. Among pattern books the most important, Serlio, is not mentioned, nor is there any realization of the influence of French architecture on England in the mid sixteenth century. There is nothing about Symonds, Stickles, Lyming, Arnold, Holt, Spicer, Hawthorne, Kirby, or Hancock – indeed about any Elizabethan architect-craftsmen except Robert Smythson, briefly mentioned on the penultimate page, and of course John Thorpe. But although Gotch devoted a great deal of space to Thorpe in one publication or another, he never unearthed any of the mass of biographical information which was lying waiting for the first person with a nose for historical research who came to look for it.

Yet it would be a pity to be too caustic about Gotch. He measured and illustrated an enormous number of Elizabethan and Jacobean buildings, many for the first time. In the course of fifty years a great deal of new material (including the Smythson drawings) came into his net. Above all he was an enthusiast, who examined, recorded, and described with both care and love. As an architect with a busy practice and no historical training it was not to be expected that his researches would rise above an amateur level. He was still to a large extent in the old tradition of architect-historians, who looked on the architecture of the past primarily as a source of ideas for that of the present. So, for that matter, were his main contemporary rivals in the field of the 'English Renaissance', Jackson and Blomfield. Architect-historians have been replaced by architectural historians only in the last thirty years. It is not perhaps coincidence that the same period has seen the end (in spite of Lord Nuffield) of any likelihood of another Elizabethan revival.

1. *Early Renaissance Architecture*, p. 5.

John Evelyn and Architecture: A First Inquiry

BY KERRY DOWNES

JOHN EVELYN's strictly architectural original writing is limited to the *Account of Architects and Architecture* appended to his translation of Fréart's *Parallel*,[1] together with the dedications of both works. The *Account*, which amounts to a cursive glossary of architectural terms of his time, was intended by Evelyn to take its place beside the lexicons (his word, used in the Preface) of the natural sciences then being produced by various of his fellow-members of the Royal Society. Its relation to other theoretical and practical writings on architecture needs examination in the larger context of seventeenth- and eighteenth-century architectural literature, but we can learn a little of Evelyn's own views on the art of building and the buildings of his own and former times from the preliminary pages – though they run from hyperbole to near-bathos – as well as from the *Account* itself. If we want to know more, we must turn to those writings which he did not intend for publication: his surviving correspondence and his diary.

This field is very large and not much explored, and architecture forms only a small and scattered part of it. This essay is concerned only with Evelyn's attitudes to the art as they appear in the Diary,[2] which covers in some detail over sixty years of his

1. *A parallel of the antient architecture with the modern . . . by Roland Fréart, Sieur de Chambray; made English . . . to which is added an account of architects and architecture, in an historical, and etymological explanation of certain tearmes . . . by John Evelyn Esq; Fellow of the Royal Society* (London, 1664). The second edition (1707) has a much enlarged revision of the *Account*; this has its own sub-title-page dated 1706 and a dedication to Wren dated 21 February 1696/7. I have relied on this edition and references are to it.

For Evelyn's writings see Geoffrey Keynes, *John Evelyn: a Study in Bibliophily and a Bibliography* (Cambridge, 1937).

2. The standard edition is now that by E. S. de Beer (Oxford, 1955), to which all volume and page numbers here refer. It provides the first adequate working text of the Diary, and I am heavily indebted both to the annotations and to the Introduction to vol. 1. This volume also contains Evelyn's revision of the early part of the Diary (*De vita propria*), which differs significantly from the corresponding part of the original *Kalendarium*. In quotations I have omitted Evelyn's eccentric use of italic.

long life; while the letters are by no means without value, it is to the Diary that one refers almost at the outset of any English historical inquiry into the second half of the seventeenth century. Its value as a major source of information, often primary, on the history of art, is limited only by two factors: first, the very breadth of the diarist's interests, which left him time to record only a fraction of the events he witnessed or heard about and the opinions he formed; and secondly the process of amendment and revision which went on throughout the compilation of the Diary, as a result of which few of the notices (especially the earlier ones) can be assumed to be exactly contemporary – and some are demonstrably not so. Given the great mass of material available in the Diary and its writer's assured permanent place in the history of his age, a picture of Evelyn as an observer and critic of architecture is worth drawing from it, even if it is often disappointingly and sometimes tantalizingly negative.

The Diary is in fact – as its definitive editor points out – a record of Evelyn's many interests, and through them of his own personality. Private means relieved him of the necessity to work for gain and allowed him to develop and mature without haste. Born in 1620, he spent most of the Civil War period on the Continent, feeling apparently, like many adherents of old régimes, that he could be of most use in the comparative freedom and safety of voluntary exile: the incidental gain to him was a virtual Grand Tour through the Netherlands and France to Italy, as far south as Campania. After the Restoration, of which he was a negotiator, he was a frequent and respected adviser of the King, and had the use and later right of lodgings in Whitehall. While he was on terms of friendship with Charles II, he was in general loyal to the crown rather than to its wearer, and rode out the Revolution of 1688. He was staunchly loyal to the Church of England, socially strongly pro-Establishment, and rather a name-dropper; one feels that dinner with a peer or a word from His Majesty made his day. He was constantly engaged in philanthropic schemes, the last and one of the most important being Greenwich Hospital, of which he was treasurer between 1695 and 1703. He was evidently a compulsive writer; the Diary was written and revised in the interstices of a busy literary life. His published works are more remarkable for usefulness and informativeness than for originality or style, but they cover many fields. To judge from the Diary he was a listener and observer rather than a reader, but he read omnivorously for information. His interests naturally changed over the years. In the sixties the Diary is full of 'our Society' (the Royal Society) and he designed the frontispiece of Sprat's pioneer history of it.[1] In later years the record of his devotional life is progressively augmented with greater details of the sermons he heard. He was a competent draughtsman and capable of laying out a garden himself. There are as many notices in the Diary of gardens and landscapes

1. Thomas Sprat, *The History of the Royal-Society of London* (London, 1667). Keynes, op. cit., p. 278, indeed suggests that Evelyn had a hand in the compilation of the work.

as of buildings. The years of travel have more about architecture than the later ones, as one might expect, but much of what he has to say there was derived, perhaps at a later date and not always accurately, from books.[1] He noticed buildings on some, but not all, of his later journeys about England; in 1654 he took his wife, English but brought up in France, on a tour to see her native country, and there are later sequences of notices (often longer ones) separated by many pages of no relevance. After 1690 the notices are fewer but longer.[2] He was by any standards a remarkable man, but not pre-eminent in the arts or any other single field. Could he have lived in our century he would no doubt have served on boards and Royal Commissions, as he did, spoken at literary luncheons and on television, and written reviews for the weekly newspapers and a column in one of the ladies' journals. Over a distance of three hundred years his articulateness and the fact of his survival allow him to speak for his own age.

Evelyn's age combined many traces of medieval thought with a new post-Baconian rationalism which sought, within the framework of theism, the explanation of all material things by experimental inquiry. This dual attitude is evident in an example from another field – the appearance of a comet in December 1680:

What this may Portend (for it was very extraordinarie) God onely knows ... I pray God avert his Judgements; we have had of late severall Comets, which though I believe appeare from natural Causes, & of themselves operate not, yet I cannot despise them; They may be warnings from God [IV. 235].

The mixture of old and new ideas informed and enlivened not only philosophy and science but the arts, fashion, and daily life. Evelyn's early enthusiasm for grottoes and for trick fountains, 'unlucky contrivances to wet the Spectators' (II. 108), belongs to the old, his writings on trees and gardening to the new. His eye for colour appreciated the medieval windows at Canterbury, which he saw before the desecration of 1644 (II. 76), the marbles of Nicola Pisano's Pisa Baptistery pulpit, the 'exquisite' one at Siena, and the sparkle of Siena Cathedral after a rain shower (II. 181, 204, 407). It saw more in the expensive overlaid colours of the seventeenth-century Chapel of the Princes at San Lorenzo than, for all his admiration for Michelangelo as the restorer of architecture, in the Medici Chapel (II. 198, 416, 214, 238, 275). The marbles of the Louvre (II. 103–5) and the churches of Genoa and Naples (II. 176, 328) seem to have impressed him more than the balance of the Farnesina ('fairly built'), where he was only really interested in the frescoes, and at least as much as the Tempietto ('of incomparable designe') (II. 288, 313). Back

1. A glaring example is Gaillon, to which according to de Beer he cannot have been, though he said he had! (II. 121).

2. This essay derives mainly from over 300 separate notices, selected from my complete reading of the Diary, but this is by no means the total.

in England, he admired the richness of the Great Hall at Hampton Court and of the plaster, terracotta, and slate decoration at Nonesuch (III. 324, 427).

In general, his appreciation of the colourful, the curious (meaning either skilful or singular), and the ingenious belong to the old attitude, but it made it possible for him and others to accept the profusion, wit, and illusion of Baroque art, more refined than the Elizabethan taste and perhaps different in kind, but equally opposed to Bacon's stern 'Houses are built to live in, and not to look on' or Evelyn's own attempts to reform and simplify men's dress.[1] Richness, wit, skill, and illusion were the qualities he saw and admired in Gibbons's carving and Verrio's wall-painting, and there is no great difference between the young man's praise of the 'agreable cheate' at Rueil, a full-size painting of the Arch of Constantine complete with sky and so life-like that birds flew headlong into it (II. 109–10), and the mature man's enthusiasm at Windsor:

That which now . . . was new & surprizing to me . . . was that incomparable fresca painting in St. Georges Hall, representing the Legend of St. George, & Triumph of the black-Prince, and his reception by Edw: the 3d, The Volto or roofe not totaly finished: Then the Chapell of the Resurrection, where the figure of the Ascention, is in my opinion comparable to any paintings of the most famous Roman Masters: The Last-Supper also over the Altar (I liked exceedingly the Contrivance of the unseene Organs behind the Altar) nor lesse the stupendious, & beyond all description, the incomparable Carving of our Gibbons, who is (without Contraversie) the greatest Master, both for Invention, & rareness of Worke, that the world ever had in any age . . . Virio the Painters Invention is likewise admirable, his Ord'nance full, & flowing, antique & heroical, his figures move . . . [IV. 316–17; further, 465].

Evelyn's story of discovering the young Gibbons working by an open window in Deptford in January 1671, and subsequently introducing him to the King, Wren, and others, is famous and one of the most attractive in the Diary, and although we may feel that somebody else would have found and promoted the young carver if Evelyn had not,[2] his continued whole-hearted recommendation of his protégé constitutes one of his best contributions to the architecture of his time. His admiration for Verrio is more embarrassing to modern taste, but from a list of the painter's work it was clearly shared by contemporaries. He was continually impressed by materials and workmanship in work of his own century. The notice of the new Amsterdam town hall, written without first-hand knowledge, long after his return from Holland, calls it 'one of the most costly, and magnificent pieces of Architecture in Europ; especialy for the materials, & the Carving, which exceeds all description' (II. 43).[3]

1. For his strictures on the French fashions and his interest in a simple 'Persian' costume see Diary, III. 465–7, and also E. S. de Beer, 'King Charles II's own Fashion', *Journal of the Warburg and Courtauld Institutes*, II (1939), pp. 105–15.   2. According to Vertue it was Lely who did so.
3. The corresponding passage in *De vita propria* has the qualification 'as I am informed it is' and a reference to the old town hall 'at my being there a very ordinary building' (I. 31–2).

He did see, and 'exceedingly admir'd', the Jesuit Church in Antwerp, 'being a very glorious fabrique without; & within wholy incrusted with marble inlayd & polish'd' (II. 63). He likewise praised Saint-Paul-Saint-Louis in Paris, particularly its 'richly carvd; and incomparable front' (II. 96). While heartily disliking the Duchess of Portsmouth, one of Charles II's mistresses, who had her apartment at Whitehall 'twice or thrice, puld downe, & rebuilt', he called the results 'splendid' and 'glorious' (IV. 74, 268, 343), and at the end of 1686 he could find nothing finer than the altar-piece and royal gallery in James II's new Popish chapel (IV. 534). Here the notice expresses religious disapproval mixed with artistic delight.

Words often failed Evelyn: on his travels he would search all Europe in vain for anything finer or statelier, sweeter or more perfect, than what stood before him; later he would leave comparisons unfinished or fall back on the word 'incomparable'. His laudatory vocabulary is limited in range but there is quite a lot of it: handsome, pretty, neat (of towns), stately (also of the cliff at Lyon), clean, strong (of castles), delicate (i.e. delightful, of Haarlem), spacious, magnificent, sweet (also of towns and country sites), beautiful, fair, remarkable, well-built, glorious, rich, nobly built, superb, exquisite, rare, princely, sumptuous, goodly, commodious. Sometimes he is less or more expressive. The fifteenth-century house of Jacques Cœur at Bourges is 'worth seeing', the Pauline Chapel in S. Maria Maggiore 'beyond all imagination glorious' and 'altogether dazles & confounds the beholders'. The Villa Borghese and its garden are 'an Elysium of delight', St Peter's 'that most stupendious & incomparable Basilicā'. At the sight of Bramante's helical ramp in the Vatican he judged that at Amboise 'nothing so spruce' in comparison. St Lawrence Jewry is 'a cherefull pile', St James, Piccadilly 'elegantly indeed built', and St Clement Danes 'prettyly built & contrived'. Adverse comment is less common, and in several cases refers to the situation of a building he otherwise likes. But Brooke House, Hackney, is 'a despicable building' and Leicester generally 'despicably built; the Chimnie flues like so many smiths forges' (III. 122).[1] He also uses mean, tolerable, ill built, ordinary. His attitude to medieval buildings and some more particular comments on contemporary architecture will be noticed later.

Evelyn's usual vocabulary is in fact never far from the Vitruvian tripos of Commodity, Firmness, and Delight or, as he put it in the *Account*, building 'handsomely, solidly and usefully'.[2] It is his approach to the useful or commodious that most clearly shows Evelyn the sober progressive F.R.S., concerned with the lie of the land for drainage, water, light, and shelter, the practical lexicographer and campaigner. Here, and in tune with Bacon, he is at his most characteristic, and this explains why collectively many of his judgements appear rather dull except in matters of decoration. An exception is that on Chambord, which he wanted to see because

1. This remark appears to be unparalleled.
2. p. 11.

of 'the extravagance of the designe': the staircase was 'very extraordinary; but of far greater expense, than use or beauty' (II. 139).

His acquaintance with European cities also convinced him of the shortcomings of London and other English towns, and while the Great Fire of London precipitated changes that pressure groups could not achieve, he was advocating reform long before the Fire. In Paris he noted the houses 'entirely of Stone, and infinitely sumptuous' and the paving-stones 'neare a foote square ... more easy to walke on than our pibbles of London', although he thought the Place Royale 'not so pleasant' as Covent Garden, which it inspired (II. 94, 100, 131).[1] He found straight wide streets and regular stone houses elsewhere, for example at Orléans, in the 'pretty Towne' of Richelieu, and at Lyon (II. 139, 150, 153), and in Florence and Siena he noted the cleanness of the streets resulting from good paving (II. 200, 202). The contrast was obvious at home, where paving was begun in Holborn[2] and Whitehall after the Restoration but most streets remained rugged (his word) and insanitary; where too it took one of the most disastrous fires of all time to stop the building of lath-and-plaster-filled timber-frame houses in London and later serious provincial fires to persuade the country to follow suit.[3] The Royal Society, with the direct interest of the King, was pressing *before* the Great Fire – Evelyn in fact tried before 1660 – for the reform of London streets and buildings,[4] and Evelyn was a member of the Royal Commission of 1662 'about reforming the buildings, wayes, streetes, & incumbrances' (III. 318).[5] He was also one of those who produced a plan for a new city soon after the Fire – as with Wren, the promptness with which he did so indicates previous thought.

Evelyn was by no means the only Englishman to visit Holland, but his experiences there probably have a direct bearing on another London scheme which was abandoned: the projected Thames Quay between the Temple and London Bridge.[6] There was nothing original in his comparison of the Amsterdam Bourse with Gresham's Exchange, except that 'in one respect it exceeds, that ships of considerable burthen ride at the very key contiguous to it'. Further, 'amost generaly the Townes of

1. His praise was fainter in the *State of France* (1652), pp. 107–14.

2. In 1663. Reference in the dedication to Denham in the *Parallel*.

3. From Evelyn's lifetime may be mentioned the fires at Northampton (1675) and Warwick (1694). A good deal of lath-and-plaster outside work seems still to have been done in Whitehall Palace in the 1670s, and the fire of 1698 there was only the last and worst of a long succession. According to Hawksmoor London in 1715 was still full of 'Dirty Rotten Sheds, allways Tumbling or takeing fire, with winding Crooked passages ... Lakes of Mud and Rills of Stinking Mire Running through them' (K. Downes, *Hawksmoor*, London, 1959, p. 242).

4. Sprat, *History of the Royal-Society*, op. cit., pp. 78, 122–3; E. S. de Beer, *London Revived* (Oxford, 1938).

5. The Commissioners for Highways and Sewers.

6. De Beer, op. cit.; T. F. Reddaway, *The Rebuilding of London after the Great Fire* (London, 1940), pp. 221–43.

Holland, are so accommodated with Grafts, Cutts, Sluces, Moles & Rivers, that nothing is more frequent than to see a whole Navy of Marchands & others environ'd with streetes & houses' (II. 46). The 'neate' effect of the stone-fronted King's Staithe at York also impressed him (III. 128) and the London scheme would similarly have united mercantile convenience and prestige with real visual civic improvement.

It is well known that Evelyn was one of the party that visited and reported on Old St Paul's a few days before the Great Fire (III. 449), and on that occasion he sided with Wren and against Sir Roger Pratt (who was prepared to re-use the old foundations for the crossing and who thought the outward list of the nave arcades was intentional for a perspective effect!). That he enjoyed the King's confidence is shown not only by the incident in 1664 in which Charles took him aside and drew for him his intentions for Whitehall (III. 387) but also by previous discussions in 1661 of 'the improvement of Gardens & buildings (now very rare in England, comparatively to other countries)' and of the projected palace at Greenwich (III. 297, 313). It was after a difference with Sir John Denham – whose official business it was – over the siting of Greenwich that Evelyn 'came away, knowing Sir *John* to be a better Poet than Architect' (III. 300–1), a circumstance which did not prevent his addressing the second dedication of the *Parallel* to him.[1] In 1664 also Wren discussed with Evelyn the designs for the Sheldonian Theatre, 'not disdaining my advise in some particulars' (III. 385). He was friendly with Hugh May, who 'by procuring a most accurate Edition of the Plates' of Fréart's book encouraged him to complete and publish his translation of the *Parallel*.[2]

Evelyn saw, and commented on, many medieval buildings, and here the attitude of the Diary is appreciably different from the strictures in the *Account*. The first edition of 1664 says nothing, but his attitude had hardened into Augustan orthodoxy by the time, towards 1697,[3] that he prepared the expanded edition published in 1707. There, a few pages after the prefatory praise of Wren and the famous 'Phoenix' reference to the new St Paul's, he launches into a wholesale condemnation of the Middle Ages which includes for contrast further praise of the works of Wren.[4] All comes under fire:

Congestions of Heavy, Dark, Melancholy and Monkish Piles, without any just Proportion, Use or Beauty, compar'd with the truly Antient...Slender and Misquine[5] Pillars, or rather bundles of Staves, and other incongruous Props ... Cut-work and Crinkle Crankle ... Mountains of Stone, Vast, and Gygantic Buildings indeed; but not Worthy the Name of Architecture: Witness ... what are yet standing at Westminster, Canterbury, Salisbury,

1. The remark about Denham may or may not be contemporary.

2. Dedication to Denham.   3. The date of the dedication.

4. For the history of the word 'Gothic' and Evelyn's use of it see Diary, VI. 1–7, and E. S. de Beer, 'Gothic: Origin and Diffusion of the Term', *Journal of the Warburg and Courtauld Institutes*, XI (1948), pp. 143–62.

5. French *mesquin*: mean, slender.

Peterborow, Ely, Wells, Beverly, Lincoln, Gloucester, York, Durham . . . Utrecht, Harlem, Antwerp, Strasburg, Basil . . . Amiens, Paris, Roan, Tours, Lyons . . . Milan, Venice, Florence . . .

And so on. But when he wrote for himself, Chichester was 'faire', Utrecht 'an incomparable Gothick fabrick', Antwerp 'very remarkable', Saint-Denis 'stately', Bruges 'well built à la Gotic', Tours no worse than 'vast', Florence 'reputed one of the noblest buildings in Europe', Fossanova 'very agreeably melancholy', St George at Windsor 'admirable', Salisbury 'the compleatest piece of Gotic-Worke in Europe, taken in all its uniformitie', Worcester 'noble', York 'magnificent', Beverley 'stately', Lincoln 'comparable to that of York it selfe', Peterborough 'exceeding faire', Newstead 'glorious', Norwich 'venerable', one of the gateways at Bury St Edmunds 'magnificent', Winchester 'a reverend pile' (this is as late as 1685). His remarks on Notre-Dame in Paris are entirely statistical, and of the Sainte-Chapelle he noted only the slenderness of the piers. At King's College Chapel, Cambridge, and the staircase at Christ Church, Oxford, it was the technical skill that he admired, as at Stonehenge, but the latter, he noted, 'appears like a castle at a distance'. St Mark's, Venice, he found rich but altogether too dark, dismal, and heavy; not only is this stricture unusual, but many of his epithets show positive, if qualified or muted, appreciation. It seems as if Evelyn inherited and perhaps transmitted, at least in private life, another facet of Elizabethan taste, an incipient medievalism, part antiquarian and part picturesque. The idea of retrospect certainly exists, for at the beginning of the Diary he calls Wotton, his birthplace, 'large & antient, suitable to those hospitable times', and later on, Beddington, 'a faire old hall but a scambling [rambling] house', becomes 'capacious, & in form of the buildings of the Age in Hen: 8 & Q. Eliz: time & proper for the old English hospitality' (II. 4; III. 221; V. 427). There are similar references to 'the antient hospitality' over the old house at Swallowfield and Mr Slingsby's house at Burrough Green (IV. 481; III. 553).

Indeed it may be said that the division between the old and the new more or less corresponds to Evelyn's private and public taste: that while he tried to lead in public, by his books, presence, and personal advocacy, there was in his efforts an element of conscience rather than inclination, of intellectual enthusiasm rather than original speculation; that his natural taste was a little old-fashioned in comparison with his contemporaries Pratt and May. He remembered the Queen of Bohemia's 'Dutch Renaissance' (as we should call it) palace at Rhenen as 'after the Italian manner' (II. 35). The quotations given by Dr Girouard in the previous essay in this volume (p. 13) show that he was able to admire Hatfield, built a few years before his birth. Charlton, the Laudian quadrangle at St John's, Oxford, Welbeck, and Worksop are on various occasions praised and even Kirby is 'very noble' and 'built à la moderne'[1]

1. 'Modern' sometimes means Gothic, sometimes post-medieval.

(III. 66, 108, 127, 133–4). He committed himself most at Audley End, which he visited in 1654. At a second visit, sixteen years later, his favourable opinion was only modified by a slightly more specific identification of its style as 'antico-moderno'.

Evelyn was not insensitive, and some of his remarks on contemporary buildings newly completed or in progress are especially interesting. New developments abroad must have been a revelation – the octagonal timber dome at Willemstad or the cupola of the Sorbonne for example (II. 60, 97) – but again he tends to understatement. There is however one appreciable notice of a progressive Roman Baroque building. Though he visited the Sapienza he is silent about Borromini's S. Ivo, begun three years previously, but he does describe S. Carlino as 'a singular fabrique for neateness as built all of a new white stone, & an excellent oval designe'. He was possibly impervious to the complexities of oval-based spatial composition – he remembered the Colosseum as circular – but in any case at least he was not shocked by the 'odd and chimerical beauties'.[1] Moreover he noted what many writers do not: the crypt with pilasters on the same plan. His further comment that the columns are 'worth the notice' is tantalizing: for their rhythm, their engagement in the wall, their diverse capitals, or something more ordinary? (II. 242). The Mansart wing at Blois, which he saw as a carcass, was 'a faire building', and having visited Maisons, the most classical French building of the time and 'a noble pile', he returned another day 'to take a more exact view of a place formerly so pleasant to me ... the body of the house not vast, but neate, & well contriv'd, especialy the staire case, & ornament of Puti about it' (II. 141, 563; III. 18).

There remain only the buildings designed by his friends and acquaintances, and in these he must have taken something of a proprietary interest, as he did in the St Paul's problem, the Highways Commission, and the Royal Society. Again his omissions are surprising and disappointing; again, although he is at times noticeably more critical and more detailed, his criticisms tend to be on grounds either of convenience or of fitness to the setting or the occasion; again he is liable to be dazzled by furniture or decoration. His sharpest comment was directed against the brusque unpedimented Doric tetrastyle temple built in the garden at Wotton by his cousin George Evelyn. George 'had ben in Italy, but was mistaken in the Architecture of the Portico, which tho' making a magnificent shew, has great faults in the Colonade, both as to the Order, which should have been Corinthian & the Ornaments' (I. 55). Further, he 'believed himselfe a better Architect than realy he was, witnesse the Portico ... he had a large mind, but over built every thing' (II. 551). Something altogether lighter, slenderer, and more decorative would have been more suitable for its position overlooking the south front of the house.

At the other extreme of competence, he approved of Wren's Winchester, Kensington, and Chelsea Hospital (v. 471; v. 237, 53) but recorded one criticism of the new

1. Introduction to *Vitruvius Britannicus*.

St Paul's, which he did not live to see completed. The single notice refers to the striking of the scaffold from the choir in 1694: he thought it otherwise 'without reproach' but took exception to the placing of columns in the upper storey above pilasters in the lower, outside the east end (v. 192). In a building he must have wanted to be a paragon of all that the new order and correctness stood for in architecture, such an irregularity was distressing, and he failed to see Wren's purpose in developing plastically the whole upper exterior of the apse.

His sense of propriety and of the occasion is strong. In other buildings less firmly rhythmical, less unavoidably prominent, he seems to have been less worried. In 1705 he reported the buildings at Greenwich to be 'now going on very magnificent' (v. 600). The unusual and unclassical elevations of the King William Block were still in scaffold but he certainly knew what they looked like; his silence cannot be due to ignorance. Moreover, two years previously the absurdly tall porticoed front of Addiscombe, being built for his son-in-law by the Greenwich mason Edward Strong and having a good deal in common with the King William Block, elicited nothing but enthusiastic praise (v. 541).

He was clearly interested in the great houses of the 1660s to the early 80s, the period dominated by Pratt and May; the Diary covers Horseheath and Clarendon House by Pratt, and nearly all May's known works, and his criticism is more detailed here than anywhere else in the Diary. Horseheath, which derived from Pratt's own Coleshill, he did not greatly like: it was costly and 'seated in a Parke, with a Sweete Prospect & stately avenue' but the water supply was poor and 'The house has also its infirmities', which he did not enumerate (III. 553). The larger Clarendon House, Piccadilly, he praised without qualification in a letter to Lord Chancellor Clarendon's son, but when writing for himself he found it 'a goodly pile, but with many defects as to the Architecture, though placed most gracefully'.[1] In retrospect, however, it acquired with the exiled and deceased Lord Chancellor the aura of the irrevocable past; when it was sold and demolished in 1683 after only sixteen years it had become (in two separate notices) 'the glorious Palace' and 'that costly & onely sumptuous Palace ... this stately Palace' (IV. 321, 338–9).

May was a more professional figure, who attempted and achieved more, but whose work has suffered as much through time as Pratt's; here Evelyn is a major source in a scanty field. Windsor he could only praise, both the Verrio–Gibbons interiors and, in 1680, 'that stately Court' (IV. 207). He visited Eltham Lodge under construction and thought it 'not well contrived', disliking the roof (possibly for the change in pitch halfway up which gives it a flare), the lowness of the rooms (a matter of commodity which he raised in the *Account*),[2] and the 'Kitchins where the Cellars

---

1. It is tempting to conclude from these opinions and the disagreement over Old St Paul's that Evelyn's estimation of Pratt, an amateur like himself, was not very high.

2. p. 12.

should be' – he was used to the ample and convenient ground-floor kitchens of earlier houses (III. 375–6). He was not displeased with Cornbury, which he saw soon after (III. 382); it is a translation of Eltham into stone, but the Diary notes neither this nor the Dutch character of both the roof and the elevation at Eltham. Berkeley House, Piccadilly, pleased him better but again lacked commodity (III. 125); he called it a palace, 'truely … very well built, and has many noble roomes, but they are not so Convenient, because it consisting of but one *Corps de Logis*, there are no Clossets, all are roomes of State'. A view of the house bears out his comment that the quadrants flanking the house were imperfectly related to the centre, for they were only three-quarters the height of the main ground storey.[1] He was less precise about Sir Stephen Fox's house at Chiswick, 'somewhat heavy & thick; & not so well understood' (IV. 294). Cassiobury he also saw before it was entirely finished (IV. 199–200) but he expected its completion to make it 'a very noble Palace', although again he thought the site (re-used from an older house) poor in most respects. In its context 'a plaine fabric' denotes approval, and significantly the feature he disliked was 'the middle Doores being round', that is round-headed and a complicating element in the elevation. He noted 'divers faire & good roomes' and the work of Gibbons and Verrio. The pediment relief, which from another source we know to be the work of a 'foreigner',[2] he thought 'cut … handsomely enough' but mentioned neither the artist nor the Dutch derivation of the feature.

Evelyn also knew Robert Hooke, through the Royal Society ('Mr Hooke of our Society'), and the Diary has notices of three of his works. The new Bedlam Hospital he called 'magnificently built, & most sweetely placed' (IV. 134) but he noted neither its foreign features nor its revolutionary planning. He said nothing about the College of Physicians beyond regretting its situation so near Newgate Gaol and 'in so obscure an hole' (IV. 307). If he failed to note Dutch influences on May and Hooke, however, he was conscious of French influence,[3] both at Euston, Lord Arlington's seat (architect unknown), and in Hooke's Montagu House, Bloomsbury. Euston had '4 great pavilions after the french, beside a body of a large house' (III. 591). 'Mr Montagues new Palace … after the French manner' interested him so much that he went to see it on three separate occasions. The second time he called it 'somewhat after the French' and the third time 'built after the French pavilion way' (IV. 90, 184, 344). The only known representation of the house, which was burnt down in 1686, confirms that the corner pavilions, *corps de logis*, and centre all had separate hipped

1. B. H. Johnson, *Berkeley Square to Bond Street* (London, 1952), facing p. 112. The house was burnt down in 1733.

2. C. H. Collins Baker, *Lely and the Stuart Portrait Painters* (London, 1912), II, p. 133. Was the carver Quellin?

3. His attitude to French fashion has been mentioned (see note 1 on p. 31); cf. also the notice of chimneypieces at Wilton based on designs by Jean Barbet, which he recognizes as 'after the French best manner' (III. 114).

roofs.[1] On this third occasion Evelyn gave a panegyric of Verrio's decorations and criticized the exterior; the elevations were 'not answerable to the inside'– presumably a matter of embellishment rather than planning – and the court was too narrow from the street and 'meanely built' and overlooked by neighbours. Once again the criticism is of convenience rather than of form.

The Diary has nothing about the future of architecture. Not only must Evelyn have speculated on the matter; with his Royal Society colleagues he was concerned with progress, artistic as well as technical. In the *Account* he enumerates some of the major writers since Vitruvius and continues:

it were I say, becoming our great Needs that some Ingenious Person did take this in Hand, and Advance upon the Principles already establish'd, and not so Acquiesce in them as if there were a *Non Ultra* Engraven upon our Columns like those of Hercules, after which there remained no more to be discovered.[2]

In this light Colen Campbell's praise of Palladio, who 'seems to have arrived to a Ne plus ultra of his art',[3] seems to look only backward.

1. K. Downes, *English Baroque Architecture* (London, 1966), figure 24.
2. p. 5.
3. Preface to *Vitruvius Britannicus*.

French Eighteenth-Century Opinion on Wren

BY R. D. MIDDLETON

THE architecture of Sir Christopher Wren is not much admired in France. Paul Biver introduces him in André Michel's *Histoire de l'art* with the words – 'un nom très illustre en Angleterre'[1] – thus disclaiming all personal or national interest. Louis Hautecœur refers to him laconically in the *Histoire de l'architecture classique en France* as 'le grand architecte Anglais'.[2] He is swiftly consigned to greatness, but nowhere is any commentary offered on the nature of this greatness, nor is any description made of the buildings that are meant to sustain it. There is no monograph on him in French. In England, of course, things are different. The amount of historical and critical writing devoted to Wren and his works is enormous. From James Elmes's pioneering memoir of 1823, C. R. Cockerell's tribute of 1838, and his friend John Clayton's compendious *Works of Sir Christopher Wren* (1848–9) – from this time onwards Wren has consistently engaged zealous, parochial minds. No fewer than seven appraisals have been published in England during the past seventeen years.[3]

Perversely, it was during the period of the English lapse in admiration, from his ousting from the surveyorship in 1718 to the Elmes revival a century later, that Wren was most appreciated in France. French eighteenth-century architects were caught by the confident calm of St Paul's. They found fault with the detail but the sheer grandeur of the building and, in particular, the evidence of Wren's easy mastery of the problems of statics won them over. Nor was this interest an aspect simply of that vogue for things English that is so important a part of French eighteenth-

1. Vol. VI, part 2, p. 772.
2. Vol. II.
3. J. Lindsey, *Wren: his Work and Times* (London, 1951); R. Dutton, *The Age of Wren* (London, 1951); Martin S. Briggs, *Christopher Wren* (London, 1951); Martin S. Briggs, *Wren the Incomparable* (London, 1953); John Summerson, *Sir Christopher Wren* (London, 1953); Viktor Fürst, *The Architecture of Sir Christopher Wren* (London, 1956); Eduard F. Sekler, *Wren and his Place in European Architecture* (London, 1956).

40

century thought. The French were studiously indifferent to most other seventeenth-
and eighteenth-century English architecture.

S. de Sorbière published his *Relation d'un voyage en Angleterre* in Paris in 1664,
including in it enthusiastic accounts of the Royal Society and Wren's Oxford
friends, but he made no mention of Wren or his early buildings. The only example
of contemporary English architecture that Sorbière thought worthy of comment
was Inigo Jones's 'sale de Witte-hall',[1] but even that was but dubiously acclaimed –
'elle paroist magnifique', he wrote, 'parce que tout le reste du Palais est mal basti'.[2]
Later seventeenth-century travellers were no less perfunctory on the subject of
English architecture, but by the end of the century they were able to include in their
list of sights a few of Wren's London churches and even St Paul's, for the first
service was held there in 1697, though the dome and west towers were not completed
for another fourteen years. In 1698 H. M. de V. published at The Hague a *Mémoire*
on an English journey, illustrating the steeple of St Mary-le-Bow – 'l'église qui
porte ce nom est, après celle de S. Paul, la plus belle de la ville de Londres'[3] – and
containing a long description of St Paul's. But the building described is the Gothic
cathedral, complete with Inigo Jones's portico, burned down in 1666.[4] Of Wren's
monument he remarks merely that it is building steadily. Similarly the author of
Les Délices d'Angleterre, printed at The Hague in 1706, referred his readers to the
Gothic building.[5] But there was no such confusion or misrepresentation in the
Lausannois Guy Miège's (1644–1718?) *Nouvel État présent de la Grande Bretagne*,
published two years later in Amsterdam. 'Pour commencer par les églises,' he wrote
of the sights of London, 'je crois pouvoir dire qu'après celle de S. Pierre, à Rome,
il n'y en a point au monde de plus grande et de plus superbe que la cathédrale de
S. Paul.'[6] His description of the building is prosaic and need not be recounted.[7]
'Le Chevalier Christophle Wren' is named as the architect, though he is not mentioned in connexion with others of his churches (St Lawrence, St Michael Cornhill,
St Mary-le-Bow, Christchurch, St Bride, St Dunstan, St Andrew Holborn, and in
Westminster, St Clement, St Anne, and St James) to which attention is directed.
Miège is the first to make the familiar comparison between St Paul's and St Peter's,
but it was invoked soon after in the random jottings *Remarques sur l'Angleterre,
faites en 1713 par Monsieur de S.G.*, in which the limited range of Wren's architecture
as exposed by the comparison is noted.

On ne dispute point le second rang à S. Paul de Londres pour la beauté et la magnificence
de l'architecture, et peut-être mérite-t-il le premier pour les ornemens extérieurs. C'est

1. Sorbière, op. cit., p. 40.　　　　　2. ibid., p. 41.

3. H. M. de V., *Mémoires et observations faites par un voyageur en Angleterre* (La Haye, 1698),
p. 298.

4. ibid., p. 337.　　　　　5. op. cit., p. 83.

6. Guy Miège, op. cit., I, p. 22.　　　　　7. ibid., I, p. 169 f.

l'ouvrage du Chevalier Christophle Wren. Il alla à Rome exprès et au retour il bâtit ce superbe temple qu'il a mis dans la perfection où il paroit.[1]

Wren's French visit of 1666 has clearly been extended to include Italy as well. But on the whole the author's comments are not ill-informed, and for sharp and compressed criticism the guide is unmatched by any other of the period. 'Les Anglois', the author records, 'ne sont ni peintres, ni sculteurs, ni architectes; mais ils sont habiles dans les arts mécaniques. Ils entendent fort bien l'échaufaudage, la charpenterie, et la menuiserie.'[2] Only one house in London is favoured, that of the Duke of Montagu.

The standard London house was described with some wonder in the *Remarques sur l'état présent d'Angleterre*, printed in 1715 in Amsterdam, though it was naturally the grander houses that were thought most worthy of the visitor's attention: those of the Duke of Montagu and the Duke of Buckingham. Wren's great church was unquestioningly accepted as *the* architectural ornament of London – 'l'église de S. Paul est ce qu'il y a de plus beau à Londres'.[3] The description that follows is longer than usual, but what is more unconformable is the detailed account of the construction of the great brick cone and the dome it supports. All the author's shrewdest comments are directed to this aspect of the architecture. He deals briefly with what were regarded as the chief failings of the building – it was too large, it was insufficiently ornamented (though it was considered that there were too many columns and pilasters bundled together around the towers), and the interior was too dark, in particular at the west end, where Wren had built up the mass with a library and upper rooms, thus obscuring the light.[4] But what nagged him most was the quality of the building work – 'non obstant cette solidité apparente', he wrote,

l'église est mal bâtie, puisqu'il se détache tous les jours des pierres de la muraille, ce qui vient de ce qu'ayant voulu faire les jointes justes, il est arrivé que les pierres n'appuyent pas également partout les unes sur les autres, mais qui portant plus sur les bords, par le poids du bâtiment, elles viennent à s'écraser.[5]

And for three pages he continued this straightforward analysis of the structural faults of the fabric, seriously questioning Wren's practical ability and concluding that it would have been wiser for him to have imitated old Roman methods of building. Here, certainly, was a connoisseur of construction. But he was one of the last to look searchingly at St Paul's; subsequent visitors looked upon it as a testament to the art of construction, sometimes, as we shall see, to their cost.

Despite the growing range of interest in St Paul's that these guide-books show and the impetus that they must have given to contemporary travel (albeit with their accounts of English learning and institutions rather than architecture) there seems to have been no further spate of exposition until, in 1733, an unidentified author, H. Le Blanc, issued *L'Architecture des églises anciennes et nouvelles*, which had for

1. op. cit., p. 13.　　　2. ibid., p. 12.　　　3. op. cit., p. 181.
4. ibid., p. 184.　　　5. ibid., p. 184.

specific purpose the advertisement of St Paul's – 'un enfant perdu que j'envoye à la découverte'.[1] The publication of this thirty-eight-page pamphlet followed soon after Béat de Murault's *Lettres sur les Anglais et les Français* (1724) and Voltaire's *Lettres philosophiques* (1726), which are generally held to have inspired a fervent French vogue for English philosophy and politics,[2] but it seems in no way to have been part of the wave of fashion for things English that followed. Limited in scope, it is yet as personal and original as Voltaire's celebrated tract. Absolutely, it provides us with the most provocative and elaborate analysis of Gothic architecture to be published in France during the first half of the eighteenth century. For it was Le Blanc's method first to analyse the architecture of the great Gothic cathedrals, in particular that at Reims, and then to compare it to that of St Paul's.

To take Gothic thus as a basis for comparison might seem odd, but in France, despite the spleen and spluttering of men of taste, Gothic had not ceased to be admired from the Middle Ages onwards.[3] Innumerable guide-books attest to its popularity. The great Claude Perrault even subscribed to a vital interest when defending his Louvre colonnade against the assaults of François Blondel. The slender, widely spaced columns, he said, were intended to evoke the arrangement of shafts in a Gothic cathedral. 'Le goust de nostre siècle,' he wrote, 'ou du moins de nostre nation, est différent de celuy des Anciens, et peut-estre qu'en cela il tient un peu du Gothique, car nous aimons l'air, le jour et les dégagements.'[4]

With this precedent and probably Perrault's design for a church of Sainte-Geneviève in mind,[5] two revolutionary theorists, Frémin,[6] author of *Mémoires critiques d'architecture* of 1702, and the Abbé J. L. de Cordemoy (1631–1713),[7] who four years later published the *Nouveau Traité de toute l'architecture*, proposed that the columnar arrangement and the proportions of Gothic cathedrals be taken as the model for contemporary church design. What they had in mind was an architecture made up in imitation of the spare, isolated columns of a Gothic cathedral, but supporting an array of horizontal lintels and, above, barrel-vaults. Though the archi-

---

1. op. cit., p. 38.

2. Louis Reynaud, *Le Romantisme: les origines anglo-germaniques* (Paris, 1926); Churton Collins, *Voltaire, Montesquieu and Rousseau in England* (London, 1908).

3. For a brief summary of this subject and a list of more detailed studies see the author's 'The Abbé de Cordemoy and the Graeco–Gothic Ideal', *Journal of the Warburg and Courtauld Institutes*, XXV, nos. 3–4 (1962); XXVI (1963).

4. Claude Perrault, *Les Dix Livres d'architecture* (1684 edn), p. 80, n. 16.

5. Michael Petzet, 'Un Projet des Perrault pour l'église Sainte-Geneviève à Paris', *Bulletin monumentale*, CXV (1957), pp. 81–96.

6. See Dorothea Nyberg, 'The *Mémoires critiques d'architecture* by Michel de Frémin', *Journal of the Society of Architectural Historians* (December 1963).

7. The dates of birth and death of the Abbé Jean Louis de Cordemoy, long confused with his brother, Louis Gerard de Cordemoy II, have now been established by Roman d'Amat, *Dictionnaire de biographie française* (Paris, 1961).

tecture was to be Gothic in inspiration it was to be Classical in appearance. Other theorists took up these ideas and there was a great deal of sharp and critical comment on the subject.[1] Le Blanc's remarks on church design show that he was well aware of the controversy. But he was no idiosyncratic enthusiast of Gothic in classical dress: he inclined rather to accept Fénelon's estimate of Gothic. In the much quoted *Lettre écrite à l'Academie Française* (before 1713), Fénelon had contrasted the satisfying air of repose and solidity of Greek architecture with what he termed the vain refinement of Gothic. A Gothic cathedral, he said, was no more than a piece of trumpery; it had the brittle elegance of a Chinese lantern.

'Le goût Gothique', Le Blanc wrote in emulation,

fait consister le capital de la batisse dans l'interruption de la massonnerie, que l'on épargne le plus qu'il est possible pour mettre à la place de grandes fenêtres, et autres ouvertures liées ensemble, par des trumeaux fort étroits, et qui paroissent à peine suffisans pour soutenir la masse; en sorte que la massonnerie employée, comme à regret, ne sert pour ainsi dire, que de bordure aux fenêtres, et aux autres ouvertures.[2]

The prime objective of Gothic architects, Le Blanc considered, was to diminish mass in architecture. Light was their guiding passion. They wished to create luminous volumes. All the elegance of Gothic cathedrals, the whittled masonry, the taut, contained details – 'miniatures et autres ornemens rentrans' – were conceived in a lunatic attempt to recreate the dim-glimmering light of the forests of Gaul, by which, he conceived, they were ultimately inspired. 'L'architecture Gothique', he wrote,

met...une église toute en fenêtres, et dérobe tant qu'elle peut la masse. On ne sçauroit, selon ses partisans, avoir trop de lumière, et trop peu de masse; mais un édifice doit il ressembler à un fallot, fait exprès pour rendre la lumière qu'on a placée au dedans?[3]

Though he appreciated the technical virtuosity of the Gothic masons, Le Blanc considered that their obsessive interest in light had driven them beyond the limits of sound construction –

l'adresse d'un pilier long et délicat est une beauté trompeuse, parce qu'il ne supporte point en effet le fardeau dont il paroit chargé. Les piliers supportent à la vérité de petits ceintres, mais ceux-ci aboutissent à un grand qui les couvre tous sans les charger en aucune façon, il prend sa force des murs qui le serrent et l'empêchent de porter sur les petits piliers; la grossièreté de cet ouvrage est dérobée par une infinité de tourillons, de moulures, de cordons et autres imperfections, qui couvre un grand défaut. Si ces piliers étaient effectivement chargées de la masse qu'ils paroissent porter, ils s'écarteroient en éclats, comme ont fait les supports de la tour de Dôle.[4]

1. See the author's article on the Abbé de Cordemoy already cited, and Dorothea Nyberg, '*La Sainte Antiquité*: Focus of an eighteenth-century Architectural Debate', *Essays in the History of Architecture presented to Rudolf Wittkower* (London, 1967).

2. Le Blanc, op. cit., p. 8.   3. ibid., p. 12.   4. ibid., p. 16.

Yet Le Blanc was clearly familiar with and moved by the Gothic cathedrals of France. He greatly admired the façade of Reims – 'ce fameux portail,' he concluded his eulogy,

quoique d'une architecture fort ancienne, a plus d'air de grandeur que les façades de S. Paul à Londres et de S. Pierre de Rome. Les *vomitora* ou *vomitores* pour rendre et recevoir le peuple, semblent faire des invitations pressants de venir au service; avantage que n'a point la façade de S. Paul, dont la porte le fait chercher à travers les colonnes, et où l'on ne soupçonne pas qu'il y ait des portes collaterales. Les façades nouvelles de S. Pierre et de S. Paul disent à vos yeux, demeurez au déhors pour nous admirer, plutôt que d'entrer dans l'église: le portail de Reims dit au contraire, entrez dans l'église plutôt que de m'admirer. Les tours du portail de Reims entrent naturellement dans le dessein, elles sont nécessaires, et elles ne pouvoient être mieux placées qu'à l'entrée, au lieu qu'à Londres on a forcé la nature du dessein pour les y faire venir.[1]

Not that Le Blanc's praise of St Paul's was less fulsome –

la façade de S. Paul à Londres est incontestablement un des plus beaux morceaux d'architecture de la Chrétienté: rien n'est plus saillant; il s'avance au devant du spectateur, lui étale de lui même sa magnificence, et semble lui présenter des beautés presque animées par leur relief.[2]

For what he admired especially in contemporary architecture was the way in which the surfaces were moulded and decorated with ornament so that the whole became a solid in *basso relievo*. But it was for the interior of St Paul's that he reserved his greatest eloquence and ingenuity of argument. Curiously, he thought it altogether appropriate that the nave should appear shorter and the vaults lower than they in fact were – 'ne croyez pas pour cela', he added, 'qu'il soit trop court, et trop bas, cela prouve seulement que les églises Gothiques sont trop hautes et trop étroites'.[3] The dome of the crossing, though, was the source of St Paul's special excellence – 'cette rose du dôme', he wrote,

vous paroît comme une place très superbe, qui au milieu d'une belle ville en rassemble au centre toutes les beautés. La proportion de cette rose est si juste, et entre si bien dans le dessein de l'édifice, pour faire corps avec lui, qu'on ne distingue point si elle est faite pour le temple ou le temple pour elle.[4]

The purpose of all Le Blanc's analysis and observation was to suggest that St Paul's, rather than the Gothic cathedrals upheld by Frémin and Cordemoy, should serve as a model for contemporary churches. But not St Paul's alone. He mentioned other churches in London (though none did he mention by name) and an odd, hybrid selection in the Low Countries, the most notable being Saint-Sepulchre at Cambrai,

1. ibid., p. 29.   2. ibid., p. 25.
3. ibid., p. 36.   4. ibid.

though local critics, he observed, considered it inferior to Saint-Martin at Tournai, from which it is said to have been copied.[1]

Le Blanc's pamphlet was reviewed in July 1734 in the *Mercure de France* by the engineer A. F. Frézier, who had earlier indulged in a furious exchange with the Abbé de Cordemoy. Frézier was delighted by Le Blanc's strictures on Gothic, but was not prepared to accept his proposals concerning St Paul's – 'si l'on doit prendre pour modèle des nouvelles églises celles des premiers siècles du Christianisme', he wrote, 'dont les novateurs ne peuvent rejetter les saints usages, on trouvera dans celle de S. Pierre des conformitez avec ces modèles qui manquent à S. Paul de Londres'.[2] Unabashed (and travel-snob that he was), he admitted that he had not seen St Paul's and was not much moved to – he knew it only from a copy of a drawing by Hulsbergh. Le Blanc's propaganda appears to have had no other immediate effect, though it might be held accountable for Contant d'Ivry's, and thus Jacques François Blondel's fertilizing interest in the churches of the Low Countries during the following decades. Certainly, no architect of importance took up his cue to imitate St Paul's – this had, however, already been done.

In 1732, the year before Le Blanc's pamphlet was published, J. N. Servandoni (1695–1766) submitted in competition and won with a design for the west façade of Saint-Sulpice that was evidently modelled on that of St Paul's (Plates 7 and 8).[3] Servandoni had been to England on at least two occasions since 1724, so that there is no doubt that he was familiar with Wren's building. During the building of the portico of Saint-Sulpice the entablature over the lower order (which in the winning design was broken into three distinct segments to correspond to the flanking towers and the central feature) was made continuous across the centre so that it overlapped the bases of the towers, making it more reminiscent yet of St Paul's (Plate 9). Subsequent changes in the design, however, made the completed work far more stark and chaste than Wren's lively original and it is difficult now to discern the relationship. Not that contemporaries were ready to acknowledge it. The Abbé J. B. Leblanc (1706–81), one of those critics, grouped around the Comte de Caylus (1692–1765), who were eager to see an 'antique' severity infused into contemporary architecture, early acclaimed Servandoni's façade. Writing in 1748, before the towers

1. Saint-Martin at Tournai is illustrated in Paul Parent, *L'Architecture des Pays Bas méridionaux aux XVIe, XVIIe, et XVIIIe siècles* (Paris–Brussels, 1926), plates XLV, XLVII; Saint-Sepulchre at Cambrai, now the cathedral, is shown in Joan Evans, *Monastic Architecture in France from the Renaissance to the Revolution* (Cambridge, 1964), plate 74. The other examples of ecclesiastical architecture that Le Blanc considered to be in the 'goût Grec' were the façade of the Dominican church (Parent, op. cit., p. 183), the façade and church of the Récollets (Parent, op. cit., p. 183), the Augustinian church (i.e. Saint-André, see J. Evans, op. cit., plates 636–7) and that of the Carmes Déchaux, all in Lille. In Brussels he admired the Carmelite church, in Antwerp the Jesuit church (i.e. St Charles Borromée, see Parent, op. cit., plate XXX).

2. *Mercure de France* (July 1734), p. 1500.

3. See the author's article, already cited, on the Abbé de Cordemoy.

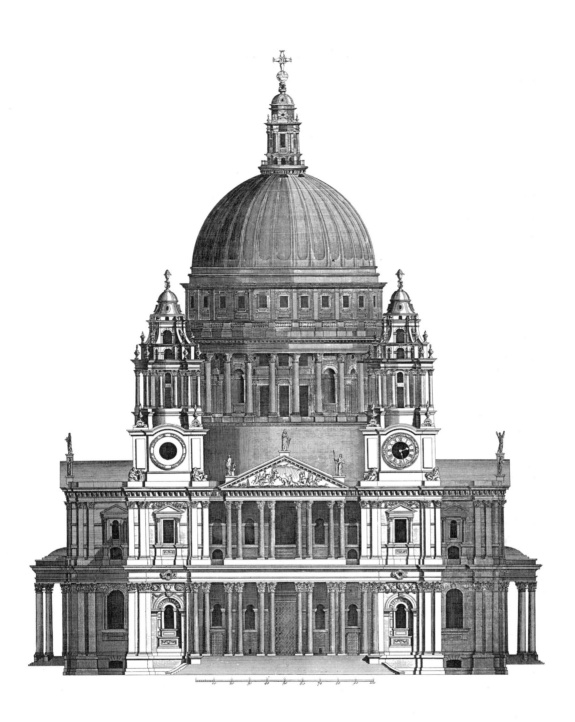

7. West elevation of St Paul's, London

or the pediment it once supported were complete, Leblanc said: 'L'élégance de sa composition, ses grandes et belles proportions, l'élevation majestueuse du parvis, nous retrace ces beaux temples de la Grèce'.[1] But he found no corresponding merit in the façade of St Paul's. In a letter written in 1737, or soon after, to the Comte de Caylus (and published in 1745 in the *Lettres d'un Français concernant le gouvernement, la politique et les mœurs des Anglais et des Français*) Leblanc described St Paul's:

L'architecte qui a bâti leur fameuse église de Saint Paul de Londres, aux proportions près qu'il a très mal observées, n'a fait que réduire le plan de Saint Pierre de Rome aux deux tiers de sa grandeur: pour peu que l'on ait de sa connoissance, il est aisé de s'appercevoir que partout où il s'est écarté de son modèle, il a commis les fautes les plus grossières.[2]

Similarly, he condemned the school of *Vitruvius Britannicus*; only Inigo Jones won his approval. P. J. Mariette (1694–1774), another member of Caylus's circle, also approved; he wrote of Jones in the *Abécédario* as 'l'un des plus célèbres architectes de ces derniers siècles', and went on to describe those of his works listed in Kent's publication.[3] In 1749 the Abbé Leblanc was chosen as *cicerone* to the Marquis de Marigny, Madame de Pompadour's brother, the future Directeur des Bâtiments. Two other more vigorous and engaging reformers, the architect J. G. Soufflot (1713–80) and the engraver C. N. Cochin (1715–90), were also appointed to accompany Marigny to Italy. The journey was of considerable importance to the future of French architecture; for Soufflot and Cochin in particular so effectively indoctrinated their charge that on their return to France in 1751 they were able to instigate a campaign of reform in the arts and architecture under his direct patronage. In January 1755, at Marigny's instigation, Soufflot was appointed to design the church of Sainte-Geneviève, now known as the Panthéon.[4] The design, approved in the following year, was intended and regarded as the embodiment of a new architectural ideal. Soufflot had in fact taken up the ideas of Frémin and Cordemoy to create a church elaborately classical in appearance, but studiously Gothic in its columnar and structural arrangement. Internally, high and slender Corinthian columns (rather than piers) supported an array of vaults and flat domes, and even the main dome was designed to appear to rest on clusters of free-standing columns. Members of the Academy considered the structure too audacious. During the early 1760s Soufflot was compelled to reassure them as to the soundness of his construction by referring to a whole range of lightly constructed churches, from Notre-Dame

1. Leblanc, *Lettre sur la peinture, sculpture et architecture* (Paris, 1748), p. 45.
2. ibid., II, p. 41.
3. P. J. Mariette, 'Abécédario', in the *Archives de l'art français*, VI (Paris, 1845–6), pp. 8 f.
4. On the history of this church see J. Mondain Monval, *Soufflot, sa vie, son œuvre, son ésthetique, 1713–1780* (Paris, 1918); Mae Mathieu, *Pierre Patte, sa vie et son œuvre* (Paris, 1940); Michael Petzet, *Soufflots Sainte-Geneviève und der französische Kirchenbau des 18. Jahrhunderts* (Berlin, 1961).

8. Servandoni's first design for the west front of Saint-Sulpice, Paris, 1732

9. Servandoni's revised design for the west front of Saint-Sulpice, Paris, engraved 1742

at Dijon to S. Agostino at Piacenza. As part of the considerable campaign launched on Soufflot's behalf the Jesuit Abbé Maior (1722–80+), known also as Père Avril, published a series of articles (there were seventeen in all) between October 1758 and December 1760 in the *Mémoires de Trevoux*. These were revised and printed together in book form in 1774, under the title *Temples anciens et modernes*. But in all essential respects they remained the same. Seven were devoted to the antiquities of Rome and Roman temple design, three were on Early Christian and Gothic churches, then followed two articles on Sancta Sophia and five on 'La Renaissance de l'architecture Gothique'. In this section, muddled together with a great deal of special pleading for Sainte-Geneviève, was an account of St Paul's. Maior was not complimentary. He regarded Wren as a tasteless bungler. 'Au milieu de l'ordonnance Corinthienne que règne dans tout l'édifice,' he wrote, 'n'apperçoit-on pas dans un grand nombre de parties de détail un mélange de maigreur et de pesanteur qui tient un peu au discordant du Gothique?'[1] The proportions were irregular, the articulation of details chaotic and inexplicable. The frieze was not carried through above the arches of the nave and the choir, and though the arches had been allowed to penetrate into this area that should have been reserved for the frieze, they were yet too broad and expansive, making the intervening piers too slender in appearance and certainly too small to receive the giant pilasters planted upon them. The dome was out of scale with the rest of the building and its interior uneasily articulated with raking columns, a licence that Maior was altogether unable to accept.[2]

Such criticism cannot be dismissed as carping connoisseurship; Wren's church was certainly failing in classical correctness. Maior's attack was prompted rather because he himself upheld an ideal of church architecture that was bold, clear-cut, and easily apprehended. He harked after those qualities of *dégagement* that Perrault was the first to value. His taste was that of the critics and architects of the first phase of the Romantic-Classical movement. He was not, moreover, unwilling to recognize Wren's positive achievements – 'Il a été grand géomètre et habile architecte', he concluded, 'il a érigé un vaste édifice noblement distribué, mais son temple est bien éloigné d'égaler St. Pierre de Rome.'

Maior's general opinion of Wren was not shared by all the members of Soufflot's circle. The mathematician Jean Étienne Montucla (1725–99), who defended the design of Sainte-Geneviève to the members of the Academy, noted Wren's architectural prowess in his *Histoire des mathématiques*, published in 1758. 'L'Angleterre', he wrote, lui doit quantité de beaux édifices, entr'autres Saint Paul de Londres, la seule basilique dans le monde Chrétien qui approche de Saint Pierre de Rome. Mais le morceau de prédilection du Chevalier Wren, est son clocher de St. Mary-the-Bows (Sainte Marie aux Arcs), l'un des plus hardis et des plus heureux morceaux en ce genre, écueil de tous les architectes.[3]

1. Maior, *Temples anciens et modernes*, p. 279.
2. ibid., p. 280.   3. Vol. II, p. 467, see also pp. 57, 59, 468, 528.

J. A. N. Rouquet, another of the Soufflot circle, an enamellist who had settled in England, was more equivocal. In the *État des arts en Angleterre*, printed in 1755 and dedicated to Marigny, he wrote: L'église de S. Paul, un des plus grands édifices de l'Europe, est, comme la plupart des grands édifices modernes, une compilation des plus belles parties de l'architecture ancienne'.[1] Rouquet discounted most English architecture, scorning especially the Mansion House.[2] The only structure he fully approved was Westminster Bridge, by the Swiss Charles Labelye, who, he noted bitterly, had not been properly remunerated.[3] And any mastery the English might have in the art of cabinet-making was due, he claimed, to the inspiration of another foreign visitor, Hubert François Gravelot, who like himself had settled for a time in England.[4] G. L. le Rouge, author of the standard handbook for French virtuosi and sightseers in London, *Curiosités de Londres*, printed first in 1763 and again in 1766 and 1770, described the Banqueting House as 'le chef d'œuvre d'architecture d'Inigo Jones',[5] and of St Paul's he wrote: 'cette église en égard à son étendue, sa beauté, sa solidité, sa figure, son architecture, tient le second rang entre S. Pierre à Rome et Sainte Sophie à Constantinople'.[6] His book is dull and unrevealing of any real interest in architecture.

J. D. Leroy's remarks on St Paul's are similarly flat and disappointing. That extraordinary book, *Histoire de la disposition et des formes différentes que les chrétiens ont données à leurs temples* (1764), which followed six years after the publication of his successful survey of the classical buildings of Greece, was probably written to lend support to Soufflot's programme of persuasion. The theories that Soufflot maintained are consistently upheld and the design of Sainte-Geneviève is several times over-praised. St Paul's, as one of the few churches comparable in size to the new Sainte-Geneviève, might, one would therefore imagine, have been dealt with at

---

1. Rouquet, op. cit., p. 145.   2. ibid., p. 152.

3. ibid., p. 153. Labelye was much admired in France by the members of Caylus's circle. Mariette includes him in the *Abécédario* and his papers were left on his death to the Comte de Caylus, who passed them on to the national library.

4. Rouquet, op. cit., p. 160: 'M. Gravelot, pendant le séjour qu'il a fait à Londres, a beaucoup contribué à inspirer le goût des formes à plusiers ouvriers anglois en tout genre.' On Gravelot see Mark Girouard, 'English Art and the Rococo', *Country Life*, 13 and 27 January and 3 February 1966. In contrast to this, Fougeret de Monbron published his *Préservatif contre l'Anglomanie* at Minorque in 1757, in which he recorded the influence of English designers on the French – and deplored it. 'Où trouvera-t-on un homme tel que le fameux Germain pour l'orfévrerie? Quelle delicatesse, quel goût, quelle noblesse règnent dans ses ouvrages. Tout est fini, tout est beau. Les Anglois n'opposent à ces chefs d'œuvres de l'art que des morceaux en filigrane surchargés d'orne-ments gotiques et confus' (p. 17).

He ends his tirade, mainly directed against the vogue for English thought and institutions inspired by Voltaire and the Abbé Leblanc: 'le seul avantage que je sache à ces gens-la, sur nous, c'est qu'ils ont d'excellens chevaux et de tres bons chiens; et n'ont ni moins ni loups' (p. 57).

5. Le Rouge, op. cit., p. 19.   6. ibid., p. 33.

some length. Leroy had not yet visited London but he corresponded with no less a man than William Chambers, who much approved St Paul's.[1] Yet Leroy's book indicates that he was interested in only one feature of the design: the way in which Wren had introduced eight rather than four arches into the crossing. 'Cette disposition', Leroy wrote,

est certainement un trait de génie de la part de l'architecte Anglois, mais il en resulte que les nefs en général paroissent trop petites par rapport à l'étendue immense du dôme; et tout ceux qui ont quelque goût et qui ont vu ce monument, rapporte que le chœur particulièrement paroît extrêmement étroit, d'ailleurs il suffit d'en considérer les desseins pour reconnoître que sa forme n'est pas à beaucoup près aussi belle que celle de Saint Pierre de Rome.[2]

In addition the cross of the plan was not clearly expressed in the relationship of the internal volumes and the façade was weakened by the superimposition of two orders. A giant order would have been preferable.

The next mention of Wren is made in the *Extrait d'une lettre sur l'état actuel des arts libéraux et méchaniques en Angleterre*, published in 1768 by Jean Claude Pingeron (±1730–95), a shrewd and strenuous traveller, who had intended to make a military career in Poland but had later turned his attention to the south, and to Rome and Naples in particular, from where he was able to venture to Sicily, Malta, and even to Greece. He was to make his reputation as the translator of works by Algarotti, Milizia, and Sestini. He eventually became the first secretary to the museum of Paris.

Pingeron's comment on Wren is brief. But his ranking of him confirms the opinion that had been established in France even before the completion of St Paul's. 'L'architecture', Pingeron wrote,

est celui de tous les beaux arts qui a fait depuis longtemps le plus de progrès en Angleterre. Inigo Jones, le meilleur élève de Palladio, le Chevalier Christoph Wren qui a bâti la fameuse église cathédrale de S. Paul et celle de Welbrok, ont décoré leur patrie de plusiers beaux monumens.[3]

That is all there is on Wren; but in view of Pingeron's wider familiarity with contemporary English architecture and his appreciation (qualified) of it, the pre-eminent position he accords to Wren, alongside Inigo Jones, is edifying. 'Palladio', he continues, 'est très goûté par les Anglois, on ne peut trop les applaudir pour cette prédilection. Cependant leurs architectes modernes font à Londres du lourd et du massif, au lieu du mâle et du majestueux, sans oublier les fenêtres à la Venitienne

1. Leroy's letters to Chambers are in the R.I.B.A., London, dated 12 October 1769, 26 November 1769; with this letter Leroy sent a book by Laugier.

2. Leroy, op. cit., p. 41. I am indebted to Aubrey Cartwright for copying this quotation and another, quoted later, by Pingeron, which were available only in the Bibliothèque Nationale in Paris.

3. Pingeron, op. cit., p. 34 – there is a long footnote on this and the following pages on the life of Inigo Jones.

(the Venetian Windows)'.[1] English gardens he praised with more fervour, though he was quick to muzzle his enthusiasm – 'ce n'est autre chose que la nature corrigée'.[2] And, venting yet more splenetic humour, he reveals the long standing of the French belief in the English as a nation of shopkeepers:

On tient peu de compte à Londres des architectes, quoi qu'il y en ait de fort bons, tels que Mm. Adam, Mylne, Payne et Chambers (c'est le second de ces artistes qui est chargé du fameux pont de *Blakfriars* qui sera le plus beau de l'Europe, et qui est presque fini). Les Vitruves Anglois sont en général peu considérés, parce qu'ils sont tous entrepreneurs, et que dans un pays aussi commerçant que l'Angleterre, on met un marchand de maisons au niveau de celui qui fait tout autre négoce.[3]

Pingeron was later to support Soufflot in his struggle to win acceptance for the design of Sainte-Geneviève. There is, however, no evidence that he justified this with reference to Wren's great church. But Soufflot himself saw affinities between the two churches and was to make them even closer.

In 1768 Soufflot heard that Pierre Patte (1723–1814), one-time engraver and architect, was preparing to travel to London together with N. H. Jardin (1720–99), who was then finalizing his designs for a vast church for Frederick V in Copenhagen, in order to measure up St Paul's.[4] Soufflot, as Contrôleur des Bâtiments du Roi à Paris, had two months earlier antagonized Patte by not appointing him to complete Servandoni's portico at Saint-Sulpice. He knew him to be a quarrelsome and bitter man (he had quarrelled furiously and professionally with the editors of the *Encyclopédie* in 1759) and shrewdly assessed that the measuring up of St Paul's would not be to his advantage. He sought to reconcile Patte. He managed after repeated invitations to get him to dine and rewarded him with an introduction to Sir William Chambers. At the same time Soufflot induced Patte to take with him a pupil, Roche, who was to measure St Paul's on Soufflot's account. The journey, undertaken in April 1769, was of considerable importance to the history of Sainte-Geneviève. In the first place Patte's study of St Paul's convinced him that the four main piers of Sainte-Geneviève would not support the ungainly dome that Soufflot had designed. A few weeks after his return from London Patte wrote the first version of *Mémoire sur la construction du dôme projeté pour couronner l'église de Sainte Geneviève*. His shattering analysis was not part of a sound mathematical argument, but was based on empirical observations on the structure of St Paul's trotted out to support a personal belief, or rather hope. Yet within a few months the most celebrated of eighteenth-century architectural quarrels had flared up, dividing the world of architecture. When in April 1770 Patte published the final version of his *Mémoire* (privately circulated up to then), Soufflot and his friends were obliged to offer a full-scale

---

1. ibid., p. 37.   2. ibid., p. 40.   3. ibid.
4. On the history of Sainte-Geneviève see Mondain Monval, op. cit., and Mae Mathieu, op. cit.

defence of the structure of Sainte-Geneviève. They adduced numerous churches that they considered to have been equally lightly and efficiently constructed. St Paul's they did not discuss, but on 2 July 1770 Soufflot showed drawings of the steeple of St Mary-le-Bow to the members of the Academy. 'Sur un plan circulaire,' he said,

cent vingt pieds de hauteur de cette pyramide sont portés sur des arcades et des encorbellements au lieu de panaches, et le couronnement de quarante-cinq pieds de hauteur est porté sur un mur de dix pouces d'épaisseur au environ, entouré de colonnes qui servent d'arcs boutants.[1]

He was interested primarily in the statics.

The fuss and intrigue occasioned by Patte's attack continued for years. In 1776 cracks were found to be developing in the main piers of Sainte-Geneviève. After an inquiry Soufflot was exonerated. Defiantly he issued a design early in 1777 for a grander dome than before, directly inspired by that of St Paul's. At the very least it must have been intended as a snub to Patte. The design of the new drum was not altogether to French taste. In May of the same year Soufflot received an unsigned letter in which the uniform and continuous circular colonnade, with which he intended to replace an earlier arrangement of columns on an octagonal plan, was vigorously attacked. It was thought dull and monotonous.

Pourquoi flattés vous les yeux du public par l'exposition d'une merveille, pour y substituer après, sans qu'on en sache la raison, une forme vulgaire et sans art, une figure monotone, un cercle en un mot, ennuyeux par sa trop grande uniformité. Vous avés trop de goût, Monsieur, pour ne pas connoître le prix de votre invention et pour le sacrifier à un dessein pauvre et commun, qu'on ne souhaiteroit pas de voir, apres avoir vu la galerie de St. Paul de Londres...[2]

But the London-inspired dome was built. And this despite Patte's far sounder and more convincing attack on the structural soundness of Soufflot's piers, presented in 1777 with all the authority of Jacques François Blondel's *Cours d'architecture*, the last two volumes of which were entrusted to Patte. There is no need to go further into the details of this well documented controversy. Suffice it to note that even in his biographical account of the work of Wréen (Christophe) at the end of volume VI, Patte found an opportunity to snipe at Soufflot. Wren, Patte wrote, 'fut à la fois un géomètre de réputation, un architecte de génie, et sur-tout le premier des constructeurs modernes'.[3] He listed his principal works – St Stephen Walbrook, St Mary-le-Bow, the Monument, Greenwich and Chelsea Hospitals, and the Sheldonian Theatre – but reserved his special praise for St Paul's –

cet édifice, le plus vaste en ce genre après S. Pierre de Rome, est un chef-d'œuvre d'intelligence et de combinaisons des pouvoirs méchaniques, que les connoisseurs ne peuvent se

---

1. Quoted in Mondain Monval, op. cit., p. 460.
2. Quoted in Michel Petzet, op. cit., pp. 57, 58.   3. Patte, op. cit., VI, p. 517.

lasser d'admirer, et, où tout, quoique de la plus grande légereté, est néanmoins reparti de la façon la plus propre à en assurer la durée.

Son style d'architecture est quelquefois peu correct: à l'exemple des hommes de génie, il négligeoit volontiers les details, et ne cherchoît qu'à plaire par le bel effet de la masse totale de ses édifices; mais de même que l'on va en Italie et en Grèce pour étudier les belles proportions et les ordonnances d'architecture des monuments antiques, il faudroit aller en Angleterre pour étudier la construction des édifices de Wréen, pour apprendre à raisonner cette partie, et à ne point opérer au hazard, comme l'on fait communement.[1]

Patte's estimate of Wren is marked by that enhanced esteem for his structural ability that was a direct consequence of the Sainte-Geneviève controversy. The account given by Jacques François Blondel himself in the historical introduction to the first volume of the *Cours d'architecture*, in 1771, is significantly different. Blondel was not interested in construction. He was devoted, though, to Christophe Wrein. Unusually impulsive, he referred to his 'talents sublimes'.[2] He provided the fullest and most accurate biography to appear in eighteenth-century France, based, not surprisingly, on that of William Dugdale. He regretted in particular that Wren had not been able to use the giant order on the west front. But despite his interest and evident enthusiasm, Blondel remembered his role of cautious pedagogue – 'ce monument,' he wrote,

tel qu'on le voit aujourd'hui, présente de la grandeur, de belles masses et beaucoup de dignité; néanmoins les connoisseurs reprochent à Wrein plusiers fautes essencielles, celles entr'autres d'avoir incorporé de petits pilastres dans les grands, de n'avoir pas élevé assez ses voûtes et d'avoir donné un diamètre trop considérable à son dôme, relativement à la grandeur de l'édifice.[3]

Blondel's treatment of Wren finds its parallel in the first volume of Dezallier d'Argenville's *Vie des fameux architectes*, printed in 1788. But the range of buildings discussed is much wider. The beauty and importance of St Paul's alongside St Peter's is accepted as an eighteenth-century commonplace. Critical asides are offhand – 'c'est une grande fabrique, d'une bonne architecture, mais trop lourd dans ses détails'.[4] The lesser buildings are more studiously extolled. The Sheldonian Theatre, surprisingly, 'passe pour un des plus beaux morceaux d'architecture d'Angleterre'.[5] The steeple of St Mary-le-Bow is judged to be 'un morceau admirable, qui n'a point son pareil dans aucune église de l'Europe'.[6] But the highest honours are reserved for St Stephen Walbrook –

ce monument, connu dans toute l'Europe, passe pour le chef-d'œuvre de notre architecte; il réunit tous les embellissemens dont le plan a été susceptible, et peut-être n'y a-t-il pas en Italie un édifice moderne qu'on puisse lui comparer pour le goût et les belles proportions.[7]

1. ibid., VI, p. 518.   2. Blondel, op. cit., I, p. 95.   3. ibid., I, p. 95; cf. also III, p. 300.
4. Dezallier d'Argenville, op. cit., I, p. 293; the account of Wren starts on p. 277, that of Inigo Jones on p. 265.   5. ibid., I, p. 285.   6. ibid., I, p. 290.   7. ibid.

Later eighteenth-century opinions of Wren add little of vital or informed comment. St Paul's is listed, together with other large buildings in London, in *Souvenirs d'un voyage en Angleterre* of 1791, by de Mesters, a Swiss living in Paris. It is illustrated in J. N. L. Durand's great *Recueil et parallèle des edifices de tout genre* (1800). The other great rationalist teacher of the period, J. B. Rondelet (1734–1829), pupil of Soufflot and completer of Sainte-Geneviève, likewise gave Wren a place in his great textbook, *Traité théorique et pratique de l'art de bâtir*, published in 1812. He devoted considerable space to a discussion of the dome, for what he was intent to show was that Wren, as an architect, was concerned primarily with efficient construction and not with the beauty of effect, which, Rondelet held, would arise naturally from a proper emphasis on the first. This focus of interest on the construction of the dome of St Paul's is evident, though less emphatically, in an observation made at this period by P. A. Paris (1745–1819). Sketching the baptistery at Pisa, he noted: 'on pourroit même croire qu'il a été connu du Chevalier Wren qui l'a imité en le perfectionnant dans la forme connique qu'il a donné a l'intérieur de son dôme de S. Paul de Londres'.[1]

Wren's reputation in France was nurtured and sustained in particular by those men who were concerned to evolve not only the theory but the style of the reformed architecture that we have termed Neo-classical. The two most important buildings of the first phase of this movement, the portico of Saint-Sulpice and Sainte-Geneviève, were both directly inspired by St Paul's. Wren's structural solutions were adduced often in the controversy which served to formulate and codify Neo-classical theory. Yet Wren's swansong was sung by that high-priest of Neo-classical orthodoxy A. C. Quatremère de Quincy (the man who tidied up Sainte-Geneviève). The account that he gave of Wren in the *Encyclopédie méthodique* in 1825 (reprinted with but minor changes in the *Biographie universelle* in 1828 and in the *Histoire de la vie et des ouvrages des plus célèbres architectes* in 1830) was based on that of Dezallier d'Argenville, but his judgements were very different. They are made in a tone of expansive authority and moral firmness. The interior of St Paul's is pronounced 'généralement médiocre'.[2] 'On n'y est véritablement frappé d'aucune sorte de grandeur, d'aucun caractère bien prononcé, soit de force, soit de sévérité, soit d'élégance et de richesse.' The exterior is considered even worse, though the dome is approved. Similarly Wren's other works are devalued and Dezallier d'Argenville is severely reproved for

1. Paris, 'Études d'Architecture', II, part II, Bibliothèque de Besançon.

2. See Quatremère de Quincy, *Encyclopédie méthodique. Architecture*, III (Paris, 1825), pp. 645 ff., *Biographie universelle* (Paris, 1828), under 'Wren', and *Histoire de la vie et des ouvrages des plus célèbres architectes* (Paris, 1830), pp. 246 ff.

Quatremère de Quincy travelled to England to see St Paul's some time between 1785 and 1787 and again in 1818; see Étienne Quatremère, *Journal des savants* (November 1853), p. 668; H. Jouin, *A. C. Quatremère de Quincy* (Paris, 1892), pp. 12 and 41; R. Schneider, *Quatremère de Quincy et son intervention dans les arts. 1788–1830* (Paris, 1910), pp. 3 and 20.

his over-estimation of St Stephen. Despite all this – or perhaps as a part of it – Wren is still judged the best – 'il était', Quatremère de Quincy writes, 'non seulement le premier, mais peut-être, dans toute l'acception du mot, le seul architecte de son pays'. No English architect since then has ranked very high in France, Wren least of all.

English Country House Guides, 1740–1840

BY JOHN HARRIS

THE innocent pastime of making the round of country houses has long appealed to the English, and is an English institution almost as old as the Reformation. Although the *Laboriouse Journey and Serche for Englandes Antiquitiees* made by John Leland from 1538[1] was principally antiquarian, he took in the castles and country houses, relishing the 'ruines of an old Maner Place', marvelling at a 'sumptuous new Building of Bricke Tymbre a fundamentis', and simply noting that here was a 'fair Park', or there 'falow Dere'. 'Laboriouse' was an understatement. We can hardly conceive the terrors and trials endured by the lonely traveller in mid-sixteenth-century England. Epithets such as 'execrably bad' or 'intolerably disagreeable' from Edward Young, two hundred years later, were restrained in comparison to Leland's experiences. Such travels were neither civilized, nor were they undertaken for the intrinsic pleasure to be gained from a tour or from a country house and its associations. If Inigo Jones did draw 'many Prospects of the old Gothick or ancient Castles' on the Progresses of James I and Charles I, as John Aubrey tells us he did,[2] he may have seen them with the eyes of a Renaissance courtier and scholar, interested as much in their families and art collections as in their architecture. Nevertheless, in early-seventeenth-century England he would have been an exception.

Country house perambulating was almost unknown until the Restoration, when social change and the rise of the wealthier merchant classes to sub-aristocratic stature brought about a new desire to travel for travel's sake. In the chronicles and diaries of Aubrey or Evelyn this new interest is beginning to take shape. They, however, are still antiquarians not prepared to travel far afield. For them country house travel had not yet become the perquisite of the educated gentleman, and in the case of Celia Fiennes[3] and her like, of the gentlewoman too. Fiennes was one of the earliest

---

1. *The Itinerary of John Leland the Antiquary*, ed. Thomas Hearne, 3rd edn (Oxford, 1768–9).
2. *Aubrey's Brief Lives*, ed. Oliver Lawson Dick (Penguin Books, 1964), p. 93.
3. *The Journeys of Celia Fiennes*, ed. Christopher Morris (1959).

of travellers, omnivorous for the sights of town and country, and untiring in her pursuit of houses and gardens. Around 1700 the discovery of England was in progress, and the new breed of discoverers was aided by the gradual improvement of roads, the appearance of gazetteers, and by the editions of Ogilby's road book, the bible of the country traveller. The *sine qua non* for Fiennes' generation, as for successive ones until the end of the eighteenth century, was to belong to the aristocracy, sub-aristocracy, or gentry. Even if a labourer could afford the entrance fee and exorbitant tips (amounting to several pounds in present-day values), the gate lodge of a Stowe or Strawberry Hill would have been firmly closed to him.

Fiennes was admittedly something of an exception around 1700, but, living until 1741, she literally saw the exception become the rule. The future scene is well set by three writers in the 1720s: John Macky, whose *Journey Through England* appeared in 1722–3;[1] William Stukeley, who published his *Itinerarium Curiosum* in 1724;[2] and Daniel Defoe in his famous *Tour Through the Whole Island of Great Britain* of 1724–6.[3] The differences between them are ones of literary style and depth of observation; and in the case of Stukeley, of a predilection for archaeology and antiquities. Their publication in this decade is no coincidence. By 1706 Leonard Knyff had drawn eighty views of country houses and royal palaces (*Le Tout dessiné sur les lieux*) which were engraved by Johannes Kip for *Britannia Illustrata or Nouveau Théâtre de la Grande Bretagne* (1707–8), and between 1715 and 1725 Colen Campbell published *Vitruvius Britannicus*, the great three-volume survey of national architecture, advertising the glories of the English country house in folios sumptuous even in comparison with Marot's *L'Architecture française*. Campbell, Leoni, Kent, and, above all, Lord Burlington, were establishing neo-Palladianism, the cult of Inigo Jones and Palladio, as a national style. Their theories initiated an architectural publishing boom the like of which was unequalled anywhere in Europe. ARCHITECTURE became every gentleman's recreation, and each vied with the other in modernizing his country house and replanning his gardens. The differences in this respect between England and France, as the two great European powers, directly stem from the relationship between the monarchy and the nobility. In France, 'le Roi Soleil' was the focus of a court life concentrated on Paris or Versailles, and this produced the most splendid period in the history of the French town house. In England, on the other hand, political life followed its leaders to the country and to the mansions whose parks spread across the face of England. A corollary to a nation bewebbed with thousands of parks was travel, and as nerve centres of social, literary, and artistic communication, houses and parks were places to wonder at. Not surprisingly, the country house guide was born in England.

1. John Macky, *A Journey through England*, 2 vols. (1722–3).
2. For Stukeley, cf. Stuart Piggott, *William Stukeley: An Eighteenth Century Antiquary* (1950).
3. Cf. the Everyman edition, *A Tour through England and Wales*, 2 vols. (1948).

From sheer necessity, portability is the first requirement of a country house guide. The prime purpose of the text is to describe features of house and garden in order of interest. At Stowe, for example, the garden and things in it obviously merit greatest attention, whereas at Wilton, house and garden are subservient to the great Pembroke collection of marbles. Sometimes, however, the compiler will merely append a catalogue of the paintings of the family. Purchased at the house, the porter's lodge, a local bookseller or stationer, or at the village inn, for prices ranging from sixpence to five shillings, they belonged naturally to the class of printed ephemera. Rarely did they attain a standard of typographical production to justify their purchase as an ornament to a library. Walpole's *Aedes Walpolianae*, his *Strawberry Hill*, Chambers's *Kew*, Blore's *Burghley*, J. Seeley's *Stowe* or Rutter's *Fonthill*, are honourable exceptions, belonging to the small group of commemorative country house quartos and folios, nearly all compiled for partisan reasons. No tourist would have been expected to stagger the five-mile circuit of Stowe with such a volume, although it might well have been displayed on the library table for visitors to examine.

The seventeenth-century predecessors of these Georgian country house monographs number but three, and all are suites of engravings without text like Kip. The earliest and most precious is *Wilton Garden*, published *c.* 1645 from drawings by Issac de Caus, who supervised the design of the gardens from *c.* 1632 until his death in 1656.[1] For once, and once only, the gardens here were the focus of attention. Then there are views of another Wiltshire house, Longford Castle, engraved *c.* 1670 by Robert Thacker, who may have been associated with near-by Salisbury; and thirdly there are the twenty-four magnificent plans, elevations, and perspective views of Audley End engraved between 1685 and 1688 by Henry Winstanley, Clerk of the Works when this Jacobean palace was a royal possession.

Accustomed as we are to the magnitude of the Palladian dissemination in the first half of the eighteenth century – a time when the country house was an object of adulation – it comes as a surprise to discover in this period only four folio monographs,[2] all compiled for partisan reasons. In 1735 and 1760 appeared the two editions of Isaac Ware's *Plans, Elevations, and Sections ... of Houghton*; in 1739 and 1746, editions of Sarah Bridgeman's *Stowe*; in 1761 and 1773, Matthew Brettingham the elder and younger's editions of *Holkham*; and in 1763 Chambers's *Kew*. Ware had been concerned at Houghton in his capacity as a colleague of Kent who decorated the interior; Sarah Bridgeman had just been widowed by the death of Charles, who had originally commissioned the Stowe views; the elder Brettingham was the builder

1. Cf. H. M. Colvin, 'The South Front of Wilton House', in *Archaeological Journal*, CXI (1954), pp. 181–90.

2. Monographs on country houses as distinct from those on specific public buildings, e.g. James Gibbs, *Bibliotheca Radcliviana* (1747); James Paine, *Plans...of the Mansion House at Doncaster* (1751); or John Wood, *A Description of the Exchange at Bristol* (1743).

of Holkham; and Chambers was the Dowager Princess of Wales's architect at Kew. All four books provided material for the compilers of smaller guides to these places: Ware was the source for Walpole's *Aedes Walpolianae*, Bridgeman for Seeley and Bickham, Brettingham for Dawson's *Stranger's Guide*, and Chambers for the plagiaristic Brentford editions of the Kew guides.

'After the purchase of a catalogue and the entrance of our names in the porter's book, we proceeded to the investigation of the house.'[1] These words, written in 1780, and the diaries and travelogues of the day are witness to a liberality of access almost assumed of a landed owner. The pace of travel varied, of course, from person to person. Such a one as Mrs Lybbe Powys was a genteel traveller, content to visit, on her way to Stourhead in 1776, Longford and Salisbury on one day, and Wilton and Fonthill on the next. 'I fancy few persons pass by Wilton,' she commented, 'as in the porter's lodge, where he desired us to set down our names and the number of our company, we saw by the book there had been to see it the last year 2324 persons.'[2] As a contrast to this slow perambulating, John Byng (later Viscount Torrington) followed the untiring footsteps of Celia Fiennes. 'I come abroad', he wrote,

to view the old Castles, old manors and old religious houses, before they be quite gone; and that I may compare the ancient structures, and my ideas of their taste, and manners, with the fashions of the present day. I enjoy a grove of venerable old oaks; feel transported at the sight of a wild water-fall; and taste the animation of a fox-hunter at the unkennelling of a fox, when I discover castle or ruin.[3]

In a typical day on a tour in 1784 he saw Malvern, Ledbury, Stoke Edith, and Hereford, and on another, Hampton Court, Berrington, and Ludlow; or on tour in the Midlands in 1789 he took in Leicester Abbey, Scrapthorpe Hall, and Quenby Hall. His diaries are the quintessence of the Georgian country house tour, and although he disliked the 'Venetian vanities' of Palladian architecture, his vicissitudes mirror those of hundreds of other tourists. At one house we will find him wandering unshepherded through the state rooms, and at another making for the gardener's cottage to buy grapes and strawberries. His reception at Chatsworth was typical of a dozen other 'great' houses. First it was necessary to tip the porter in the hope that he would be sufficiently '*obliging* to find the gardener, and the housekeeper', persons '*allways* ready to attend to strangers' providing they too received a good substantial tip. For this the gardener let loose the cascade and made the fountains play, after which the housekeeper came along to take them on another expensive tour to see

1. Esther Moir, 'Touring Country Houses in the Eighteenth Century', *Country Life* (22 October 1958), 586. My thanks go to this author, and I am especially indebted to her *The Discovery of Britain The English Tourists, 1540–1840* (1960). Cf. also her 'Georgian Visits to Landscape Gardens'. *Country Life* (7 January 1960), 6–8.
2. Mrs Lybbe Powys, *Passages from the Diaries*, ed. E. J. Climenson (1899), pp. 165–6.
3. *The Torrington Diaries*, ed. C. B. Andrew, 2 vols. (1934).

what Torrington described as the 'foolish glare, uncomfortable rooms, and frippery French Furniture of this vile house'.[1] He was typical of the travelling gentry who expected admittance wherever they called, and his peevish note on Lord Guildford's behaviour at Wroxton in 1785 nicely sums up the contemporary situation: 'Let him either forbid his place entirely; open it always; or fix a day of admission; but for shame, don't refuse travellers who may have come 20 miles out of their way for a sight of this place.'[2] A crusty Torrington need not disguise the fact that opening times were often strictly observed. When travelling through Derby, R. J. Sullivan and his friend were reminded that it was then noon, and if they wanted to see Kedleston, 'travellers have no admittance but from ten till two',[3] and at Wanstead the Rev. Stebbing Shaw and his friend found the house open only on Saturdays. At Mount Edgcumbe, on the contrary, 'A ring of the bell procures a necessary attendant who shows and explains the whole of this terrestrial Paradise'. In 1778, when this was written, no printed guide was available, but in 1821 the fame of this garden had already demanded seven editions of a *Walk round Mount Edgcumbe*, an anonymous 'Guide for the numerous strangers who visit the celebrated spot, and who may wish to take a complete survey of the various beauties in which it abounds'. The park and pleasure grounds were open daily, the flower garden occasionally in summer, 'by a particular ticket, granted only to parties not exceeding six persons', and the house was never shown. The *Walk* was even divided up into tours of various lengths, from the 'Grand Tour' of the Park of $4\frac{1}{4}$ miles, descending to ones of $3\frac{1}{4}$, $2\frac{1}{2}$, $1\frac{1}{2}$, and $1\frac{1}{4}$ miles. Similarly the park and gardens of Blenheim were always open, but there in addition the palace was open from 2 until 4 except Saturdays and public holidays. Fonthill was open from 12 until 4; Hafod, after the purchase of a ticket from the local inn, could be seen from 12 until 2.

Despite the increasing popularity of country-house touring during the first half of the century – and, as if to confirm this, Mrs Moir lists sixteen printed and manuscript tours – the few early guides are not to houses and gardens, but to art collections. Wilton was naturally a cynosure for connoisseurs of the day, and in 1730 and 1731 attracted the attention of Cary Creed and Count Carlo Gambarini of Lucca. In 1730 Creed drew and etched forty plates of the *Marble Antiquities* for sale at twenty shillings,[4] and in 1731 reissued them, adding thirty-four more to sell at thirty-five shillings. Although Creed was a nonentity both as a person and as an artist, nevertheless his charming etchings of the Pembrokian marbles were neither exceeded in number, nor hardly bettered, by J. A. Gresse's drawings for Kennedy's illustrated guide of 1769. Gambarini's *Description of the Earl of Pembroke's Pictures* (1731) accompanied an *Introduction to his Design* to engrave paintings from famous English collections. He was, according to Vertue, 'in the favour of the old Earl of

---

1. ibid., pp. 11, 37.   2. ibid., pp. 1, 23.   3. Moir, op. cit., p. 59.
4. Advertised in the weekly journals for July 1730, and commented upon by Vertue: 'the first notice I think of him in public'. Cf. Walpole Society, *Vertue Notebooks*, III, p. 43.

Pembroke'.[1] Creed's engravings sold for connoisseurs' prices, but Gambarini's little book – the first printed catalogue of the Wilton pictures – was moderately priced and would certainly have been in the hands of visitors to the state rooms. Walpole's *Aedes Walpolianae, or a Description of the Collection of Pictures at Houghton Hall in Norfolk* (1743) is also a catalogue in the Gambarini manner, but although it was intended as a 'plain description of the effects' at Houghton and a reflection of his father's taste, Walpole did provide two folding plans and elevations, dimensions of many of the rooms, and brief descriptions of the decoration. He also included his own *Sermon on Painting* and the Rev. Mr Whaley's poem, *A Journey to Houghton*. This therefore is the first catalogue or guide with literary and poetic accompaniments, the forerunner of an almost universal practice of compilation in the late eighteenth and early nineteenth centuries. It was Stowe that inspired the first comprehensive guide to a house or garden, for in 1744 J. Seeley's *Description of the Gardens of Lord Viscount Cobham at Stowe* appeared, to be followed in 1750 by George Bickham's *Beauties of Stow*. Nevertheless, there were three earlier publications on Stowe that both authors could have drawn upon: an anonymous poem, *Stowe: the Gardens . . . Address'd to Mr. Pope*, published in 1732 and now known to have been written by Gilbert West, Lord Cobham's nephew; Sarah Bridgeman's *General Plan of the Woods, Park and Gardens of Stowe . . . with several Perspective Views in the Gardens*, published in 1739, with a further edition in 1746; and a description of the gardens published as an *Appendix* by the reviser of the 1742 (third) edition of Defoe's famous *Tour*.

West's poem – referring in its opening lines to Pope's exclamation, 'a work to wonder at – perhaps a Stowe', in the *Epistle to Lord Burlington* (1731) – is almost the sort of guide which could be read out loud as one wandered round the gardens. Being an intimate of the place, West gave to 'Kent's judicious hands' or to 'lamented Vanbrugh' their dues of responsibility, so frequently forgotten in the later guides.

Because of its folio size, Bridgeman's *General Plan* was in no sense a guide. Nevertheless, it was the first published work on Stowe to contain a map, and even if parts of this map are fictitious, it must surely have been known to Bickham, who published the first guide-map in his second edition of the *Beauties* in 1753. The genesis of the Bridgeman book is obscure, but it seems to have taken shape under Charles Bridgeman's direction soon after Rigaud, the draughtsman, arrived in England in 1734.[2] Even if West and Bridgeman had been studied by Seeley, there can be little doubt that his first *Description* in 1744 was modelled upon the *Appendix* that followed the 1742 Defoe. This edition of the *Tour* was meant specially for the traveller, for not only was it reduced to pocket size, but it contained various aids for quick and easy reference. Given a title-page, this anonymous *Appendix* would have been Stowe's first separately published guide. The compiler, whoever he may have been, supplied

1. ibid., p. 157; and IV, p. 19.
2. ibid., III, p. 69. Rigaud's drawings are now in the Metropolitan Museum of Art, New York.

correct information which was not noted by Seeley and was only entered in Bickham's 1753 edition: for example, in West and Defoe the Doric Pavilions at the south entrance are correctly given to Vanbrugh and the Boycott Pavilions to Gibbs.

When Seeley produced his *Description* in 1744 he called himself Writing Master in Buckingham, the local town. It was published by Dicey of Northampton and sold by Seeley and George Norris, Peruke Maker, of near-by Newport Pagnell. Seeley methodizes the rather haphazard appendix in the 1742 Defoe, adding a dedication to Lord Cobham, and in more elegant type sets the pattern for perambulating the gardens. The second edition of 1743 is slightly amplified, and in the 'correct'd and enlarg'd' third edition in 1746 Seeley describes himself as bookseller and stationer, and states that his guide can be purchased in London, at Rivington's in St Paul's Churchyard. The 1747 edition is the same, as is the fifth (in fact editions are never numbered) in 1748. In 1749 a new edition appeared, again 'corrected and enlarg'd'. Up till now there had been no illustrations, but in 1750 – in emulation, as we shall see, of Bickham – an edition appeared, retitled *Stow: the Gardens*, containing views of the garden buildings and two elevations of the house. Presumably for the benefit of owners of earlier editions, the illustrations could be purchased separately,[1] as could the *Description*, and also a newcomer upon the scene, called the *Dialogue upon the Gardens*. This *Dialogue* had appeared in the same year as the edition of 1748, and was printed for Seeley and sold by Rivington. Although this edition and the second (1749) and third (1751) remained anonymous, the *Dialogue* is known to have been written by the Rev. William Gilpin.[2] In the guise of Polython and Callophilus, the learned Gilpin, brought up on Shaftesbury, Pope, Addison, and Hutcheson in matters of philosophical and aesthetic taste, has attempted to interpret the Stowe landscape in aesthetic and pictorial terms. In the *Dialogue* can be discovered the seeds of Gilpin's later Picturesque theory.

In 1750 cosmopolitan London intruded upon Seeley's pastoral Buckinghamshire scene in the person of George Bickham, very much the professional rival anxious to cash in on the gardens' popularity. His *Beauties of Stow*[3] very cleverly contained thirty 'Designs, or Drawings', decidedly an added attraction to a potential purchaser, and was printed by E. Owen of Holborn. Seeley must have been hard hit, for not only was Bickham's guide more compact and more personally worded, but its 'cuts' were attractive if crude, and it contained the first account of the house, over-

1. The complete guide comprised three parts: I. *Forty Views of the Temples* for two shillings and sixpence; II. *A Description of all the Buildings* for sixpence; III. the *Dialogue* for one shilling. At Sayer's, the famous London bookseller, a bound copy could be purchased for five shillings.

2. William D. Templeman, *The Life and Work of William Gilpin* (University of Illinois Press, Urbana, 1939), pp. 33–5.

3. The 1750 edition cost four shillings and could be bought at 'Mr. Hoskins at the New Inn going into ye Gardens', where was retailed Bickham's set of sixteen views of the gardens costing a 'Guinea Plain & 2 Guineas Coloured'.

looked by Seeley in his earlier editions. Bickham considered Stowe the 'wonder of our Days, and the most charming Place of all *England*'. At the end of his account he rhapsodizes upon the 'surprising Greatness' of the gardens of Gubbins in Hertfordshire, and upon Blenheim, a house to figure a few years later in his *Tour from Stow to Blenheim and Ditchley*,[1] also printed at Owen's shop. Bickham's second edition of the *Beauties* in 1753 is invaluable for its 'Curious General Plan of the Whole Gardens', but except for a reworded title-page is unchanged textually. In 1756, however, a third and new edition appeared with a text reworded to occupy a larger format, running to forty instead of sixty pages, and with new drawings of the Palladian Bridge, the Lady's Temple, the Grecian Temple, Captain Grenville's Monument, the Shell Bridge, the Egyptian Pyramid, and the Artificial Rockwork.

Meanwhile Seeley, as we have seen, had issued a second edition of the *Dialogue*. He may have issued an edition of the *Description* in 1752, but this is uncertain, and the next documented edition is that of 1756,[2] with a map – an improvement, incidentally, upon Bickham's map. This was followed by a reprint in 1762 and, in 1763, by a new edition 'With all the Alterations and Improvements that have been made therein, to the present Time'. It also contained a 'Description of the Inside of the House'.[3] This latest guide is much more professional, Seeley having learnt something from Bickham and capitalized upon it: the house is shown in an accurately dimensioned plan and south elevation, many views have been engraved anew,[4] the map has been revised, and the illustrations are accompanied by seven pages of measured plans of the temples and garden buildings. Preceding the tour of the gardens is a careful description of the house in no less than eleven pages, while inserted in the tour is a new poem, 'On her Royal Highness the Princess Amelia's arrival at Stowe'. Very noticeably the garden has been better documented: Kent is credited with the Hermitage, the Grand Gateway between the Boycotts, and the niches and court gateways on the north front of the house; Leoni is given the garden gateways to the courts, and Vanbrugh's Rotunda is stated to have been altered by Borra. The statues of Cain and Abel have gone, as have the Fane of Diana, a statue of Venus, the Witch House, and the Imperial Closet. The Grecian Temple has been renamed Concord and Victory, and its place in the Grecian Valley is discussed in relationship to General Wolfe's monument.

Work at Stowe was proceeding at such a pace that a 1766 edition demanded alterations to the text and new engravings of the Castle (an ornamented farm), the

1. An edition was also titled *The Grand Midland Tour, or, a Companion to Stow, Ditchley and Blenheim*, and published in London.

2. This 1756 edition cost sixpence without the plan, one shilling with, and five shillings bound with the views engraved in 1750.

3. Mr Hoskins at the New Inn has now been replaced by T. Hodgkinson, to be the retailer for many years.

4. Two views were engraved in 1759, possibly for an aborted edition.

Wolfe Obelisk, the Gothic Temple, and the Palladian Bridge. There was also added a plan and elevation of the Triumphal Arch at the south approach designed by Lord Camelford. The text has received the accession of a poem 'On Gardening', dedicated to Lord Temple. In 1769 and 1773, although the texts have been re-arranged and some illustrations re-engraved, the editions are the same as in 1766, although in 1773 the Lady's Temple was described as 'now altering'. By 1777 the whole south front of the house had been rebuilt, and new rooms formed behind it. This demanded a new map, a mass of textual alterations to cover the work of Blondel and Adam,[1] and a more interested attitude towards the house. We are now given a splendid plan and two perspectives that show Adam's front and Blondel's great rotunda Saloon. In the 1783 edition changes are minor ones. Blondel's Saloon, for example, has been 'finished According to a Design of Signor Waldre'.[2]

In the 1777 and 1783 editions, Gibbs's Lady's Temple has made way for a neo-classical one by Blondel, and the Temple of Friendship has been given a new square-capped roof. Whereas previously Kent had been credited with the four gate-ways to the court, two are now given to Valdré. In the 1788 edition Seeley had to record a new owner of Stowe, for in succession to Earl Temple, George Grenville Nugent Temple was now Marquis of Buckingham. We are still witness to an almost continuous process of change in the gardens, and change also in attributions. Poor Vanbrugh's authorship of the Doric Pavilions has been long forgotten, and they are (wrongly) attributed to Kent, but with later alterations given (correctly) to Borra, who is now stated to have altered the domes of the Boycotts, given (wrongly) to Vanbrugh. Kent's gateways near by have been extended by Valdré. In Seeley's Illustrations this gateway replaces the Egyptian Pyramid and St Augustine's Cave, two ornaments presumably consigned to history. In the Elysian Fields we can see that Kent's Shell Bridge has been replaced by a Stone Bridge, and his Grotto rebuilt within an embankment. Moving to the Grecian Valley, Seeley relates the history of the Temple of Concord and Victory – that it was unfinished inside until completed by Borra in 1763. More information is added to the description of the house, particu-larly about the work of Domenico Bartoli in the Saloon and Music Room, the latter a new addition designed and painted by Valdré. Seeley now advertises himself as Bookseller, Binder, Stationer, and Printer; since 1773 he had printed the guide him-self in Buckingham.[3]

He had long witnessed the Stowe scene, from 1744 as a humble writing master, to

1. For Blondel, cf. John Harris, 'Blondel at Stowe', in *The Connoisseur* (March 1964), pp. 173–6.

2. For Valdré, cf. E. Croft-Murray, 'Un Decoratore Faetino in Inghilterra', in *Studi Romagnoli*, VIII (1957); and Michael Gibbon, 'A Forgotten Italian at Stowe', *Country Life* (4 August 1966), pp. 260–3.

3. In 1788 the description of the house and gardens cost one shilling; with a plan of the gardens, one shilling and sixpence; with the garden plan and with views of the house two shillings; and all in boards four shillings, or bound and gilt five shillings.

1788 as a prosperous local dignitary. These forty-four years had been the most eventful of the park's history, and we have seen how in a stream of editions Seeley faithfully recorded the changes, almost as season succeeded season. After his death his two sons took over the business, J. Seeley remaining in Buckingham, and L. B. Seeley setting up in Paternoster Row. In 1797 there was still a demand for guides, for tourist travel had still to reach its peak, so Messrs Seeley's new edition was an entirely new typographic venture, transforming the charming yet nevertheless crudely printed guide of 1788 into a most sophisticated one illustrated by T. Medland, and produced in both expensive and cheap editions. As if to mirror the slowing up of work in the gardens, the only alterations since 1788 are the disappearance of Nelson's Seat and Dido's Cave, and the renaming of the Lady's Temple (given a new interior in 1790) as Queen's Temple. The outcome of this new guide was a second edition in 1827 and a third in 1832, when the printer was R. Chandler, probably in succession to J. Seeley, who had died. It was sold by L. B. Seeley, now '& Son', established in grander premises in Fleet Street. This is the last Seeley guide[1] and commemorates the end of a family's connexion as press agents to a great dynasty and house.

By the mere virtue of its international fame, Stowe attracted visitors as do Woburn and Longleat today. Few houses or gardens – perhaps only Wilton and Blenheim – could vie in popularity with a place demanding no fewer than thirty-one editions of guides. The appeal of Wilton's collections diminished only after 1800. Following Gambarini's picture catalogue of 1731 came Richard Cowdry's *Description* in two successive editions (1751[2] and 1752), and then James Kennedy's *New Description*, which saw at least ten editions or issues between 1758 and 1786. Kennedy, the Wilton agent, was interested only in describing the marbles and pictures, as was the author[3] of the *Aedes Pembrochianae*, a 'New and Critical' account whose popularity, exceeding even Kennedy's, demanded thirteen editions between 1774 and 1798. There were many such connoisseur's guides, unconcerned with the architecture of a house or the charms of a garden, but contributing nevertheless to the appreciation of a Georgian seat and its ambience.

Blenheim is the only possible valid comparison with Stowe, and a poor one at that

---

1. It was followed by the concluding guide to Stowe, Calkin and Budd's dreary unillustrated one of 1838.

2. On 28 January Cowdry issued his *Proposals for printing by subscription, an account of the pictures . . . at the earl of Pembroke's house at Wilton | For the convenience of those who go to see the House, the Pictures, Statues etc. are regularly named after the manner they are ranged in every Room.* Publication was intended in March 1751 at a cost of two shillings and sixpence (Bodleian, Rawlinson, 707).

3. The author of the *Aedes Pembrochianae* is often given as George Richardson. This is not so, and is due to a misreading of the ambiguously worded title-page, which refers to the inclusion of Jonathan Richardson's 'Rules to Judge of the Goodness of a Picture', and his 'Science of a Connoisseur'.

in terms of illustration and description. The compiler of its guide was Dr W. F. Mavor, the 'laureat' of Blenheim, Mayor of Woodstock, and tutor to Lord Blandford. His new *Description of Blenheim* in 1787 is prefaced by a turgid poem of 516 lines on the house, happily dropped by the fourth edition of 1797, when it was replaced by a mundane 'Preliminary Essay on Landscape Gardening'. This edition also sought to make itself more attractive by the accession of some views by Metz. Mavor's guide is disappointing, for he was totally uninterested in the artistic aspects of the place. It never improved, and after 1806 his name was conveniently forgotten by the new 'Proprietors', who continued to turn out virtually the same old guide until 1836. But then Blenheim, after all, was no evolving Stowe.

With Stowe, Wilton, Blenheim, and Fonthill as outstanding exceptions, most houses required only one edition of a guide. Wardour Castle is a typical example. With the flood of visitors to near-by Fonthill Abbey, John Rutter, in the same year as his Fonthill guide, obviously tried to catch the overflow of visitors at Wardour. His *Historical and Descriptive Sketch* of 1822 was published at his Shaftesbury printing house. Unlike Fonthill, open only by virtue of its impending sale, the 'advertisement' to the Wardour guide informs us that the 'well known liberality' of its noble owner allowed the house to be seen by entrance at the main door from 11 to 5 daily. By now the guide-book formula was well established and Rutter's possesses the three essentials: a study of the genealogy of the family, a description of the gardens, then of the house, and finally a room-by-room account of the pictures. This type recurs frequently: at Duncombe in 1812, Knole in 1817, Goodwood in 1822.

A few guides are outstanding for their literary, typographical, or historical contents. Chatsworth, Strawberry Hill, and Fonthill are three obvious examples. The sixth Duke of Devonshire's *Handbook of Chatsworth and Hardwick* is perhaps the rarest account of any English country house, and being the Duke's own personal compilation is not really a guide for the tourist. Beautifully printed and bound by Frederick Shoberl, Prince Albert's printer, it was an *élite* book meant as a gift for the Duke's friends. It belongs to a category either too expensive to purchase at the Inn or Lodge or too large to carry about. Britton's Cassiobury and Toddington, excellent as they may be as historical monographs, would never have been on sale to the tourist. In many ways this also applies to the most renowned guide of all, Walpole's *Description* of Strawberry Hill printed by Kirgate at the Strawberry Hill Press in 1774. It uniquely reflects the antiquarian tastes of its compiler, and is as redolent of him as the Chatsworth book is of the Duke, or *Rosamond's Bower* of Crofton Croker, who deliberately parodied the Strawberry Hill guide.

Walpole is to Strawberry Hill as Beckford is to Fonthill. By retreating to a hill near Fonthill House, encircling it with a wall, and building there from 1796 his Gothic Abbey, Beckford escaped from the tourist route that passed the classical portico of the older house. He was most reluctant to allow visitors access to the

Abbey, and could hardly have approved of James Storer's guide, printed in 1812, unless it was meant to commemorate a pseudo-phase of completion, preceding the building of the great Eastern Transept. It may be that Storer's twenty-four pages and two illustrations were allowed on the grounds of being a sop to a curious public. It was quite another matter in 1822, when Christies announced their Fonthill sales for September and October, and after their cancellation in September 1823, when Phillips announced a new sale for John Farquhar, the purchaser of the Abbey. This meant an incursion of thousands of visitors and brought the guide writers hurrying to the Wiltshire downs. In 1822 Rutter's smaller *Description* went through six issues or editions, and Whittaker's *New Guide* through many more. In 1823 Rutter capitalized on this, and brought out his extremely elegant *Delineations*. In so doing he showed up adversely John Britton, whose *Graphical Illustrations* of the Abbey had come out in the same year. We are told by Rutter that his 1823 book was meant as a 'more perfect record' than the earlier edition made 'amidst the hurry of the view' in 1822. It has become, of course, a library monograph in descent from Houghton or Holkham, as is Britton's book.[1]

When Britton published his *Cassiobury* in 1838 and his *Toddington* in 1840, he may have been aware that the fashion for perambulating houses was on the wane. Indeed, the fashion was as characteristically and exclusively Georgian as the architectural pattern books or Rowlandson prints. If supply may be taken to reflect demand, statistics based on known new guides and editions prove this point. For the decades beginning in 1760, 1770, 1780, and 1790 the numbers are 12, 8, 14, and 10. They then jump up in the 1800s to 14, and up to 24 in the 1810s. After a slight decrease to 19 for the 1820s, they plunge to 12 in the 1830s, and to 9 in the 1840s. This is very roughly supported by Mrs Moir's bibliography, which shows a high point in 1790, decreasing in 1820 and suddenly dropping in 1840. Not surprisingly, perhaps, the period 1790 to 1820 is the period of greatest interest in theories of the Picturesque and in the production of colour plate travel-books.

The Victorian country house guide did not exist, although catalogues to art collections, such as the Hendersyde one, did. Except for the few very great houses, the mansions of our Victorian ancestors were generally closed to the public. Lord Torrington's grandson could never have perambulated them with the same ease as his grandfather, nor would he have found a liberal reception. It is surely significant that one can name no typical country house tourist of the Victorian age as one could a Torrington, a Pococke, or a Powys for the preceding one, nor can one discover much interest on the part of house-owners in architecture. There seem, for example, to have been no owners who were amateur architects in the Georgian sense.

1. For accounts of Corsham, Fonthill, Toddington, and Cassiobury cf. Britton's *Autobiography*, part second, the *Descriptive Account of the Literary Works of John Britton*, by T. E. Jones (1849), pp. 13 ff., 61, 62.

The age of country house touring was over, at least until after the Kaiser's War, when the National Trust began to issue guides to its properties. The Hitler War completely changed the social circumstances of country house travel, turning the tables, so to speak, upon the noble owner, for whom plebeian half-crowns are both an item of revenue and a pledge of public appreciation such as the state may underwrite. We can still buy local apples and pears, but hardly grapes and oranges; we can still wander unmolested through saloons or, alternatively, curse, in true Torrington fashion, some tedious conductor. Fortunately our half-crown liberates us for ever from the bane of tipping. The successors to the Georgian guides are the familiar leaf-green National Trust booklets, the Pitkin 'Pride of Britain' books, or the 'English Life' publications; or if we are touring state-owned properties, the guides published by Her Majesty's Stationery Office. At most they cost us three shillings or, exceptionally, five. We may, if we wish to bestow on ourselves a lofty sense of status, still tour Stowe with Bickham or Seeley. They are obtainable, here and there, at a trifle over £50.

A CONCISE BIBLIOGRAPHY OF
GUIDES TO COUNTRY HOUSES, WITH SOME
CATALOGUES OF COLLECTIONS

Place of publication is London unless otherwise stated, or unless – as in the case of Mount Edgcumbe and Hawkstone – editions are known but copies of the guides are not available. This bibliography is based principally upon the author's own collection, with additions from the British Museum and the Bodleian Library, and upon information supplied from local sources, particularly public and county libraries.

ALNWICK CASTLE (Northumberland) – *A Description of Alnwick Castle*, (1) Alnwick, 1796; (2) 1800
   A descriptive ... View ... of Alnwick Castle, Alnwick, 1822

ALTHORP (Northamptonshire) – *Aedes Althorpianae*, 2 vols., 1822. By T. F. Dibdin
   Catalogue of the Pictures, 1836

AMMERDOWN (Somerset) – *Description of the Mansion, Marbles and Pictures at Ammerdown*, Bath, *c.* 1818

APPULDURCOMBE (I.o.W.) – *Museum Worsleyanum*, 2 vols., 1794. By Sir Richard Worsley. Edn in 1824 by Septimus Prowett

ARUNDEL CASTLE (Sussex) – *The History and Description of Arundel Castle*, (1) 1817; (2) 1818. By C. Wright

BLENHEIM PALACE (Oxfordshire) – *New Description of Blenheim*, (1) Woodstock (and for succeeding edns), 1787; (2) 1789; (3) 1793; (4) 1797; (5) 1800; (6) not dated; (7) 1806; (8) 1810; (9) 1811; (10) 1817; (11) 1835; (12) 1836; (13) 1846. French edn in 1791. By W. F. Mavor and later editors
   Six Views of Blenheim ... with an Historical Description, 1823. By J. P. Neale

BROMLEY HILL (Kent) – *Bromley-Hill The Seat of the Right Hon. Charles Long*, 1816.
By George Cumberland

BURGHLEY HOUSE (County of Huntingdon and Peterborough) – *A History or Description . . . of Burghley House*, Shrewsbury, 1797. By J. Horn
A Guide to Burghley House, (1) Stamford, 1815; (2) Stamford, 1816. By J. Blore
Burghley, Stamford, 1847. By W. H. Charlton

CASSIOBURY (Hertfordshire) – *The History and Description . . . of Cassiobury Park*, 1838. By John Britton

CHATSWORTH (Derbyshire) – *Handbook of Chatsworth and Hardwick*, 1844. By William Spencer, 6th Duke of Devonshire

CORSHAM (Wiltshire) – *An Historical Account of Corsham House*, 1806. By John Britton

CROOME COURT (Worcestershire) – *An Historical . . . Account of Croome D'Abitot*, Worcester, 1824. By W. Dean

DEEPDENE (Surrey) – *An Account of the Deep-Dene*, 1826. By J. P. Neale

DUDLEY CASTLE (Staffordshire) – *A Descriptive . . . Account of Dudly Castle*, 1825. By Luke Booker

DUNCOMBE PARK (Yorkshire) – *A Description of Duncombe Park and Rivalx Attempted*, (1) Kirbymoorside, 1812; (2) with a description of Helmsley Castle, Kirbymoorside, 1821

EATON HALL (Cheshire) – *The Eaton Tourist*, Chester, 1825. By J. Seacombe
Views of Eaton Hall, 1826. By J. and J. C. Buckler

ENVILLE (Staffordshire) – *A Description of Envil*, 1777. By Joseph Heeley
See also HAGLEY

FELIX HALL (Essex) – *Descriptive Sketch of Ancient Statues, Busts, &c At Felix Hall*, Chelmsford, 1833

FISHERWICK PARK (Staffordshire) – *See* HAGLEY

FONTHILL ABBEY (Wiltshire) – *A Description of Fonthill Abbey*, 1812. By James Storer
A Description of Fonthill Abbey, Shaftesbury and London, 1822. 6 edns in the year; 'new' edition 1823. By John Rutter
Fonthill Abbey . . . An Historical Description, 1822. Published by Weale
The New Guide to Fonthill Abbey, 1822. By G. & W. B. Whittaker
Delineations of Fonthill and its Abbey, Shaftesbury and London, 1823. By John Rutter
Graphical and Literary Illustrations of Fonthill Abbey, 1823. By John Britton
Historical Notices of Fonthill Abbey, 1836. By J. B. Nichols

GOODWOOD (Sussex) – *A Visit to Goodwood*, Chichester, 1822. By D. Jacques
Goodwood Its House Park and Grounds, 1839. By W. H. Mason

GROVE HILL (Kent) – *Grove-Hill, A Descriptive Poem*. (Included because it contains notes on the house.)

HAFOD (Cardiganshire) – *An Attempt to describe Hafod*, 1796. By George Cumberland
A Tour to Hafod, 1810. By James E. Smith

HAGLEY (Worcestershire) – *Letters on the beauties of Hagley, Envil and the Leasowes*, 2 vols., 1777. By Joseph Heeley. German edition, Leipzig, 1779
A Description of Hagley Park, 1777. By Joseph Heeley

A Companion to the Leasowes, Hagley, and Enville: with a sketch of Fisherwick, Birmingham, 1789; Birmingham, not dated, *c.* 1800?

A Description of Hagley, Envil and the Leasowes, Birmingham, *c.* 1800

Catalogue of the Pictures, Statues & Busts . . . in Hagley Hall, (1) Stourbridge, 1804; (2) Stourbridge, 1811; (3) Stourbridge, 1822

See also LEASOWES

HAREWOOD (Yorkshire) – *The Tourist Companion . . . of Harewood*, Leeds, 1819. By John Jewell

HAWKSTONE (Shropshire) – *A Description of Hawkstone*, Shrewsbury, 1766

A Description of Hawkstone, (1) Shrewsbury, 1783; (2) Shrewsbury, 1784; (3) 1786; (4) London, 1792; (6) London, 1799; (7) London, 1802; (9) 1807; (10) London, 1811. By T. Rodenhurst

HENDERSYDE PARK (Roxburghshire) – *A Descriptive Catalogue of the Collection of Pictures, Sculptures, Bronzes, &c at Hendersyde Park*, (1) Edinburgh, 1835; (2) Kelso, 1859

HOLKHAM HALL (Norfolk) – *The Plans . . . of Holkham*, (1) 1761, by Matthew Brettingham the elder; (2) 1773, revised by Matthew Brettingham the younger

A Description of Holkham House, Norwich, 1775

The Stranger's Guide to Holkham, Burnham, 1817. By J. Dawson

New Description of Holkham, Wells, 1816. By J. Blome

HOUGHTON (Norfolk) – *The Plans . . . of Houghton*, (1) 1735; (2) 1760. By Isaac Ware

Aedes Walpolianae, (1) 1743; (2) 1752; (3) 1767. By Horace Walpole

THE HYDE (Essex) – *Museum Disneianum*, 1846. By John Disney

INCE BLUNDELL (Lancashire) – *An Account of the Statues . . . and Paintings at Ince*, Liverpool, 1803. By Henry Blundell

Engravings and Etchings of . . . Sepulchral Monuments . . . at Ince, 2 vols., 1809. By Henry Blundell

KEW GARDENS (Surrey) – *Plans . . . of Kew Gardens*, 1763. By Sir William Chambers

A Description of the Gardens and Buildings at Kew, Brentford, not dated, but before 1771. By George Bickham and P. Norbury. Later edns

KNOLE (Kent) – *An Historical . . . Sketch of Knole*, (1) 1817; (2) 1821. By John Bridgman

The Visitor's Guide to Knole, Sevenoaks, 1839. By J. H. Brady

Abridgement of the Visitor's Guide to Knole, Sevenoaks, 1839. By J. H. Brady

KNOWLE COTTAGE (Devon) – *Guide to Illustrations of Knowle Cottage*, Sidmouth, 1834. By C. F. Williams

LEASOWES (Worcestershire) – *Description of the Leasowes*, 1764. By R. Dodsley

A Description of the Leasowes, 1777. By Thomas Heeley

See also HAGLEY

LEE PRIORY (Kent) – *List of Pictures . . . at Lee Priory*, Lee Priory, 1817

LEIGH COURT (Somerset) – *A Catalogue of the Pictures at Leigh Court*, 1822. By John Young

MOUNT EDGCUMBE (Devon) – *A Walk round Mount Edgcumbe*, (1) Plymouth, *c.* 1808; (2) 1810; (3) 1812; (5) 1817; (6) Stonehouse, 1819; (7) London, 1820; (8) Plymouth,

1821; (?) 1825; (?) Devonport, 1831; (9) Devonport, 1836; (10) Devonport, 1837; (11) Devonport, 1840; (12) Devonport, 1840; (13) Devonport, 1841

NUNEHAM COURTENAY (Oxfordshire) – *Nuneham-Courtenay*, 1783. By Horace Walpole? *Description of Nuneham-Courtenay*, (1) 1797; (2) 1806. From notes by Horace Walpole

ROSAMOND'S BOWER (Middlesex) – *A Description of Rosamond's Bower, Fulham*, 1843. By T. Crofton Croker

STOKE PARK (Buckinghamshire) – *An Historical ... Account of Stoke Park*, 1813. By Henry Hakewill

STOURHEAD (Wiltshire) – *A Description of the House and Gardens at Stourhead*, Salisbury, 1800

A Description of the House and Gardens at Stourhead, Bath, 1818. Revised by R. Colt-Hoare

STOWE (Buckinghamshire) – *Stowe: the Garden*, (1) 1732; (2) 1753; (3) undated. By Gilbert West

A General Plan of the Woods, Park and Gardens of Stowe ... by Sarah Bridgeman, (1) 1739; (2) 1746

Tour Through the Whole Island of Great Britain (by Defoe), 3rd edn, 1742, appendix on Stowe (anon.)

A Description of the House and Gardens ... at Stow, (1) Northampton, 1744; (2) Northampton, 1745; (3) Northampton, 1746; (4) Northampton, 1747; (5) Northampton, 1748; (6) Northampton, 1749; (7) 1750; (8) 1752?; (9) 1756; (10) 1759; (11) 1762; (12) 1763; (13) 1766; (14) 1768; (15) 1769; (16) 1773; (17) Buckingham, 1777; (18) Buckingham, 1780; (19) Buckingham, 1783; (20) Buckingham, 1788; (21) Buckingham, 1797, in two printings; (22) Buckingham, 1798; (23) Buckingham, 1817; (24) Buckingham, 1827; (25) Buckingham, 1832. By Benton Seeley. After 1797 by John Seeley. 1832 by R. Chandler and J. Seeley

A Description of the Gardens, 9th edn, 1751, a plagiarized Seeley edn by E. Owen and S. Wasey

The Beauties of Stow, (1) 1750; (2) 1753; (3) 1756. By George Bickham

A Dialogue Upon the gardens ... of Stow, (1) Buckingham, 1748; (2) Buckingham, 1749; (3) Buckingham, 1751. By W. Gilpin

Stowe. A Description..., 1838. By Calkin and Budd

STRAWBERRY HILL (Middlesex) – *A Description of the Villa ... at Strawberry Hill*, (1) Strawberry Hill, 1774; (2) Strawberry Hill, 1784. By Horace Walpole

TODDINGTON (Bedfordshire) – *Graphical Illustrations ... of Toddington*, 1840. By John Britton

WARDOUR CASTLE (Wiltshire) – *An Historical ... Sketch of Wardour*, Shaftesbury, 1822. By John Rutter

WESTON UNDERWOOD (Buckinghamshire) – *Cowper Illustrated by a series of Views in or near the park of Weston Underwood*, (1) 1803; (2) 1804; (3) 1810

WHITE-KNIGHTS (Berkshire) – *A Descriptive Account of the Mansion and Gardens of White-Knights*, c. 1809–10. By Mrs B. Hofland and Thomas Hope

WILTON (Wiltshire) – *A Description of the Earl of Pembroke's Pictures*, 1731. By Count Carlo Gambarini

A Description of the pictures, statues, bustos . . . at Wilton, (1) 1751; (2) 1752. By Richard Cowdry. Italian edn by Antonio Pillori, 1754

A New Description of the Pictures . . . at Wilton, (1) Salisbury, 1758; 1764; 1768; (6) 1776; (7) 1776; (9) Salisbury, 1779. By James Kennedy

A Description of the Antiquities and Curiosities in Wilton House, (1) Salisbury, 1769; (2?) Salisbury, 1786. By James Kennedy

Aedes Pembrochianae, (1) 1774; 1778; (10) 1784; (11) 1788; (12) 1795; (13) 1798

WOBURN ABBEY (Bedfordshire) – *An Historical . . . Account of Woburn*, (1) 1818; (2) 1844; (3) 1850. By Stephen Dodd

Outline Engravings and Descriptions of the Woburn Abbey Marbles, 1822

A Guide to Woburn Abbey, Woburn, 1831. By J. D. Parry

A 'Retrospective View' by John Clerk of Eldin, with some Comments on Adam's Castle Style

BY JOHN FLEMING

An unsigned and unfinished manuscript giving 'a short retrospective view of the state of architecture in Great Britain previous to Mr. Adam's time together with an account of the style by him introduced' is preserved among the Clerk of Penicuik Papers in H.M. Register House, Edinburgh.[1] It appears to be in the hand of Robert Adam's brother-in-law, John Clerk of Eldin[2] – the amateur etcher of picturesque Scottish views and author of an influential *Essay on Naval Tactics* (privately printed 1782, published 1790) – and was probably written shortly after Robert Adam's death for a projected memorial publication with which various unfinished draft lives of Adam by John Clerk are also presumably connected. Unfortunately the manuscript breaks off before reaching the promised account of Adam's style, but the surviving 'retrospective view' is of unusual interest, being largely concerned with medieval architecture and ending with the opening shots of what was clearly going to be an onslaught on Inigo Jones and the English neo-Palladians.[3] Written at a time when the *Gentleman's Magazine* was carrying almost monthly effusions on the beauties of Gothic, it expresses a remarkably level-headed attitude towards the current fashion

1. No. 4983 in the Clerk of Penicuik Papers. I am indebted to Sir John Clerk Bt for permission to quote from these papers. I have modernized the spelling and regularized the punctuation and capitalization. The gaps in the first and last paragraphs appear in the original.

2. John Clerk of Eldin (1728–1812) was the seventh son of Sir John Clerk, 2nd Bt. He was the exact contemporary of Robert Adam, whose sister Susan he married in 1753. Their son became Lord Eldin. For John Clerk's biographical sketch of Robert Adam see my *Robert Adam and his Circle* (1962), pp. 3 and 323. Only one of the drafts appears to be in John Clerk's hand.

3. Some indication of John Clerk's opinion of Inigo Jones and the English neo-Palladians may be gleaned from his draft biographical sketch of Robert Adam (see preceding note): '... that dull and elaborate [floridity?] which universally prevailed in the buildings of this island till the time of Mr. Adam's return from abroad. Nor is it a little singular to say that we do not recollect to have ever seen, during the whole course of our investigations into this subject, one suite of apartments from the time of Inigo Jones down to the period we have now mentioned, where convenience, elegance and variety are united, or even attempted'.

75

and in fact condemns outright the use of Gothic for any but religious buildings. In this Clerk was, so far as I know, unique among British writers of his day, though of course perfectly in line with French and German theorists.[1] Furthermore, Clerk was here almost certainly reflecting views held by Robert Adam towards the end of his life – views which Clerk had frequent opportunities to hear and discuss during Adam's annual summer visits to Scotland when he stayed with the Clerks in Edinburgh. Indeed it is tempting to suppose that Clerk's 'retrospective view', with its sympathy for Norman or Romanesque architecture and its antipathy to Gothic, was intended as an apologia for the buildings upon which Adam was then engaged, those curious 'castle-style' houses which do not seem to have been greatly admired at the time and have been consistently condemned, or just ignored, by all writers on Adam ever since.[2] However, Clerk's views require a deal of interpretation in so far as they refer to this last and most problematical period of Adam's work, and it will be best to leave discussion of them until after reading the text, which now follows.

We think a short retrospective view of the state of architecture in Great Britain previous to Mr. Adam's time together with an account of the style by him introduced, will be useful and entertaining. Laying aside the consideration of the Druidical productions in this island, which are rather matters of curiosity than instruction and more the object of the antiquary than the Man of Taste,   first led to work of the Romans in this country and though if there are here now no capital remains to boast of yet it is not to be imagined that the energy and enterprise of that great people could abstain here from works of grandeur and magnificence. Their walls across the country from sea to sea, and their stations where mosaic pavements and other antiquities are still discerned, show that they had likewise left memorials of their art behind them. Anterior to the Gothick architecture in this country the Saxons had established a kind of rude art of their own, where little ornament but great strength and magnitude prevailed. It is remarkable that in this they seldom or never had

1. See W. Herrmann, *Laugier and Eighteenth-Century French Theory* (1962), especially chapters V, VI, and VII; and W. D. Robson-Scott, *The Literary Background of the Gothic Revival in Germany* (1965), *passim*. See also the quotation from Laugier in Dr Lang's essay in the present volume, p. 86.

2. Mr Alistair Rowan's unpublished thesis on the castle style includes a chapter on Adam's castle-style buildings and deals with them in some detail for the first time. I am greatly indebted to Mr Rowan for allowing me to read his thesis, though my interpretation of Adam's intentions differs from his. Previous comments on Adam's castle-style buildings range from J. C. Loudon (*Country Residences*, 1806, I, p. 115): 'To unite in the same mass forms so opposite as those which characterize Grecian and Gothic architecture may justly be thought so ridiculous as never to have been attempted...' to Arthur T. Bolton (*The Architecture of Robert and James Adam*, 1922, I, p. 94), who thought it more than doubtful if Robert Adam had ever 'grasped the significance of the structure and growth of the old castles in relation to their sites' and considered that in general the 'whole castle building movement was essentially false and ended in nothing and it has now no importance except as a record of the side issues of the social life of the last half of the eighteenth century and of their echo in the first quarter of the nineteenth'. Of course Bolton regarded the castle style as 'the first stirrings of the Gothic Revival'.

recourse to the arches of the Gothick form which, rising from two centres, finish in an acute angle at the top, but adhered to what they no doubt had learnt from their late masters of this country in forming their arches, like them, semicircular.

Our ancestors till the time of Inigo Jones, seem to have had no knowledge of what is called Grecian Architecture, by which we understand the introduction of Grecian orders, nor were they indeed very solicitous about regularity in their castles or private dwellings. Where these were really intended for strength and resistance, which was the case with most of them, they seem principally to have been directed by situation and to have adapted their plan to the circumstances of their site without attending to regularity or considering it as leading to beauty. We are indeed far from thinking them blameable for this omission, which might often have interfered with and cramped their ideas of utility and defence, objects much more interesting than regularity, symmetry and proportion which are qualities more properly attached to the Grecian architecture. From the great and noble remains of these castles in every part of this island, from their lofty towers and pendulous turrets and battlements, we still view them with great admiration as sublimely picturesque and beautiful, the stupendous productions of a warlike age.

Coeval with this in Britain is what is commonly distinguished by the name of Gothick architecture, a style which seems by our ancestors to have been peculiarly dedicated to religious purposes in so much that even in castles where the general tenour of building was perfectly different, yet when a chapel was introduced it immediately assumes the Gothick, both in its external form and internal decoration. The same may be observed with respect to convents and other religious houses, even to crosses in market places, which, being always surmounted by the cross, partake also of the Gothick style. Some modern architects, misled by the circumstance of both these styles being the productions of a remote period, have very improperly blended them in their works. Morris, a minor architect of this country, designed a castle for the duke of Argyll at Inveraray – not a Barons' castle nor even in the Queen Elizabeth style, but a Gothick one – not what he wished it to be but what he was ignorant how to accomplish.

The ancient architects of Gothick buildings seem to have arrived at regularity in their designs but were not bigotically attached to it. It is certainly susceptible to great grandeur, pomp, solemnity and gloom, and therefore peculiarly adapted to religious worship. But those modern artists who have transferred it to garden seats and other diminutive objects have shown much want of taste and propriety.

Subsequent to the Barons' castles, another style took place and was first introduced into this country during the reign of Henry VIII and continued under his immediate successors. This is what we have distinguished above by the name of the Queen Elizabeth style and may be properly enough termed a refinement of the Barons' castle. For it is to be observed that during the reign of Henry VIII the government of England began to take a more settled and steady appearance and castles for defence being less necessary they gradually gave way to palaces and houses where there was some attention paid to the convenience and size of appartments with some regularity of design and windows of such dimentions as to admit abundance of light. Those palaces and houses were not, however, divested of the principal decorations of the old castle: they were still flanked by towers and surmounted with turrets and battlements, and though their regularity and situation deprived them generally of the picturesque contour of the former yet they continued, from their grandeur and effect, to be pompous and interesting objects. Of this species of building we have here a splendid display in the Heriot's Hospital of this city, where it is worthy of observation that even in this late period the chapel partakes of pure Gothick.

No one ever more completely adopted the spirit of this species of building than Mr. Adam, of which Culzean Castle and that of Thomas Kennedy Esquire at Dulquharran in the shire of Ayr and Lord Hyndford's at Mauldsley in Lanarkshire and many others in this country are incontrovertible proofs.

But to return, Inigo Jones gave the first blow to this Castle Architecture and certainly succeeded in banishing it from England by introducing the Grecian architecture with the regular orders and therefore the time of his flourishing under Charles the first and second and Oliver Cromwell the Protector makes an era in the architectural history of this island.

Inigo Jones was born in the year —— and died in —— having been the first to bring about a thorough revolution in the taste of this country. He thereby acquired a high degree of reputation which has been handed down, with great enthusiasm, to our own times. Every production of his, however paltry or insignificant, has been praised and considered till now as a   of art. At this present period however I believe we may venture to say the fascination established by novelty wears off and we may dare to criticize his works like those of other men. Availing ourselves of this lately acquired privilege we will take a critical survey of some of his principal works, of which, though never carried into execution, we look upon the design for the Royal Palace of Whitehall to be the most considerable.

But for the mention of Heriot's Hospital, this retrospective view would require little interpretation or comment. The general meaning and drift are clear enough: only when Clerk associates Adam's late castle-style houses (e.g. Culzean, Dulquharran, and Mauldslie) with the Elizabethan prodigy houses and specifically with that curious and unlovely epigone of Scottish Jacobean architecture, Heriot's Hospital, does he become difficult to follow. For although Heriot's Hospital and, say, Culzean, might be compared in a very loose sense as examples of similar syncretic solutions to the stylistic problems involved in designing a non-classical yet regular and symmetrical secular building, the comparison would be false since the aims and mental processes of the architects were clearly so different. And again, although occasional similarities of detail can be found between Heriot's Hospital and Culzean (e.g. in the turreted stable block of the latter), nevertheless the two buildings have exceedingly little in common either in plan, elevation, or general conception. Indeed they cannot be intelligibly compared.

If it is difficult to understand how Clerk could have associated such diverse and incongruous buildings in his mind in any meaningful way, it is quite impossible to imagine that Robert Adam did so. And if, as seems probable, Clerk was to some extent reflecting his brother-in-law's views, this inconsistency becomes all the more difficult, and all the more necessary, to explain.

The explanation is to be found, I think, quite simply in careless writing. The manuscript does not seem to have been revised or corrected, except very cursorily as it was written down. That Clerk intended to revise it, but never did so, is suggested by his leaving occasional blanks such as those for the birth and death dates of Inigo Jones. It is therefore possible that the repetition of the phrase 'this species of building' – first in connexion with Heriot's Hospital and again in the next paragraph – was unintentional and would have been corrected in a revision, when its misleading effect would have become immediately apparent. If we make this small correction – it would be sufficient to substitute 'type' for 'species' the first time the offending phrase is used – the difficulty is at once removed. The comparison made by Clerk would no longer be between Adam castle-style houses and Elizabethan and Jacobean prodigy houses but between the Adam castle style and the whole non-Gothic secular tradition in British architecture, which, according to Clerk, derived from Roman architecture (especially Roman military architecture), achieved its robust maturity in Norman or Romanesque buildings, which he calls the Barons' castles, and persisted in the Elizabethan and Jacobean styles which he thought 'may be properly enough termed a refinement of the Barons' castle'.[1]

As I mentioned earlier, Adam's castle-style houses have always been treated very warily, if at all, by writers on his work. The buildings are not attractive and are superficially so unlike Adam's other work that many of them have been ignored altogether on the assumption that they are merely an old man's aberrations of taste it were kinder to overlook, and, in any case, had probably been mangled in execution by local builders. For it has been assumed that Adam merely provided the designs and had no control over their execution. This is untrue. In the case of Seton Castle (Plate 10), which is the most fully developed and best preserved example of the style and for which ample documentation survives, Adam retained as close personal supervision over every stage of the construction as he did in any of his recognized master-

---

1. Humphry Repton made an interesting 'Inquiry into the Changes in Architecture' which may be usefully compared with John Clerk's 'retrospective view' (*Repton's Landscape Gardening*, ed. J. C. Loudon, 1840, pp. 383–5). Repton is not so radical in his approach as Clerk, but he gives some prominence to what he calls the 'Queen Elizabeth or House Gothic' – a 'mixed style' – which he thought the best for modern houses 'if they must be in any style of what is called Gothic'. Yet, he goes on, 'a mixed style is generally imperfect: the mind is not easily reconciled to the combination of forms which it has been used to consider distinct, and at variance with each other: it feels an incongruity of character, like an anachronism in the confusion of dates'. Repton did not approve of Adam's castle-style buildings, for it was surely with them in mind that he remarked on 'the spruce affectation of symmetry so fatal to the Gothic character' (op. cit., p. 281).

It may be observed, in connexion with Clerk's comments on the Queen Elizabeth style, that in the comparative views accompanying Richard Payne Knight's *The Landscape* (1794), the Capability Brown type of landscape, of which he disapproved, surrounds a classical style country house, whereas the picturesque type of landscape, of which he approved, surrounds an Elizabethan or Jacobean style 'prodigy house'.

pieces of earlier years.[1] May we then, with the help of Clerk's 'retrospective view', gain a new and better understanding of Adam's intentions in these rebarbative but powerful buildings?

The first obstacle to an understanding of them has been their association with the Gothic Revival. Any non-classical building erected during the late eighteenth and early nineteenth centuries is quite naturally interpreted in this way. And in Adam's case an apparently obvious precedent was to hand in Inveraray Castle,[2] where he himself had worked as a young man and which had inspired his elder brother John's design for Douglas Castle a few years later.[3] Moreover Robert Adam had intermittently worked in an elegant, flippant neo-Gothick style, notably at Alnwick.[4] It might therefore seem reasonable to suppose that his later non-classical houses were a development of this Adamesque neo-Gothick style. But Clerk makes it very clear that this supposition would be mistaken. Adam's intentions were quite otherwise. He had come to realize the falsity of neo-Gothick – Morris is condemned for his 'ignorant' use of it at Inveraray – and that a soundly based and 'correct' non-classical style for domestic buildings in Britain should be founded on a historically accurate understanding of medieval architecture.

The problem and the attitude of mind which Adam brought to it recall Payne Knight, who was building Downton during the late 1770s. Like Adam, Payne Knight thought it incorrect to build houses with capitals and columns in the English countryside:

> But let no servile copyist appear,
> To plant his paltry imitations here;
> To show poor Baalbec dwindled to the eye,
> And Paestum's fanes with columns six feet high!

1. The building contract for Seton, between the client Alexander Mackenzie and the Edinburgh builders Adam and Thomas Russell, is dated 12 November 1789 (Clerk of Penicuik Papers, H.M. Register House, Edinburgh). The existing castle or peel tower was to be demolished, the site cleared, and the new house built at a total cost of £3,400 with a penalty of £200 should it not be finished by Martinmas 1791. The Russells were to be placed 'under the inspection and supervision of Robert Adam Esq. or in his absence of Mr. John Paterson, clerk to the said Robert Adam Esq.'. An account of the building history is contained in the surviving Adam–Paterson correspondence now in the possession of Dr David C. Simpson, who has very kindly allowed me to read it though not quote from it.

2. For Inveraray see my *Robert Adam and his Circle* (1962), *passim*.

3. Douglas Castle was never completed and is now demolished (partly in 1935, completely in 1961). Undated plans and elevations for it are in the collection of Sir Alec Douglas Home, The Hirsel, Coldstream. These correspond in general though they are not identical with the elevation published in *Vitruvius Scoticus*, plate 82. The foundation stone inscribed '1757' is recorded by Pennant in his *Tour in Scotland in 1769* (1772, II, p. 132). According to S. H. Maxwell, *A History of the House of Douglas* (1902), II, p. 243, the building was not begun until 1758.

4. See my article 'Adam Gothic' in *The Connoisseur* (October 1958), in which are illustrated the remarkable Adam neo-Gothic buildings in the park of Alnwick Castle.

10. Robert Adam: Seton Castle

11. Robert Adam: Unexecuted design for Brampton Bryan (Sir John Soane's Museum, London)

With urns and cenotaphs our vallies fill,
And bristle o'er with obelisks the hill!
Such buildings English nature must reject.[1]

But whereas Payne Knight was to seek his 'correct' style in the imaginary buildings depicted by Claude and Poussin and out of them evolve an ingenious syncretic solution,[2] Adam's approach was much more radical and rational. He went back to first principles, to what he believed to be historically valid origins, and, whatever one may think of the results, there can be little doubt that Adam had the better understanding of the problems involved.

The impetus to confront these problems afresh and find a new and radical solution to them was not, as might be expected of Adam, an entirely disinterested one. By the mid 1770s his reputation was in urgent need of repair. The first volume of *The Works* had come out in 1773 and Adam no longer held a monopoly in the elegant, light, sophisticated style of neo-classical interior decoration on which his career and fame were based. To reassert himself he hoped to launch a new Adam style, one founded on neo-classical principles and yet not out of sympathy with the increasingly medieval sensibilities of the period and, above all, one which was as patently novel and original as his neo-classical style had been twenty years earlier.

But if his motives may have been ambiguous, the attitude of mind which lies behind Adam's solution is clear and direct. This was quite foreign to that which motivated the Gothic Revival. Adam was not inspired by any romantic longings for a chivalrous Baronial past with knights in armour, troubadours, and wimpled ladies. His approach was strictly rational, and he reached his solution by a logical process of thought, based on historical precedents whose authenticity and original function could be archaeologically ascertained. This rational approach to the search for a 'correct' style is, of course, typically neo-classic and it is in a neo-classic and not in any romantic neo-Gothic context that the late Adam castle-style buildings should be examined and appreciated.

The robustness and solidity of these astylar though regular and symmetrically planned buildings, combined with the gradual elimination of all specifically medieval features such as battlements, are indeed very suggestive of Romanesque architecture. But may we perhaps go even further – at any rate in the case of Seton – and suggest that here Adam was adumbrating a new Romano-British style, derived especially from Roman military architecture – the architecture to which, according to Clerk, the secular tradition in British architecture can ultimately be traced back? Comparison of Seton with, for example, Adam's reconstructions of the fortifications of Spalatro, especially the corner towers, or with his drawings of the walls of Rome

1. R. P. Knight, *The Landscape, a Didactic Poem* (1794).
2. See N. Pevsner, 'Richard Payne Knight', in *Art Bulletin* (December 1949), pp. 293–321. Also Dr S. Lang's essay in the present volume, pp. 85–97.

12. Jacques-Louis David: The Intervention of the Sabine Women (Musée du Louvre, Paris)

itself and of towers and fort-like tombs (e.g. that of Theodoric at Ravenna), are certainly very striking.[1] The similarity is even closer in his unexecuted design for Brampton Bryan[2] (Plate 11). That he intended Seton to have any recognizable colouring of Roman military architecture is, in the absence of any documentary evidence, impossible to maintain. But it would not be out of harmony with what we know of his mind – and of that of such Edinburgh lawyers as Alexander Mackenzie, his client at Seton – to suppose them to have indulged the pleasing fancy that they were here reviving a Roman station guarding the easternmost end of a vanished Roman Wall. Nor would they have been alone in such fancies and aspirations. For during these same years very similar projects were being made by other architects, of a similar neo-classical cast of mind, in France. Boullée's inspiration was on occasion Romanesque, of an unusual type peculiar to himself,[3] and L. J. Desprez produced designs which are quite astonishingly close to Adam's.[4] Indeed Desprez, in such projects as that for a state prison (dating from the late 1780s), clearly drew his inspiration from the remains of Roman military architecture which he had sketched in Italy and of which he later drew reconstructions. Thus both source and the use made of it provide a remarkable parallel with Adam. And finally there is J.-L. David himself, who included in the background of his great neo-classical masterpiece *The Intervention of the Sabine Women* (Plate 12), painted in 1796–9, an imaginary reconstruction of the walls of Rome whose affinity with their northern provincial outpost at Seton is unmistakeably germane.

1. Plates x and xi in Adam's *Ruins of the Palace of the Emperor Diocletian at Spalatro* (1764). For his Italian drawings see my article in *Connoisseur* (November 1960), pp. 186–94. Reconstructions of Roman military architecture by Adam's Roman friend Gavin Hamilton are also relevant here, e.g. the background of his *Achilles dragging Hector's Body around the Walls of Troy*, known from the engraving by Cunego, 1766.

2. Sir John Soane's Museum, London: Adam Collection, vol. XXXVII, no. 39.

3. See H. Rosenau, *Boullée's Treatise on Architecture* (1953).

4. See N. Wollin, *Desprez en Italie* (1934). His design for a state prison is reproduced on p. 81 after an engraving by Beskow. For his sketches and reconstructions of Roman military architecture see, for example, his drawings entitled 'Agrigente antique, reconstruction' and 'La Capitulation' on pp. 171 and 181. Desprez was in Italy from 1777 to 1784. The design for the state prison is undated but was presumably made in the late 1780s, see his somewhat similar design for a 'Monument d'homme illustre' which is dated 1787.

Richard Payne Knight and the Idea of Modernity

BY S. LANG

Richard Payne Knight was all but rediscovered by Nikolaus Pevsner nearly twenty years ago.[1] His paper was concerned principally with the man and his aesthetic conceptions and ideas. This essay is to be more modest and to relate only to one particular aspect of Knight's many interests, namely what – in lieu of a happier name – will be called the 'mixed style'[2] – a style which mixes the two seeming opposites, the Grecian and the Gothic.

R. P. Knight lived in the heyday of revival architecture, the Gothic, the Doric, the Egyptian, etc. To these were added exotic styles – the Moorish, the Indian, the Chinese.[3] Early in life – from 1774 on – he had built himself a house,[4] Gothic without, Grecian within, thus combining the picturesque aspect of the exterior with Grecian elegance inside. Yet not for him the nostalgia of the past: he wanted to be a modern, but the idea of throwing overboard all these styles of the past and creating one of the present never occurred to him.

For Knight there was only one way to 'create' a new style – by mixing the existing ones; long after he had built his house he defended the mixing of styles in his *Principles of Taste*:

It is now more than thirty years since the author of this inquiry ventured to build a house ornamented with what are called Gothic towers and battlements without, and Grecian

1. N. Pevsner, 'Richard Payne Knight', *Art Bulletin*, XXXI (1949). Cf. also W. J. Hipple Jr, *The Beautiful, the Sublime and the Picturesque in Eighteenth Century British Aesthetic Theory* (Carbondale, 1957), for a discussion of R. P. Knight.

2. This not very attractive term seems more appropriate than 'eclectic'. The question of the mixed style has also been discussed in passing by J. J. Mayoux, *Richard Payne Knight et le Pittoresque* (Paris, 1932), p. 100, who saw in it an emanation of Romanticism and the Picturesque.

3. The Doric Revival, the Egyptian Revival, and aspects of the Chinese reception have been discussed by N. Pevsner and S. Lang in the *Architectural Review* of 1948, 1956, 1949, reprinted and amended in N. Pevsner, Studies in *Art, Architecture and Design*, I (London, 1968).

4. Cf. Pevsner, loc. cit. (note 1 above), pp. 293 f.

85

ceilings, columns, and entablatures within; and though his example has not been much followed, he has every reason to congratulate himself upon the success of the experiment; he having at once, the advantage of a picturesque object, and of an elegant and convenient dwelling; though less perfect in both respects than if he had executed it at a maturer age.[1]

Knight might have felt justified in such an arrangement by Laugier's suggestion:

Je ne sçai si dans l'intérieur de nos Eglises nous ne ferions pas mieux d'imiter et de perfectionner cette Architecture gothique, en réservant l'Architecture grécque pour les dehors.[2]

But he may in the first place have been inspired by the buildings in Claude's and Poussin's landscapes:

The best style of architecture for irregular and picturesque houses, which can now be adopted, is that mixed style, which characterises the buildings of Claude and the Poussins; for as it is taken from models, which were built piecemeal, during many successive ages; and by several different nations, it is distinguished by no particular manner of execution, or class of ornaments; but admits of all promiscuously from a plain wall or buttress, of the roughest masonry, to the most highly wrought Corinthian capital.[3]

And, elsewhere:

in the pictures of Claude and Gaspar, we perpetually see a mixture of Grecian and Gothic architecture employed with the happiest effect in the same building.[4]

Knight seems justified in his advocacy of a mixed style because nobody can give a definition of pure Gothic:

At this time, when the taste for Gothic architecture has been so generally revived, nothing is more common than to hear professors, as well as lovers, of the art, expatiating upon the merits of pure Gothic; and gravely endeavouring to separate it from those spurious and adscititious ornaments, by which it has lately been debased; but nevertheless, if we ask what they mean by *pure Gothic*, we can receive no satisfactory answer: there are no rules – no proportions – and, consequently no definitions: but we are referred to certain models of generally acknowledged excellence; which models are of two kinds, entirely differing from each other; the one called the castle, and the other the cathedral or monastic.[5]

In advocating a mixed style Knight implied that Gothic and Grecian were opposed to each other; curiously enough, however, he derives Gothic from the classical styles, perhaps to make the idea more palatable, and calls it a

1. R. P. Knight, *An Analytical Inquiry into the Principles of Taste*, 3rd edn (London, 1806; 1st edn London, 1805), p. 223.

2. M. A. Laugier, *Observations sur l'architecture* (The Hague, 1765), p. 117.

3. Knight, op. cit., p. 225. See also E. M. Manwaring, *Italian Landscape in Eighteenth-Century England* (New York, 1925), who first pointed out that the English landscape garden had been inspired by paintings of Claude, the Poussins, and Salvator Rosa. C. Hussey, *The Picturesque* (London, 1967), p. 214, has drawn attention to Knight's sources: the models he had in view were the buildings shown in the backgrounds of pictures by such men as Claude and Gaspar, in which Grecian and Gothic were mixed with the happiest effect.

4. Knight, op. cit., p. 160.   5. ibid., p. 162.

corruption of the sacred architecture of the Greeks and Romans, by a mixture of the Moorish or Saracenesque, which is formed out of a combination of Aegyptian, Persian, and Hindoo. It may easily be traced through all its variations, from the church of Santa Sophia at Constantinople, and the cathedral of Montreale [sic!] near Palermo, one of the sixth, and the other of the eighth century, down to King's chapel at Cambridge, the last and most perfect of this kind of buildings; . . .[1]

He goes on to compare Gothic with various oriental styles and maintains that the

pointed arch, which we call Gothic, is the primitive arch; of which, the earliest instance known in Europe is the emissarius of the lake of Albano, built during the siege of Veii, long before either the Greeks or Romans knew how to turn any other kind of arch: for as this may be constructed without a centre, by advancing the stones in gradual projections over each other, and then cutting off the projecting angles, its invention was obvious, and naturally preceded those constructed upon mechanical principles; . . .[2]

Knight's description of the Gothic arch as the primitive arch is interesting and may throw some more light on his idea of a derivation of Gothic from classical architecture.

Throughout the eighteenth century the 'Gothic Ages' had been compared to the early and not so early periods of Greece. Bishop Hurd in his *Letters on Chivalry* ponders on

a remarkable correspondency between the manners of the old heroic times as painted by their great romancer, Homer, and those which are represented to us in the books of modern knight-errantry.[3]

And elsewhere he points out that

Now in all these respects Greek antiquity very much resembles the Gothic. For what are Homer's Laestrigons, and Cyclops, but bands of lawless savages, with each of them, a Giant of enormous size at their head? And what are the Grecian Bacchus, Hercules, and Theseus but Knights-errant, the exact counterparts of Sir Launcelot and Armadis de Gaule.[4]

And a little later:

Nay, could the very castle of a Gothic giant be better described than in the words of Homer:
> High walls and battlements the courts inclose,
> And the strong gates defy a host of foes   (Od. XVII, 318).[5]

Bishop Hurd finally sums up:

The purpose of the casual hints, suggested in my last letter, was only to shew that the resemblance between the heroic and Gothic ages is very great.[6]

1. ibid., p. 165 f.; while reading this paragraph, the Brighton Pavilion seems to rise before one's eyes.   2. ibid., pp. 166 f.
   3. R. Hurd, *Letters on Chivalry and Romance* (London, 1762), Letter IV, p. 26, quoting 'the xx. tom.' of the *Memoirs of the Academy of Inscriptions and Belles Lettres*.
   4. ibid., p. 31.   5. ibid., p. 32.   6. ibid., Letter V, p. 38.

Bishop Hurd could base himself on Addison, with whom he must have been well acquainted, as he edited his works and added notes (on the essayist's stylistic inaccuracies) to them.[1] Addison had compared the ballad of Chevey Chase to ancient poems, particularly to Virgil:

The Sentiments in that Ballad are extreamely Natural and Poetical, and full of the majestick Simplicity which we admire in the greatest of the ancient Poets.[2]

In the following lines Addison goes even further:

If the reader compares the foregoing six lines of the song with the following *Latin* verses, he will see how much they are written in the spirit of *Virgil*.[3]

It is probably true to say that Addison was mainly concerned with extolling the English ballads when comparing them to Virgil or Homer:

The thought in the third stanza . . . is such an one as would have shined in *Homer* or in *Virgil*.[4]

Yet underlying it all was a belief that early English ballads were equal to early Greek and Roman work.

Knight could thus base his ideas on authors preceding him, and it is very likely that he did so. However, Addison and Bishop Hurd had discussed poems and ballads, not the visual arts or architecture; but this was certainly no impediment at a time when Horace's 'Ut pictura poesis' was still valid.

Summing up, he says:

It has already been observed that the architecture of the Gothic castles, as they are called, is of Grecian or Roman origin: but, if it were not, there could be no impropriety in employing the elegancies of Grecian taste and science, either in the external forms and proportions, or interior decorations of houses built in that style: for, surely, there can be no blamable inconsistency in uniting the different improvements of different ages and countries in the same object; provided they are really improvements, and contribute to render it perfect.[5]

Knight will have been aware that he was not the first one to mix the Gothic and the Grecian. In England, Batty Langley had done so when creating his Gothic orders,[6] and Kent before him; one must assume that he too had not perpetrated his

1. J. Addison, *The Works*..., with notes by R. Hurd, various edns.
2. Addison on Chevey Chase, *Spectator*, no. LXXIV (25 May 1711).
3. ibid.   4. ibid.   5. Knight, op. cit., pp. 222 f.
6. B. and Th. Langley, *Gothic Architecture Improved by Rules and Proportions*, ... *to which is added an Historical Dissertation on Gothic Architecture* (London, 1742). Langley there published designs for five Gothic orders with several variants for some of them; he intended these orders for use in 'Frontispieces, Doors, Windows, Chimney-Pieces, Insides of Rooms etc. in the Gothic Manner' (plate 1).
In 1751 Batty Langley published *The Builder's Director or Bench-Mate being a Pocket Treasury*

sins in innocence.[1] Vanbrugh, too, had added medievalizing features to Italianate houses,[2] and such houses did in fact exist in Jacobean England. Again there was no doubt that Vanbrugh knew what he was doing and mixed his styles deliberately; perhaps he did so in order to follow Shaftesbury's demand for a national style, though there is no documentary proof.[3] The case was different in Tudor and Jacobean architecture. When the Italian Renaissance first came to England its outward signs – the orders, the round arch, the colonnade, the pediment, etc. – were grafted on to the stem of the indigenous architecture; the result was a hybrid, neither Italian Renaissance nor English Gothic. This particular mixture was, however entirely unpremeditated and 'naive', and in no way consciously contrived.

Towards the end of the century this idea of a mixed Grecian–Gothic style is taken up in England on a conscious level and on a bigger scale, in part centring round a re-appraisal of Vanbrugh. Reynolds in his Discourse of 1786 greatly praises the architect's imagination, and in an oblique way alludes to Vanbrugh's mixing the styles:

To pass over the effect produced by that general symmetry and proportion, by which the eye is delighted, as the ear is with musick, Architecture certainly possesses many principles in common with Poetry and Painting. Among those which may be reckoned as the first, is, that of affecting the imagination by means of association of ideas. Thus, for instance, as we have naturally a veneration for antiquity, whatever building brings to our remembrance ancient costume and manners, such as the Castles of the Barons of ancient Chivalry, is sure to give this delight. Hence it is that *towers and battlements* are so often selected by the Painter and the Poet, to make a part of the composition of their ideal Landskip; and it is from hence in a great degree, that in the buildings of Vanbrugh, who was a Poet as well as an Architect, there is a greater display of imagination, than we shall find perhaps in any other; and this is the ground of the effect which we feel in many of his works, notwithstanding the faults with which we feel in many of them are justly charged. For this purpose Vanbrugh appears to have had recourse to some principles of the Gothic Architecture; which though not so ancient as the Grecian, is more so to our imagination with which the Artist is more concerned than with absolute truth.[4]

of the Grecian, Roman, and Gothic Order; the Preface is dated 1746. On p. vii Langley says the following: 'In the last Part of this work I have given a great variety of *Gothick* Moldings for the *Bases* and *Capitals* of *Columns*, *Arches*, *Weatherings*, *Jaumbs* for Doors, Windows, Chimney-Pieces, etc., and the Manner of describing them geometrically of any Magnitude desired: Which being entirely new, I hope will be favourably received.'

1. For William Kent's 'mixed' style see in particular J. Vardy, *Some Designs of Mr. Inigo Jones and Mr. William Kent* (n.p., 1744), plates 22, 48, 49, 51.

2. Cf. S. Lang, 'Vanbrugh's Theory and Hawksmoor's Buildings', *Journal of the Society of Architectural Historians*, XXIV (1965).

3. Cf. preceding note.

4. J. Reynolds, *Discourses on Art*, ed. R. R. Wark (Huntingdon Library, San Marino, 1959), Discourse XIII, 1786, lines 405 ff., pp. 241–2.

Uvedale Price some years later, in 1794, that is several years before Knight wrote, discusses Vanbrugh at length:

It appears to me that at Blenheim, Vanbrugh conceived and executed a very bold and difficult design; that of uniting in one building, the beauty and magnificence of Grecian architecture, the picturesqueness of the Gothic, and the massive grandeur of a castle; and that in spite of the many faults with which he is very justly reproached, he has formed, in a style truly his own, a well-combined whole, a mansion worthy of a great prince, and warrior. . . . And, lastly, having probably been struck with the variety of outline against the sky, in many Gothic and other ancient buildings, he has raised, on top of that part, where the slanting roof begins in many houses of the Italian style, a number of decorations of various characters. These if not new in themselves, have at least been applied and combined by him in a new and peculiar manner; and the union of them giving a surprising splendour and magnificence, as well as variety to the summit of that princely edifice.[1]

In a later passage Uvedale Price becomes censorious, possibly having remembered the necessity of rules:

An architect who is thus notorious for his violation of rules, his neglect of purity and elegance, and his licentious mixture of styles and ornaments, certainly ought not to be held up as a model for imitation: but on the other hand, an artist who, in any art, produces new and striking effects, well deserves to have their causes investigated.[2]

Richard Payne Knight puts forward two more good reasons for favouring a mixed style. At the beginning of his treatise he discusses the Sense of Taste and comes to the conclusion that 'Very young children are almost always fond of pure sweet; but as the palate grows adult, it requires some mixture of acid and bitter to vary it, and give it pungency, or it becomes vapid and disgusting.'[3] Thus one must draw the moral that the adult palate prefers a mixture of food and hence also a mixture of styles, not 'pure' styles.

His other reason is less abstruse and rather avant-garde. He believes that a style should be 'of its time' and not imitate a style of the past;[4] 'pure' Gothic would be such an imitation, but by mixing styles one arrives at a new one and can create a 'gentleman's house of the nineteenth century'.[5]

In all marked deviations from the ordinary style of the age and country in which we live, the great difficulty is to avoid the appearance of trick and affectation; which seem to be, in some degree, inseparable from buildings made in imitation of any obsolete or unusual style; for, as the execution, as well as the design of almost every age and country, has a particular character, these imitations are scarcely ever in perfect harmony and congruity

1. U. Price, *Essays on the Picturesque* (London, 1794–8), II, pp. 251 ff.
2. ibid., pp. 255 f.
3. Knight, op. cit., p. 21.   4. ibid., p. 223.
5. C. Hussey, op. cit., summarizing Knight's ideas.

throughout; but generally proclaim themselves, at first sight, to be mere counterfeits; which, how beautiful soever to the eye, necessarily excite unpleasant ideas in the mind. A house may be adorned with towers and battlements, or pinnacles and flying buttresses; but it should still maintain the character of the age and country, in which it is erected; and not pretend to be a fortress or monastery of a remote period or distant country: for such false pretensions never escape detection; and when detected, necessarily excite those sentiments, which exposed imposture never fails to excite. Rustic lodges to parks, dressed cottages, pastoral seats, gates, and gateways, made of unhewn branches and stems of trees, have all necessarily a still stronger character of affectation; the rusticity of the first being that of a clown in a pantomime, and the simplicity of the others that of a shepherdess in a French opera. The real character of every object of this kind must necessarily conform to the use, to which it is really appropriated; and if attempts be made to give it any other character, it will prove in fact to be only a character of imposture: for to adapt the genuine style of a herdman's hut or a ploughman's cottage to the dwellings of opulence and luxury, is as utterly impossible, as is to adapt their language, dress, and manners to the refined usages of polished society.[1]

This passage contains a combination of various theories: for one, the classicistic idea of propriety, then the idea of honesty, here obviously derived from the idea of being out of character,[2] and above all the idea that '... the design of almost every age and country has a particular character...' and that '... it [the house] should still maintain the character of a house of the age and country, in which it is erected'.

When Knight was writing, Hegel had not yet formulated his ideas and cannot have been an influence.[3] A possible source of inspiration may have been Herder, who believed that 'Gothische Baukunst aus dem Geist der Zeiten erklärbar ist'[4] and was certain that Ossian could not be a forgery: 'so was lässt sich in unserm Jahrhunderte nicht dichten'.[5] Herder also held that Greek drama could only originate in the South, and Shakespeare's and Sophocles' plays have hardly more than the name in common.[6]

1. Knight, op. cit., pp. 223 ff.

2. This idea of honesty found its fullest expression in Pugin's writings.

3. Hegel's *Vorlesungen über die Aesthetik*, devised since 1818, were first published in 1835; cf. G. W. F. Hegel, *Sämtliche Werke*, ed. H. Glockner (Stuttgart, 1927–40), XII, pp. 3 and 12.

4. *Ideen zur Philosophie der Geschichte der Menschheit*, book XX, ed. Suphan, XIV, p. 488: '... im Ganzen aber wird die bessere Gothische Baukunst am meisten aus der Verfassung der Städte und dem Geist der Zeiten erklärbar'.

5. J. G. von Herder, *Von deutscher Art und Kunst* (Hamburg, 1773), ed. B. Suphan (Berlin, 1877–99), V, p. 160. See also D. W. Jöns, 'Begriff und Problem der Historischen Zeit bei Johann Gottfried Herder', *Göteborgs Universitets Arsskrift*, LXII (1956), no. 5.

6. *Von deutscher Art und Kunst*, ed. Suphan, V, pp. 209 f. 'In Griechenland entstand das Drama, wie es in Norden nicht entstehen konnte. In Griechenland wars, was es in Norden nicht seyn kann. In Norden ists also nicht und darf nicht seyn, was in Griechenland gewesen. Also Sophokles Drama und Shakespears Drama sind zwei Dinge, die in gewissem Betracht kaum den Namen gemein haben.'

Herder also said (in *Torso* of 1768; Suphan, II, p. 265): '[Jeder Author] trägt die Fesseln seines

Payne Knight might, however, also have been influenced by Voltaire's idea that 'Tout homme est formé par son siècle.'[1] It is more than probable that Knight had read some works by Voltaire, and the *Essai sur les mœurs* may well have interested him. He could have known about German thought and Herder through the painter Hackert, whom he accompanied on a tour through Sicily;[2] Knight had probably acquired some knowledge of German on this tour, so that he could have remained in touch with what happened in German intellectual, literary, and artistic circles. Knight pleading for a 'modern 'style is, by implication, advocating an original style.

He ends his *Principles of Taste* with a discussion on Novelty. While it is difficult at times to gauge precisely Knight's opinion, it does seem that he comes out on the side of 'Novelty' rather than 'Imitation',

for when the novelty of the first impression is over, and the interest of curiosity and surprise has subsided, mere imitation of common objects begins to appear trifling and insipid; and men look for, in imitative art, something of character and expression, which may awaken sympathy, excite new ideas, or expand and elevate those already formed.[3]

This passage should be compared with one of the final sentences of the essay:

The source and principle of it is, therefore, *novelty*; the attainment of new ideas; the formation of new trains of thought;...[4]

Richard Payne Knight can hardly not have been aware of Edward Young's ideas on originality. Young contrasts the original and the imitations, genius and learning;[5] he holds that 'Originals can arise from Genius only'.[6]

The strongest influence on Knight was most likely William Duff's essay. Duff, writing a few years after Young, in 1767, refers more directly to architecture:

A Talent or Genius for Architecture is discovered by a proper union of Imagination and Taste, directed to the accomplishment of the ends of this art...Human ingenuity hath as yet discovered only five orders in this art, which contain all the various forms of grandeur and beauty, consistent with regularity that have ever been invented; and our modern artists have confined their ambition to the study and imitation of those illustrious monuments of Genius left them by their predecessors, as if it were impossible to invent any other superior or equal models. To invent new models of Architecture would, we confess, require great compass of Imagination...To unite in one consummate plan the various orders of ancient Architecture requires indeed a considerable share of Imagination....[7]

Zeitalters dem er sein Buch zum Geschenk darbeut: er steht in seinem Jahrhundert, wie ein Baum in dem Erdreich, in das er sich gewurzelt, aus welchen er Säfte ziehet, mit welchem er seine Gliedmaassen der Entstehung decket.'

1. Voltaire, 'Essai sur les mœurs', II, *Œuvres complètes*, XII (Paris, 1878), p. 66.
2. Pevsner, loc. cit. (note 1 on p. 85), p. 293.
3. Knight, op. cit., pp. 101 f.   4. ibid., p. 475.
5. E. Young, *Conjectures on Original Composition* (London, 1759), pp. 19 ff. and passim.
6. ibid., p. 34.   7. W. Duff, *An Essay on Original Genius* (London, 1767), pp. 42 f.

Duff considers the Gothic architects as worthy of attention because they were original inventors:

The architects, who first planned those edifices though unacquainted with the polite arts, or with the *Grecian* and *Roman* Architecture, were doubtless great Originals in their profession, since they planned them by the unaided strength of their own genius. Their untutored imaginations prompted them to aspire to the Solemn, the Vast, and the Wonderful; and allowing an unbounded scope to the exercise of this faculty, they were enabled to give to their buildings that awful, though irregular grandeur, which elevates the mind, and produces the most pleasing astonishment. These Gothic edifices shew the inventive power of the human mind in a striking light and are sufficient to convince us, that excellence in Architecture was not confined to the *Greeks* and *Romans*, but may be sometimes displayed among a people in other respect barbarous.[1]

However grand classical architecture was, its imitation was not worthy of an original architect:

No improvements have been made in this art by our modern Architects, whose greatest ambition and excellence hath been, to understand and to copy those venerable remains of ancient Architecture.[2]

For a modern architect to be modern there is really only one way out:

yet we may remark, that after all the improvements: which Architecture received in the age of Pericles and Augustus, it seems susceptible of one important improvement, from the union of the awful Gothic grandeur with the majestic simplicity and graceful elegance of the *Grecian* and *Roman* edifices; and that by such an union ORIGINALITY of GENIUS in this art might be signally displayed.[3]

Duff wrote in 1767, a few years before Knight built Downton, though nearly forty before the *Principles of Taste* were published.

Duff does not plead here for a mixture of stylistic modes but rather echoes the Abbé de Cordemoy's tenets: he advocates the Greco-Gothic ideal, something more exalted and sophisticated, a marriage of ideas and principles rather than of forms and shapes.[4] Duff must have been imbued with French theory, but Knight brought his ideas down to earth and attempted to create an actual modern idiom, perhaps in a somewhat clumsy manner. But just because he made a definite suggestion, his ideas were taken up and could be followed by practising architects. Knight found

1. ibid., p. 257.   2. ibid., p. 253.

3. ibid., p. 258. Knight had probably also read A. Gerard, *An Essay on Taste* (London, 1759), to which had been added translations of Voltaire's, d'Alembert's, and Montesquieu's essays on taste.

4. J. L. de Cordemoy, *Nouveau Traité de toute l'architecture*, 2nd edn (Paris, 1714), p. 241: 'Ordre Gothique'. The whole problem of the relation of Gothic and Grecian in France in the eighteenth century has been fully discussed by R. D. Middleton, 'The Abbé de Cordemoy and the Graeco-Gothic Ideal: A Prelude to Romantic Classicism', *Journal of the Warburg and Courtauld Institutes*, XXV, XXVI (1962, 1963).

an immediate disciple in E. J. Willson, who had owned the *Principles of Taste*.[1] Though a pure and unadulterated Gothic Revivalist, he realized that Gothic must be adapted to present-day methods; but he did not go so far as to advocate a new 'mixed' style.

By a judicious attention to appropriate models a modern residence, of whatever size or character, may be constructed in the Gothic style, without departing from sound principles of taste. Some modifications of ancient precedents must be allowed, for an absolute fidelity will frequently prove incompatible with convenience; but as few deviations as possible should be gone into; and above all, nothing should be attempted which is inconsistent with the situation and character of the place, or which cannot be executed on a proper scale of dimensions...[2]

He objects to

a servile adhesion to ancient models, exclusive of all invention, which cannot reasonably be required. Modern edifices must be adapted to modern habits of life and the wants and wishes of the present generation. At the same time, it must be remembered, that ignorance or neglect of the rules and precedents of architecture whether the Grecian, Roman, or Gothic style be adopted will inevitably produce extravagance and bad taste.[3]

The idea of wanting to be a 'modern' gained momentum as the nineteenth century went on, probably much furthered by the publication of Hegel's *Vorlesungen über die Aesthetik* (devised since 1818) in 1835. In the same year Thomas Hope argued for a 'contemporary architecture'.[4] And judging from Donaldson's lecture at University College of 1842, mixing the styles was the predominant method of creating a new architecture:

By the contemplation of nature's self, free from the false laws of established systems, he may strike out an original path, founded on the internal resources of his own powers of observation. A recurrence to first principles was never more essential than at this moment. For not only our own school, but those of our continental neighbours have reached a most critical period. We are all in fact in a state of transition. There is no fixed style now prevalent here or at Paris, at Munich or Berlin. There is no predominant predilection nor acknowledged reason for adopting any one of the old styles of Art. We are wandering in a labyrinth of experiments, and trying by an amalgamation of certain features in this or that style

1. This is evident from the sale catalogue of Willson's library (not listed in Lugt's *Repertoire des catalogues de ventes publiques*, but of which there is a copy in the library of the Society of Antiquaries, London). The sale was conducted by Mr Weir at Lincoln on 21–23 November 1854.

2. E. J. Willson and A. C. Pugin, *Specimens of Gothic Architecture* (London, 1821–3), II, pp. xxii f.

3. E. J. Willson, A. C. Pugin, and A. W. N. Pugin, *Examples of Gothic Architecture* (London, 1831 etc.), II (1836), p. xix.

4. Quoted by P. Collins, *Changing Ideals of Modern Architecture, 1750–1950* (London, 1965), p. 128.

of each and every period and country to form a homogeneous whole with some distinctive character of its own, for the purpose of working it out into its fullest development, and thus creating a new and peculiar style.[1]

Donaldson's essay confirms what the reader of this paper might have guessed already, that much or some of the eclecticism of nineteenth-century architecture should be looked at with kinder eyes than has been done so far. This is not the place to examine the events in nineteenth-century architecture in any detail, but one might be justified in assuming that Payne Knight's demand for a modern idiom in the form of a mixed style may well have induced architects to try their hand in such concoctions and have emboldened them to carry out feats of novelty and originality denied to architects of other ages.[2]

G. G. Scott, on the face of it and according to some of his own writings a pure eclecticist for whom styles become hardly more than playthings later on, proves in his early *Remarks on Secular and Domestic Architecture* that he too had not remained untouched by the idea of a modern style; he even discusses the architecture of the future.[3] In the Preface he gives the programme:

And, finally, to shew to the public that we aim not at a dead antiquarian revival, but at developing upon the basis of the indigenous architecture of our own country, a style which will be pre-eminently that of our own age, and will naturally, readily, and with right good will and heartiness, meet all its requirements, and embrace all its arts, improvements, and inventions.[4]

A later passage proves that the demand for a new style was in the air, but that Scott thought it not possible to invent one:

The advocates of a new style of architecture suited to the nineteenth century have here a good card to play; and I am not disposed to join issue with them upon their general theory, but only as to the mode in which it is to be carried out. I freely admit that buildings whose uses and origins belong especially to our own day have, on that ground, a pre-eminent claim to be treated in a manner at once new and characteristic of the age which they repre-sent. And I am as ready to admit that we shall be equally far from effecting this by binding ourselves closely to the style of the mediaeval Hotel de Ville, the Roman Palazzo, or the palace (*in nubibus*) of Inigo Jones. Are we, then, to invent a spick-and-span new style to suit them? This involves two other questions: – first, Is it morally possible to invent such

1. T. L. Donaldson, *Preliminary Discourse on Architecture* (London, 1842), p. 29.

2. The problem of eclecticism has been fully treated in C. L. V. Meeks, *The Railway Station* (London, 1956).

3. G. G. Scott, *Remarks on Secular and Domestic Architecture, Present and Future* (London, 1858). Professor Pevsner has drawn attention to G. G. Scott's book and its significance in connexion with the problem of eclecticism and modernity in 'Möglichkeiten und Aspekte des Historismus', in L. Grote (ed.), *Historismus und bildende Kunst, Studien zur Kunst des Neunzehnten Jahrhunderts*, I (Munich, 1965), p. 23.

4. Scott, op. cit., p. vii.

a style? secondly, Are these buildings to differ in their character from others of their own age? My reply to both is in the negative. No age of the world has ever deliberately invented a new style, nor yet made use of a style for one class of buildings different from what it applies to others. If, then, my arguments as to style in general hold good, they avail equally for these as for any other class of buildings.[1]

Yet he makes plans for a future style:

I think we may, in the first place, lay down for our architecture of the future, that it must unite in itself the two great normal principles of construction – the lintel and the arch . . . In the next place, I think it is equally certain that in *arched* construction *all* reasonable forms of arch must be held admissible; – knowing all forms, we are at liberty to reject any which may be shewn to be capricious, unsightly, or contrary to principles of sound construction; but we are not at liberty to proscribe any which are free from these objections. We have no right to limit the legitimate elements of construction – nor could we do so if we tried. Especially must our future architecture embrace, and that heartily, the two leading forms – the round and the pointed arch.[2]

Finally he comes very near to suggesting a mixture of styles:

Assuming in each country of Europe its own Gothic of the best period as a centre, it will, we would predict, become enriched by the *best ideas* of all other periods and countries. Not only must the different varieties of the architecture of Western Europe be laid under contribution, but the great Eastern branch of Christian art be brought to aid our own, and especially must we fill up the one great hiatus in our Northern styles by making that most noble feature, the *dome*, to form a conspicuous element in our future developments. . . . Our architecture must unite within itself all that can be learned from the past, all that is demanded by the present, and all which will be developed by the future, – the style we select for our starting-point being the bond of union which will cement all these elements into one perfect and homogeneous whole.[3]

In reading G. G. Scott one feels that he was acquainted with Knight's *Principles*, but tried to steer away from their tenets though he could not quite escape their impact. He repeatedly stresses that present-day buildings should be built in a present-day style. He was too convinced a Gothicist and too much under the influence of Pugin to advocate a mixing of styles, yet he admits that different forms should be combined in a future style.

The last faint echo of Knight's ideas – if an echo it was and not a derivation from Scott – appears in a passage in Voysey's *Individuality*. It may be quoted here in conclusion:

It is obviously unwise under these circumstances to tie the architect down to any style of the past. If the Tudor arch is still the most graceful and still the most frank avowal of practical needs, and best fitted to the material nearest at hand, and meets all requirements

1. ibid., pp. 203 f.   2. ibid., pp. 266 f.   3. ibid., pp. 272 f.

and conditions of modern life, why not adopt it and use it if need be in conjunction with the round arch or the lintel, if either of the latter can be justified on the same grounds. But the traditionalist is shocked by what he calls the mixture of styles.[1]

Is it too bold to assume that Knight's demands for a new style and his suggestions how to arrive at one influenced much theoretical writing and beyond it the practice of the nineteenth century? Perhaps not. Even if he, as we have seen, did not wholly invent these ideas, he formulated them in such a way that they could be taken up by others and thus perpetuated.

1. C. F. A. Voysey, *Individuality* (London, 1915), p. 86.

H²

John Britton and the Genesis of the Gothic Revival

BY J. MORDAUNT CROOK

THE English Gothic Revival can be divided into four periods: the Rococo, the Picturesque, the Ecclesiological, and the Eclectic. Of these four phases only the second and third concern us here, that is the shift from Gothick to Gothic between the 1790s and the 1830s. Apart from liturgical considerations, this transition represented the triumph of archaeology over romanticism. Yet its hero was neither an archaeologist nor a romantic but a pot-boiling publisher named John Britton (Plate 13).

Both the Greek and the Gothic Revivals began as Romantic diversions and ended as academic systems. But their rates of progress were very different. Sanderson Miller's sham ruin at Hagley Park (1747) was built ten years before James Stuart's neighbouring Doric temple.[1] Yet the Greek Revival became respectable two generations sooner than its Gothic counterpart. Before Wilkins's work at Haileybury and Downing (1806–7), the Grecian style was merely one of several exotic modes produced by the romantic impulse; after Smirke's rebuilding of Covent Garden Theatre (1809), it rapidly became the yardstick of architectural orthodoxy.[2] Meanwhile the rival movement remained relatively static: James Wyatt's progress from Lee Priory (1783–90) and Sheffield Park (c. 1785) to Fonthill (1796–1807) and Ashridge (1808–13) was compositional rather than stylistic. When *The Ecclesiologist* eventually appeared in 1841 the Greek Revival was nearly finished. These differing rates of progress can be explained quite simply in terms of archaeological publications. It was not until the 1830s and 1840s that the Gothic Revivalist possessed a quarry of stylistic precedents comparable to the volumes of Greek antiquities published between 1760 and 1800. What Stuart and Revett were to the Greek Revival, Carter and Britton were to the Gothic. And just as Revett's lack of ambition left the field clear for James Stuart, so Carter's emotional approach was less effective than Britton's

1. N. Pevsner, *An Outline of European Architecture* (Penguin Books, Jubilee edn, 1960), pp. 594–5, plates 500–1.
2. J. Mordaunt Crook, *Haileybury and the Greek Revival* (Hoddesdon, 1964).

98

13. John Britton (1771–1857), topographer and gothicist. The frontispiece to his *Autobiography* (1850), showing the author surrounded by mementoes of his career: busts of Shakespeare and Aubrey, a plan of Stonehenge, and his own design for a monument to Chatterton

hard-headed business sense. It was Britton's phenomenal series of publications, not Carter's letters to the *Gentleman's Magazine*, which swung the Gothic Revival from romanticism to archaeology.

John Britton was a self-made man, and he never let his readers forget it. In his own words his career showed 'what may be effected by zeal and industry, with moderate talents, and without academic learning'.[1] He was born in 1771 at the village of Kington St Michael near Sodbury in Wiltshire, the birthplace of John Aubrey.[2] When he left school at thirteen to help in his father's baker's shop he knew little except the alphabet and the Bible. When he left Wiltshire for London in 1787 he had never seen a newspaper or a dictionary. As a penniless apprentice he spent five years in the cellar of a Clerkenwell wine-merchant, corking and bottling and secretly studying by candlelight. 'Buried alive,' he tells us, 'I contrived to do as much work in six hours as my fellow-apprentices did in ten.'[3] Not surprisingly, he developed the symptoms of consumption. These he countered with a stiff diet of Cheselden's *Anatomy*, Buchan's *Domestic Medicine*, and Tissot's *Essay on Diseases incident to Sedentary People*.[4] 'Thus', he claimed, 'I owe prolongation of life to reading'.[5] At the same time he set out to subdue an impulsive temperament by studying Watts's *Logic* and *An Essay on the Conduct of the Passions and Affections*.[6] This exercise seems to have been rather less successful: towards the end of his apprenticeship he fell in love with a visiting lady's maid and vainly followed her on foot 216 miles into the heart of Devonshire.[7] Already he seemed destined to be a topographer. But first came a curious episode in Britton's life which goes some way towards explaining the character of his early publications and the absurdity of his style. He set his heart on becoming an actor.

After leaving the Jerusalem Tavern in Clerkenwell, Britton joined two more wine-merchants as a cellarman before enrolling as a clerk, first with an attorney in Gray's Inn, and then with a firm of solicitors. He now had more time at his disposal, and his evenings were spent in the company of actors and demagogues. He soon developed a taste for public speaking, singing, and recitation. At an eating house in Great Turnstile, Holborn, he met up with eccentrics like the Chevalier d'Éon and Sir John Dinley.[8] At a 'spouting club' at Jacob's Well, Barbican, he met agitators like John Gale Jones and reformers like Thelwall, Hardy, Godwin, and Holcroft. And here he made his name by reciting the comic poems of Peter Pindar, Colman, Collins,

---

1. J. Britton, *Autobiography* (1850), II, Appendix, p. 1; P. Ferriday, 'John Britton', *Architectural Review*, CXXII (1957), pp. 367–9.

2. Cf. Britton's *Memoir of John Aubrey* (1845) and his edition of Aubrey's *Natural History of Wiltshire* (1847).

3. *Autobiography*, I, Appendix, p. 6.

4. Britton, *Beauties of Wiltshire*, III (1825), p. 25.

5. *Autobiography*, I, p. 328.   6. *Beauties of Wiltshire*, III, p. 22.

7. *Autobiography*, I, p. 74.   8. ibid., pp. 80–5.

and O'Keeffe.[1] Through Mark Lonsdale, stage manager at Sadler's Wells, he met Thomas, Charles, and T. F. Dibdin, John and Charles Kemble, Grimaldi the clown, and Master Betty, the young Roscius, as well as entertainers of lighter kind, such as Richer the rope dancer, Dubois the egg-hornpipe performer, and G. B. Belzoni the Patagonian Samson.[2] Oddly enough, it was Belzoni's bizarre career which pointed the way to Britton's future. This muscular antiquary and inveterate traveller built up an international reputation as an Egyptologist before dying of dysentery on the road to Timbucktoo.[3] His chief discovery, the Belzoni sarcophagus, eventually found its way into the Soane Museum. To the impressionable Britton he was a living reminder of the potential connexion between archaeology and publicity. And an opportunity existed for developing just such a combination in the shape of De Loutherbourg's Eidophusikon. After acting as Garrick's scene-painter, De Loutherbourg had invented a new form of entertainment involving movable scenery lit by argand lamps and accompanied by elaborate sound effects. As one critic put it, 'he introduced a new art – *the picturesque of sound*'.[4] Fashion later encouraged a number of imitations, such as the Diorama and the Colosseum in Regent's Park, the Cosmorama in Regent Street, the Paecilorama at the Egyptian Hall, and the Panorama in Leicester Square.[5] In 1799 an impresario named Chapman bought up De Loutherbourg's equipment and engaged John Britton at three guineas per week to write, recite, and sing an appropriate commentary.[6] Three years later Britton collaborated with Lonsdale in putting on a show at the Lyceum Theatre. Gas was used for the first time in a theatrical setting, and Britton's monologues accompanied panoramic views of Egyptian antiquities recently published by Denon.[7] A similar scheme failed soon afterwards; but the baker's son had found his métier. It merely remained to translate these illustrated monologues into the dignity of print.

During the next half century Britton moved on from showmanship to scholarship. But he never lost the accents of the music-hall chairman. Joseph Hunter remembered

1. ibid., pp. 92–3. He also frequented the Odd-Fellows Club, the School of Eloquence in Cheapside, and the Shakespearian Theatre in Tottenham Court Road.   2. ibid., pp. 100 f.

3. 'Collections relating to Sadler's Wells', XIV, B.M. press mark Cracherode I, Tab 5 b; Belzoni, *Discoveries ... in Egypt and Nubia* (1820); *European Magazine*, LXXXII (1822), pp. 97–107; *The Times* (14 January 1834), p. 7; J. Harris, *Travels of Belzoni* (1825 edn); T. J. Smith, *A Book for a Rainy Day* (1861 edn), pp. 174–9; J. Halls, *Henry Salt* (1834); C. Redding, *Past Celebrities* (1866), I, p. 268, and *Recollections* (1885), I, pp. 138–9.

4. Ephraim Hardcastle [W. H. Pyne], *Wine and Walnuts* (1823), I, p. 296. De Loutherbourg's technique was much admired by Reynolds and Gainsborough.

5. Cf. Britton's *Picture of London* (1827), pp. 317–18, and *Brief Account of the Colosseum* (1829).

6. *Autobiography*, I, pp. 97–9.

7. ibid., pp. 100–1. For some time Britton considered the theatre 'the most fascinating place of rational amusement in the world' (ibid., p. 127). He seems to have been 'cured ... through seeing Macbeth miserably butchered by a strolling company, who performed in a cow-shed at Maidenhead' (*Bristol Mercury*, 10 September 1853).

him as 'something between a Book-maker and a Book-seller', and an exponent of the theory 'that there was great virtue in advertising'.[1] His advertisements certainly read like theatrical posters: 'at an expense hitherto unparalleled ... the Author has now produced four volumes ... at an expense hitherto unknown and inexperienced in literature ... ', etc. His commentaries are littered with archaic Latinisms like 'castrametation', 'lusorial', and 'domiciliated'. In fact he managed to combine the egoism of a born actor with the verbosity of a self-taught pedant. Like some archetypal figure out of Samuel Smiles, he wrote his autobiography three times over and larded his chapters with quotations from Martin Tupper: 'Great is the dignity of authorship ... O, books! ye monuments of mind'. His energy was stupendous. As a correspondent he was tireless.[2] In fifty years he produced more than one hundred volumes.[3] But few of them sold well, and he seldom made a profit. What spurred him on was the status and prestige attached to learning, 'the passion for study, the delight in books, the desire of solitude and celebrity ... the triumphs and disappointments of literary glory'.[4] He delighted in recondite references, exquisite engravings, and fine typography. He was also something of a prig.[5] It was one of the ironies of his career that his most widely read works were a flimsy pamphlet on the Great Western Railway[6] and a comic production with crude illustrations by Rowlandson.[7] But whatever his faults, Britton was neither a charlatan nor a recluse. Charles Knight remembered him leading choruses at Frogmore between bouts of topography, 'kind-hearted ...

1. J. Hunter, Notices of Contemporaries, B.M. Add. MS. 36527, f. 169, 25 September 1834. For examples of Britton's advertising technique cf. Bliss Corresp., B.M. Add. MS. 34567, ff. 245, 301; Bodleian MS. Don. d. 87, ff. 245–59.

2. E.g. letters to George Woodful, B.M. Add. MS. 27781, ff. 132, 134, 136; Rev. Joseph Hunter, Add. MS. 24866, f. 11; Rev. R. Yates, Egerton MS. 2372, f. 228; Thomas Hill, Add. MS. 20081, f. 41; Philip Bliss, Add. MS. 34567, ff. 266, 299; Sir Francis Madden, Egerton MSS. 2839, f. 82, 2841, ff. 249 and 340, and 2844, f. 116; Charles Babbage, Add. MSS. 37185, f. 94, and 37187, f. 155; John Martin, Add. MSS. 37965, f. 59, and 37967, f. 106; George Baker, John Le Keux, Henry Thomas Hope, Dawson Turner, and S. W. Singer, Add. MS. 38794 ff. 159, 164, 166, 172, 175.

3. For a full list of Britton's publications, compiled by T. E. Jones, see *Autobiography*, II, Appendix, pp. 187–92.

4. Isaac D'Israeli, *The Literary Character* (1822), I, p. 5. See also Britton's *Toddington* (1840), p. xi.

5. 'I never saw a person either slightly or fully intoxicated without shuddering' (*Autobiography*, I, pp. 348–51). He condemned Fonthill as 'a sum of the utmost licentiousness and debauchery among the servants, male and female, from the steward to the grooms, all the females prostitutes etc.' (Mitford Note Books, VIII, B.M. Add. MS. 32566, f. 38).

6. *A Lecture on the Road-Ways of England* (Bristol, 1833). This eulogy of steam power was delivered to the Bristol Literary and Philosophical Society and later presented to the railway directors. They distributed thousands of copies *gratis* but paid the author nothing (*Autobiography*, II, p. 200).

7. *The Pleasures of Human Life: investigated cheerfully, elucidated satirically, promulgated explicitly and discussed philosophically in a Dozen Dissertations on Male, Female and Neuter Pleasures ... by Hilaris Benevolus & Co., Fellows of the London Literary Society of Lusorists* (1807). This was a riposte to Beresford's *Miseries of Human Life* (*Autobiography*, II, pp. 188–90).

indefatigable, good-tempered, self-satisfied, pushing and puffing'.[1] Lysons and Farington envied his 'Sunday evening parties for artists'.[2] George Godwin recalled a 'singularly active and penetrating mind, extraordinary powers of arrangement and organisation, an excellent memory and a *kind heart*'.[3] His ambitions as a scholar far outran his talents. But architectural historians have cause to be grateful to the man Beckford once called 'that highly ridiculous, highly impertinent Britton, the Cathedral fellow'.[4] Digby Wyatt claimed that he revolutionized topographical illustration: 'his labours were incessant, his memory extraordinary, his system admirable, his clearness of understanding and liveliness of fancy ... vigorous, his affections warm, his habits exemplary'.[5] T. L. Donaldson called him 'the Father of British Antiquities'.[6]

Britton's earliest publications stem from his theatrical phase: essays in the *Attic Miscellany* and *Sporting Magazine*, collections of lyrics like *The Thespian Olio* and *The Odd-Fellows' Song Book*, and *Sheridan and Kotzebue: the Enterprizing Adventures of Pizarro* (1799). Prompted by Sheridan's *Pizarro*, *Sheridan and Kotzebue* already showed some grasp of historical method and an early interest in the techniques of printing and illustration.[7] But the first real hint of a topographical career came in 1798, when the printer and bookseller John Wheble suggested a work on the scenery and antiquities of Wiltshire. Undaunted by reference books which seemed 'almost as unintelligible as if couched in Greek',[8] Britton set about gathering information.

With maps, a pocket-compass, a small camera-obscura...two or three portable volumes, an umbrella, and a scanty packet of body-linen etc., I commenced a walk from London on 20 June [1798], and returned ... on 30 Sept. During that excursion, I visited Windsor, Oxford, Woodstock, Stratford-upon-Avon, Warwick, Kenilworth, Birmingham, Hagley, the Leasowes and Church Stretton. Thence I made diverging excursions to Shrewsbury, Welshpool, and several other places ... ; and returned through Ludlow, Leominster, Hereford, Ross, down the Wye, to Chepstow, to Bristol and Bath; thence to several different parts of Wiltshire, and back to London. This long and toilsome, but extremely interesting and attractive journey, cost me only eleven pounds, sixteen shillings and ninepence![9]

1. C. Knight, *Passages of a Working Life* (1864), I, p. 31; II, p. 307; III, p. 43.

2. Diary of Joseph Farington, B.M. Print Room Typescript. p. 4474, 24 February 1810.

3. *The Builder*, XV (1857), pp. 22–5.

4. B. Alexander (ed.), *Life at Fonthill, 1807–22* (1957), pp. 228–9, 21 October 1817. After seeing Mackenzie's 'celestial' drawings, Beckford decided 'Britton does not displease me'. For Britton's correspondence with Beckford cf. Bodleian MS. Eng. misc. d. 222, ff. 1–90. I owe this, and several other Bodleian references, to Mr Peter Howell.

5. *R.I.B.A. Reports and Papers* (1856–7), p. 57.

6. *Autobiography*, I, p. 16 n. For an early memoir and portrait cf. *European Magazine*, LXXVII (1820), pp. 195–200; Bodleian MS. Don. d. 87, ff. 239–41.

7. *Autobiography*, II, pp. 184–8.   8. ibid., I, p. 238.

9. ibid., p. 137. For Britton's inadequate maps cf. ibid., p. 319.

At Windsor Castle he encountered Benjamin West, at Bowood the Marquess of Lansdowne, at Downton the redoubtable Payne Knight, and at Foxley he met Uvedale Price before moving on to Tintern Abbey. While at Oxford he first entered the Bodleian and paid 2s. 6d. to inspect Blenheim Palace, 'the first large country house I had ever seen'.[1]

The Beauties of Wiltshire appeared in two volumes in 1801. They were roundly censured by Gough as flimsy and flippant, and Britton later admitted the justice of this criticism.[2] His high-flown introduction on the theory and practice of topography only made matters worse.[3] An expanded excerpt on Corsham House, published separately in 1806, merely demonstrated that he had yet to develop any real understanding of architecture.[4] But he was already making prodigious efforts to remedy his deficiencies as a scholar. After struggling through Gough's edition of Camden's *Britannia*, Cox's *Magna Britannia*, King's *Munimenta Antiqua*, and Wyndham's *Doomsday for Wiltshire*, he was relieved to find Warner's *Walks Through Wales* 'fluent, familiar and pleasant', not 'encumbered and confused by technical terms, or dull details of genealogy, manorial and parochial history, and useless lists of rectors and vicars, with long inscriptions on tombs in Latin, Greek and bad English'.[5] Gilpin's *Forest Scenery*, Reynolds's *Lectures*, Payne Knight's *Landscape*, Repton's *Landscape Gardening*, Price on *The Picturesque*, and Burke on *The Sublime and the Beautiful* all helped to mould his taste. But his feeling for exact and appropriate illustration was developed by reaction rather than by imitation. He deplored the conventions of Walker's *Copper-Plate Magazine*, the '*pretty* aquatint prints' in Ireland's *Warwickshire Avon*, and the 'tasteless and trivial' scenes contained in Grose's *Antiquities*. If he had a model in the field of illustration it was John Harrison's *Novelist's Magazine*, with its drawings by Stothard and the elder Smirke and engravings by Heath, Sharpe, and Grignon.[6] Britton's slow development from littérateur to topographer was well demonstrated by the contrast between the early volumes of the *Beauties of Wiltshire* and the third volume which appeared in 1825. By that date he had already embarked on two memorable projects which moved forward from topography to archaeology and from archaeology to architectural history, the *Architectural Antiquities* and the *Cathedral Antiquities*. But before these could be completed he had first to finish a multi-volume work which made his name

1. ibid., pp. 168, 188, 197, 353, 362. Britton's description of his reception at Bowood is a gem.
2. *Gentleman's Magazine* (1801), part II, pp. 631–5, 905–6; J. Brewer, *Introduction to . . . Beauties of England and Wales* (1818), p. xiii n.; *Autobiography*, II, pp. 5–7.
3. *Beauties of Wiltshire*, I, pp. vi–x. For a wiser statement of topographical theory cf. Britton's *Essay on Topographical Literature* (1843).
4. *Historical Account of Corsham House* (1806); *Autobiography*, II, pp. 16–18; *Review of Publications of Art*, I (1808), pp. 223–31.
5. *Autobiography*, I, pp. 135–7.
6. ibid., p. 257.

as a writer but restricted his development as a historian, *The Beauties of England and Wales*.

Early in 1800 the publishers Vernor and Hood first suggested to Britton that he should undertake a topographical survey of the whole country. Thomas Hood, father of the poet, had recently done well with the *Monthly Mirror* and *Poetical Magazine*. He now hoped to copy the success of a profitable piece of plagiarism published by Alexander Hogg under the title of Boswell's *Antiquities of England and Wales*.[1] Britton would have none of this, nor would his co-author Edward Wedlake Brayley (1773–1854). It was in a Clerkenwell bookshop in 1789 that Britton first met up with Brayley, then apprenticed to Henry Bone the enameller. Together they composed a satirical lampoon called *The Powder Tax, or a Puff at the Guinea Pigs*. This was the start of a partnership lasting sixty-five years and extending to such well documented works as *The History of Surrey* (5 vols., 1840–8), *Memoirs of the Tower of London* (1830), and *The Ancient Palace and Late Houses of Parliament at Westminster* (1836). Brayley was much more of a natural scholar than Britton, meticulous, cautious, and quite untouched by his partner's flair for publicity. 'Mr. Brayley was constitutionally of a healthy and hardy frame', wrote Britton,

and was thus enabled to endure and surmount great bodily as well as mental exertion. I have known him to walk fifty miles in one day, and continue the same for three successive days. After completing this labour, from Chester to London, he dressed and spent the evening at a party. At the end of a month, and when pressed hard to supply copy for the printer, he has continued writing for fourteen and for sixteen hours, without sleep or respite, and with a wet handkerchief tied round a throbbing head.[2]

The two authors certainly made a formidable combination. One critic called them 'the Castor and Pollux of Topographers'.[3]

What Hood had in mind was a six-volume compilation appearing in monthly instalments over a period of three years. In the end *The Beauties of England and Wales* ran to twenty-seven bound volumes and took twenty years to complete. Understandably, the publishers were not amused. The authors attempted to produce a comprehensive account based on original sources and illustrated by accurate engravings of antiquities. Whereas Hood stipulated '*seats and wood-scenery*, considering these the principal *beauties* of the country',[4] from the start Britton set himself a different brief, adding 'Delineations, Topographical, Historical and Descriptive' to the original title. By 1802 he was beginning to justify delay by pleading his determination to make the work 'as original, accurate, and interesting as possible'. In 1805

1. ibid., I, pp. 238, 258, and II, pp. 48–9; *Introduction to . . . Beauties*, p. xiv.

2. *Gentleman's Magazine* (1854), part II, pp. 538, 582–8; *The Athenaeum* (1854), p. 1170; *Autobiography*, I, p. 69.

3. *Gentleman's Magazine* (1831), part II, p. 47.

4. *Introduction to . . . Beauties*, p. xiii.

he accused Hood of 'undue interference' and began the independent production of *Architectural Antiquities*. Only Hood's death in 1811 allowed the surviving share-holders to persuade Britton to re-enter the project. The names of Britton and Brayley alternately precede each other on the title pages of the first six volumes: *Bedfordshire, Berkshire and Buckinghamshire* (1801), *Cambridge, Cheshire and Cornwall* (1801), *Cumberland and Derbyshire* (1802), *Devon and Dorset* (1803), *Durham, Essex and Gloucester* (1803), and *Hampshire, Isle of Wight and Hereford* (1805). The labour of preparing the letterpress fell largely upon Brayley. Britton was responsible for some of the historical commentaries, and for 'the principal travelling, correspondence, labour of collecting books and documents, direction of draughtsmen and engravers'.[1] Responsibility thereafter was more distinct. Volumes seven and eight, *Hertford, Huntingdon and Kent* (1808), went to Brayley; volume nine, *Lancashire, Leicester-shire and Lincolnshire* (1807), went to Britton. Scarcely had Brayley begun *London, Middlesex and Westminster* when he fell foul of Hood's successor, John Harris. Of the first five volumes (1810–16) on the metropolis, Brayley contributed two before giving way to Joseph Nightingale and J. N. Brewer. Meanwhile some of the work prepared by Britton was completed by the Rev. J. Evans as *Monmouthshire, Norfolk and Northamptonshire* (1810). Then came *Northumberland and Nottinghamshire* (1813) by the Rev. J. Hodgson and F. C. Laird; *Oxford and Rutland* (1813) by Brewer; and *Staffordshire* (1813) and *Shropshire and Somerset* (1813) by Nightingale. In the absence of Britton and Brayley there was less care and greater speed. The publishers could even claim that 'this work is executing with unparalleled dispatch'. The final volumes certainly came with a rush. *Yorkshire* (1812) was farmed out to John Bigland, *Suffolk, Surrey and Sussex* (1813) to Frederick Shoberl, *Warwickshire* (1814) to Brewer, *North Wales* (1812) to Evans, and *South Wales* (1815) to Rees. Britton completed *Wiltshire* in 1814, and in the same year he joined with Brewer, Hodgson, and Laird to finish *Worcestershire and Westmorland*. Finally, Brewer added an introductory volume containing a historical survey of British antiquities, a formidable bibliography, and an exposé of the trials and quarrels which had punc-tuated the whole work.

These quarrels had been conducted in public. In 1814 Britton announced that 'over the paper, printing and embellishments, I had no control, and am therefore not responsible'. His attempts to give the series a 'more strictly and properly ... topographical and antiquarian character' were 'thwarted by the obstinacy and cupidity of a publisher: who at length carried his hostility towards me so far, as to force me to give up my share in the work'.[2] Not to be outdone, the publishers inserted a biting notice in Britton's own volume on Wiltshire. This complained of 'the scandalous insinuations of these *Antiquarian Quacks*' and 'the turpitude of Mr. Britton and his

1. *Autobiography*, II, pp. 54–5.
2. ibid., p. vii.

106

co-adjutor' in daring 'to throw out aspersions' which displayed 'a malevolence of heart, only known, it is hoped, to persons like themselves'.[1]

But the series was remarkable in several other ways. In the first place the cost of production (some £50,000) was enormous.[2] So was the labour involved. For the first five volumes alone the authors travelled 3,500 miles. Between 8 June and 20 September 1800 they walked 1,350 miles. Starting out from London, their itinerary was as follows: Fulham, Richmond, Hounslow Heath, Weybridge, Oatlands, Chertsey, St Ann's Hill, Eton, Stoke Poges, Virginia Water, Newbury, Donnington Castle, Marlborough, Savernake Forest, Tottenham Park, Avebury, Marlborough Downs, Salisbury Plain, Stonehenge, Amesbury, Old Sarum, Salisbury, Frome, Bath, Wells, Glastonbury, Wookey Hole, Cheddar, Mendip Hills, Bristol, Thornbury, Berkeley Castle, Gloucester, Ross, Hampton Court, Holme Lacy, Hereford, Ludlow, and Church Stretton. At this point they parted, hoping to meet up again at Welshpool. However, after crossing Wenlock Edge and visiting Much Wenlock, Broseley, and Coalbrookdale, Brayley fell ill. So Britton completed his 'walk round North Wales' alone, calling at Newtown, Llanidloes, Aberystwyth, the Devil's Bridge, and Hafod.[3] But this was only the beginning. When the publishers decided to deal with the counties in alphabetical order, the authors discovered that they had begun at the wrong end of the country. The spring of 1802 saw Britton in Devon and Cornwall. In August 1803 he was in Gloucestershire; in September 1804 in Hampshire; and in 1806 in Lancashire, Lincolnshire, and Northamptonshire. His exertions were noted with approval by the National Institute of France.[4] Not since Camden had such a comprehensive survey been produced. Grose and Gough had been relatively selective. All volumes contained critical bibliographies, and several were accompanied by an 'Illustrative Appendix' entitled *The British Atlas* (1804–9). The text is occasionally strident and personal and the arrangement haphazard. But by attempting to make the series both scholarly and readable the authors performed a double function: in the words of George Ormerod the Cheshire historian, it was 'a popular work for general entertainment and utility', as well as 'a focus to collect the scattered rays of information'.[5]

1. *Wiltshire* (1814), p. 1; Bodleian MS. Don. D. 87, ff. 219–36.

2. The series retailed at £30. 2s. 6d. per standard set. For detailed reviews cf. *Annual Review*, I (1802), pp. 456–64; II (1803), pp. 422–7; III (1804), pp. 438–40; IV (1805), pp. 426–8; VII (1808), pp. 76–9.

3. *Autobiography*, I, pp. 238–42.

4. ibid., II, pp. 52–4.

5. *Introduction to . . . Beauties*, p. xii. For amusing examples of Britton's lack of objectivity, see his accounts of the battle of Naseby and of the Easter bottle-kicking ceremony at Hallaton, Leicestershire (*Lancashire, Leicestershire and Lincolnshire*, pp. 436–7). For his methods of obtaining information from local gentry cf. Cumberland Papers, B.M. Add. MS. 36499, f. 12, 22 March 1801; Windham Papers, B.M. Add. MS. 37916, f. 59, 8 December 1806.

In the long run it was the seven hundred illustrations which made the greatest impact. And for this Britton justifiably claimed the credit. It was only towards the end of the series that he handed over responsibility to the ubiquitous J. P. Neale. 'We sought a new style of *embellishment*', Britton recalled, 'in which accuracy of representation should be combined with picturesque effect.'[1] Hollar, Loggan, and Burghers had been interesting rather than accurate. Aubrey, Dugdale, Plot, Carew, Lambard, Burton, and Thoroton had all produced valuable information lacking in pictorial impact. Stukeley had been the first topographer to introduce plans and sections of buildings. Kip, Knyff, and Buck had been limited by the conventions of their bird's-eye surveys. 'The "cuts" ... in Grose's *Antiquities*' were but 'caricatures in topography' and 'only tolerable in the very infancy of literature and art'. The scenes in Gilpin's *Tours* had no more than 'a certain degree of prettiness and pictorial effect'. And in recent years only Pennant, Cordiner, Hearne, and Byrne had produced illustrations of the requisite standard.[2] Carter's sketches made little attempt to appeal to a wider public.[3] As one of Britton's advertisements modestly put it, his plates 'effected a memorable improvement' and 'greatly assisted in rendering *local history* an object of fashionable study'. A new school of artists and engravers grew up under his direction. The watercolourists Samuel Prout (1783–1852)[4] and Frederick Mackenzie (1788?–1854)[5] made their debut in *The Beauties of England and Wales*. So did the engravers John and Henry Le Keux (1783–1846 and 1787–1858).[6] Later on they were joined by Edward Blore (1787–1879),[7] George Cattermole (1800–

1. *Introduction to ... Beauties*, p. x.   2. ibid., p. xi.

3. Britton respected Carter's scholarship. He produced a new edition of *Ancient Architecture* in 1837 and collected many of Carter's drawings, e.g. B.M. Add. MS. 27322 (*Autobiography*, II, p. 213; *The Times*, 26 July 1830, p. 4).

4. Haydon introduced Prout to Britton, who took him on a walking tour of Cornwall and trained him for two years at his house in Clerkenwell. Despite ill health he became famous for his Continental sketches and survived to be a friend of Ruskin (*Art Journal*, XI, 1849, pp. 76–7; *Gentleman's Magazine* (1852), part I, pp. 419–20; J. Ruskin, *Notes on S. Prout and W. Hunt* (1879); J. L. Roget, *Old Water Colour Society* (1891), I, p. 340, II, p. 50, 459; Bodleian MS. Eng. litt. e., ff. 120–1).

5. Besides Britton's works, Mackenzie contributed to Ackermann's *Westminster Abbey* (1812), *Oxford* (1814), *Cambridge* (1815), and *Winchester and Eton* (1846); Havell's *Seats* (1816–19); Westall's *Abbeys and Castles in Yorkshire* (1820); Ingram's *Oxford* (1837); Heath's *Picturesque Annual* (1839); Wright and Jones's *Cambridge* (1841), and Tilt's *Churches of London* (1837–9). Like Britton, he made little profit from his talent (*Old Water Colour Society*, I, p. 371, II, pp. 84, 455).

6. Both brothers had been apprenticed to James Basire (1730–1802), who succeeded Vertue as engraver to the Society of Antiquaries. Henry abandoned engraving in 1838 but John's son, J. H. Le Keux (b. 1813), continued the tradition. (Obituary by Britton, *The Builder*, IV, 1846, pp. 289–90; Dodd's History of English Engravers, B.M. Add. MS. 33402; *Gentleman's Magazine*, 1846, part I, p. 647).

7. Antiquary, architect, and Gothicist, employed by Britton on the *Architectural* and *Cathedral Antiquities*; later 'special architect' to William IV and Queen Victoria (H. M. Colvin, *Dictionary of English Architects*, 1954, pp. 78–82).

68),[1] R. W. Billings (1813–74),[2] Henry Shaw (1800–73),[3] and several others who built independent reputations on the training they received.

Britton's obituary of perhaps his favourite protégé, W. H. Bartlett (1809–54), reveals something of his training methods. Bartlett joined the other pupils at the age of fourteen in 'a comfortable and pleasant office in the midst of a garden – a rarity in London ... provided ... with all necessary materials, and also numerous books, drawings, prints and sketches for study' after the 'best specimens by Hearne, Alexander, Cotman, Girtin and Turner'.[4] Britton demanded sketches 'based on the principles of truth and daylight, and with forms and colours which were referable to the laws and effects of nature'. The young apprentice was conducted round Gloucestershire, Somerset, and Yorkshire and dispatched to Essex, Kent, Bedfordshire, and Wiltshire in the footsteps of Prout, Cotman, and Mackenzie. Then he worked at Bristol, Gloucester, and Hereford for the *Cathedral Antiquities* and joined up with Penry Williams for Britton's projected volume on Deepdene,[5] and with Le Keux for Britton's *Picturesque Antiquities of English Cities* (1828–30). Later on Bartlett travelled extensively abroad and became distinguished in his own right. But four years before his death he assured his old master,

I have a vivid ... recollection of the awakening of the antiquarian spirit within me under your tuition; of drives and walks about the Wiltshire downs, and of the great gig-umbrella, swaying to and fro, and the danger of all being capsized, of cromlechs, stone temples, old churches, and old gateways, and a host of other objects.

Britton's own drawings were seldom more than competent.[6] But his standards as an

1. Placed with Britton at the age of fourteen; worked on the *Cathedral Antiquities* with his brother Richard. Praised by Ruskin for his 'powerful genius...antiquarian feeling...pure, earnest and natural' (*Modern Painters*, 1888, I, p. 114). Also illustrated Lawson's *Scotland Delineated* (1847–54) and Hall's *Baronial Halls* (1848) (*Art Journal*, N.S. III, 1857, pp. 209–11; VII, 1868, pp. 180–1; IX, 1870, pp. 92–3; J. Sherer, *Gallery of British Artists*, 1879, I, pp. 97–106).

2. Apprenticed to Britton between the ages of thirteen and twenty. As an artist he worked with Godwin, Mackenzie, and Le Keux; as an author and topographical publisher he produced works on the *Temple* (1838), *Brancepeth* (1841), and *Kettering* (1843) churches, on *Carlisle* (1840) and *Durham* (1843) cathedrals, and on the *Antiquities of Durham* (1846) and *Scotland* (1845–52); as an architect he directed restorations in Scotland, notably that of Edinburgh Castle chapel (*The Builder*, XXXII, 1874, pp. 982, 1035).

3. Architectural draughtsman, engraver, illuminator, and antiquary. After working for Britton on Wells and Gloucester Cathedrals, he produced numerous illustrated works on medieval architecture and antiquities (W. T. Lowndes, *Bibliographer's Manual*, ed. H. G. Bohn, 1864, III, pp. 2371–2).

4. *Art Journal*, N.S. I (1855), pp. 24–6. For Bartlett's review of Britton's *Autobiography* cf. *Sharpe's London Journal*, XII (1850), pp. 214–20. For an account of Britton's house (17 Burton Street, St Pancras) cf. *Autobiography*, II, pp. 155–60.

5. MS. volume (1825–6), R.I.B.A. Drawings Collection.

6. E.g. *Beauties of England and Wales: Cornwall*: St Michael's Mount, St German's church, Probus tower, and Truro church; *Wiltshire*: Bowden Park, Malmesbury abbey church, Chippenham church, and the Manor House, Stanton St Quintin.

editor were rigid and exacting: the early sketches of Prout and Cattermole were rejected as insufficiently accurate. His combination of enthusiasm and discipline certainly brought out the best in his pupils. And by merely uniting the names of Mackenzie and Le Keux he came near to making himself immortal.[1]

Britton's knowledge of antiquities, as well as his quest for higher standards of illustration, had been restricted by the *Beauties'* cursory format. His next series, the *Architectural Antiquities of Great Britain,* gave full rein to his ambitions as an architectural archaeologist. He set out to exhibit 'collectively... specimens of the various styles' of medieval architecture by 'correct delineations and accurate accounts ... drawn and engraved with scrupulous accuracy' and by 'enlarged representations of particular parts and ornaments, with ground plans etc.'[2] His co-publishers, Messrs Longman and Taylor, were co-operative.[3] His engravers, notably Smith, Roffe, Rawle, Woolnoth, and the Le Keux brothers, were supremely competent. And his list of 'scientific artists' was dazzling: Prout, Nash, Alexander, Hearne, Wyatville, Porden, Wilkins, Cotman, Buckler, Gandy, Wild, Westall, Dayes, Fielding, West, Turner, Shee, Repton, Blore, and Mackenzie. The result was possibly Britton's most successful undertaking, and certainly his most profitable.[4] The first four volumes appeared fairly quickly in 1807, 1809, 1812, and 1814. Volume one contained measured drawings of the Temple Church, Malmesbury Abbey Church, the chapel at King's College Cambridge, the ancient crosses at Hereford, Gloucester, Coventry, Cheddar, Malmesbury, Chichester, and Winchester, and the Eleanor crosses at Waltham, Northampton, and Geddington. None of these had been previously engraved with such accuracy. The system of elevation, measurement, plan, cross-section, and commentary was continued in volume two with Henry VII's Chapel at Westminster, as well as with several examples of Tudor domestic architecture: Audley End, Hengrave Hall, Holland House, Tabley Hall, Wollaton, Oxburgh Hall, and Longleat. Volume three did the same for St George's Chapel Windsor, Waltham abbey church, the Redmount Chapel and St Nicholas Chapel at Lynn, Norwich Cathedral cloister, Hedingham Castle, and the Roslyn Chapel in Scotland, for which Sir Walter Scott supplied some of the information. Volume four was largely devoted to castellated examples: Conisborough, Caernarvon, Warwick, Kenilworth,

1. They first appeared together in *Architectural Antiquities,* II (1809).

2. *Autobiography,* II, pp. 110–11, 116–17.

3. As with most of Britton's major publications, Messrs Longman kept the accounts and allocated profits. Josiah Taylor, the architectural bookseller, acted as a focus for the employment and entertainment of architectural historians. His catalogue included works by Stuart and Revett, Soane, Malton, Richardson, Nicholson, Lugars, Gwilt, Gandy, Aiken, and Plaw, as well as Gothicists like Milner, Dallaway, Warton, Bentham, Gunn, and Hawkins (*Autobiography,* I, pp. 247, 265, 268, 304–5).

4. As author he received £1,800 over twenty-one years for the five volumes; as joint owner he received £3,266 (*Autobiography,* II, p. 204).

Rochester, Thornbury, Norwich, Ludlow, Bolton, and Castle Rising. But the abbeys of Glastonbury and Croyland were also included, along with Crosby Hall, London. Material collected on St Mary Redcliffe was published separately as an independent volume in 1813; and this in turn justified a companion volume on Bath Abbey Church, published in 1825.[1]

The first four volumes of *Architectural Antiquities* supplied an obvious want. The ichnography of British medieval building had been popularly demonstrated for the first time. In Sir Kenneth Clark's words, 'the old fantastic parodies of Gothic were no longer possible. Britton killed Ruins and Rococo'.[2] The engravings were generally praised as 'a real honour to the country ... scientific enough to excite professional attention, and sufficiently picturesque and diversified to afford an ample treat to the general reader'.[3] But there was one fundamental criticism. A miscellany of medieval antiquities, however well produced, was no substitute for a systematic survey of Gothic architecture. Britton had embarked on an essay in the comparative method without first clarifying his chronology. To remedy this deficiency he eventually produced a fifth volume in 1827 entitled *A Chronological History and Graphic Illustrations of Christian Architecture in England*. Begun in 1818 and laboriously compiled over the next nine years, it posed as 'something like a grammatical or scientific treatise'. Its contents included a chronological commentary illustrated by plans, sections, elevations, and views; an alphabetical list of medieval architects; a chronological list of churches, monuments, crosses, etc.; and a dictionary of architectural terms. The main body of the work was prefaced by a diffuse historical introduction plus an elaborate attempt to define the origin and stylistic terminology of Gothic architecture. As regards these notorious controversies Britton had the advantage of writing just as the dust was beginning to settle. Skating over the theories of some sixty combatants, he steered his way between Wren's 'Saracenic', Warton's 'Absolute Gothic', Milner's 'Pointed', Sayers's 'Norman', Mitford's 'Plantagenet', and Gunn's 'Romanesque', and contented himself with a few criticisms of his contemporaries. Carter was censured for confusing Saxon and Norman; Rickman for adopting the term 'Perpendicular' and for illustrating it with examples of his own work rather than from original specimens.[4] On the whole, Britton contributed little

1. *Autobiography*, II, pp. 144–5 and 148–50. For a favourable review cf. *Literary Gazette* (1825), p. 260.　　　　　2. Sir K. Clark, *The Gothic Revival* (Pelican edn, 1964), p. 66.

3. *New Annual Register* (1815), p. [423]. For other favourable notices cf. *Anti-Jacobin Review*, XXI (1805), p. 427; *European Magazine*, XLVIII (1805), pp. 217, 380; *Critical Review*, V (1805), pp. 82–5; *Annual Review*, IV (1805), pp. 388–92, V (1806), pp. 724–5. One critic, 'a powerful and hostile drawcansir', was the engraver John Landseer, father of Sir Edwin (*Worcester Cathedral*, p. xxvii; *Review of Publications of Art*, I, 1808, pp. 320–43; Bodleian MS. Autogr. d. 21, f. 265).

4. *Architectural Antiquities*, V (1827), pp. i, 37, 39, 68, 129, 170; *Redcliffe Church* (1813), pp. viii–ix. In private he dismissed Rickman as a 'Quaker quack' (Soane Museum, Private Correspondence III/i/93, 7 November 1833).

on the interpretative side, falling back on the terms 'Saxon', 'Norman', and 'Pointed' (rather than 'Gothic'). He lacked an original mind. He was strongest in precise dating and documentation, and in the presentation of visual evidence. The sections of mouldings, capitals and spandrels, the spires and arches arranged in stylistic sequence, the scaled-down drawings of windows, fonts and piscinas, all were superbly engraved in outline, mostly by John Le Keux. As an architect's textbook the volume was invaluable. It was certainly 'the *first* attempt at a *coherent history* of *English* Gothic'.[1] Britton announced that its publication constituted 'an epoch' in his life: 'henceforth it will be my aim to guard against the temptations of novelty, and endeavour to reduce my labours to six or eight hours, instead of twelve or fourteen per day . . . having passed the fifty fifth year of my age, it is time to calculate on a little respite'.[2] But in 1827 he was in fact only half way through a work which proved to be his *magnum opus*, the *Cathedral Antiquities of England*.

Britton was the first to attempt a complete survey of English cathedrals since Browne Willis (1727–42). Carter's series (1797–1801), sponsored by the Society of Antiquaries, had proved abortive.[3] Storer's *Cathedrals* (1812) had been popular but inadequate. Only two masters held the field: Bentham's *Ely* (1771) and Milner's *Winchester* (1798). Almost from the start Britton limited himself to the medieval English cathedrals. St Paul's, St Asaph, Bangor, St David's, and Llandaff were postponed indefinitely. Even so, the series remained incomplete, and a parallel range of pocket guides got no further than the Norwich Cathedral *Vade Mecum* (1817). The series aimed not at Bentham's combination of ecclesiastical and antiquarian history but at a summary of all available evidence, administrative, biographical, and architectural, in which 'the descriptions and engravings [should] mutually illustrate each other'.[4] A few of the cathedrals were already well documented. None had previously been subjected to the analysis of measured plans, 'sections and strict geometrical elevations'.[5]

Salisbury (1814) was the first volume and the most successful. Despite competition from a rival publication by William Dowdsworth and Henry Hatcher, the £2,200

1. P. Frankl, *The Gothic* (1960), p. 498.

2. *Architectural Antiquities*, v (1827), pp. ii, vi.

3. The series has been belatedly revived: J. A. Repton and W. Wilkins Sen., *Norwich Cathedral*, ed. S. Rowland Pierce (1965).

4. *Peterborough Cathedral*, p. vi; *Gloucester Cathedral*, p. viii. For a friendly review by Southey cf. *Quarterly Review*, XXXIV (1826), pp. 305–49.

5. *Lichfield Cathedral*, p. 6. 'Had this species of illustration been adopted by a Hollar, a Loggan, or a Vertue', or by 'the writers on Christian architecture in the 17th or 18th centuries . . . much irrelevant dissertation and trifling controversy would have been avoided' (*Canterbury Cathedral*, p. i). 'Had . . . Gough, Grose, Whitaker etc. . . . understood this species of elucidation, they could have shortened and simplified their own writings, and furnished more accurate and satisfactory information to readers' (*Wells Cathedral*, p. vii).

spent on production was repaid with interest.[1] Dowdsworth and Hatcher may have been more scholarly, but Britton's book was a joy to handle. Like the final volume of *Architectural Antiquities* and the entire *Cathedrals* series, it was a product of Charles Whittingham's Chiswick Press. Britton certainly had a fine eye for typography, printing, and binding, as well as for drawing, etching, and engraving. Even more than the Moyes and Bensley editions of his works, the Whittingham volumes merit the title of 'books... which are among the greatest... glories of British book design'.[2] Next came *Norwich* (1816) and *Winchester* (1816–18), with engravings of customary distinction by the Le Keux brothers and drawings by Mackenzie, Cattermole, J. A. Repton, and Blore. With *York* (1818–19) the series reached its peak: the engravings more numerous and the text more comprehensive than ever before or afterwards. *Lichfield* (1819–20) showed no drop in quality, but gave rise to a quarrel between Britton and Mackenzie which turned out to be irreparable. In attempting to cut back production costs Britton presumed too much upon the good will of his draughtsmen and engravers. On the wrapper of the second number he even went as far as publicly threatening them with dismissal. But Mackenzie had already taken his revenge. In plate XVI 'of this very number, a view of Chantrey's famous monument, the Sleeping Children, a confused inscription had been surreptitiously inserted in one of the painted windows, embracing the words, "a fine drawing spoilt by John Britton"'.[3] Rather than provoke still further this 'cabal or combination' of artists, Britton apologized in the following number.[4] But the damage had been done. *Oxford* (1821) appeared late, with inferior drawings by George Cattermole. *Canterbury* (1821–3) rescued the series with a splendid set of geometrical sections by two young architects, G. L. Taylor and Edward Cresy.[5] But with *Wells* (1823–4) and *Exeter* (1825–7) the problem of vanishing profit margins reappeared in graver form. New artists were engaged, notably T. Wyatt, J. S. Cotman, H. Shaw, and J. Gandy, and a new publicity drive was set in motion. W. H. Bartlett, Henry Asted, and Penry Williams

1. Britton was not offended by competition; he subscribed to the rival volume and later wrote Hatcher's obituary (1847). But he objected to the way his own artist, Nash, had been 'seduced by the Verger [Dowdsworth] to make other drawings for a similar publication' (*Worcester Cathedral*, p. ix). For favourable reviews of Britton's *Salisbury* cf. *Literary Panorama*, N.S. III (1816), pp. 563–71; *Gentleman's Magazine* (1815), part I, pp. 152–3 and ibid. (1816), part I, pp. 52–8, 139–40; *Eclectic Review*, N.S. V (1816), pp. 450–7.

2. R. McLean, *Victorian Book Design* (1963), pp. 2–6. Bensley produced *Redcliffe Church* and Moyes *Bath Abbey Church*. Whittingham was also responsible for the superb printing of *Fonthill* (1823), *Cassiobury* (1837), and *The Union of Architecture, Sculpture and Painting* (1827). See *Autobiography*, I, pp. 298–300, II, pp. 207–8.

3. *Autobiography*, II, p. 131 n.

4. Mackenzie lobbied several artists and writers in an attempt to defeat Britton (Elmes Corresp., B.M. Add. MS. 42864, ff. 46–7).

5. *Canterbury Cathedral*, p. ii; G. L. Taylor, *Autobiography of an Octogenarian Architect* (1870), I, pp. 161–2.

were engaged for *Peterborough* (1827–8) and the same young team was responsible for illustrating *Gloucester* (1828–30). At Gloucester, however, the fifty-six-year-old author 'experienced a compound fracture of the right leg', from which he never fully recovered.[1]

At this point an attempt was made to reconstitute the series on the basis of local subscriptions. *Bristol* (1829–30) would never have appeared had it not been for this expedient.[2] But the impetus generated by local support for *Hereford* (1830–1)[3] petered out with *Worcester* (1832–5), the last of the Three Choirs volumes. Rochester, Durham, Chichester, Chester, Carlisle, Ely, and Lincoln never appeared. For Ely there was of course Bentham's pioneer work. And for Lincoln Britton eventually re-edited C. Wild's volume in 1837. But it is a measure of his overall achievement that for those cathedrals which escaped his survey we must still rely on accounts which are by comparison second-rate: Ormerod for Chester, Dallaway for Chichester, Carter for Durham, Lysons for Carlisle, and Hasted for Rochester. Britton blamed the collapse of his project on clerical apathy. At Exeter, Hereford, and Wells he encountered indifference and hostility.[4] The 'timid' Dean of Hereford even advised him 'not to trouble himself about Hereford Cathedral, as ... it might be likely to involve him in further losses'.[5] The author's final plea for assistance was almost uniformly ignored.[6]

However the real reason for the collapse of the series was the changing state of the book market. Britton had made his name with expensive and scholarly works, meticulously edited and exquisitely produced. He made a name but not a fortune. Reviewers described the engravings contained in *The Fine Arts of the English School* (1809–12) as 'transcendently good'.[7] But the volume made a loss of £1,000.[8] The losses involved in publishing *The Union of Architecture, Sculpture and Painting* (1827) resulted in one of several squabbles between the author and his old friend Sir John Soane.[9] And just as Britton's publicity techniques were beginning to take

1. J. Hunter, 'Notices of Contemporaries', B.M. Add. MS. 36527, f. 169, 25 September 1834; *New Monthly Magazine*, XXI (1822), p. 492; *Gloucester Cathedral*, pp. v–vi.

2. Subscribers included William Beckford, George Ormerod, and several members of the Bristol Chapter and Corporation.

3. Subscribing gentry included the Biddulph family, Viscount Eastnor, Sir Uvedale Price, Charles Hanbury Tracy, and J. R. Meyrick of Goodrich Court.

4. *Worcester Cathedral*, pp. xi–xii and xxi; *Exeter Cathedral*, p. ii; *New Monthly Magazine*, XXI (1827), p. 182.   5. *Hereford Cathedral*, p. vi.

6. A request to guarantee the remaining seven volumes was sent to forty-four Bishops and as many Deans and Chapters; only six replies were received (*Worcester Cathedral*, p. xvii; *Gentleman's Magazine*, 1835, part II, pp. 403–5).   7. *British Critic*, XL (1812), p. 434.

8. Britton's *Magazine of the Fine Arts* (1821) was also a financial failure (*Autobiography*, II, pp. 178–81). For profit and loss accounts of most of his works cf. *Autobiography*, II, pp. 205–6.

9. Both men were prickly and egocentric. They also quarrelled in 1821 over a review in the *Magazine of the Fine Arts* and in 1836 over Britton's non-appointment as Registrar of the Royal

effect, the bottom fell out of the copper-plate market. An expanding audience co-incided with a technical revolution, the substitution of steel engraving for copper-plate.[1] Britton had outgunned Grose and Carter, but he met his match with Shepherd and Neale. Nevertheless he decided to compete at the same level. In 1829 he put out two money-spinning volumes containing mass-produced steel engravings: *Bath and Bristol*, published by Jones & Co., with drawings by Shepherd; and *Modern Athens or Edinburgh in the Nineteenth Century*, a work which managed to combine the attractions of Neale's *Seats* and Elmes's *Metropolitan Improvements*.[2] Three years later came *Descriptive Sketches of Tunbridge Wells*, and *Devonshire and Cornwall Illustrated*, containing 'Views of Cities, Towns, Public Buildings, Streets, Docks, Churches, Antiquities, Abbeys, Picturesque Scenery, Castles, Seats of the Nobility etc. etc.'.[3] Britton had been more or less compelled to enter this new market by the recent failure of two volumes of copper-plate engravings, *Picturesque Views of English Cities* (1826–7) and *Picturesque Antiquities of English Cities* (1828–30). *Picturesque Views* was born during the publishing crisis of 1825–6 and was produced without letterpress in order to avoid contributing eleven fine copies to the copy-right libraries.[4] *Picturesque Antiquities* contained a scholarly commentary as well as views 'under the varied effects of meridian sun-shine, cloudy and dark skies, sun-rise, sun-set, twilight, rainbow etc.'. But it proved to be 'the most losing speculation he ever embarked in. Had it been published in 1810, instead of 1830, it would have been eminently popular and profitable'.[5] In an attempt to keep afloat he therefore re-edited a volume of memoirs, a standard guide-book, and a comic poem: *A Narrative of Memorable Events in Paris ... in 1814* (1828);[6] *The Picture of London* (1825–33);[7]

Academy. On the first occasion Soane endorsed Britton's apology: 'no answer, silent contempt'. On the second, Britton answered: 'we shall *never* meet again'. The coquettish Mrs Britton ('little B') acted as mediator on such occasions, sending 'half a dozen bottles of. . . Wiltshire Ale and a few Portugal onions' to Lincoln's Inn Fields (Soane Corresp. III/i/18, 53, 109). See also *Autobiography*, II, pp. 83–4, 167–8; A. T. Bolton, *Portrait of Sir John Soane* (1927), *passim*; Bodleian MSS. 25424 Montagu d. 24 and Eng. litt. d. 113, ff. 64–5.

1. *Hereford Cathedral*, p. v; *Worcester Cathedral*, p. xiv.

2. *Autobiography*, II, pp. 96–8.   3. ibid., pp. 99, 101–2.

4. For favourable reviews cf. *New Monthly Magazine*, XXI (1827), pp. 46, 373; *Literary Gazette* (1828), pp. 492, 634; *Gentleman's Magazine* (1827), part I, pp. 136–8. Britton's *Rights of Literature* (1814), which attacked the copyright laws of 1710 and 1801, was vindicated in 1837 when the copyright privilege was withdrawn from Syon College London, the King's Inns Dublin, and the four Scottish universities, leaving the British Museum, Oxford, Cambridge, Trinity College Dublin, and the Advocates' Library Edinburgh (Copyright Pamphlets and MSS., B.M. press mark 515 1 20; Bodleian MS. 25557, Top. Gen. e 41; *Autobiography*, II, pp. 190–7).

5. *Autobiography*, II, pp. 69–73.

6. These memoirs, by an English détenu named T. R. Underwood, had previously appeared in the *London Magazine* (1825) and *Révue britannique* (1826). Cf. *Literary Gazette* (1828), p. 280.

7. First published by Sir Richard Phillips in 1802 and caustically reviewed by Britton (*Annual Review*, I, 1802, pp. 479–83), it was chiefly designed for 'the foreigner and strangers' and carried

and *The New Bath Guide* (1830).[1] There was still a market for lavish publications on the lines of his earlier *Fonthill* (1823).[2] But the superlative illustrations in *Cassiobury* (1837), *Toddington* (1841), and *Windsor* (1842) all depended on subscription lists or private subsidies,[3] and similarly the celebration lithographs of the *London and Birmingham Railway* (1838–9).

Towards the end of his career Britton faced criticism as well as bankruptcy. His *Dictionary of the Architecture and Archaeology of the Middle Ages* (1831–8) claimed to be the culmination of twenty-five years' work.[4] And in many ways it improved upon its predecessors, such as those by Robert Stuart, Peter Nicholson, and James Elmes. The comparative plates by Cattermole and Le Keux are particularly valuable. But critics took pleasure in exposing a number of errors and omissions, particularly with regard to foreign terms. One dismissed it as 'a trashy compilation, crammed with anilities, senilities, and puerilities, with the grossest blunders and the most startling absurdities'.[5] Still, it deserved a better fate than being first remaindered by Bohn & Nattali and then pirated by Parker of Oxford. Less excusable was the author's incorrigibly pompous style. 'Really', remarked one reviewer of *Cassiobury*, 'it is full time that a stop should be put to all that sort of inane, schoolboy pomposity, and commonplace hoisted upon stilts.'[6] But Britton was not the sort of man to wilt under criticism. At times he positively courted controversy: he even tried to elucidate the origin of Stonehenge,[7] the identity of Junius,[8] and the authorship of Shakespeare's plays.[9]

warnings against 'hypocrites, sharpers, and rogues of various orders' including 'the frail sisterhood' (pp. viii and xi).

1. Bodleian MS. 25445 Montagu d. 21., ff. 45–6. This edition of Christopher Anstey's comic classic contained etchings by George Cruickshank and woodcuts by Samuel Williams.

2. Seven out of eleven copper plates were destroyed to protect the monopoly of subscribers who included Nash, Rennie, Robert and Sydney Smirke, Thomas Hope, Rickman, Blore, Godwin, Goodridge, George and Joseph Gwilt, Hakewill, G. L. Taylor, and Lewis and Jeffry Wyatt.

3. *Cassiobury*: drawings by Turner and Pugin produced in aquatint by Hill and Lewis. *Toddington*: lithographs by J. C. Bourne; engravings by Kitton and Billings. *Windsor*: drawings by Gandy and Baud; lithographs by Hawkins, Bourne, and Moore; geometrical elevations by Winkles.

4. *Autobiography*, II, pp. 152–5.

5. *Architectural Magazine*, V (1838), pp. 522–3; *Civil Engineer and Architect's Journal*, I (1837–8), pp. 336, 404, and II (1839), pp. 44, 172. For favourable notices cf. *Architectural Magazine*, II (1835), p. 546, and V (1838), pp. 417–18.

6. *Civil Engineer and Architect's Journal*, I (1837–8), p. 125.

7. 'Ancient Barrows' (*Autobiography*, II, Appendix, pp. 49–59); articles in Abraham Rees's *New Cyclopaedia* (1802–19) and Charles Knight's *Penny Cyclopaedia* (1832 etc.). Britton's monument in Norwood Cemetery was designed by George Godwin à la Stonehenge.

8. *Junius Elucidated* (1848) nominated Barré as author, Shelburne and Dunning as advisers, and Greatrakes as amanuensis (*Autobiography*, II, pp. 170–2; Madden Corresp., B.M. Egerton MS. 2844, f. 276, 8 October 1847; Bodleian MS. 25458, Montagu Illus. 200*).

9. *Remarks on . . . Shakespeare* (1814); 'Essays on . . . Shakespeare' (*Autobiography*, II, Appendix, pp. 1–48).

Among Britton's later publications was one which satisfied creditors as well as critics, making a profit of £1,400: *Specimens of Gothic Architecture* (2 vols., 1820–5). The entire credit for this work has generally gone to A. C. Pugin – so much so that the development of Regency Gothic has usually been explained in terms of Britton's *Antiquities* serving an amateur audience and Pugin's *Specimens* educating the professional architect. In fact Britton was well aware of the growing specialist market for diagrammatic illustration, a market largely created by his own earlier works. It was his energy as an editor and his experience as a publisher which guaranteed the *Specimens'* success, just as much as the drawings by A. C. Pugin and the documentation by E. J. Willson. In his own words, he arranged to

write parts of the work, advise as to the drawings and engravings, and conduct the business details of printing, publishing and examining the proof sheets of the literary matter contributed by Mr. Willson...I declined to place my name in the title-page...as my engagements ... in the 'Architectural and Cathedral' volumes required nearly every working moment ... [But] I soon found that nearly the whole business department devolved on me, for [A. C. Pugin]...had not, at that time, any knowledge of its routine and details; and Mr. Willson, like myself, was often incapable of working from severe headaches ... The titles, dedications, prefaces, indexes, and other writings were by myself, and also some of the description and historical matter. The drawings were all made by Mr. Pugin's pupils.[1]

As a sequel to the two volumes of *Specimens*, Britton and Pugin began work on *The Public Buildings of London* (2 vols., 1825) and *The Architectural Antiquities of Normandy* (1825–8). The *Normandy* volume bore a title-page with the names of Britton, Pugin, and Le Keux; otherwise it followed the diagrammatic format successfully established by the *Specimens*.[2] *The Public Buildings of London* was much more of a co-operative venture, and the recorded loss was £460. Its model was Legrand's *Paris et ses édifices* (1806–9). No less than eleven professional architects supplied drawings and information: Nash, Soane, Robert and Sydney Smirke, Joseph Gwilt, John Shaw, Philip Hardwick, John Newman, James Burton, Samuel Ware, and David Laing. Britton supplied most of the text and Pugin supervised the drawings. But several sections were written by E. W. Brayley, J. B. Papworth, C. R. Cockerell, and W. H. Leeds, who also produced a supplementary volume in 1838. Nearly one and a half centuries later, Britton and Pugin are still our most reliable guides to Regency London.[3] But they never co-operated again.

1. *The Builder*, XIII (1855), p. 5; four MS. volumes of preparatory sketches, R.I.B.A. Drawings Collection. Britton's part in editing the *Specimens* went unnoticed at the time, e.g. *Quarterly Review*, XLIX (1821), p. 116; *Edinburgh Review*, XLIX (1829), p. 423.

2. *Gentleman's Magazine* (1828), part II, pp. 519–21. Engravings and letterpress were published separately: by charging for the plates and distributing the text *gratis*, Britton avoided presenting eleven copies to copyright libraries.

3. For detailed reviews cf. *Gentleman's Magazine* (1827), part II, pp. 134–7, 247–51, 529–33, and ibid. (1828), part I, pp. 343–6, 442–4.

In the progress of these publications, the draughtsman [A. C. Pugin] and his friend the engraver, Mr. Le Keux, became involved in the meshes of a law net, which was thrown by the first over, and entangled the author [Britton] in tantalising litigation. A separation took place, and Mr. Pugin commenced his *Examples of Gothic Architecture* [2 vols., 1826] on his own responsibility and under the advice and authorship of Mr. Willson.[1]

During the last twelve years of his life Britton published little except a rambling two-volume autobiography. His first wife died in 1848; and after remarrying he was so short of money that he had to resign his membership of the Society of Antiquaries. Disraeli came to the rescue with a Civil List pension of £75 in 1852.[2] Apart from his literary achievements, he merited this reward on grounds of public service. As adviser to the Royal Literary Fund for forty years he dealt with twelve hundred applications for relief.[3] As a member of the Art Union committee he was regularly involved in the management of funds and distribution of prizes.[4] Waltham Cross, Stratford Church, and St Mary Redcliffe owed their restoration to his efforts.[5] For many years he campaigned for governmental protection of ancient monuments.[6] He shared in the foundation of the London Society of Architects and Antiquaries, the Royal Institution, the Wiltshire Topographical Society, the London Institution, the Royal Geographical Society, and the Russell Institution.[7] The Birmingham Athenaeum, the London Mechanics Institution, and the Literary and Philosophical Institutions at Reading, Bristol, and Bath were only a few of the local societies to which he lectured.[8] He was one of the strongest contributors to the movement which led to the foundation of the R.I.B.A.[9] And the list of subscribers to the Britton

1. *The Builder*, XIII (1855), p. 5. 'I am now endeavouring to separate all accounts and connection with Pugin and Taylor, both of whom have acted meanly and dishonourably towards me. The *Normandy* and *London Buildings* being finished, I shall never again have connection with either' (Soane Corresp. III/i/68, 22 November 1828).

2. *The Builder*, XV (1857), pp. 22–5; *Gentleman's Magazine* (1852), part II, p. 65.

3. *Gentleman's Magazine* (1857), part I, p. 191. See also Britton's *Poetical Address written in behalf of the Artists General Benevolent Fund* (1818).

4. Minutes of Art Union Committee, II–III (1840–3), B.M. Add. MSS. 38866–7 *passim*.

5. See Britton's *Appeal for . . . Redcliffe Church* (1842). The work was executed by Hosking and Godwin (*The Builder*, II, 1844, p. 274; *Civil Engineer and Architect's Journal*, VI, 1843, pp. 11–15).

6. On the lines of Guizot's scheme of 1837. See Britton's 'Letter to Joseph Hume on . . . pre-serving . . . ancient monuments'; his scheme for 'The Guardian of Antiquities'; and his proposal for a National Historical, Archaeological, and Topographical Institution (*Autobiography*, I, p. 15, and II, Appendix, pp. 73–81, 103–4, 140–1).

7. ibid., II, pp. 36–47; *The Times* (25 December 1834), p. 4; *Worcester Cathedral*, p. xxvi. See also Britton's *Address read before the Society of Architects and Antiquaries* (1821) and the society's records, Bodleian Gough Adds. London 8°, 415.

8. Soane Corresp. III/i/93; *Autobiography*, I, pp. 148–9, 153, 207, 221, and II, p. xiv; *Worcester Cathedral*, p. xxiii.

9. Soane Corresp. III/i/27, 8 December 1822. See also Brayley and Britton's *Westminster* (1836), pp. iii–viii, and Britton's *Union of Architecture, Sculpture and Painting*, p. xiv. He considered his

Testimonial in 1845, twelve years before his death, reads like a roll-call of mid-Victorian architects: Barry, Burton, Cockerell, Cubitt, Donaldson, Ferrey, Fowler, Godwin, Gwilt, Hardwick, Hosking, Kendall, Pennethorne, Richardson, Scott, Smirke, Taylor, and Tite.[1]

As a draughtsman Britton was undistinguished. As a designer he was second-rate: his scheme for a Gothic mausoleum in the middle of Trafalgar Square is fussy and overloaded.[2] But as editor, publisher, and publicist his influence on the development of the English Gothic Revival ranks with that of A. W. Pugin and John Ruskin. He seldom ventured abroad, but his influence radiated at least as far as Germany.[3] The latest expositor of Gothicism calls him 'the first exponent of the *topographical* method on a large scale, if not ... its creator'.[4] Nearly a hundred years ago the first historian of the movement remarked that 'he did more to promote the due appreciation of Medieval Art than any contemporary writer'.[5] 'Before a national taste can be made effective,' added Eastlake, 'it must be instructed, and before it is instructed it must be created.' More than any other architectural writer, Britton was responsible for this creation.

honorary membership of the Institute (1835) 'more gratifying to his feelings than any public compliment he ... ever received' (*Worcester Cathedral*, p. xxviii). At his death in 1857, the Council of the R.I.B.A. attended his funeral at Norwood Cemetery and later erected a memorial in Salisbury Cathedral (*Building News*, III, 1857, pp. 63, 110, 137, 300, 1172; *Gentleman's Magazine*, 1857, part I, pp. 126, 203, 258; *Civil Engineer and Architect's Journal*, XX, 1857, p. 57).

1. At the presentation dinner the speakers (including Britton) went on so long 'that to take notes was out of the question' (*The Builder*, III, 1845, p. 325; *Autobiography*, I, pp. 503 f., and II, Appendix, pp. 193–7).

2. His design for a cenotaph to Thomas Chatterton was equally unsuccessful (*Autobiography*, II, pp. 60–72; *Civil Engineer and Architect's Journal*, III, 1840, p. 105).

3. W. D. Robson-Scott, *Literary Background to the German Gothic Revival* (1965), p. 265.

4. P. Frankl, *The Gothic* (1960), p. 496.

5. C. L. Eastlake, *History of the Gothic Revival* (1872), pp. 80–8.

The Sources of Pugin's *Contrasts*

BY PHOEBE STANTON

THOUGH A. W. Pugin prepared the plates and wrote the text of *Contrasts; or, A Parallel Between the Noble Edifices of the Fourteenth And Fifteenth Centuries, And Similar Buildings Of The Present Day; Shewing The Present Decay of Taste* in 1836, the genesis of the idea of *Contrasts* appears in a signed and dated drawing of 1832 which shows three house façades, one dated 1470, another 1532, and the third 1832.[1] Pugin drew the nineteenth-century example to seem paltry compared with its neighbours. By August 1835 he had begun the book, and he had decided to entitle it *Contrasts*,[2] but in the autumn he laid the project aside temporarily to work for Charles Barry and Gillespie Graham. When this employment ended Pugin left London on 5 December and went to Salisbury. *Contrasts* still had to wait; the future of *Examples of Gothic Architecture* was a time-consuming problem, for E. J. Willson had failed to deliver the text, the subscribers were annoyed by the delay in publication, and Ackermann was asking for the third volume of the illustrations of medieval ornament, which were receiving favourable notice.

Established at St Marie's Grange, Pugin set to work in January 1836, and, in a few days of intense concentration, prepared the drawings for *Designs for Gold and Silversmiths*. *Contrasts* was on his mind, however, for with the drawings he sent Ackermann an unsolicited and 'curious letter-press relative to the magnificent church plate formerly belonging to the ecclesiastical establishments in this country'.[3] The manuscript of this contribution does not survive, but its content must have been close to the text which ultimately appeared as *Contrasts*. Pugin's temper was short. A visit to Highcliffe Castle to give an opinion on the new buildings erecting there had confirmed his view of architectural practice in the nineteenth century. He found

1. From a sketchbook. Reproduced in the *Journal of the Royal Institute of British Architects* (December 1952), p. 48.
2. Letter, Pugin to E. J. Willson, written from Salisbury, 16 August 1835.
3. Letter, Pugin to E. J. Willson, written from Salisbury, 4 January 1836.

120

that 'through bad management and want of knowledge' the project had gone awry, for Lord Stuart de Rothesay had purchased

the remains of the great house at Andelys and part of the Abbey of Jumièges and these fine remains were brought over to be reconstructed in his new house, but the architect Mr. Donthorne could not have had the slightest idea of Gothic architecture as he has turned Norman capitals upside down to serve for bases to the latest style of Louis 12 and Francis 1 and made sad havoc with everything.[1]

Pugin prepared the drawings for *Contrasts* between 23 February and 5 March and sent them immediately to Talbot Bury to be etched. By 2 May the revisions of the plates were completed and Pugin began the text portion, which he finished on 30 May.[2] Thomas L. Walker refused to associate himself with the book and Pugin disposed of his complaint that *Contrasts* was too harsh by saying that Walker's rejection did not 'arise from conviction but from his applying some of the contents to himself. I did not mean any part to apply to him in the least, but those whom the cap fits let them wear it'.[3] Pugin was convinced that the letterpress was 'very severe but not a bit too much so', and he announced that he was happy in the position he had taken, for he said,

I know my assertions are true, it is time these Church of England men were held up in their true Light and I trust I have done it effectively. I have likewise exposed the degraded state of architecture in the title. . . .Architecture and decoration is a *trade* at present and no great results can be produced while such a system lasts.[4]

Contrasts appeared in August 1836; it was published by its author from St Marie's Grange.

Though he was prepared for the adversaries he half-hoped would respond to *Contrasts*, Pugin was, nonetheless, somewhat daunted by the violence of the attack when it came. Less than a month after the book was issued he was aware that it had generated 'a vast deal of rage' and he described himself as 'a marked man here at Salisbury'. By mid October he felt besieged in his new house, for charges of 'infant Papist, juvenile apostate, young Jesuit and inquisitor' rained around him.[5] *Contrasts* was a success, the people it challenged had responded, but it was also a product of the literary, philosophical, and artistic environment in which Pugin lived. Few of its observations and propositions were new. The power which *Contrasts* possessed to provoke, wound, and attract an opposition resided in its lack of complication, the clarity and message of the plates, the declarative letterpress, and the date of its publication.

1. ibid.   2. Dates from the diary of A. W. Pugin.
3. Letter, Pugin to E. J. Willson, written from Salisbury, 5 September 1836.
4. Letter, Pugin to E. J. Willson, written from Salisbury, 2 August 1836.
5. Letter, Pugin to E. J. Willson, written from Salisbury, 18 October 1836.

Pugin did not invent the idea that architecture had become a 'trade'. E. J. Willson had said much the same thing in 'Remarks on Gothic Architecture and Modern Imitations' which constituted the preface to volume II of *Specimens of Gothic Architecture*, published in 1823. With the agreement of his collaborator, A. C. Pugin, Willson had decried frivolous flirtation with various styles, and pointed out that 'commerce had replaced the humble but significant art of the mason and carpenter' and that

an ingenious lad, the son of a substantial yeoman when put apprentice to a master-builder, sinks, for a time at least, beneath the rank of his family; he is hardly company for his brother, who stands six days in the week, in full dress, behind a linen-draper's counter; and yet he has chosen a profession which requires a hundred times more intellect.

Though the younger Pugin altered Willson's observations by introducing a religious bias and historical explanations and by stressing the need for professional dedication on the part of architects, the crux of one argument in *Contrasts* had long been Pugin family property.

In the *Foreign Quarterly Review* an author had, in 1831, in a review of Seroux d'Agincourt's *Histoire de l'art par les monumens* and *Histoire de la vie et des ouvrages des plus célèbres architectes du XI siècle jusqu'à la fin du XVIIIe* by Quatremère de Quincy used the occasion to denounce the state of architecture and the calibre of architects in England. There were marked similarities between this article and *Contrasts*.

The reviewer declared that it seemed, superficially, that architecture in England was receiving all the encouragement it required, and so it was if 'mere building' was the index and encouragement was defined as 'nothing more than pounds, shillings and pence'.

Were architecture no more than shoe-making or coat-making, this would be all very well; the patronage it receives sufficiently ample. The *Trade* flourishes, but the *art*, how are we to finish the sentence? By encouragement we understand something more than employment, conceiving it to mean an intelligent appreciation, and liberal patronage of the powers of architecture as a fine art.

The architect in England was enduring an experience comparable to what 'a singer would feel in exerting his powers before a room of deaf spectators'. Copying fine examples of earlier architecture was no remedy for the crisis in taste; it was time to understand the spirit of the finest work and to copy this rather than the tangible forms building had once assumed. He found the English school, as represented by Soane, inferior to the Continental standard established by Ledoux, von Klenze, and Schinkel.

When *Contrasts* came to the attention of the *Foreign Quarterly Review* in 1837 it delivered Pugin a glancing blow, for it referred to him as that 'preter-pluperfect

Goth' and said nothing about his book. The reviewer was a doubting reader who had decided Pugin was a quixotic person, incapable of doing harm. *Contrasts* was too amusing to be made fun of and too accurate in its view of English architecture to be attacked.

Any number of old and new sources could have suggested the system of comparisons used in the plates of *Contrasts* and the image of the balance with which it concluded. By 1836 Pugin had read widely and begun to assemble his library of fifteenth-, sixteenth-, and seventeenth-century books. In 1834 he bought a 1493 edition of the *Nuremberg Chronicle* and a beautiful sixteenth-century edition of the *Golden Legend* which contained more than three hundred woodcuts. He was particularly pleased with the illustrations in both. He could have encountered symbolic use of the balance in the *Nuremberg Chronicle*, for St Michael is shown weighing souls, or in caricatures and book illustrations he saw as he explored the history of the Reformation in preparation for *Contrasts*.[1] At the beginning of the second volume of John Daye's 1576 edition of Foxe's *Book of Martyrs* Justice appears weighing 'Gods most blessed word, against the doctrines and vanities of mans traditions'. Pugin owned Timothy Bright's *An Abridgement of the Booke and the Actes and Monumentes of the Church* (1589) which did not carry the fifty fine woodcuts of the Daye edition, but it seems likely that, in view of his developing interest in sixteenth-century illustrations and prints, he had examined the unabridged version published by Daye.

The caricatures of Cruikshank certainly inspired the style of Pugin's satiric plates on nineteenth-century building and the design of 'Selections from the Works of Various Celebrated British Architects'. *Life in London, or the Day and Night Scenes of Jerry Hawthorn and His Elegant Friend, Corinthian Tom* had a frontispiece in which the foibles of man and society were displayed in an architectural frame (Plate 14). Cruikshank's notion of the ups and downs, the top and the bottom of London life, the ins and the outs, related closely to the system of comparisons Pugin chose. The use of the column and the name 'Corinthian Tom' was humour with an architectural flavour. Throughout his life, when he was provoked beyond words by the inadequacies of others, Pugin illuminated his letters with minute drawings in the manner of Cruikshank, so he could hardly have overlooked the illustrations in the *Comic Almanack* in which the architecture of London as much as its people conveyed a sense of tawdry elegance and human frailty (Plate 15). From Cruikshank Pugin surely learned how to use the notices posted on buildings as an opportunity for bitter puns, and he must have perceived Cruikshank's regret for the loss of the medieval world. In 'London going out of Town, or The March of Bricks

1. M. D. George, *English Political Caricature to 1792* (Oxford, 1959), p. 5. Miss George notes that 'In the long succession of English political prints, countries or persons, documents or symbols are weighed in the balance...' She describes the balance as 'an outstanding example of the medieval image transformed by the Reformation and passing into the language of political allegory'.

14. *Life in London*, by Pierce Egan with illustrations by I. R. and G. Cruikshank,
appeared in an edition of 1821

15. Illustration for August 1835, *The Comic Almanack*, by George Cruikshank

16. London going out of Town, or The March of Bricks and Mortar, by George Cruikshank, 1829

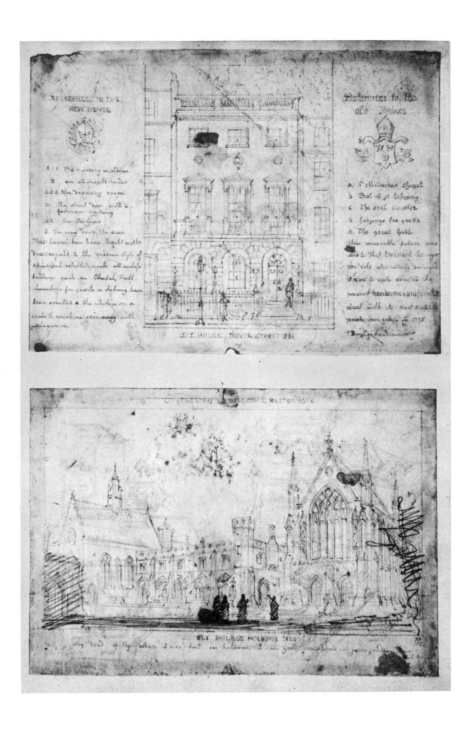

17. Drawing in pencil by A. W. Pugin for 'Contrasted Episcopal Residences', done between 23 February and 5 March 1836, at St Marie's Grange, Salisbury, for *Contrasts*, 1836 edition

ELY HOVSE DOVER STREET.1836

CONTRASTED EPISCOPAL RESIDENCES

ELY PALACE HOLBORN 1536

18. Proof of the etching 'Contrasted Episcopal Residences' for which Plate 17 was the drawing

and Mortar', and in others of Cruikshank's drawings, medieval churches could be seen surviving precariously, engulfed by smoke and threatened by the endless rows of new houses which were invariably presented as unprepossessing, cheap pastiche (Plate 16).

By 1836 Pugin had become something of a scholar; the ways in which he used his reading and the interpretations he placed upon his sources were singularly specialized. He studied topographical history, literature, and primary source materials on the Middle Ages, to find descriptions of the past with which he could, in his imagination, recreate life as it had been before modern anonymity, irresponsibility, and ugliness had destroyed the humane relationships he was convinced existed before the Reformation.

The original drawings and trial impressions of the etchings for *Contrasts* indicate that Pugin spent more time on 'Ely Palace, Holborn, 1536' than on the others. There were eighteenth-century prints which showed the building as it had been immediately before it was pulled down in 1775. Pugin had found these, and he worked generally from them when he prepared his drawing. But the beautiful group of buildings he illustrated as Ely Palace bore little resemblance to the fragmentary remains that had survived into the eighteenth century. He restored the building in his illustration of it, straightened walls, replaced roofs and crosses, repaired the broken niches and put sculpture into them. The drawing was free in style and content. He put trees in the right foreground, and in the distance neighbouring Gothic buildings rose. The sky was filled with clouds. Across the lower portion Pugin wrote, 'My Lord of Ely, when I was last in Holborn, I saw good strawberries in your garden there', for, interpreting the lines from *Richard III* literally, Pugin pointed out, by quoting them, that there had once been a time when the Bishop of Ely owned a garden in London, instead of a town-house in a narrow street (Plate 17). The first etched impression retained the clouds and the trees (Plate 18). The second and final version omitted these refinements and brought the plate into conformity with the others in the sequence.

It was possible for Pugin to read Stow's *Survey of London* and Dugdale as forthrightly as he had *Richard III*. Stow could be understood as the record of a world changing from good to bad, as a sad comparison between an age of generosity, piety, and kindliness and one bent upon destruction, sacrilege, and cruelty. The *Survey* provided information on the history of Ely Palace and the Bishops, recounting how Thomas Arundell had rebuilt the palace, 'augmenting it with a large port, gatehouse, or front towards the street or highway', and giving in astonishing detail the menus and guest lists of the 'great and solemn feasts' held there. Much of *Contrasts* was a lamentation over the loss of patronage for the arts, and in Stow's lists of private gifts Pugin found ample grounds for grief. The plate contrasting public conduits was certainly suggested by Stow's statement that in the east end of this street standeth the great conduit of sweet water, conveying by pipes of lead under ground from Paddington for the service of the city, castellated with stone, and cisterned with lead, about the year 1285, and again new built and enlarged by Thomas Ilam, one of the sheriffs 1479.

Beneath the etching of the conduit Pugin placed the name of its donor and the date Stow assigned to the gift.

Pugin owned fine seventeenth-century editions of Dugdale's *Baronage of England* and *History of St Paul's*, and his *Monasticon Anglicanum* was a first edition. Their Hollar illustrations were intact, and by 1836 Pugin had begun to acquire his collection of Hollar London views. The appendix of *Contrasts* shows that Pugin used the text of Dugdale as he did Stow's, but it was the Hollars that, in the end, made Pugin's imaginary journey a reality. Though they were a picture of seventeenth-century London, they gave an impression of the city as it had been before its medieval character had quite disappeared. Hollar's delineations of Gothic architecture, his views on the Thames and of Islington, became the models after which Pugin fashioned his drawing style.

Pugin had begun to read the careful histories of the abbeys issued by the Benedictine Congregation of St Maur. Dom Jean-François Pommeraye's *Histoire de l'église cathédrale de Rouen*, a masterpiece among the Maurist studies, was Pugin's particular favourite in 1836. Pommeraye was essentially a historian, but he appreciated the beauties of the churches of Rouen. The 1662 edition which Pugin owned was equipped with folding plates by Jean Toutin, which, though by no means as fine as the Hollars, enriched the book. The buildings were shown in the bird's-eye views customary in Baroque illustrations which conveyed a reasonably accurate impression of the relationship between the churches and their satellite buildings. Pommeraye was a necessity in the war Pugin had declared on the subject of the Reformation. When, in September 1836, E. J. Willson asked if he might borrow the book, Pugin refused, saying he had 'too much need of Dom Pommeraye to be able to part with it even for a short season'.

Many of the authorities cited in *Contrasts* belong to the period in historical writing which James Westfall Thompson has defined as 'The Age of Erudition'.[1] They were, and still are, standard sources for the serious student of the Middle Ages. In his study of the English scholars of the seventeenth century, David Douglas says: 'in modern times the greatest English medievalists have been precisely those who have held seventeenth century scholarship in the highest esteem'.[2] At the age of twenty-four Pugin was already fortifying his architectural brilliance and reputation as a Gothic enthusiast with an admirable command of the history of the period he had chosen.

1. J. W. Thompson, *A History of Historical Writing*, 2 vols. (New York, 1942), II, chapter xxxvi.
2. D. C. Douglas, *English Scholars* (London, 1939), p. 367.

The letterpress of *Contrasts* was not as well conceived as the plates. There was justice in the remark of one critic who said when he reviewed it: 'Mr. Pugin ought never to write, when he can draw so much better ... Nature made him a first rate architect, but amerced him of logic.' Pugin certainly made mistakes in judgement and in fact which invited criticism and maddened his opponents. His choice of the fifteenth century was a result of youth and the fact that he had, in 1836, only begun to acquire his knowledge of history and the history of art. A not entirely unfriendly critic was able to question the whole premise of the book because of this admiration for the fifteenth century.

Johnson called Goldsmith 'inspired idiot'; but our author goes a step further than that fascinating poet in his absurdities. Goldsmith only ventured to say

> A time there was ere England's griefs began
> When every rod of ground maintained its man.

Much fruitless labour having been spent to ascertain the chronology of this golden era, Mr. Pugin has set the question forever at rest by assigning it to the fifteenth century i.e. the desolating Wars of the Roses.[1]

The way in which Pugin attributed to the Reformation every fault he perceived in his own time was a gross over-simplification, but he shared it with many a more mature and intellectually astute contemporary. The Reformation was not in fashion in the 1820s and 1830s; its popularity had declined as interest in the Middle Ages rose.

Despite its inherent weaknesses, *Contrasts* deserves to be understood as part of a pattern of English thought, already well established by 1836. The major contributors to these ideas were more famous than Pugin. Their skill as writers in a polemic style exceeded his. Their knowledge of history and its implications was more accomplished than his. It is to Pugin's credit that he was able to find a place for himself in such gifted company and that his first book established itself as part of the literature on 'The Age'.

The early nineteenth century was an uneasy time. French experience in the Revolutionary and Napoleonic periods seemed to mean that eighteenth-century philosophical formulations were potentially destructive of discipline and dissolving of tradition. Authoritarian arguments abounded, and the extreme Catholic conservatism of de Maistre existed beside the diametrically opposed but equally rigid and sweeping recommendations of Saint-Simon. As the quantity of historical writing increased and its quality improved, knowledge of history became the property of any thoughtful man. Inevitably those who thought seriously about the state of contemporary life and approached its problems conscientiously sought insight by comparing the present with the past. Virtually every author who commented upon and lamented the characteristics of 'The Age' used history as a tool of social criticism.

1. This quotation and that preceding it are from a long review of *Contrasts* by T. Mozley, which appeared in the *British Critic and Quarterly Theological Review* in April 1839.

Comparisons did not encourage optimism. The panoramic view provided by the historian gave an appearance of orderliness to earlier ages. With such models at hand, the nineteenth century seemed to its occupants singularly disordered and lacking in greatness and scale. Preoccupation with the past became a symptom of and a cause for discontent. Feelings of responsibility for 'The Age' and hopes for and concern over its destiny were commonplace; 'The Age' should be 'great' everyone agreed, but 'greatness' was an elusive quality. Generally most people who used the term or one similar to it meant that they hoped their time would attain coherence and assume a distinctive character and that it would find a solution for the social distress that any reasonably unselfish person could see around him if he but looked.

When Pugin declared at the end of *Contrasts* that he had intended 'to pluck from the Age the mask of superior attainments so falsely assumed' and 'direct the attention of all back to the real merit of past and better days', he placed his remarkable book in its proper context. Pugin apparently thought of his achievement as an isolated phenomenon, and he encouraged others to do so. In one sense he was correct and in another he was not. He had brought into architectural commentary arguments and a method of reasoning which had been present in other writing for more than a decade and a half.

The Saint-Simonians had taken a position on the character of 'The Age' and the meaning of the Middle Ages, and their observations and recommendations were part of the 'climate of opinion' in which Pugin grew. They perceived a pattern in European history; periods of 'organic' wholeness alternated with times of transition and 'critical' change. They described the centuries that had elapsed since the Reformation as 'critical', and they pronounced the medieval period as one which had been 'organic'. Though they admired the social and philosophical structure of the Middle Ages, they accepted the 'critical' chaos which followed it and they were not impressed by the advocates of a return to medieval life as a solution to the malformations of 'The Age'. The arts were, they said, but one expression of any civilization. It would benefit no one to revive or even to preserve the art of a past age; they stated emphatically that 'the artists who mourn the demolition of the old cathedrals and castles ... must not have understood that these buildings must disappear with the ideas of which they were symbols'. Revival was servile and survival useless, but art and the artist were instrumental and necessary to constructive social change. Art, they said, was a means by which 'man could be induced to social arts and brought to see his private interest in the general interest'.

In a book entitled *Le Nouveau Christianisme*, published in 1825, Saint-Simon himself had examined the Protestant Reformation and found it wanting. Luther, he said, had failed notably in his reorganization of Christianity once his revolution had taken effect. Secularization of religious experience had eliminated art and made the Church prosaic.

131

It is interesting that there was such significant pressure to revive medieval life that in 1831 the Saint-Simonians delivered a verdict concerning it. Their decision that the Reformation was 'critical' must have fostered further rejection of it. Pugin's conception of his task as an artist-reformer, his rather top-heavy theory that architecture revealed the inner spirit of a society, and his appraisal of the Reformation, resembled ideas that were floating freely in England. He certainly was no Saint-Simonian and he would have found their position on the possibility of a revival distasteful, but it should be noted that in the first edition of *Contrasts* Pugin did not really recommend revivalism. He aimed, rather, to show the harm the Reformation had done and to condemn the stupidities perpetrated in the name of Gothic.

The decade before the publication of *Contrasts* had produced many English criticisms of 'The Age'.[1] John Stuart Mill's *The Spirit of the Age*, published in 1831, Thomas Carlyle's two essays of social commentary, *Signs of the Times* (1829) and *Characteristics* (1831), and *Sartor Resartus* of 1834, and finally Robert Southey's *Sir Thomas More: or, Colloquies on the Progress and Prospects of Society*, published between 1829 and 1831, are some of the distinguished contributions to this literature.

Mill's essays for the *Examiner*, which, as a group, were entitled *The Spirit of the Age*, give some idea of the nostalgic feeling for the Middle Ages and despair about 'The Age' current at the time Pugin first thought of *Contrasts*. Mill wished to 'point out in the character of the present age, the anomalies and evils characteristic of the transition from a system of opinions which had worn out, to another only in process of being formed'. He was, of course, indebted to Saint-Simonianism. Mill defined a particular contemporary problem, saying: 'the idea of comparing one's own age with former ages, or with our notion of those which are yet to come, had occurred to philosophers; but it never before was itself the dominant idea of any age', and he announced that he had little patience for

those men who carry their eyes in the back of their heads and can see no other portion of the destined track of humanity but that which it has already travelled, imagine that because the old ties are severed mankind henceforth are not to be connected by any ties at all; and hence their affliction, and their awful warnings.

Mill approached the future with optimism, and though the state of things left much to be desired, he refused to join the despairing chorus to which Southey belonged. He described *Colloquies* as 'a very curious and not uninstructive exhibition of one of the points of view from which the spirit of the age may be contemplated'.

Carlyle was gloomy, for he found that 'Mechanism has now struck its roots down into man's most intimate, primary sources of conviction; and is thence sending up, over his whole life and activity, innumerable stems – fruit-bearing and

1. The authoritative discussion of nineteenth-century attitudes to 'The Age' is W. E. Houghton, *The Victorian Frame of Mind, 1830–1870* (New Haven, 1957).

132

poison-bearing'. The arts were casualties in a common disaster, for 'in defect of Raphaels, and Angelos, and Mozarts, we have Royal Academies of Painting, Sculpture, Music; whereby the languishing spirit of Art may be strengthened, as by the more generous diet of Public Kitchen'. Even the philosophers and historians had 'no love and no hatred', but instead 'stand among us not to do, nor to create anything, but as a sort of Logic-mills to grind out the true causes and effects of all that is done and created'. He summarized his view in a brilliant image: 'by arguing on the "force of circumstance" we have argued away all force from ourselves; and stand leashed together, uniform in dress and movement, like the rowers in some boundless galley'. He did not share Mill's conviction that 'whatever we may think of the present age we cannot get out of it', nor was Carlyle inclined to play a passive role as history made its inevitable rounds.

Pugin must have read Carlyle, and agreed with him; in the 'Conclusion' of *Contrasts*, he declared there 'never was a period when there were so many lectures, academies, drawing schools' and he described the uninspired education of the men who entered the architectural profession by the academic route.

Robert Southey had said as early as 1819 that he had 'a great deal to say upon the dangers and prospects of society', for he had 'thought a good deal upon the parallel of circumstance of this age and of Henry VIII and probably my frame of mind and way of thinking very much resemble what Sir Thomas More's were in his day'. Southey believed 'it well worth any student of history's while to consider well the Life of Sir Thomas More and to dwell soberly on his *Utopia*'. This preoccupation with More was part of a rebirth of interest in More and the Reformation, and it was possible to read *Utopia* as a description and defence of the Middle Ages.[1]

In *Colloquies*, Southey explored his belief that the great 'operating causes in the age of the Reformation and in this age of revolutions are similar'. Using a plan suggested by Boethius, he wrote his book as a series of dialogues between himself and More. Southey consciously attempted to 'draw the parallel between that age and this', for he hoped 'a great many home truths may be brought into view'. At the outset More defined the nineteenth century as 'portentous and monster breeding, one of the grand climacterics of the world'. He found the people of England in a condition little better than they had been when Caesar arrived. Cities bred disease of body and spirit, and the working classes were

less religious than in the days of the Romish faith; and if we consider them in relation to their immediate superiors we shall find reason to confess that the independence which has

1. R. W. Chambers, in *Thomas More* (London, 1935), points out that 'More was the last man who lived the whole of his life with the England of the Middle Ages yet undestroyed around him; a land of great libraries which had been accumulated since Anglo-Saxon times, of ancient religious houses where the walls were covered with painting and the windows shone with glorious glass of the fourteenth and fifteenth centuries; a land of schools and hospitals more plentiful than they were to be again for many a day'.

been gained since the total decay of the feudal system, has been purchased by the loss of kindly feelings and ennobling attachments.

Southey was convinced that the feudal system had lost its inhumanity just as it was swept away by the Reformation and that the fifteenth century was 'a most important age in English history, and till the Reformation so fearfully disturbed it, in many respects a happy and enviable one'. He joined others of his generation in praising the part monastic institutions played in the medieval polity:

The great abbeys vied with each other in architectural magnificence and in this more especially, but likewise in every branch of liberal expenditure, giving employment to great numbers, which was better than giving unearned food. They provided as it became them, for the old and helpless also. That they prevented the necessity of raising rates for the poor by the copious alms which they distributed and by indiscriminately feeding the indigent, as has been inferred, because those rates became necessary immediately after the suppression of the religious houses.

On the subject of the Reformation Southey was intemperate. He said it had 'lowered the standard of devotion, lessened the influence of religion, not among the poor and ignorant alone, but among all classes, and prepared the way for uncontrolled dominion of that worldly spirit which it is the tendency of the commercial system to produce and foster'. Through the words he and More speak he warned that 'they who care nothing for their ancestors will care little for their posterity . . . indeed little for anything except themselves'.

In *Colloquies*, Southey dealt only occasionally with the arts, but when he did so his views were close to those of Pugin. Southey feared that democratization would have a levelling effect upon the human mind and stunt all creativity, until, in the end, it would be 'fatal to excellence and favorable to mediocrity', a comment for which Pugin's plate dedicated to 'The Trade' might well have been an illustration.

Two other authors had contrasted past and present and discussed 'The Age' in terms similar to Pugin's appraisal of it: the works of William Cobbett and Kenelm Digby played their part in the creation of *Contrasts*.

Two books of Cobbett's many are relevant here, his *History of the Protestant Reformation*, first issued between 1824 and 1827 in a series of letters and a list of abbeys and priories dissolved or granted in the Reformation, and *Rural Rides*, which also appeared first in parts and was published in book form in 1830. G. D. H. Cole has described the *History of the Protestant Reformation* as a 'brilliant philippic'. Inspired by living issues, harsh agrarian problems of poverty and displacement of the countryman, irresponsible political leadership and Catholic Emancipation, Cobbett mounted a massive attack on the Reformation. It had, he said, 'impoverished and degraded the main body of the people'; the truth about it should be brought to light 'in bare justice to our well fed and well clad Catholic forefathers' and 'for

134

mercy to ourselves, their unfortunate, half-famished, ragged, pauperized descendents'. The *Protestant Reformation* was read widely in English Catholic circles, and comparisons between it and the text portion of *Contrasts* show that Pugin was one of its admirers. The sources cited by Cobbett and Pugin are identical, though any writer who set out to discredit the Reformation would have drawn on Heylyn, Strype, and Stow. More revealing are the cases in which the actual wording and sequences of ideas in *Contrasts* are closer to Cobbett than to the books used by both authors. When he described the violations of the churches under Edward VI Cobbett had paraphrased Heylyn:

Every church altar had, as I have before observed, more or less of gold and silver. A part consisted of images, a part of censers, candlesticks and other things used in the celebration of the *mass*. The mass was, therefore, abolished and there was no longer to be an *altar*, but a *table* in its stead. The fanatical part of the reformers amused themselves with quarrelling about the part of the church where the table should stand; about the shape of it, and whether the head was to be placed to the North, the East, the West, or the South; and whether the people were to stand, kneel or sit at it! The plunderers, however, thought about other things: they thought about the value of the images, censers and the like.

In his chapter on the Church under Edward VI Pugin made the following observation:

But an altar, which with its daily lighting and decoration entailed a considerable expense, and as its rich appendages formed no inconsiderable plunder, it is condemned to be pulled down, and a common square table set in its place, as being, forsooth, agreeable to apostolic use.

These two statements, when they are compared with Heylyn, show that Pugin was closer to Cobbett than to his original source material. The word 'plunder' does not appear in Heylyn who had, however, quoted Hooper's sermon demanding that the magistrates 'turn the altars into tables'. Cobbett omitted the reference to Hooper and italicized *table*, while it is Pugin who introduced the notion of 'a common square table'. Neither Cobbett nor Pugin saw fit to mention a point made by Heylyn, that, several years after the spoliation of the churches, an inquiry into the whereabouts of Church treasures was ordered by the Crown to discover 'what jewels of gold and silver, or silver crosses, candlesticks, censers, chalices, copes, and other vestments, were then remaining in any of the cathedrals or parochial churches; or otherwise had been embezzled or taken away'.

Rural Rides revealed Cobbett's feeling for the land, for the relationships between the men, the landscape, and the buildings of England, and the nostalgia which swept over him when he recovered, for a moment, a trace of what England had once been. His account of the gardens at Albury is justly famous and typical of his descriptive power at its best; it is a strange coincidence that Pugin was ultimately to work at Albury. Cobbett visited Reigate in October 1825, just as he was working on the *Protestant Reformation*, and wrote a comment which could well have been the inspiration for the plate illustrating medieval and modern residences for the poor which Pugin prepared for the 1841 edition of *Contrasts*.

This town of Reigate had, in former times, a Priory, which had considerable estates in the neighbourhood; ... We all know how long it has been the fashion for us to take it for *granted*, that the monasteries were *bad things*; but, of late, I have made some hundreds of thousands of good Protestants begin to suspect, that monasteries were better than *poor-rates*, and that monks and nuns, who *fed the poor*, were better than sinecure and pension men and women, who *feed upon the poor*.

The second important additional plate in *Contrasts*, 1841, was that comparing the Catholic town of 1440 and the same town in 1840. Again, in *Rural Rides*, Cobbett supplied Pugin's inspiration, for in 1830 he visited Leicester and found it pleasing in some ways and discouraging in others.

Leicester is a very fine town; spacious streets, fine inns, fine shops, and containing, they say, thirty or forty thousand people. It is well stocked with jails, of which a new one, in addition to the rest, has just been built, covering three acres of ground! And, as if *proud* of it, the grand portal has little turrets, in the castle style, with *embrasures* in miniature on the caps of the turrets. Nothing speaks the want of reflection in the people so much, as the self-gratulation which they appear to feel in these edifices in their several towns. Instead of expressing shame at these indubitable proofs of the horrible increase of misery and crime, they really boast of these 'improvements', as they call them. Our forefathers built abbeys and priories and churches, and they made such use of them that jails were unnecessary. We, their sons, have knocked down the abbeys and priories, suffered half the parsonage-houses and churches to pretty near tumble down, and make such uses of the remainder, that jails and tread-mills and dungeons, have now become the most striking edifices in every county in the kingdom.

Cobbett died in June 1835, the summer Pugin began to work on *Contrasts*. Cobbett's style, his vocabulary, his sentence structure in which fact was piled upon fact, his method of organizing paragraphs, evolving them from a challenging opening proposition, became part of Pugin's style. The plates were, however, very much Pugin's own, for using architecture as his evidence he set out to right the wrongs Cobbett had described. Architecture was, after all, what Pugin knew and drew best.

Kenelm Digby was a gentleman of independent means who spent his long life (he was born in 1796 and died in 1880) upon research and literary pursuits. He gradually explored the literature and history of the Middle Ages until, by 1830, he had become an efficient and productive scholar. Two of Digby's books may be related directly to Pugin's development. The first, *The Broad Stone of Honour: or, Rules for the Gentlemen of England*, appeared in three editions between 1822 and 1829. Curiously, Digby did not really rewrite each: he merely added new information to the text of the earlier version. The third edition was much more complex than the earlier two, for it was published in four volumes between 1826 and 1829; volume 3 appeared first, volume 2 was issued next, and 1 and 4 came out together in 1829. The third was dedicated to Sir Thomas More. The other major work by Digby, and one which Pugin surely knew, was *Mores catholici: or, Ages of Faith*, a massive eleven-volume assemblage of documents and records from and on life in the Middle Ages. Each volume was organized around one of the Beatitudes. The third, which appeared in 1833, contained a long chapter on medieval architecture.

Digby became a Roman Catholic in 1825, after he had published the first two editions of *Broad Stone* and while he was still associated informally with Cambridge, where he had obtained his degree at Trinity College in 1819. In 1828 he went to France, where he studied intensively. These were fruitful years both in education and friendships, for, though he returned for a time to England in 1830, he lived for the most part abroad for the rest of his life, returning to England periodically.

The Broad Stone of Honour described and recommended the medieval way of life, contrasting it, by implication and directly, with that of the nineteenth century. Digby was no polemicist; he was too good-natured and mannerly for that. His intellectual bearing was elevated but not disdainful. He found 'the ancient orders of Christendom are superseded by clubs and associations' and 'avarice and ambition' prevalent. He said 'we live in an age of system and of civilization pushed to an extreme. Too much is expected from the operation of the law and too little from the virtue of individuals'. His response to art and architecture in the earlier editions of his book was not analytical, but he recommended that Englishmen stop visiting 'Classic lands' and turn instead to Germany, France, and England where they could see the works of 'their rude but generous ancestors'.

In the first edition the authorities cited by Digby were largely those any educated gentleman might have employed; they were, in the main, Roman authors. A few revealing references showed, however, that Digby was in contact with thinking of another kind, for he referred to Madame de Staël's *Germany* and disclosed the fact that he had begun to read the Schlegels. He was also using Joinville, Froissart, Brantôme, and Saint-Palaye. There were several references to Byron.

By 1823 *Broad Stone* was quite a different book, for Digby had encountered Julius Hare and the *Lay Sermons* by Coleridge. Suddenly Digby found his views corroborated. Wider reading had introduced him to Jeremy Taylor, Isaac Barrow, and Bishop Bull. His explorations of French writing had led him to Mezeray, Sismondi, and de Maistre. His attitudes on art were still tangential rather than essential to his argument. He admired Salisbury Cathedral, but he agreed with Madame de Staël that 'the view of St Peter's is like continual music'.

The third edition was a sternly Catholic work, ardently and declaratively opposed to the Reformation. Nor was it easy to read, for Digby had embedded the two earlier editions in a mass of new documentation. *Broad Stone* had become an encyclo-pedic compendium of fact and fable, arranged, as he later organized *Mores catholici*, under general headings. His sources had expanded enormously. German historians – Voigt, von Raumer, Büsching – appear in force, and Digby had also read Count Stolberg and Schleiermacher. He knew the works of the Schlegels and quoted them extensively, without the intervention of Madame de Staël, whose place in this edition is not prominent. Digby had also begun to collect the raw materials of medieval history. Alcuin is quoted, and Digby had encountered Suger through his reading in André Duchesne. He had used Baluze on St Gall. Finally, Digby's acquaintance with French writers had led him to the Maurist histories and to Chateaubriand. His English references are particularly interesting. Coleridge appears, for Digby had found that his statement 'I have not a deeper conviction on earth than that the principles, both of taste, morals and religion which are taught in the commonest books of recent composition are false, injurious and debasing' agreed precisely with his own view of things. Bishop Hurd is mentioned only to be condemned, but Southey's *Letters from England: by Dom Manuel Espriella* are praised. The edition cites more than four hundred authors.

The chapter on medieval architecture in *Mores catholici* appeared after Pugin had decided to write *Contrasts* and before he began serious work on the book in 1835. It is a glowing report of the hundreds of buildings Digby had visited, a kind of personal catalogue rather than a history. As usual, many scholarly authorities appear, and there are ample quotations from medieval sources. A note of asperity crept into Digby's discussion when, after quoting Chateaubriand's assertion that France had once had 1,872,926 monuments from the Middle Ages, Digby turned to look at the architecture of his own time:

Remark, too, that the religious, civil and military architecture of these ages rose aloft and struck the eyes, unlike the modern which is flat and levelled, like the ranks of our social state. Chateaubriand asks, will our age leave such a testimony of its passage? We have no longer the faith which moved so many stones. We raise exchanges, bazaars, coffee houses, club houses.

From these books a portrait of Digby emerges. He would have been capable of steering Pugin's developing interests in scholarship and he would have been sympa-thetic with Pugin's despair over the state of his art. Ambrose Phillipps de Lisle and Digby were life-long friends and members of the circle of Catholic leaders with whom Pugin associated himself. That Pugin knew Digby by 1837 can be established from an entry in Pugin's diary for that year, but, whether or not he knew their author in 1835 and 1836, it seems impossible that Pugin could have overlooked *The Broad Stone of Honour* and *Mores catholici* as he read in preparation for *Contrasts*.

There are sources cited in *Contrasts* which are not discussed here, but they do not contradict what has been said. Pugin admired Dr Milner's *Letters to a Prebendary*, which he first read in January 1835. It should also be noted that ten years before Pugin began his project Charles Butler had written, in the *Book of the Roman Catholic Church*, a description which might have been the theme of *Contrasts*:

England was covered with edifices raised by the sublimest science and dedicated to the most noble and most salutary purposes; commerce prospered, agriculture, literature, every useful and ornamental art and science was excellently cultivated and was in a state of gradual improvement. The treasury overflowed with wealth, there was no debt, and one fourth part of the tithes in every place being set apart for the maintenance of the poor, there was no poor law. Such was the temporal prosperity of England when the Reformation arrived. Will it suffer on a comparison of it with the condition of England at any subsequent era, or even with its present?

That Pugin drew on sources which a recent Catholic convert who was also an aspiring architect would have known in no way qualifies the significance of *Contrasts*. It merely places the book in the stream of ideas to which it belongs. *Contrasts* was of the deepest importance for Pugin and his career. It demonstrated his capacity to take hold of ideas and turn them effectively to his dogmatic purposes. It showed, also, that he possessed gifts which none of the literary or historical commentators upon whom he drew could claim. As an artist-illustrator, Pugin performed at the top of his capacities in *Contrasts*. The plates were wonderful, and it is significant that he worked on them first, as though he forged his ideas through their preparation. Pugin never withdrew his support from these illustrations, and he repeated all but one of them in his subsequent edition of the book. Pugin did not change his mind; he merely elaborated the theme he had discovered between 1832 and 1836.

James Fergusson

BY MAURICE CRAIG

T H O S E who earn their living at a subject they enjoy are sooner or later faced with the question: which books to keep in the office and which to keep at home. I keep most of my architectural books in the office; but Fergusson I keep at home. By 'Fergusson' I mean of course the four-volume *History of Architecture* published between 1862 and 1876. To be sure, not all the reasons for this are entirely to Fergusson's credit. The book is out of date, and therefore expendable for serious purposes. It can be enjoyed for its vigorous opinions, and we can all relish the pleasure of patronizing Fergusson as our editor did when he called him 'an incorrigible and wildly prejudiced amateur'. At home, in the evening, something crops up and we look it up in Fergusson. It will probably be there all right: but the attribution or the date can no longer be relied on. No matter, we can look it up tomorrow in a proper book. But it will have to be a very proper book indeed. Any expert, if his field be narrow enough, can always beat the amateur whose field is wide. But in the meantime the amateur may make some very large circles round the expert. In its vast synoptic sweep, Fergusson's book still stands alone in the English language. It is also endlessly stimulating.

James Fergusson was an amateur and a Victorian, born eleven years before the Queen-Empress, the second son of an Inspector-General of Military Hospitals. As a young indigo merchant in Calcutta he looked, with rational and unencumbered eyes, at the buildings of India and China, what Banister Fletcher was later to call the 'non-historical styles'. For history, in this sense, Fergusson cared not a fig, regarding it as a crippling burden to the architect and a misleading will-o'-the-wisp to the critic. His first book, published when he was thirty-seven and had made his fortune in business, was about Indian architecture, and he followed it up with another two years later. Two years later again he wrote *The True Principles of Beauty in Art* (1849), illustrated by the buildings of Egypt, Assyria, Greece, Etruria, and Rome. Pugin's *Contrasts* had already been out for a dozen years, his *True Principles*

140

were already published. Ruskin was by now on the warpath. Fergusson, with his coarse, businessman's mind, was to canvass many of the same ideas as they, but from an independent, indeed a philistine standpoint. It is more than possible that he succeeded in giving them a wider currency than either of these writers, for his books are still exceedingly common.

The three books already published were to grow, gradually, into the four volumes of the *History*.[1] Besides the *History* and the various monographs which cluster about

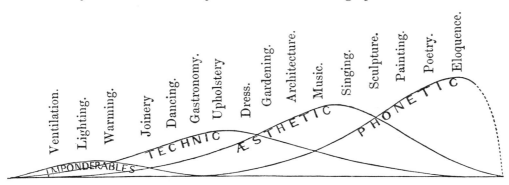

and support it he wrote a once famous book on *Rude Stone Monuments* and three patriotic and strictly practical books on artillery-fortification. He ended up as an F.R.I.B.A. and recipient of the Institute's Gold Medal.[2]

The roles of theorist and of encyclopedic historian are not usually combined in this field. Fergusson's wide travels and his early grasp of the camera's value as a synoptic tool,[3] combined with an impressive philosophic scaffolding, enabled him to stand alone in this respect. By any standards he deserves full marks for his provision of plans and sections, which was far ahead of his time.

Much of his philosophic scaffolding looks groggy to our eyes, and some of it is not merely absurd but also offensive. We may laugh at his little diagrams according marks to the 'technic, aesthetic, and phonetic' elements in a given art or specimen of

1. The *History of Architecture* started life as the *Handbook of Architecture* in 1855, and was expanded and republished in two volumes in 1865 and 1867 as the *History*. In the meantime the *History of the Modern Styles of Architecture* (the insertion of the word 'styles' is significant) had appeared in 1862 and thereafter was treated as volume IV of the *History*. The volume on *Indian and Eastern Architecture* (from which Plate 19 is taken) appeared in 1876 (but was an expansion of earlier works) and thenceforward was described as volume III of the whole *History*.

2. From 1856 to 1858 he was General Manager of the Crystal Palace Company. When Sir Henry Layard, the archaeologist, became First Commissioner of Works in 1868 he invited Fergusson to become his secretary, and soon made him 'Inspector of Public Buildings and Monuments'. But when Fergusson found that he was not even allowed to see the drawings for Street's Law Courts, he resigned the empty honour.

3. He had an extremely large private collection of photographs, said to be still existing in the possession of his descendants.

building, like an examiner at the 11-plus; but there is no harm in using such a scaffolding to assist analysis, so long as you throw it away when it comes to the point, and Fergusson's system is not as silly as it looks. However, the ethnographic or racialist element is worse than silly, with its claptrap about the Turanian race and its 'strong architectural instincts'. In Fergusson's defence it may be urged that in a much more refined and acceptable form such theories may be found in the work of such an intelligent writer as Robert Byron. We may snort when we read in Fergusson of Frederiksborg Castle that it 'is another warning not to look for true Art among peoples of such purely Teutonic blood as our cousins the Danes', but, substituting for the word 'blood' another more acceptable to our beliefs, is there not a residue of common sense lurking in even such an offensive observation as this?

Fergusson's obstinate common sense is continually coming to his aid. 'It has often been objected', he says, 'to the principle of educating the poor, that we are only making them clever devils, and giving them tools for their own destruction. With ten times more force', he continues, 'might this be objected to our system of educating the rich.' We are almost, but of course not quite, in the world of Wildean epigram.

Fergusson's great strength, to our way of thinking, is his freedom from any sort of reverence. He remains unimpressed by prestige in any shape or form. No matter what sacred niche any building occupies in the pantheon of the cultivated, his approach to it is fresh. I believe[1] that this is largely because the first buildings he looked at critically were those which did not belong to the European tradition. It is clear, though he never says so in so many words, that he found Greek architecture boring. Out of the thousand-odd pages of his *History*[2] proper he gives fifty pages to Greece: hardly an over-generous ration for a public saturated with the superiority of the Elgin marbles and their setting. Like all good judges, he finds Aya Sofia more nearly worthy of reverence than almost any other building. But this does not stop him from pointing out a fault which 'might easily be remedied in a second attempt'.

He did in fact devote two specialized monographs to Greek problems: one to the problem of the lighting of Greek temples and the other to the old problem of the reconstruction of the Mausoleum of Halicarnassus.[3] But clearly these interests did not spring so much from an admiration for Greek building as such, as from a typically Fergussonian desire to tackle a problem in logic.

His grudge against the Greeks is twofold. The first count (which even Fergusson would admit is not their fault) is that they have been loaded with too much reverence and therefore need to be taken down a peg or two. In the preface to his *Modern Architecture* he seems to believe that the intention of classicizing (or for that matter

1. Two passages in the Preface to vol. 1 of the *History* go far to confirm that this was so and that Fergusson knew it to be so.   2. i.e. the two volumes.

3. Though Fergusson is still worth reading on these topics, his conclusions are not accepted by recent qualified opinion.

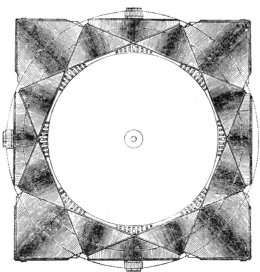

19. Section and plan of the pendentives of the Tomb of Mahmud at
Bijaipur, India, from Fergusson's *Indian and Eastern Architecture*.
Fergusson greatly admired the way in which, in this sixteenth-century
Indo-Saracenic building, the weight of the dome is hung inside the build-
ing, exerting no side-thrust

of gothicizing) Victorian architects is to deceive, and he fears that in this they may succeed. We, on the other hand, do not believe either that this was their intention, or that, had it been, they could have succeeded in it.

His second charge against the Greeks is that they were uninterested in the organization of space. We, if not Fergusson, may feel that that was not their fault either. For him, it deprived Greek architecture of almost all that makes architecture interesting. The Greeks (before Byzantium) were content with simple internal spaces, and in consequence they neither faced nor solved the structural problems posed by the monumental roofing of large and complex spaces. Having solved to his own satisfaction the problem of the lighting of Greek temples, he is said to have caused a building to be erected at Kew embodying his solution. This building, the Marianne North Gallery, turns out on examination to be a rather dull little structure showing no device more startling than a row of clerestory windows filled with obscure glass. When I visited it on a bright July day the attendants had the strip-lighting already switched on.

Historians of architecture, especially before the days of scientific excavation, were perforce historians of the most conspicuous surviving architectural forms. This, in practice, meant temples, baths, or churches with the occasional large basilica or palace hall thrown in – anything which by its size or durability refuses to be ignored. For Fergusson, therefore, the archetypal building is a single hall, with or without supporting spaces, and preferably vaulted. It is no use trying to impress him with a building such as Wanstead or Zakharov's Admiralty: they are, he would reply, merely aggregations of living, working, or display space over which has been thrown, more or less skilfully, a conventional garment of pediments, pilasters, balustrading, and the like. In the words of a later writer, it is merely playing around with the Renaissance box of bricks. No great constructional problem is either posed or solved.

We have recently been reminded by Dr Krautheimer that 'To consider vaulting an improvement over timber roofing is a nineteenth-century prejudice'. A similar or at least related point was made with his customary trenchancy by Goodhart-Rendel: 'To call a building beautiful while you believe it to be of stone and to declare the same building ugly directly anyone tells you it is really faced with cement shows an odd conception of the meaning of the word beauty.'[1] Maybe so:

1. Or, as Fergusson himself put it (*History*, I, p. 20), 'Persons will travel hundreds of miles to see a great diamond or wonderful pearl, who would not go as many yards to see paste models of them, though if the two were laid together on the table very few indeed could distinguish the real from the counterfeit.' Apropos of cement, one of the more startling discoveries which lie in wait for the casual reader of Fergusson is that he recommended that the tiles should be stripped off the dome of S. Maria del Fiore and replaced by a covering of cement, preferably coloured cement (*Modern Architecture*, p. 573 n.). This is the same Fergusson whose obituarists give him credit for having helped powerfully to dissuade the Dean and Chapter of St Paul's from veneering the inside of St Paul's with marble and covering the vaults and dome with mosaics.

but Fergusson is closer to Lethaby than to either of these writers. For him, the merit of a building is partly made up of actual knowledge of its nature. The most romantic castle I have ever seen, silhouetted on a sea-girt promontory, turned out on closer inspection to be a fish-curing establishment. Yet I hold the curing of fish to be, as Dr Johnson said of the making of pickles, a harmless object, which is more than can be said of the purposes for which most castles were built.

Fergusson insists on knowing a building from the inside outwards before he will judge it (Plate 20). In nothing is he more Scotch, Victorian, moralistic, and indeed modern, than in this. And surely he is right. Our admiration of St George's Hall cannot fail to be enhanced by the knowledge that over that splendid space is a proper vault made of monumental materials. When we admire Pearson's churches we do so not for his nasty bourgeois runs of carving, nor even wholly for his splendid large-scale geometry, but largely for his determination to cover them with proper vaults. Years ago an old Irish architect told me with reverence in his voice that Bentley rejected the use of steel reinforcement in his domes at Westminster not because steel is a base material, but because, though its coefficient of expansion is almost exactly that of concrete, 'almost' was not good enough. Whenever I look at Bentley's cathedral the moral beauty of this decision comes into my mind and adds to my enjoyment.

But Fergusson was not happy with this position. Far from it. In nothing was he less Scotch than in his freedom from complacency. The texture of his vast work, synoptic in intention and encyclopedic in achievement, is laced with the tension of moral anxiety. Consider these passages:

The old Scandinavian or Dutch settlers [in America] built their meeting-houses for prayer, or their neat quaint dwellings, in utter ignorance[1] of the precepts of Palladio, and with the same supreme contempt for Mediaeval Art as it prevailed in Europe for three centuries after it ceased to be a real art; and the Puritan Pilgrim Fathers, who followed and superseded them, showed the same Anglo-Saxon indifference to Architectural ornament as has characterized their race at all times... The consequence of this was, that from the time of the earliest colonisation of this country, till after the termination of the war of 1812–14, there was hardly one single building erected in Northern America which is worthy of being mentioned as an example of Architectural Art.

Sixteen pages later in the same work:

... though Classicality or Mediaevalism may do very well for churches, managers of theatres are in earnest, and their audiences insist on both seeing and hearing what is going on, and will not be content with being told that it is correct to sit behind a pillar where nothing can be seen, or under a roof where every sound is lost ... The result has been that modern Theatres, so far, at least, as concerns their internal arrangements, are the only

1. Fergusson was of course himself ignorant of the process whereby Palladio, via Gibbs and the copy-books, did in fact filter through to the colonists, not to mention Thomas Jefferson.

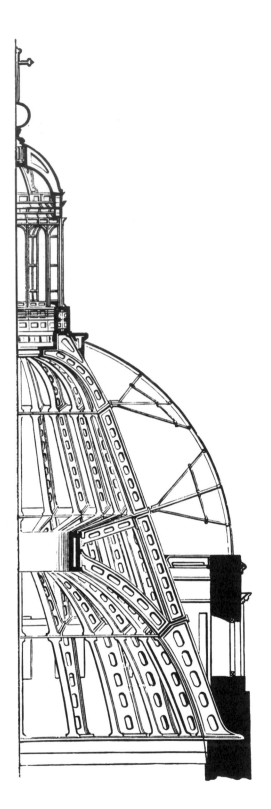

20. Half-section of the dome of St Isaac's
Cathedral, St Petersburg, by Ricard
Monferran, from Fergusson's *Modern Styles
of Architecture.* Though approving the use
of cast and wrought iron here, Fergusson
criticized its application as showing 'little
constructive skill'

important buildings in modern times designed wholly without reference to precedent, and regarding which an architect really must think what is best to be done and how he can best do it. It hence arises that in speaking of them we must revert to our old principles of criticism,[1] and explain their peculiarities as if they were the works of reasoning men and not the products of copying machines.

In other words, the New England builders are to be despised for their ignorance of Palladio, while the theatre-architects are commended for throwing him out of the window. But why? Is it because the New England builders were not rich, so that their buildings are small and simple and made of wood? Some colour is lent to this idea by the fact that Fergusson goes on to say 'our Theatres would be by far the most satisfactory of our Architectural productions if it were not that, in almost all cases, economy is one of the first exigencies to be attended to . . . one consequence of which is, that no theatre in Europe is constructed internally of such durable materials as are requisite to architectural effect. The boxes and fittings are generally of wood . . . with a temporary look about them very destructive of grandeur'. A few pages later he laments the fact that though theatre interiors are to be taken seriously because of their rationalism, 'their exteriors have unfortunately been handed over to the "dealers in Orders" in the same manner as other civil buildings'. From this we might be led to suppose that Fergusson is resolutely opposed to the dolling up of functional buildings. In the diagram on p. 148, for instance, from the Introduction to volume 1 of the *History*, we might be pardoned for supposing that his purpose is to show a progressive degeneration through the loading on of ornament, reading from left to right. We should, however, be wrong. 'Let us suppose the Diagram', he says, 'to represent a cotton-factory, a warehouse, or any very commonplace utilitarian building.' Section A, he says, is bad building (which is to go a good deal further than merely to say it is not architecture). Section B is better, and so on until at D we reach 'architecture', while E, we are invited to agree, is better architecture still. Elsewhere he praises the apartment blocks of Second Empire Paris. 'In some instances', he admits, 'the old disease of pilasters breaks out with an unmeaningness worthy of the age of Henri Quatre; but as a general rule the dressing of the windows, their balconies, and the string courses which mark the floors, are left to tell the story; and when this is the case, it is really impossible to go wrong.'

As usual, Fergusson is not such a fool as he looks. He is perfectly well aware that a formula with which it is 'impossible to go wrong' will not produce High Art: but he also knows that an apartment block in a street façade is no proper place for art of great pretension. He knows quite well that on the plane of mere building a wall is a wall is a wall, but that by modelling and inflexion a wall may be made to speak, and that this eloquence (or in certain contexts the pointed want of it) is the language

1. By 'our old principles of criticism' Fergusson means the principles applicable to 'real' architecture, and hence used in the first two volumes of the *History*.

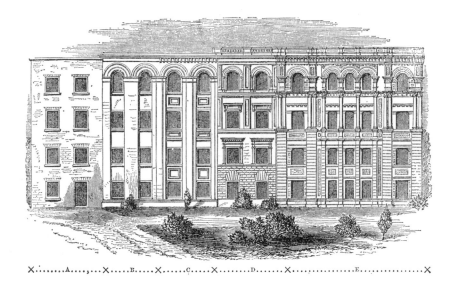

X········A····,···X·····B·····X······C·····X·······D······X··········E···············X

of architecture. But he is very much disturbed by the thought that to the man in the Victorian street this language has no meaning. In the main text of his *Modern Architecture* he has nothing but the warmest praise for St George's Hall, of which he thinks as highly as I do. He even refrains from his customary asides about the absurdity of erecting replicas of the antique in an industrial society. But in the Introduction to the volume he has something rather different to say about this building.

The learned in Art . . . go into ecstasies on observing the purity of style and correctness of composition which pervade every part of St George's Hall, Liverpool. It recalls every association we ever felt in contemplating Classical Art, and reproduces all we ever dreamt of as great or good in the best age of that school. But common people do not feel this . . . The absence of windows does not strike them as a beauty; on the contrary, they think that it gives a gloomy and prison-like aspect; and, in spite of all our preaching, they feel that a far more convenient and suitable building might have been got for half the expense.

Like Dr Johnson, Fergusson would rejoice to concur with the common reader, if only it were possible. But he sees the gulf between the 'unlearned millions' and the educated world yawning ever wider, and the prospect fills him with gloom. After writing nearly 600 pages on Modern Architecture, 'the retrospect, it must be confessed, is sufficiently melancholy and discouraging'. There are two obvious possibilities in this situation. One is for the educated classes to throw all their Greco-Roman lumber overboard and become converts to reason; the other is for the toiling masses to be educated, not in the classics, but in architectural values. He sees no immediate prospect of either. No wonder he was despondent.

148

With the other classic dilemmas of architectural theory Fergusson fares no better, impaling himself upon their several horns visibly, painfully, and repeatedly. He is, for example, continually tempted by the proposition that good engineering equals good architecture. Yet time and again he turns away from the conclusion, and always for a different reason.[1] Faced with the façade of King's Cross station, which he cannot help admiring, all he can find to say is that 'the style is so simple and grand that it ought to have been executed in granite, while it is carried out in simple brick'. In granite, he continues, the offsets in the great arches could have been omitted, 'and if the money saved in material had been employed in ornament, a more architectural façade might have been attained'. He does not, as we might expect, criticize the tower for being too slender to resolve the duality of the elevation. He cannot but praise the great trusses of the roof, but insists again that to be made into architecture the trusses should have been given more mass to make them look stronger, or ornamented, or have bits added to them to change their proportions. But in what style? Having spent so long in telling his readers to forget about style, he is at a loss for an answer. Next door, at St Pancras, is a dreadful object-lesson in what not to do. 'On the other hand, when engineers attempt decoration they generally fail.' (This is not our experience of the Victorian engineers, but by now we are used to Fergusson's distaste for some Victorian productions which seem to us to have passed the test of time.)

He shows some disposition to plump for what the Victorians called the 'Italian' style – 'that compromise between classicality and common sense which is called Italian'. At the end of *Modern Architecture*, and almost at the end of his tether, he clutches at it as at a straw: 'there is yet one other style within whose limits progress still seems possible. The Renaissance Italian is by no means worked out'.[2] It is not an encouraging picture: the richest, most resourceful society the world has ever seen, reduced to quarrying away at the one remaining deposit, holding off bankruptcy for a few short years. Nor, to be fair, is this his final word. After a page or two of (for him) unusually woolly argument, he ends with the hope that 'taste (even if not innate) may result from the immense extent of our knowledge'.

He is much too intelligent to suppose that an 'ought' proposition (taste) can ever be derived from an 'is' proposition (knowledge). He knows, we all know, that knowledge is more often the enemy of taste than its nurse. But let us be fair to Fergusson. It is not 'archaeological' knowledge of which he is here speaking, except in the sense

1. As for example when he says of the Basilica of Maxentius ('Temple of Peace') that it is 'so clever a piece of engineering that it must always have been a failure as an architectural design'. An extraordinary judgement.

2. 'It has also this immense advantage, which the Gothic never can possess, that it requires and demands that the highest class of Art in painting and sculpture should be associated with it, instead of the crude barbarism of the Middle Ages.'

that knowledge of what has been done in the past three centuries is a guide to what not to do. He is thinking of an intimate and profound knowledge of the essence of building, which he hopes may again be raised, as it has been in other ages, to a higher power to become architecture.

His instincts tell him that salvation, if it is to come at all, will come from the engineers.[1] Indeed, but a few lines back, he has been gloomily speculating on whether the engineers will succeed in converting the architects to their own gospel of common sense, or whether (as he seems to think more likely) as the engineers rise in society they will, through snobbery, join in the old vicious game of make-believe.

Like other theorists, and especially perhaps like others of his time, Fergusson is driven from time to time to postulate a golden age, a time before the fall when architecture was untrammelled by the falsities which so oppress him. In so doing he talks a good deal less nonsense than most of his contemporaries about the merry pious masons doing everything just right because they lived in an unclouded age of faith. As so often, his common sense saves him from absurdity. When he speaks of 'anonymous' art he does not fall into the common trap of supposing that nobody designed it. The anonymity, he insists, amounts only to this: that nobody thought it significant to make a fuss of the designers by name. He likens the building of a medieval cathedral to that of an Atlantic liner. In both cases a number of highly skilled people discharge their grave responsibilities in the light of their experience; but they do not get their names in the papers.

'Ship-building,' he says, ' ... though totally distinct, is still so nearly allied to architecture, as to make a comparison of the two easy and intelligible.' Nor did it escape his notice that the ships of his time, especially towards the end of his life (he died in 1886), were much cleaner, more rational, and better architecture than most of the buildings on land. Yet he denies them the name of architecture.

Why? Several possible explanations suggest themselves in the light of Fergusson's known beliefs. One is that, since no ship is ordinarily expected to last more than thirty years or so, they lack the durability which he regards as an essential attribute. Another is that since the conditions to be satisfied are so closely similar in ship after ship, they tend to consist of the same elements in the same arrangement, and there is little scope for originality. Yet they are not more like one another than, say, basilican churches, and they are certainly less like one another than terrace-houses, or for that matter Corinthian columns. The beauty of a ship, Fergusson would urge, is the product of necessity. Symmetry, which Fergusson prizes in land buildings, is virtually forced on the ship designer. It follows that the designer cannot take the credit for it. A ship is so circumscribed by the forces of nature that it is nearly as

1. As when Justinian called in a steam-engineer to design the Church of the Holy Wisdom (R. Krautheimer, *Early Christian and Byzantine Architecture* (Pelican History of Art) (Harmondsworth, 1965), p. 153).

difficult to design an ugly ship as to design an ugly harp, and for similar reasons. Yet ugly ships have been, and still more, are being built, and some have been built which, like the *Aquitania*, are more serious and more successful works of art than the land architecture of their time. They satisfy Fergusson's demand that the architect should imitate Nature's methods and not her forms; that he should not be afraid to house dissimilar and asymmetrical organs within a symmetrical envelope, as happens in the human body. Major functions should be expressed in elevation only when this is appropriate: minor functions need not be.

We have already seen that Fergusson arranges the arts in a spectrum according to the part played in each by the technic, aesthetic, and phonetic elements. He observes that whereas progress is to be expected in the technic arts, there is no progress at the phonetic end of the spectrum. Poetry has not become any better since Homer, merely different. A ship of 1860, on the other hand, is better than one of 1760, which is in turn better than one of 1660, and so on. By the phonetic element in a building he means that part of the building's message which can be paraphrased, however inadequately, in words. A young Irish architect (at least he was young then) once said to me that every time we see an architrave round a doorway we are reminded of the Roman Empire: we feel the lead, as it were, being tugged against our collar. On a cruder level there is or was a convention, still used in the popular theatre and in cartoons, that a pointed arch indicates an ecclesiastical context.

If Fergusson had seen the *Vasa* raised from her oozy bed in Stockholm harbour he would, I am sure, have agreed that she makes assertions about the majesty of the Crown of Sweden quite as unequivocal as those made by the Royal Palace. He would no doubt have added that pilasters, tabernacle-frames, and heraldic gingerbread are not made any more acceptable by being plastered round the sterncastle of a man of war rather than across a palace façade – rather the contrary. The *Vasa* is an example of ship design gone wrong through trying too hard to look like a building on land. What Fergusson would like to see is that land-buildings should become as rational as ships.

So why, once again, are ships not 'architecture'? What Fergusson actually says is this:

If we could imagine any nation ever to construct ships of God, or to worship on the bosom of the ocean, ships might easily be made such objects of beauty that the cathedral could hardly compete with them.

Rather than waste time ridiculing this absurd proposition, I prefer to hazard a paraphrase, and suggest that what he is really saying is that all architecture, including the secular, derives its artistic purpose from temple architecture, and that some of the language of temple building 'rubs off' on to secular building. But this is clearly not true of the Roman architecture which Fergusson so much admires; for not only is Roman temple architecture relatively insignificant (except of course for the Pantheon), but it is precisely when the architecture of the baths, palaces, and basilicas borrows the language of the temple that Fergusson finds it guilty of falsity, or at best of making trivial what should be grand and sublime. If Fergusson had lived long enough to be able to contrast the splendid exterior of the *Aquitania* with the assortment of Louis XIV and Tudor interiors, we may be sure that his criticism would have been along these lines.

Perhaps Fergusson's position makes better sense if religion is left out of the equation, especially since we have already caught him seeming to imply, in his remarks on theatres, that going to the theatre is a more serious business than going to church. He seems to be demanding that architecture should not only be stable, durable, and convenient, but should also truthfully reflect, in its decorative system, the aspirations, the sense of direction, and the community sense of the society which produces it. This is such a banal formula that nobody would disagree with it, which is almost tantamount to saying that it has no value. Yet Fergusson is able to see that the workmen who built the *Great Eastern*, and their wives and families, were able to 'understand' the designer's purpose in a way in which those similarly involved in Street's Law Courts could not 'understand' the architect's. In his efforts to imagine a rational architecture, Fergusson comes near to demanding that society itself should first become rational. However blundering, at times insensitive, at times self-contradictory his writing may be, at the back of his mind there is the vision, vague and blurred no doubt, but doggedly persistent, of an architecture proper to an industrial democracy.

Among the obituaries printed at his death is one (in *The Architect*) which, spending only a line or two on the usual courtesies, launches into a bitter attack on him for having been a prime agent in making the public discontented with the architecture served up to it by the architects. Important as is the task of comforting the afflicted, it has been said that the task of afflicting the comfortable is sometimes equally urgent. Fergusson helped to discharge this task, and the fact that for him personally there was no comfort in it is the saving quality that keeps his memory green.

Nineteenth-Century Architectural Periodicals

BY FRANK JENKINS

It would be difficult to over-estimate the part played in history by the communication of ideas. In a sense, history is the accumulation of these ideas; and the movement of history, its rate of change, has been determined by the speed and completeness with which ideas have been communicated. This is true of architecture as of any other human activity. The invention of language, alphabets, and printing were all steps of tremendous importance in man's struggle to know and to inform. Less fundamental, but nevertheless of considerable significance, were the improvements which came about in printing methods in the early part of the nineteenth century. To a large degree through the great increase in printed material which they brought about, they account for the variety, the restless search for new forms of expression, and the unprecedented rate of stylistic change which characterize nineteenth-century architecture. Over the same period they contributed towards the democratization of architectural taste, and without them the 'international style' of the present century could not have been realized.

For something like four centuries printing techniques changed little. Type was still set by hand in the early nineteenth century at the rate of about 1500 letters per hour. But in 1800 iron, for the first time, took the place of wood in a hand press and the next forty years witnessed a complete revolution in printing methods. In 1841, with the invention of the Pianotyp, it was possible to set in an hour 6,000 letters – about four times the rate which had been possible a few decades earlier – and with the advent of Koenig's printing cylinder and the aid of steam power, *The Times* in 1814 was producing hourly no less than 1,000 impressions, increasing this fourteen years later to 4,000 when it installed the Applegath press.

Apart from their effect upon newspaper production, these developments brought into being a new type of literature, the modern magazine, lavishly illustrated, inexpensive, and published at regular, frequent intervals: neither book nor newspaper, and quite different from eighteenth-century periodicals like *The Gentleman's*

Magazine. Two famous examples were Charles Knight's *Penny Magazine* (1832–45), which at one stage reached a printing of 180,000 copies a week, and *The Penny Cyclopaedia* (1833–44), while *Punch* (commenced 1841) and *The Illustrated London News* (commenced 1842) followed the same basic pattern but were directed to a different public.

At the same time, within a period of less than six years, at least three architectural magazines appeared, all very well illustrated and remarkably inexpensive: the monthly *Civil Engineer and Architect's Journal* (commenced 1837), the *Surveyor, Engineer and Architect* (commenced 1840), and the most influential architectural periodical of the last century, the weekly *Builder* (commenced 1842). More will be said about these shortly, for they provided the roots from which the modern architectural journal has grown. But first it is necessary to look at some earlier publications of a somewhat different type.

As early as the 1770s there had appeared *The Builder's Magazine*, but this was very different in character from *The Builder* of the following century, as its sub-title indicates – *A Monthly Companion for Architects, Carpenters, Masons, Bricklayers, Etc., as well as for Every Gentleman who would wish to be a competent Judge of the elegant and necessary Art of Building*. It was in fact a pattern book, not dissimilar to those published by Langley and Halfpenny, and when completed included a dictionary of building terms and 185 plates of details and buildings, ranging from a 'Malt-house' to a 'Bone-house', engraved by John Carter. It was originally issued in monthly parts and then re-issued as a complete work in 1774, when the Building Act of that year was added to the text.

In the eighteenth century this was a fairly common practice. For instance, *The Connoisseur*, first published on a weekly basis starting on 31 January 1754, was later reprinted in complete volumes – achieving a sixth edition in 1774. *The Builder's Magazine* was reprinted again in 1779, its sub-title being altered to *A Universal Dictionary*, and re-issued as late as 1820 with new type and the addition of a list of building prices as *The New Builder's Magazine and Complete Architectural Library* by George Andrew Cook, Architect and Builder.

The Builder's Magazine can hardly be regarded as a periodical in our present sense, and the first work which concerns us, devoted entirely to architectural matters, was *The Architectural Magazine*, conducted by John Claudius Loudon, which commenced monthly publication in March 1834 and ran for five years. In appearance it was octavo size, and it followed the pattern of other more general periodicals like *The Gentleman's Magazine* and *The Monthly Magazine*, both of which incidentally contained an appreciable amount of architectural intelligence of popular appeal. Loudon's magazine – its full title was *The Architectural Magazine and Journal of Improvement in Architecture, Building, and Furnishing and in the various arts and trades connected therewith* – was published by Longman, Rees, Orme, Brown, Green

154

and Longman and modelled on its conductor's earlier but very successful *Encyclopaedia of Cottage, Farm and Villa Architecture*. It was intended however to cover a much wider field than the *Encyclopaedia*, since 'in addition to the private dwellings of every class of society residing in the country, it will include also dwellings in cities and towns, and public buildings, in a word, the whole of civil architecture, building and furniture'.

On the completion of the first volume of *The Architectural Magazine*, Loudon provided a preface which stated the object of the magazine, which was 'to second the effect produced by the *Encyclopaedia*, by improving the public taste in architecture generally, by rendering it a more intellectual profession, by recommending it as a fit study for ladies, and by inducing young architects to read, write, and think, as well as to see and draw'. Apart from miscellaneous reviews and reports, the magazine published articles of three types: those aimed at popularizing 'the subject of architecture as a matter of taste'; those familiarizing 'the general reader with what are technically called the Elements of Architectural Design'; and papers of 'a practical nature'. The first number for instance contained a particularly hard-hitting criticism 'On the present State of the Professions of Architect and Surveyor, and of the Building Trade in England' by 'Scrutator', who was to become a regular contributor; E. Trotman 'On the Extent to which the elementary Forms of Classic Architecture are, from their Nature and Origin, fixed or arbitrary'; and, moving from the realms of theory to a more homely level, I. J. Kent's 'Instructions for choosing a Dwelling-House'.

For five years the magazine maintained this catholicity of subject matter, reporting on important buildings in this country and abroad (it seems to have been particularly well informed on American works, giving, for instance, an excellent account of T. U. Walter's Girard College);[1] providing information on technical matters (in 1837 it published an important article 'On the effect which should result to Architecture, in regard to Design and Arrangement, from the general Introduction of Iron in the Construction of Buildings');[2] and keeping a watchful eye on matters of professional integrity and decorum (in 1835 it ran an interesting series on architectural competitions).[3] If there was an editorial bias it was towards the struggling movement for higher professional standards among architects – the magazine made a point of reporting the meetings of the Architectural Society and the Institute of British Architects – and against the style of the New Westminster Palace. Significantly among its many contributors, two names make a regular appearance, J. A. Hansom and George Godwin, both of whom were later to play leading parts in British architectural journalism as editors of the *The Builder*.

In 1834, in his first contribution to *The Architectural Magazine*, 'Scrutator' had made a plea for the formation of an architectural society 'not for eating and drinking

1. loc. cit., v, pp. 446–59.   2. ibid., IV, pp. 277–87.   3. ibid., II, pp. 12, 197, 481, 484.

or backbiting their brethren [presumably a dig at the Architects' Club, which had existed since 1791] but to make rules for the governance of the profession'. Later that year such a body came into being with the founding of the Institute of British Architects.

One of the objects of the new Institute was 'the publication of such communications as may be curious and interesting to the Public and to the Profession', and in the autumn of 1836 the first number of the Institute's *Transactions* was published by John Weale. Apart from the Institute's regulations, its first annual report and a list of contributors to its collection, library, and funds, the volume included a number of 'communications' from members and others. The Honorary Secretary, T. L. Donaldson, contributed a paper on Vitruvius; J. B. Papworth, Vice-President, wrote 'On the Benefits resulting to the Manufactures of a Country, from a well directed cultivation of Architecture, and the Art of Ornamental Design'. Other papers were either archaeological, for instance 'On the Polychromy of Greek Architecture', or more strictly practical. Among the latter George Godwin's name once more appears as the author of a prize essay on 'The Nature and Properties of Concrete, and its application to Construction up to the present period'. The volume was well illustrated with cuts and lithographs, and one fine *colour* plate of German origin.

The second volume was not published until 1842, by Longman's, and the third appeared in 1853. After this date publication was on a regular basis. In 1885 new series were initiated of both the *Transactions* and the *Proceedings*, the latter containing notices and reports of meetings and similar matters, and in 1893 the two were amalgamated to form *The Journal of the R.I.B.A.*, Third Series. With very few lapses, the Institute's publications maintained high standards of scholarship and writing and were excellently illustrated. Successive editors clearly took their responsibilities seriously in providing members with information which was as full and as accurate as possible.[1]

October 1837 saw the appearance of the first number of *The Civil Engineer and Architect's Journal*, which was to continue monthly publication for the next thirty years. As its title suggests, the journal was slanted towards architects with an engineering bent, and it made no pretence at covering the more esoteric areas of archaeology and architectural theory. For this reason it is particularly valuable as a source of information on nineteenth-century buildings and building techniques. It was clearly directed to the American profession as much as to the British, listing a New York publisher on its title-page, and gave good coverage of building activity in the U.S.A., the first issue including an article on railways in America. But what was most striking about the journal was its size and the number and excellence of its illustrations. On

1. For a more detailed account of the Institute's publications see Edward Carter, 'The R.I.B.A. Journal', in *The Growth and Work of the R.I.B.A.*, ed. J. A. Gotch (1934), pp. 141–56.

concluding the first volume the editor could note with pride that in it there were 'above four hundred pages and two hundred engravings, presenting a mass equal to two thousand magazine pages or eight volumes of octavo novels'.

Three years later, in 1840, another, very similar, journal made its appearance, *The Surveyor, Engineer and Architect*, conducted by Robert Mudie. Mudie's intention was to provide a journal which related the activities of the architect, surveyor, and engineer. 'All the journals professing to contain similar matter', he explained in a preliminary address, 'have struck us as resembling the untied bundle of rods – containing the quantity of material, but destitute of union which gives strength, and in which chiefly the real value of such a journal consists.' But Mudie was swimming against the tide of history. It was the age of professional definition and separation, and the complexity of practice was such that a return to the 'unity' of the eighteenth-century building scene was impossible. His journal, which became increasingly orientated towards surveying and civil engineering, lasted for three years, and in closing the final volume in 1843, with a touch of pathos Mudie noted: 'It is more difficult to speak of the future than of the past....'.

But already another publication had entered the field and had been given an extremely encouraging reception. On the last day of 1842 there appeared the 'Precursor Number' of *The Builder, An illustrated weekly magazine for the Drawing-room, the Studio, the Office, the Workshop, and the Cottage.*

Its editor and proprietor was the architect Joseph Aloysius Hansom, inventor of the vehicle which bore his name, who eight years earlier had been declared bankrupt, having rashly stood surety for the contractor for the great neo-classical town hall he had designed at Birmingham. Although his new venture was to bring further financial difficulties, Hansom embarked upon it with gusto. His prefatory message glowed with enthusiasm – and philanthropy. 'There are', he wrote,

in England, Scotland, and Wales, one hundred and twenty thousand Carpenters[, in] . . . Ireland thirty thousand more . . . exclusive of apprentices . . . who, in common with the other co-operating Building Artificers require to read and study . . . For these hundreds of thousands there has hitherto been no retailing of proper food for the mind; no books at moderate prices, and in suitable parcels . . . The 'Architectural Magazine' by Mr. Loudon, indeed, did wonders in its way . . . but what is there . . . for the workshop, and for the fire-side circle of the Building Artisan?

When the second issue appeared on 18 February 1843 – at the remarkably low price of 3*d*. (unstamped) and 4*d*. (stamped) – it contained complimentary letters from an architect, a surveyor, a plasterer, and a joiner. *The Mechanic's Magazine*, however, was not encouraging: 'Another new journal...but little original strength.' Nevertheless its strength was to grow, although soon it lost its original 'self-help' character and became very much more a professional journal.

During 1843, Alfred Bartholomew, best known perhaps for his *Specifications for Practical Architecture* (1841), a strongly rationalistic treatise on architectural theory, became editor. Bartholomew retired through ill-health towards the end of 1844, and was succeeded by George Godwin, who for a number of years ran the journal virtually single-handed, contributing himself a great part of the text of each issue.

For the third volume (1846), the sub-title of *The Builder* was changed to 'An illustrated weekly magazine for the Architect, Engineer, Operative and Artist', and in December 1850 a fifty per cent increase in the size of future issues was announced. The following year the title was changed once more and the journal no longer made any pretence of catering for building tradesmen. It was now directed to 'the Architect, Engineer, Archaeologist, Constructor and Artist'.

Under Godwin's editorship *The Builder* prospered. Its illustrations, taking advantage of the many technical improvements of the period, were superb. In 1863 a further change was made in the sub-title when 'Art-Lover' was substituted for 'Artist', and again, five years later, when 'Sanitary Reformer' was included between 'Constructor' and 'Art-Lover'.

In October 1883, after thirty-nine untiring and productive years of service, Godwin retired. To mark the occasion his colleagues presented him with an address 'enclosed in a neat gilt frame, representing an emblematic "bundle of sticks" tied with a love-knot'.

The new editor was Henry Heathcote Statham, who had come to London from Liverpool some years previously at Godwin's suggestion and who gave for twenty-five years editorial service as distinguished as his predecessor's. As the end of the century approached *The Builder*, which throughout its history had clearly and honestly reflected its times, acknowledged the new movement of Beardsley and C. R. Mackintosh and introduced an elegant Art Nouveau title-page to its now bi-annual volumes.

A journal of a very different type and of a very much shorter life was *The Architectural Quarterly Review*. Its aims were extremely lofty. 'To effect regeneration [of architecture]', its prospectus declared, 'two things are peculiarly important:- the one, sensibility on the part of Architects to "the form and pressure of the time" by acquaintance with every contribution to the knowledge of the past, and with the progress of opinions and discoveries; and the other, clear insight into the philosophy of Art – those unvarying principles supposed to be applicable to the styles of all ages.' The *Review* proposed to assist architectural 'regeneration' by publishing key articles, ranging over every aspect of architecture, but even before publication its editor seems to have had doubts as to the likely success of the venture. On 16 December 1850 he wrote to the Secretary of the Institute of British Architects, enclosing a copy of the prospectus and recalling that 'energetic support [from the profession] has sometimes failed in the case of undertakings confessedly of high merit and importance – a circumstance which has much interfered with the enterprise of publishers – in the issue of works *peculiarly* calculated for professional readers'. The first volume appeared in 1851 with articles on 'The Great Exhibition and its influence upon Architecture', 'Truefitt's designs for country churches', Klenze's designs for the museum at St Petersburg, Assyrian architecture, and Ruskin and the *Stones of Venice* – an extraordinarily mixed bag. Despite this, professional support was not apparently forthcoming, and only one issue seems to have been published.

There were other more successful undertakings. *The Building News, a weekly illustrated record of the Progress of Architecture, Metropolitan Improvements, Sanitary Reform, &c. &c. &c.* commenced in 1855, becoming *The Building News and Architectural Review* in 1860, and *The Building News and Engineering Journal* in 1863. Eventually in 1926 it amalgamated with *The Architect* to become *The Architect and Building News*.

The Architect itself had been founded in 1869 under the editorship of T. Roger Smith. This 'weekly illustrated Journal of Art, Civil Engineering and Building' was lively, informed, and well illustrated – its first number contained an article on 'The Co-operation of Architects and Engineers', a subject that had been growing in importance throughout the century. In 1893 it became *The Architect and Contract Reporter*.

Another important and particularly well produced journal was *The British Architect*. Published in Manchester, it commenced in 1874 and continued until 1917. The immense amount of important work being carried out in the provincial centres in the second half of the century, particularly in the north, warranted a fuller coverage than existing journals could provide. To meet this need was one of the expressed aims of *The British Architect*. Its outlook was extremely practical and was succinctly stated in the first number: ' ... we shall give more prominence to facts, data and principles in connection with actual practice than to theories, opinions, and criticisms upon general topics ... Our Journal will be definitely local in application and detail, yet thoroughly national in purpose and comprehensiveness'. This policy was adhered to, and today the journal provides an extremely valuable, but often overlooked, source on late-nineteenth-century architecture.

In February 1895 the first number of another periodical appeared, *The Builder's Journal, An Architectural Review*, becoming the following year *The Builder's Journal and Architectural Record*. After two more changes of title it settled down in 1919 to *The Architects' Journal*, the title which it still retains.

On the day which saw the first change in the title of *The Builder's Journal*, 11 November 1896, the same press embarked on another venture, *The Architectural Review, for the artist and craftsman*. More splendidly produced than any previous architectural periodical, it was clearly directed to the 'man of taste' and its full title acknowledged the now firmly established Arts and Crafts movement. Despite this, it had about it something of that quality of opulence and 'empire' which is so readily associated with England of the 1890s; at the same time it reflected the period's comfortable, Voyseyesque attitude to life. Discreetly designed, beautifully printed on glossy paper with a new high standard of photographic reproduction, *The Architectural Review* closes the story of nineteenth-century architectural periodicals.

It was concerned with architectural criticism rather than providing technical information, a policy which was the antithesis of that stated by the editor of *The British Architect*. A product of the age of the aesthetic movement and the *Yellow Book*, it was the architectural equivalent of *The Studio*, which had commenced in 1893, although it tended to be more conservative than the latter. The first issue included an urbane and full account by J. E. Newberry of the work of J. L. Pearson, Aston Webb's restoration of St Bartholomew the Great, and excellent drawings by Rickards and Joseph Pennell.

Over the century architecture had achieved a new status. From ranking virtually as a trade to the majority of people at the beginning of the century, by its end it had become a highly respected profession, being accepted by one university as a fit discipline for undergraduate study. *The Architectural Review* reflected this status. It answered too the question asked by those practitioners who were opposed to the statutory registration of architects, in particular the Bill of 1891. Was architecture primarily a profession or an art? Manifestly, to the *Review*, it was both.

W. R. Lethaby

BY P. FERRIDAY

Perhaps no English architectural writer, Pugin apart, has had more influence than
W. R. Lethaby; his views, or crude summaries of them, were everywhere current
in the nineteen twenties and thirties. Many of those who were assiduous in promoting
Lethabyism have seen the dubious consequences, and his name is no more a much
quoted one. In a time of reaction from his ideas as to the nature of architecture it
might seem suitable to suggest that he wrote two of the masterpieces of our architectural literature, his first book on Westminster Abbey and his life of Philip Webb.

That Lethaby and his friends stood for something inimical to the prevailing ideas
of the time in relation to work and its organization and to economics and art is evident
in everything he wrote. The background of his attitudes was described in *Philip
Webb*, of all English architectural biographies the most memorable and endearing.
It was perhaps the last significant work by a contemporary in the literature of
Pre-Raphaelitism, taken not in the strict sense of the Brotherhood but as signifying
that larger group influenced by Rossetti either personally or through his work.
Lethaby was enchanted by the gaiety, by the casualness, by the unprofessionalness
(in the qualifications, frock-coat sense) of the Rossetti, Morris, Webb, Burne-Jones
set. That enchantment and loyalty so suffused his life of Webb that all the freshness
and spontaneity of the century seem to be theirs alone. He inherited, uncritically,
their feelings and reactions of the eighteen fifties. A key, perhaps *the* key, feature of
Morris and his friends was a horror of the destruction – the blotting out – of one
England by another that they saw, and significantly the first chapter of the Webb
biography was titled 'Oxford before the railway'. The sordidness and squalor of
industrialization for a generation not observing its seeming heroic youth but power-
lessly watching the inexorable mechanistic progress – the very trees and their
childhood country were dying round them – was agonizing to the sensitive. The
mere number of things, of people, of products, the number of issues and of problems,
the pressures, inventions, causes, the unstoppable and unrelenting commerce, all this

seemed to be poisoning peace of mind and the immemorial. These reactions Lethaby communicated in his biography, not simply as nostalgia and retreat (though those were natural and sensible), but as a struggle to redeem the times, to make well and beautifully in a world of Brummagen rubbish. But Lethaby was insufficiently aware of the immediate tradition of Morris and Webb, a tradition no older than industrialism – that of the Gothic Revival and literary Romanticism. The tradition of the later Pre-Raphaelites, deriving partly from Pugin, partly from Ruskin, partly in reaction to contemporary events, and not at all from historians, was a fantasy medieval world ('The age of Romance' Lethaby styled it) where there was no war, no pestilence, no starvation, no cruelty, no deformities, and nothing Chaucer would have recognized. The fantasy – and such men as Ruskin and Morris were hardly innocent self-deceivers – was worth its keep; to be set against the slag heaps, company promoters, and villas. The value of the fantasy was to be measured by its products. Behind considered fantasies of this sort lie purposeful and needful thinking; Ruskin's and Morris's thinking on the nature of wealth and the conditions of labour were the intellectual content of the fantasy. Morris's peculiar brand of socialism, freebooter socialism, affected, by the example of his marvellous life, all those who were fortunate enough to come into contact with him. The effect on Webb as the architect of the group is clearly shown in the biography as an attempt to seek a way out of the style-battle morass with a fundamental rejection of the institution and terminology of the architecture of his time, with a return to the local and vernacular, with a vision of architecture as a corporate craft building operation, a natural growth from bottom to top, from soil to silhouette. The curious combination of the Gothic Revival tradition, craft socialism, and nostalgia is beautifully embodied in *Philip Webb*. That Lethaby's valuation of Webb's own buildings and those of his contemporaries might now be accepted by few is not necessarily a serious criticism; his gift was, as here exemplified, for bringing out the spirit, the liveliness, the sensitiveness of a group who lived through desperate times, and who made things of beauty. *Philip Webb* remains an experience of the past, a vivid and encouraging portrait.

The Ruskin–Morris–Webb–Lethaby notion of architecture as a craft building operation was largely derived from their vision of the conditions of Gothic, and it is hardly surprising that their views were most convincingly embodied in their writings directly about Gothic. The masterpiece of the tradition is *Westminster Abbey and the King's Craftsmen: a study of medieval building*, published in 1906. That other important studies, by Lethaby himself, by Westlake, Bond, Rackham, and the Royal Commission on Historical Monuments, followed it has not affected its place as the outstanding study of any one of our medieval buildings; its richness of historical feeling and evocation are unique. It was the multiple significance of the Abbey that Lethaby bound together in one narrative: a significance formally architectural, a significance of monarchical history, a significance as a European creation – where

English, French, Italian, German, and Flemish work is combined – a significance of the long endurance of a faith. To bring forth all this required very special responsiveness, acute architectural perceptiveness, and wonderful scholarly aptitude.

The central feature of the book, and what gave it its momentum and activity, was the study of the building's progress as seen through the records of the masons and artists. Although a good deal relating to the craftsmen was already in print (in Scott's *Gleanings* for example), it was Lethaby who collected it and added to it from the records and put it in order – a considerable work of scholarship in itself. But this proper historian's work is not what makes Lethaby so different – it would have been done by other historians. The details of the craftsmen's work, names, pay were the consequence of an apprehension of how Gothic could be written about – not as a dissection of parts, details, influences, styles, all classified and tabulated, but as an active creation. The Abbey, through the craftsmen, is built; it comes from Henry III's reconstruction personally and actively to date. The organization of the building trade was indicated (that was to be much amplified by Messrs Knoop and Jones and Mr Harvey), but the very paucity of information about some of the masons – John of somewhere, Henry of somewhere else – has a kind of poignancy and adds to the sense of so many almost forgotten who had combined and succeeded each other in making what was once not only structurally superb but decoratively splendid. 'If I think, again of this place, / And of people, not wholly commendable, / Of no immediate kin or kindness. / But some of peculiar genius, / All touched by a common genius / . . .' And it was through the old accounts in the Public Records Office and in the Abbey that Lethaby, one thinks partly at least beneath the level of *conscious* intention, recreated so far as possible on paper the making of a work of art of a people, 'all touched by a common genius', of the past.

The life of the book, the correspondence with the active making of its subject, depends as well on Lethaby's use of his various sources. He had an impeccable sense of quotation from medieval sources, a phrase or a sentence; touches of sudden vividness such as the description of Wolsey receiving the Cardinal's hat in 1515. And additionally – and this is rather a different point – because of the destructive restorations he had to reconstruct from the accounts of earlier scholars: from Camden, Norden, Keepe, John Carter, Neale, Gilbert Scott, Burges, and many others. So, almost without aforethought, the building is given a continuous history through the last three centuries, often in the language of those centuries. In describing the original form of the outside of the north transept, restored in the Wren works, then by Scott, and cruelly by Pearson, Lethaby used as evidence Wyngaerde's view (*c.* 1560), Speed's map (*c.* 1610), Hollar's etching of 1654, Keepe's description of 1683, a print by Collings of 1689, an engraving for Strype's edition of Stow, Wren's report, and a measured drawing probably by Dickinson. These sorts of references, particularly quoted descriptions, form a subsidiary theme, of antiquarian history and more particularly of continuing care for the building; a theme of observation and scholarship echoing the making by the craftsmen.

Of the narrower excellencies may be instanced the fine balance in discussing the relations of Westminster to the French cathedrals (though at the time it was not known that Master Henry was Henry of Reyns) and the occasional asides that illuminated the history of Gothic – such a one being: 'We are usually told that the Perpendicular style is especially a product of Gloucester, and it does seem probable that the large work of applying slight *casings* there to the earlier building may have influenced the turn the style took. On the other hand, the Chapter House of St. Paul's of 1332 seems to have approximated very closely to the Perpendicular manner, so also did St. Stephen's Chapel, and I should expect the first word in fashions to have been said by the King's Masons of London.' *That* point is still under discussion.

The adequacy of Lethaby's views as to the nature of art and architecture, the provenance of which were described in his *Philip Webb*, were tested when he came to write what was his most influential book, *Architecture* (1912). *Architecture*, one of the volumes of the Home University Library of Modern Knowledge, purported to be a history of architecture from the beginning, in 251 small pages. Gothic is finished on page 228, the Renaissance occupies the next eight pages, and 'The Modern Position' completes the story in fifteen; that is, post-Gothic architecture is hardly allowed an existence at all. The explanation of the proportions of the book is a simple one in that Lethaby identified architecture with building construction – great architecture was adventurous engineering. Where there was little or no development in structure, then architecture was stagnant: 'It must, I think, be admitted by those who have in part understood the great primary styles, Greek or Gothic, that the Renaissance is a style of boredom. However beautiful single works may be, it tends to be blind, puffy, and big-wiggy. Its highest inspiration was good taste, it was architect's architecture.'

If certain premises produce such evidently ridiculous conclusions one may infer faulty premises. It would not be difficult to produce instances of special pleading and false argument from *Architecture*, but the curiosity is that Lethaby was incapable of re-examining his premises. The identification of architecture and engineering was located in the survey of Gothic: 'The builders made an effort to do all that might be done in stone, and the possibilities of rearing stones one upon another were explored to the utmost. The structure, as Morris has well put it, became organic. This was the law of growth in Gothic architecture.' Such a version (really of the insensate leading the sensate) has a kind of specious convincingness, but at every particular and detail fails to explain. It misses out too many buildings – nearly all later Gothic for example – and ignores too many differences (let alone other national kinds of stone building), including those between contemporary Gothic buildings. Why were the west fronts of Peterborough and Salisbury designed as they were? – any explanation would

164

involve other considerations ('taste' and 'design') than Lethaby would allow for. And if the Lethaby notion of Gothic was pushed to its natural conclusion, there was no Gothic in England, unless French-designed, as the American C. H. Moore showed. Lethaby stopped short of this conclusion presumably because he did not want to reach it, but he left unexamined the premises from which the conclusion could be drawn. What Lethaby had done was to remove from architects choice and sensibility. That this was the consequence of the reaction of Webb and Morris to the style war and profusion of historical quotation of forty and fifty years earlier there can be no doubt when reading the life of Webb.

The irony of Lethaby's work is that he should have come to propound views on architecture which diminished it, and that his views forced him to dismiss a major part of the architectural heritage. The double irony is that his equation of engineering and architecture should have been so readily accepted in the nineteen twenties and thirties under the notion of functionalism. To read the progressive journals of the thirties is to re-read Lethaby's version of Gothic. Instead of stone, concrete and steel were to guide, or irresistibly lead, architects to a new organic architecture; loyalty to the possibilities of the material was to solve all formal problems and difficulties. This ingenuous anticipation was paralleled by the speciousness of Lethaby's theory of architectural development; it was not surprising that the young architects of the time found him congenial reading.

There was in Lethaby an incapacity for seeing where his own speculation would take him, or at least an astonishing naivety in thinking, and a remarkable sense of history in its particularity; to this last and rare quality of mind and feeling we are indebted to him for two precious books.

Ruskin and American Architecture, or Regeneration Long Delayed

BY HENRY-RUSSELL HITCHCOCK

Ruskin regenerated art, 'as an appeal to moral order always must'.
Montgomery Schuyler,[1] quoting Emerson

The eloquent prose of John Ruskin's *Stones of Venice* and *Seven Lamps of Architecture* ... was almost solely responsible for the shift of architectural taste from English to Italian mediaeval prototypes.
Samuel M. Green[2]

THERE is surely no English writer on architecture so famous as John Ruskin, and even Nikolaus Pevsner has not yet been as widely and continuously read in the United States.[3] Ruskin's most important books and lectures concerned with architecture belong to the five years 1849–54. He himself, moreover, by the late 1850s was already turning against the newer directions the Victorian Gothic had been

---

1. 'The Work of Barney & Chapman', *Architectural Record* (September 1904); as reprinted in Montgomery Schuyler, *American Architecture and other Writings*, eds. William H. Jordy and Ralph Coe (Cambridge, Mass., 1961), p. 134. The editors, generally so successful in tracing Schuyler's references however minor to their sources, were unable to locate the phrase in Emerson's writings. By this date, Schuyler was quite disenchanted with Ruskin, so that the quotation is somewhat ironic. See below, p. 204.

2. This brief quotation from p. 323 of the latest general account of American art and architecture, that by Samuel M. Green: *American Art, A Historical Survey* (New York, [1966]), expresses clearly current opinion as to the effect of Ruskin's writings on American architecture.

3. The most extensively published American writer on architecture was Asher Benjamin (1773–1845). Of his books, 115 editions and issues have been located in major libraries and others may well exist. Ruskin's American editions and issues come a close second – there are, at the least, more than a hundred up to 1895. The runner-up for second place, A. J. Downing, comes far behind with fewer than fifty: H. R. Hitchcock, *American Architectural Books, A List of Books, Portfolios, and Pamphlets on Architecture and Related Subjects published in America before 1895* (Minneapolis, [1962]), pp. 9–13, 31–4, 85–92.

166

taking – in some part, at least, as a result of his influence. Yet his was a name much conjured with in relation to architecture wherever the English language was used throughout the rest of the nineteenth century, and even in such places as Barcelona, Brussels, and Berlin,[1] where other Victorian critics were surely little read, well into the twentieth century.

The thirty-nine volumes of the Library Edition of the *Life, Letters and Works of John Ruskin*, edited by E. T. Cook and Alexander Wedderburn and published over the years 1903 to 1912, consecrated Ruskin's position in English life and letters and paralleled the appearance of a spate of biographies following after his death: Alice Meynell's and J. Spielmann's already in 1900, Frederic Harrison's in 1902, G. W. Kitchin's in 1904, E. T. Cook's and also A. C. Benson's in 1911. It was at the opening of the century, moreover, that Marcel Proust was translating Ruskin, bringing out in 1904 *La Bible d'Amiens* on which he had begun to work some five years before. But Proust never tackled the major books on architecture Ruskin had written in the late 1840s and early 50s, for his interest in Ruskin was essentially aesthetic and literary. *The Seven Lamps of Architecture*, however, had already been translated into both French and German in 1900; and *The Stones of Venice* was available from 1898 in German and in 1905 in French.[2]

When a new cycle of books on Ruskin began to appear a generation ago with Amabel Williams-Ellis's *Tragedy of John Ruskin* (London, 1928) and R. H. Wilenski's *John Ruskin: An introduction to the further study of his work* (London, 1933), the emphasis was biographical and psychological; for Ruskin's architectural theories, so resoundingly damned in 1914 by Geoffrey Scott,[3] no longer seemed of current relevance. More recently, Ruskin studies have been largely taken over by students of Victorian literature whose interests rarely extend to his concern with architecture. Only those writers who, like myself, are concerned with mid-nineteenth-century architectural developments pay much attention to him as a critic of architecture, and, in our writings, the references are quite likely to be no more than recurrent use of the vague term 'Ruskinian'. An important exception to this, however, is a paperback anthology of extracts from *The Art Criticism of John Ruskin*, edited and

1. Antoni Gaudí i Cornet apparently spoke only Catalan, but the Güell circle he frequented knew English. According to George Collins in *Antonio Gaudí* (New York, 1960), p. [126], n. 56, 'Ruskin had been appreciated by the Renaixença movement for some time and was being translated into Catalan over the year 1900.' Many Germans, encouraged by Hermann Muthesius, read Ruskin in the years 1900–10. The title of Henry Van de Velde's article, 'Artistic Wallpapers', reporting on the exhibition of them in 1892 in Antwerp, would seem to indicate that this Belgian 'Ruskinian' knew English. The article is found in *L'Art moderne* (1893), pp. 193–5, and also in *L'Émulation* (1893), pp. 150–1.

2. Translations of Ruskin are really irrelevant to this article, but it is clear that after 1900 much of Ruskin's writing became available in the principal European languages and even, as has been noted, in Catalan.

3. *The Architecture of Humanism* (London, 1914; 2nd edn, 1924).

with an introduction by Robert L. Herbert (Garden City, N.Y., 1964). Part II of this – some hundred pages – is devoted to the writings on architecture.

I am here concerned not with the central story of Ruskin as an English critic of architecture and his influence on the modulation of Victorian Gothic architecture in England during the 1850s and early 60s when that influence was strongest,[1] but rather with the evidences of a quite exceptionally prompt interest in his architectural writing in America and the surprisingly slight influence that writing seems to have had on actual building in the United States before the early seventies and after those years from 1880 onwards.

It was necessarily Ruskin's early writing concerning another art than architecture – volumes I and II of *Modern Painters*, which appeared in London in 1843 and 1846 respectively – that first came to the attention of Americans even before American editions of them, based on the third revised London edition of volume I and the second edition of volume II, both of 1846, were brought out in New York in 1847 and 1848 by the firm of Wiley and Putnam.[2] (It may well be that the reputed quotation from Emerson at the head of this article refers only to the art of painting and not to

1. This matter was discussed at some length in the last chapter, 'Ruskin or Butterfield? Victorian Gothic at the Mid-Century', of my *Early Victorian Architecture in Britain*, 2 vols. (New Haven, 1954), and with particular reference to Street in 'G. E. Street in the 1850s', *Journal of the Society of Architectural Historians*, XIX (December 1960), pp. 145–71. The books in preparation on Butterfield by Paul Thompson and on Street by R. J. Lambert should have much to add to the story, with confirmation or correction of some of my own surmising. The story of the commissioning, designing, building, and decorating of Butterfield's All Saints, Margaret Street, has already been considerably amended by Thompson in 'All Saints' Church, Margaret Street, Reconsidered', *Architectural History* (1965), pp. 73–94.

2. The firm of Wiley and Putnam, founded in 1837, broke up in 1848 after the publication of the second volume of *Modern Painters*. George P. Putnam 'conducted a branch of the business in London and acted as English representative', and literary titles formed an important part of the firm's lists: *The First One Hundred and Fifty Years, A History of John Wiley and Sons, Incorporated 1807–1957* (New York, [1957]), p. 16. However, in 1842 the firm had issued their first architectural book, A. J. Downing's *Cottage Residences*. J. G. van der Poel's brief account of the early ventures in architectural publishing of the firm (op. cit., p. 159) contains several inaccuracies: The first edition of Downing's *Architecture of Country Houses* was published by the Appleton firm in New York and Philadelphia in 1850, not by Wiley and Putnam in 1848; and Robert Dale Owen's *Hints on Public Architecture* carries the imprint: New York and London, George P. Putnam, 1849, indicating publication after Wiley and Putnam had parted company.

In 1844 Putnam amazed Elizabeth Barrett by proposing to issue her poems in New York at his own risk and give her ten per cent of the profit. Robert Browning was even more flabbergasted when she 'miraculously received' a remittance from Wiley and Putnam in New York. To Thomas Carlyle, Putnam offered 'a true royalty arrangement, one of the first on record – ten percent "on the selling price of all copies of 'Cromwell' sent into the market by them" – and also on reprinted editions of his former works, or some of them' (op. cit., p. 33). One might have supposed that Ruskin would have been glad to accept a similar arrangement, but this was not the case: 'Ruskin was among the famous writers who have refused to make use of the offices of a professional publisher. Ruskin employed an agent to look out for details, but got out his own editions, and book-

architecture at all.) In the present context, however, the books concerned with architecture that came out in London first – but usually at once in New York also – in the decade between the publication of the second volume of *Modern Painters* (in which Ruskin was first revealed as the author) and the eventual appearance of the third and fourth volumes in 1856 and the fifth in 1860 are much more relevant.[1]

It is unlikely that many Americans read at the time they appeared Ruskin's earliest writing about architecture, the series of articles entitled 'The Poetry of Architecture' that J. C. Loudon published in his *Architectural Magazine* during the course of 1837–8. The material was still a fairly conventional presentation of late Picturesque ideas and ideals and the eighteen-year-old author was then identified only by the pseudonym 'Kata Phusin'.[2] The American landscape-gardener Andrew Jackson Downing (1815–52) would soon, beginning with the publication of his *Treatise on the Theory and Practice of Landscape Gardening* in 1841,[3] be offering

sellers had to buy off him direct, at a very small discount from the retail price. Moreover, Ruskin was a frank hater of America and her ways [but see below, pp. 180–1]. Wiley [presumably after he and Putnam had separated] had a very short reply from him [Ruskin] to a letter proposing the issuance [in New York] of an authorized edition, on terms such as Carlyle had readily accepted. Under the conditions Wiley felt justified in going ahead . . .' (op. cit., p. 34). The author of the chapter from which these quotations are taken is Henry Walcott Boynton.

1. As *Modern Painters* was not included among the list of Ruskin titles on architecture I circulated to American libraries some quarter of a century ago when compiling *American Architectural Books* I do not have the detailed information concerning the American publishing history of that work nor such knowledge of the location of the successive editions and issues as I have of Ruskin's books dealing with architecture.

First, a word about the English editions: The dates of the initial and later appearances of the various volumes seem to be as follows: vol. I [1st edn], 1843; 2nd edn, 1844; vol. II [1st edn], 1845; vol. I, 3rd rev. edn, vol. II, 2nd edn, 1846; 4th edn, 1846; 5th edn, 1851; vols. III and IV [1st edns] January and April, respectively, 1856; vol. V [1st edn], 1860. There is no need to give collations here. Further London editions of certain volumes were brought out in 1860, 1868, and 1869, and in 1873 a New Edition of the whole.

The publishing history of *Modern Painters* in America is somewhat less complicated. After the first edition of 1847–8 by Wiley and Putnam of vols. I and II the Wiley firm brought out further editions of vols. I–IV in 1857 and of vols. I–V in 1860, 1862, 1864, 1869, and 1885. The 1885 Wiley edition of the [*Works*] included not only the Prefaces to the first three London editions but also the Preface to the New Edition of 1873. In all the issues of this Wiley edition vol. I occupies vol. 1; vols. II and III, vol. 2; vol. IV, vol. 3; and vol. V, vol. 4. Thus the first American publication of vols. I and II is certainly that of 1847–8; vols. III and IV became available in a Wiley edition, a year after their 1856 London appearance, in 1857; and vol. V in 1860, the same year as the London edition of that terminal volume. For this work therefore, as for *The Stones of Venice*, all five volumes were available in American editions by that later date and, in this case also, included eventually all four Prefaces.

2. Κατά Φύσιν = according to nature.

3. New York & London, Wiley and Putnam; Boston, C. C. Little & Co., 1841, 451 p., front.; 2nd edn rev. and newly ill., New York & London, Wiley & Putnam, 1844, 497 p., illus., 16 pl. incl. front.

much the same Loudonian principles of house-design, first in a chapter on 'Landscape or Rural Architecture' in that book and, the following year, in a new work concerned with *Cottage Residences*.[1] This included eleven plates[2] of projects for cottages and villas, some of them designed by himself but mostly by two architects among his close friends, A. J. Davis (1803–92) and the Scottish-born John Notman (1810–65). Two later editions of each of these books appeared before 1849 when Ruskin's more mature writing on architecture first reached the English and American public under his own name. 'The Poetry of Architecture' was, however, serialized in 1855 in *The Crayon* in America, probably with Ruskin's permission.[3] Not until 1873 was an American edition of *The Poetry of Architecture* brought out as a book by John Wiley and Son,[4] but this preceded any such publication in England. Nine additional Wiley issues to 1890 give evidence of the continued market for even this earliest of Ruskin's writings. The demand for his books must have been, in the opinion of the publisher, at something of a peak in 1873 to have justified the reprinting of such juvenilia already available to Americans in the files of *The Crayon*.

The Wiley firm had from the first made the publication of Ruskin's works a speciality. The imprint was Wiley and Putnam to 1848, John Wiley until some time in 1864, next John Wiley and Son to 1875, and then John Wiley and Sons, as it is still today when the firm continues to be an important publishing house, especially in scientific fields. John Wiley's edition of *The Seven Lamps*,[5] complete with all the original plates, was brought out in New York in the same year, 1849, as the first London edition. That had not been true for *Modern Painters*, volumes I and II, despite Putnam's presence as agent in London. The rapidity with which a new

1. New York & London, Wiley and Putnam, 1842, 187 p., illus., 11 pl. incl. front.

2. The eleven plates are of designs for ten houses in this and the 2nd (*sic*) edn of 1844, which is properly a mere re-issue of the 1st with no changes. With the 3rd edn of 1847 the collation changes to 180 p., illus., 15 pl. incl. front. (1 col.), since designs for fifteen houses are provided. These three editions are all by Wiley and Putnam, Wiley alone taking over in this case only with the first issue of the 4th edn in 1852. On the other hand, beginning with the 4th edn of 1849 of the *Treatise*, publication of that work was carried on by George P. Putnam in New York in association with Longman, Brown, Green & Longmans in London.

Further publishing history of these two Downing books is irrelevant here; but Downing's *Architecture of Country Houses*, New York, D. Appleton & Co.; Philadelphia, G. S. Appleton, 1850, 484 p., illus., 36 pl., with eight further issues, all New York, D. Appleton & Co., to 1866, might be mentioned.

3. See below, p. 180–1.

4. 246 p., illus., in all Wiley issues. The *Poetry* is found bound with other Ruskin material in vol. 4 of an 1891, Philadelphia, Renwee, Wattley and Walsh edition of the [*Works*] on pp. [3]–178, as also in an 1894, New York, Bryan, Taylor & Co., 'Edition de luxe'. The latter seems to be a re-issue of the Philadelphia edition. The Brantwood edition, despite Allen's arrangement with the Merrill firm in New York, I consider an English and not an American imprint.

5. 186 p., 14 pl., in all Wiley issues before 1880; 206 p., 14 pl., in the later Wiley edition and its successive issues to 1891.

English work could then be produced without authority, one might say pirated, in the United States is remarkable considering that today we often have to wait a year or more even when sheets are imported. Before a second American edition – or issue, for it was identical with the first except for the imprint date 1852 – was brought out the Wiley firm was already publishing the first volume of *The Stones of Venice*.

But first the publishing history of *The Seven Lamps* in America over the next forty years should be summarized. Before 1885, when another New York publisher, John B. Alden, began to issue an edition of the [*Works*][1] in rivalry with Wiley's twelve-volume edition of 1884 (indicated as *The Works of John Ruskin* only on the bindings), there had been sixteen Wiley issues, including the first of 1849 and those included in the [*Works*] from 1884 on. Only the 1857 issue carries the imprint of Wiley & Halsted, a very brief partnership of John Wiley with Oliver Halsted, a cousin. The 1876 issue was already bound with other Ruskin material – as is true again of that of 1884 and the five later Wiley issues – in [volume 14] of the [*Works*].[2] There is no need to carry the story beyond 1891 for, thanks in good part to the new American copyright law of that year, Charles E. Merrill & Co. in New York were then able to bring out the authorized 'Brantwood' edition by arrangement with George Allen, Ruskin's publishing agent, and Wiley's effective monopoly came to an end. Finally the Cook and Wedderburn edition made all earlier ones, English or American, obsolete.

It is not certain, of course, that there were no more Wiley issues than those referred to above and recorded in *American Architectural Books*, which includes all located in major libraries. The occasions when *The Seven Lamps* was issued in successive years – 1865, 1866; 1876, 1877; and 1884, 1885, 1886 – would seem to indicate, in the first and second cases at least, that those were points when interest was still as great or greater than in the mid fifties shortly after the book was first published. The appearance of the rival Wiley and Alden editions of the [*Works*] in the mid eighties, however, suggests that by then a change had come in the character of the market for such books, as also a change in the status of their author: Ruskin was no longer considered by Americans to be a revolutionary critical writer but rather an established literary figure, as regards his writing on painting and on architecture at least, if not on political economy.[3]

1. In the 1885 Alden edition *The Seven Lamps* is bound with other Ruskin material in [vol. 1] of the [*Works*] with separate title-page, 210 p. and 14 pl.

2. The collation of both of these late editions is the same as for the Alden edition of 1885: 210 p., 14 pl.

3. But there can be no question that these books were now far more readily available than in the 1850s, especially in the many American public libraries that were founded in the 1870s and 80s. Moreover, a new cycle of Ruskin influence on men born in the 1860s began at this point. See below, p. 206.

An unfortunate 'Ruskin Commonwealth' founded by J. A. Wayland, editor of the journal *The*

In 1851 the first volume of *The Stones of Venice*, sub-titled by Ruskin 'The Foundations', was published in London. As with *The Seven Lamps*, Wiley in the same year brought out an American edition,[1] but with a serious omission. For the former he had been able to provide all the illustrations as well as the text. This time, although the text cuts were included and even the 'List of Plates', the plates themselves are missing. The *Stones* did not, apparently, have at first the same appeal to mid-nineteenth-century Americans as the *Lamps* – I would, indeed, concur with their implicit judgement. No further American editions or issues of volume I of the *Stones* appeared before 1860, though Wiley issues of the *Lamps* came out in 1852, 1855, 1857, and 1859. Moreover, after volumes II and III of the *Stones* were published in London in the course of 1853, Wiley did not offer them to American readers until 1860. Was there, perhaps, some temporary breakdown in the methods by which early copies, sheets, or proofs were expeditiously obtained from London that had made possible simultaneous New York editions of the *Lamps*, of *Pre-Raphaelitism*, and of volume I of the *Stones* before, and would again? The omission of the plates from the Wiley edition of volume I of the *Stones* in 1851, which was not repaired in later Wiley issues, may perhaps suggest that such difficulties had already begun that soon. On the other hand over the years 1855 to 1860 *The Crayon* in New York was publishing many extracts from Ruskin's writings, including the above-mentioned serialization of 'The Poetry of Architecture', with Ruskin's at least implicit authorization.

However that may be, in 1860 Wiley did issue a complete three-volume edition[2] of *The Stones of Venice*, though still without the plates, as has been noted above. (There was no complete new English edition of the whole work before 1874.) Though not as popular over-all in the United States as the *Lamps*, new Wiley issues of the *Stones* appeared in successive years in 1864 and 1865, in 1872 and 1873, and, most surprisingly, in every year from 1880 to 1890!

Coming Nation (circulation 60,000), attempted to carry out Ruskin's economic theories in the 1890s. The story is briefly told by D. H. Dickason in chapter 16 of *The Daring Young Men* (Bloomington, Ind., 1953). Wayland's settlement, at first of nineteen families, was outside Tennessee City, Tenn. It collapsed in 1901.

1. 435 p., illus. Ruskin's *Pre-Raphaelitism* was also published in New York by Wiley in 1851.

2. All issues in 3 vols., illus., until 1885. The volumes of the 1882 issue are indicated on the binding as vols. 5, 6, 7 of the [*Works*]. The 1885 edition is 3 vols. in 2, with binding indications that these are vols. 5 and 6 of the [*Works*]. In the Alden edition of that year vols. I and II form [vol. 5] of the [*Works*] and vol. III is bound with other Ruskin material in [vol. 6] of the [*Works*]. In the Renwee, Wattley and Walsh edition, Philadelphia, 1891, of the [*Works*] the *Stones* occupy vols. 1, 2, and 3, as also in the 'Edition de luxe' of the *Complete Works*, New York, Bryan, Taylor & Co., 1894.

The Saint Louis Public Library alone reports an 'Illustrated Holiday Edition' (Boston, Estes & Lauriat, 1894). As Lauriat was, later at least, primarily a bookseller one must suspect this is merely the New York, Bryan, Taylor edition of that year with a special title-page. Even Saint Louis lacks vol. 2 of this.

This bit of publishing history suggests that *The Stones of Venice* was not as familiar to interested Americans in the 1850s as *The Seven Lamps*, particularly not the second and third volumes, which had to be imported from London, despite the six excerpts in volume II of *The Crayon*.[1] However the work took its proper place in the Ruskinian canon in America as soon as the Civil War was over – a war in which Ruskin's personal sympathies had been with the defeated, and henceforth architecturally unproductive, South rather than with the triumphant North.[2] Further evidence of this rising interest is the fact that Wiley picked up and published in 1866, the year William Robert Ware (1832–1915) initiated professional instruction in architecture[3] in the United States at the Massachusetts Institute of Technology in Boston, *An Inquiry into some of the Conditions affecting 'The Study of Architecture in our Schools...'*,[4] which Ruskin had read before the Royal Institute of British Architects at the Ordinary General Meeting of 15 May 1865 and which was printed in the *Sessional Papers* of the R.I.B.A., vol. XIX (1864–5). Never very popular, this was usually bound from 1875 on with other Ruskin material in the Wiley issues, though always provided with a separate title-page. As in the case of *The Poetry of Architecture*, there was no separate English publication of the *Inquiry* in book form.

Far more important in the Ruskin architectural canon than the *Inquiry* were the *Lectures on Painting and Architecture*, delivered by Ruskin at Edinburgh in November 1853, which were first published in London in 1854. In the clarity with which they present the Ruskinian architectural message at the point when he himself was most assured of its importance, they rival *The Seven Lamps* and outrank volumes II and III of *The Stones of Venice*, which had appeared in London the year before. One can commend Wiley's judgement in issuing these lectures at once in New York in

1. Evidence of such rapidly growing interest before and even during the Civil War is the appearance of a Ruskin anthology: *The True and the Beautiful in Nature, Art, Morals and Religion*, 'selected from the works of John Ruskin ... by Mrs L. C. Tuthill', which Wiley published in 1858 and of which there was a 2nd edn in 1860 and a 3rd in 1863 – the two last properly merely new issues, I believe. Louisa Caroline Huggins Tuthill (1798–1879) had earlier written a *History of Architecture* (the first to include that of the United States), Philadelphia, Lindsay and Blakiston, 1848.

2. The Louisiana-born H. H. Richardson (1838–86), who had first studied at Harvard before the war, settled in New York after his return from Paris in the mid 1860s, moving in 1874 to Brookline, Mass. The Georgia-born John W. Root (1850–92) was in Liverpool in 1868–70; he then studied briefly at the College of the City of New York, and in 1872 went to Chicago to work for the firm of Carter, Drake & Wight (Asher Carter [1805–77], William H. Drake, and Peter B. Wight, concerning whom more will be said below).

3. Although Ware's architecture was, on occasion, somewhat Ruskinian (see below, p. 201), his programme for the M.I.T. School was closer to that of the Paris École des Beaux-Arts: W. R. Ware, *An Outline of a Course of Architectural Instruction* (Boston, J. Wilson & Sons, 1866), 36 p.

4. 29 p. Later issues 1869, 1872, 1875, 1882, 1884, 1885, 1886, 1889, 1891, and the usual Alden and Renwee, Wattley and Walsh editions of 1885 and 1891, respectively, though not included apparently in the Bryan, Taylor 'Edition de luxe' of 1894.

1854,[1] the same year as the first London edition. Yet the *Lectures* were never in as much demand in the United States as the two longer works to judge from the spacing of the fifteen Wiley issues that followed from 1856 to 1891, and they appeared in successive years only in 1884, 1885, and 1886.[2]

Many other works of Ruskin are, of course, concerned in part with architecture. His ideas on the subject kept changing, moreover, as emendations in the later English editions, far less frequent than the recurrent American issues, give evidence. But of the decade when his influence was first reaching America only one other work published in America need be mentioned: *The Two Paths*, which appeared from Wiley in New York in 1859,[3] the same year as the first London edition. This included, as chapter IV, 'The Influence of Imagination in Architecture' and, as chapter V, 'The Work of Iron in Nature, Art and Policy'. The work is of special significance in that it evidently suggested the title of *The New Path*,[4] an intentionally 'Ruskinian journal' edited, among others, by the architect Peter Bonnett Wight (1838–1925), to which Russell Sturgis (1838–1909), then Wight's partner, was a frequent contributor. In their work of the 1860s at least, these two have about the best claim to be rated as disciples of Ruskin in architecture.

The earliest linking of Ruskin's name with architecture in the United States is probably the mention of the 1847–8 American editions of *Modern Painters*, volumes I and II, and of the 1849 American edition of *The Seven Lamps* in an article on 'Church Architecture', signed J.W.P., that appeared in two parts in the *New-York Ecclesiologist*[5] in 1849. The Ruskin books were not reviewed but merely listed in what was, in effect, the bibliography of the article together with E. A. Freeman's *History of*

1. 189 p., 15 pl. incl. front. Later issues 1856, 1859, 1864, 1866, 1870, 1872, 1875, 1880, 1882, 1884, 1885, 1886, 1889, 1890, 1891, and also the Alden edition of 1885 and the Renwee, Wattley and Walsh edition of 1891. Beginning with the 1872 issue all later issues and editions are bound with other Ruskin material, usually *The Seven Lamps* but possibly in 1880 and 1891 with *An Inquiry*. The *Lectures* are in vol. [14] of the 1884 Wiley edition of the [*Works*] and later issues, but in vol. 1 of the Alden edition of 1885, and in vol. 5 of the Renwee edition of 1891. The *Lectures* seem to have been omitted from the Bryan, Taylor & Co. 'Edition de luxe' of 1894; at least no library reported such a holding.

2. The highly critical account of *The Opening of the Crystal Palace* was published in America only in the 1885 Alden edition of the [*Works*], vol. [10], 16 p., with separate title-page.

3. 217 p., front., illus., 1 pl. Later issues in 1865, 1866, 1869, 1870, 1872, 1875, 1876, 1881, 1883, 1884, 1885, 1886, 1887, 1888, 1891, and also in the 1885 Alden edition of the [*Works*], bound with other Ruskin material in vol. [9], in the 1891 Renwee edition in vol. 13, as also in the 1894 Bryan, Taylor edition. Beginning in 1865 the Wiley issues are often bound with other Ruskin material, in 1869 in vol. [1] of the [*Works*] and in 1885 and 1886 in vol. [8].

4. The *New Path* appeared considerably later and only for two years (1863–4) so that it has less importance than *The Crayon*, which first appeared in January 1855 and continued for six years.

5. Vol. I, no. 6, pp. 179 ff., and vol. II, no. 1, pp. 9 f. The publication year of the *New-York Ecclesiologist* was irregular, since vol. I, no. 1 had appeared in October 1848; the two parts of this article are dated August and October 1849.

Architecture (London, 1849), James Fergusson's *Historical Inquiry into the True Principles of Beauty in Art*, part I (also London, 1849), all the nine volumes of the English *Ecclesiologist* that had thus far appeared, and, curiously enough, Browning's *Paracelsus*.

The *New-York Ecclesiologist*, which ran only to a fifth and last volume – so announced for 1853 – was as specialized in its interests as its English model. With such vital matters to consider as the wearing of stoles by deacons and the 'Spirit of Christian Symbolism', its coverage of architecture was extremely limited. Its columns, like those of the English *Ecclesiologist*, chiefly provided descriptions, often very condemnatory, of new Anglican churches rather than reviews of books on architecture or general discussions of architectural theory. Frank Wills (b. 1827), the ablest of the few English church-architects who emigrated early to the United States, after in his case first working in Canada, provided a conventionally Camdenian article on 'Reality in Church Architecture' in volume I, number I.[1] This he supplemented, in the double number II–III for January 1849,[2] with a briefer note, signed with initials only, that included five church plans – the first illustrations of any sort in that journal. J. W. P.'s article which has just been mentioned came out later in that year.

More closely related to the latest developments in English church architecture, if not specifically to Ruskin, was an article in the *New-York Ecclesiologist* by the Rev. William A. McVickar on 'Brick as a Material for Churches' that appeared in November 1852.[3] In concluding, McVickar mentioned that he had 'intended to give an account of a few of the old brick churches of Lombardy, but the time [would] not allow'. This interest in Italian brick architecture, preceding by three years the appearance of G. E. Street's extremely influential *Brick and Marble Architecture of the Middle Ages*, was certainly premonitory. But for those Anglican enthusiasts who were following closely the English *Ecclesiologist* and therefore already aware of Butterfield's designs for All Saints, Margaret Street – of whom McVickar was probably one – it need not constitute evidence of any direct influence from *The Seven Lamps* or *The Stones of Venice*.

The clue to the *New-York Ecclesiologist*'s tepid interest in Ruskin perhaps lies in a misapprehension. The author of the unsigned article on 'The Spirit of Christian Symbolism' in the terminal number of the journal for December 1853,[4] while ready to cite Ruskin in this particular connexion, states that he is a Presbyterian![5]

One must look elsewhere for the earliest evidence of the impingement of Ruskin's ideas on men actually practising architecture in the United States. Gervase Wheeler, an English architect perhaps not long settled in America but already somewhat

---

1. pp. 34–40.   2. pp. 53–4.   3. Vol. IV, pp. 168–75.   4. Vol. VII, p. 187.

5. The High Anglicans in England doubtless considered Ruskin 'no better than a Presbyterian'; but he was, of course, a member of the Church of England, despite his violent anti-Popery that so distressed ecclesiologists in the fifties.

Americanized, as his house-plans and his ready acceptance of wooden construction indicate, was certainly one of the first to mention Ruskin in a book on architecture. In the preface to his *Rural Homes: or Sketches of Houses suited to American Country Life, with original plans, designs, etc.* (New York, Charles Scribner, 1851), a work so successful that it was many times re-issued in New York and elsewhere,[1] he wrote:

In conclusion, I would say that, in the hope of infusing something of its spirit herein, I have mentally headed every page with a sentence suggested as a matin and a song to every architect and amateur – Mr. Ruskin's great maxim, 'Until *common sense* finds its way into architecture, *there can be but little hope for it.*'

Common sense, one must allow, is not the quality either the American or the English followers of Ruskin in the third quarter of the century usually learned, at least from him, to apply in their buildings. There is, however, a good deal of already outmoded 'common sense' of a sort in Wheeler's house designs, for most of them are quite as much in the post-Loudon tradition as Downing's.

My own copy of Wheeler's book carries on the flyleaf a rather long handwritten dedication to Miss Alice Rudd:

A little pebble could bear but small share toward building a stately Temple, – and yet, duly mixed with mortar might be an atom of its foundation; – so, a little book how unpretending so ever it may be, – if but heartily written – can scarcely fail to contribute some one idea which, blending with a something in the reader's mind already there, may be the initiative to the perfect embodiment of a new and useful thought.

Wheeler's humility was doubtless sincere; and it is also true that by mentioning Ruskin in a house-pattern book, even if of a very modest and retardataire sort, he did contribute an 'atom' to the High Victorian Gothic architecture which would only begin to flourish in the United States some ten years later.

The next event of consequence, even though its connexion with Ruskin's ideas is more than debatable, was the building of All Souls Church in Fourth Avenue at 20th Street in New York (Plate 21). Even had the *New-York Ecclesiologist* not ceased publication in 1853, the year this was commissioned, it is unlikely its editors would have given much attention to what was, in their Camdenian terms, only a 'Socinian conventicle'. All the same, All Souls was a major addition to the church architecture of New York City as Unitarian churches had long been generally along the eastern seaboard. But the architect of the 'Church of the Holy Zebra', as it was jokingly called almost from the first, was English like Gervase Wheeler.

Jacob Wrey (or Wray) Mould was born in 1825.[2] He studied under Owen Jones

1. In 1852, 1853, twice in 1854, in 1855, and twice in 1868, as well as in undated editions by Charles Scribner and by other publishers in New York (Geo. E. Woodward and American News Co.), in Auburn, N.Y. (Alden, Beardsley and Co.), in Rochester, N.Y. (Wanzer, Beardsley and Co.), in New Orleans (Burnett & Bostwick), and in Detroit (Kerr & Doughty). The collation of all issues is: 298 p., front., illus., 9 pl.   2. d. 1884.

21. J.W. Mould: All Souls' church, New York City, commissioned 1853, built 1854–5; demolished

(1809–74) and is even reputed to have accompanied Jones to Spain in connexion with Jones's monumental publication of the Alhambra.[1] This must have been on a late trip, as the first volume was already completed and issued by 1842, when Mould was only seventeen, although the second volume did not come out until 1845. Young Mould's collaboration on the *Grammar of Ornament*, Jones's other major work, may have been of more consequence even though that did not appear until 1856, three years after Mould had settled in the United States. It is not impossible, moreover, that he had assisted Jones in the decoration of the original Crystal Palace with colour in 1851 and also in the preliminary designing of the various 'courts' – Alhambra Court, Greek Court, etc. – that were set up by Jones in the Crystal Palace at the time of its reconstruction at Sydenham in 1852–4.[2] Mould certainly did not need to read Ruskin in order to become aware of the potential importance of polychromy in architecture; it is also evident that he came neither from the Camdenian milieu of Butterfield nor from the Pre-Raphaelite group of painters and their friends with which Ruskin was so closely associated in the early 1850s.

Mould reached New York from England in 1853; late that year All Souls was commissioned,[3] and the church was built over the years 1854–5. Two years later he began the Second Unitarian Church at Clinton and Congress Streets in Brooklyn. After the Civil War in 1867 Mould became the assistant to Calvert Vaux (1824–95), a well established English-born architect, who was then Chief Architect of the Public Parks of New York City, and in 1870 succeeded him.[4]

1. Jones's named co-author for the first volume, J. Goury, was French. Their study of the Alhambra began in 1835–7.

2. The *New York Weekly Review* for 28 February 1865 noted that Mould had 'under Owen Jones, made color his early, especial and thorough study'. I owe this reference to Ellen Kramer and, indeed, without her generous assistance and special research the account of all the New York City buildings mentioned here would have been sadly incomplete.

David Van Zanten, who has been studying the life and work of Mould, informs me in a letter that Mould probably 'earned his bread as Jenny Lind's song writer' before he came to America. 'Her famous Shepherd's Song, for example, appears to be his craftsmanship.'

3. In a report given in a seminar which I conducted in the spring of 1957 at the Institute of Fine Arts of New York University, Alan Hodge provided the information that the members of the church set up a building committee in October 1852 which was superseded by a new committee in the following year. Moses Grinnell, a member of the second committee, was responsible for bringing Mould to New York. The church was dedicated on Christmas Day 1855. Mrs Kramer, to whose seminar notes I owe this information, further recalls that in the discussion following Hodge's report influence from Léon Vaudoyer's cathedral of Marseille, begun in 1852, was suggested, as also from the German Rundbogenstil. The Vaudoyer design seems no more likely a source than Bindesbøll's boldly striped church of 1850–2 at Hobro in Denmark, which was not mentioned.

4. Undated and almost certainly demolished works of Mould in the late fifties were the banking house of Matthew Morgan in William Street in New York and other unidentified things in Lenox, Mass., and Meriden, Conn. (*Architects' and Mechanics' Journal*, 16 March 1861, p. 233).

Mould's All Souls is of almost exactly the same date as the east end that G. G. Scott added in 1853 to Camden Church, Camberwell, the first new production with which Ruskin is believed to have been directly associated. Like the remodelled interior of that modest Georgian meeting-house in the Peckham Road – which was the Ruskin family's church, and to which Ruskin himself is supposed to have contributed the design of the windows in the apse – All Souls might be described as 'Round-arched High Victorian Gothic' except for the fact that, unlike the Camden Church, it is really not Gothic at all. It is, moreover, as the nickname indicates considerably more polychromatic, especially on the exterior. Not only are the arches banded, as at Camberwell, but all the walls are of alternating stripes of Caen stone and red brick. Once Street's *Brick and Marble Architecture* appeared, in the year All Souls was finished, and reached America – there was never an American edition, but it was doubtless soon known to all those interested – All Souls struck observers as being very Italianate, and hence in a loose way Ruskinian. Actually, with its rather chunky plan – totally unecclesiological naturally – and its broad, squat lantern over the crossing, it is more Byzantine[1] than medieval Italian in character. All Souls, therefore, is not properly to be considered evidence of the early influence of Ruskin. And it would be *very* early, even in English terms, since only All Saints, Margaret Street, among major English High Victorian Gothic churches, was under way before it was commissioned; while the University Museum at Oxford, in which Ruskin took so great an interest, was designed by Benjamin Woodward only in the year the New York church was completed. Deane & Woodward's earlier museum for Trinity College, Dublin, was begun in 1853, but that, while distinctly Venetian in evident response to the *Stones*, is even more definitely *quattrocento* than All Souls was Byzantine.

Mould's church for the Second Unitarian Society in Brooklyn was built in 1857–8.[2] A building committee was organized on 7 May 1857 and ground was broken the following month. The dedication was on 2 March 1858. In the *Church Register* for 1919 of the Second Unitarian Society there is the following description: 'Mr. Mould's design was one of great originality in its day; a replica, so far as American building resources then made it possible, of a typical chapel in Northern Italy, with its apse and campanile.' Mould may well, this time, have drawn on Street's book, and actual Ruskinian influence seems somewhat less improbable here than at All Souls. The variegated slate roof, later removed, sounds especially High Victorian, and the whole concept parallels once again a nearly contemporary English design, Burges's competition-winning project of 1856 for the Crimean Memorial Church in Istanbul based on S. Andrea at Vercelli. Moreover, by 1857 it

---

1. In the *Architects' and Mechanics' Journal* (9 February 1861), p. 186, there appeared an illustrated article on 'Byzantine Windows' in which the claim was made that the 'Holy Zebra' was 'the most excellent ecclesiastic specimen' of Byzantine design in the United States.

2. I owe the facts concerning this Brooklyn church to the assiduous research of Mrs Kramer.

is likely that the members of the building committee had read *The Seven Lamps*, if not all three volumes of *The Stones of Venice*.

A more certain result of the reading of Ruskin by Americans in the fifties was the beginning of the seven-year run of a magazine devoted above all to propagating the ideas of the Pre-Raphaelites for whom Ruskin had for some years been such an eloquent spokesman. This was *The Crayon: A Journal Devoted to the Graphic Arts, and the Literature Related to Them*. William J. Stillman (1828–1901), the editor, was a painter and poet who had graduated from Union College, Schenectady, in 1848. While working later that year with Frederic E. Church,[1] the painter who was soon to be recognized, not alone by Americans, as a worthy heir to Turner (still alive, of course, at that point), Stillman came on *Modern Painters* of which the Wiley and Putnam editions of the first two volumes had just appeared. In 1849 he set out for London where, through Griffith, Turner's dealer, he met the master and, even before that, his apostle Ruskin. Later, in the summer of 1860, he accompanied Ruskin on a prolonged Alpine excursion.

Although unillustrated *The Crayon* was, in the words of Frank Luther Mott,[2] 'the best art journal of the period'; and while Stillman – and also his associate John Durand, the son of the painter Asher B. Durand – were especially interested in painting and poetry, *The Crayon* dealt considerably more with architecture than the *Cosmopolitan Art Journal*, which began the following year and ceased publication after five years, or the earlier *Bulletin of the American Art Union*[3] which, in the forties, had barely mentioned Ruskin.

But *The Crayon* was devoted to Ruskin, even though their idol refused – if in extremely cordial terms – to be a regular contributor and recommended W. M. Rossetti to be their London correspondent. Ruskin wrote Stillman thus:

I have much to thank America for – heartiest appreciation and a better understanding of what I am and mean, than I have ever met in England. Nothing gives me greater pleasure than the thought of being of use to an American; and, if I can, in any way, oblige any of your friends who are interested in Art, I beg that you will call on me.[4]

One may, therefore, consider that the inclusion of extracts from Ruskin's writings in *The Crayon*, including the serialization of 'The Poetry of Architecture', was at

1. For Church, see D. C. Huntington, *The Landscapes of Frederic Edwin Church* (New York, 1966); for Stillman, see Dickason, op. cit., chapter IV, pp. 33–46; for *The Crayon*, Dickason, op. cit., chapter V, pp. 47–64.

2. *A History of American Magazines* (Cambridge, Mass., 1938), II, p. 193.

3. During the years *The Crayon* was being issued there were some references to Ruskin in magazines of a more general character: *Putnam's Monthly Magazine* for September 1855 carries a relevant letter from the editor on pp. 335–6; and in July 1857 there is an article, probably by the well known art journalist Clarence Cook, that deals especially with Ruskin on pp. 108–9. Ruskin is mentioned again in 'Our Houses', in *Harper's Magazine* (September 1859), pp. 513–18.

4. *The Crayon*, I (2 May 1855), p. 283.

least implicitly authorized. Many of the extracts concern painting, but in volume II there is a series of six passages from *The Stones of Venice* that have to do with architecture. Other articles in volume II may be considered definitely Ruskinian in subject and tendency: 'Brick';[1] 'Colored Slates';[2] and 'Our Building Stones'.[3]

The article 'Brick in Architecture'[4] in volume III is really a review of Street's *Brick and Marble Architecture*, which had appeared the previous year. Moreover the author, reputedly the Bohemian-born architect Leopold Eidlitz (1823–1908),[5] recognized the significance of Mould's newly completed church as an example of the stylistically advanced use of brick (p. 23):

In the new Unitarian church . . . an attempt of this kind has been made, but, we think, unsuccessfully, owing in the first place to the unfortunate choice of materials, which are Caen stone, and a very dark red brick, giving too violent a contrast and no harmony of color [Eidlitz, of course, had not seen All Saints, Margaret Street, and his own extreme exercise in polychromy (Plate 22), the so-called 'Church of the Holy Oil-Cloth', would not be designed and built until the early 1870s]; and, again, to the fact, that the bands are of the same width which gives a formal air to the whole, and destroys all breadth of effect. Nevertheless, this is a step, though an imperfect one, in the right direction [surely pure Ruskinian criticism!]. We intend shortly to take up this subject of using colored materials, and discuss it thoroughly, believing that our architects have heretofore neglected a most important element of beauty in their designs.

Following this came a paragraph in support of 'structural polychrome' quoted from Street's book.

In that year, 1856, and the next *The Crayon* published, as promised, the series of articles on 'Our Building Stones',[6] and also one on Ruskin by Brownlee Brown.[7] Ruskin himself was represented only by his notes on the 1857 Royal Academy Exhibition.[8] In 1858 the editors returned to the subject of the 'Holy Zebra',[9] quoting that nickname in a humorous defence of All Souls and concluding with the statement that '. . .if premature for our present tastes, it will be abundantly appreciated by the

1. *The Crayon*, II, pp. 271 f.   2. ibid., II, pp. 115 f.
3. ibid., pp. 10, 53, 355, 367.   4. ibid., III, pp. 23 f.
5. Although his book, *The Nature and Function of Art, more especially of Architecture* (New York, 1881), appeared relatively late in his career, Eidlitz was an important figure among New York architects in the fifties and already an active critical mind. He was until recently rather forgotten, since most of his prominent works have been demolished, but Schuyler had devoted a three-part article to him some months after his death in the *Architectural Record*, XXIV (September, October, November 1908), pp. 164–79, 277–92, 365–78, that William Jordy has reprinted nearly in full in Schuyler (Jordy and Coe, eds.), op. cit., I, pp. 136–87. Jordy has much to say about Eidlitz in his 'Introduction' – especially on pp. 21–34 – and there attributes to him this article in *The Crayon*. Eidlitz was by no means a devout Ruskinian; he once told his good friend Schuyler, however, 'By all means an architect ought to read Ruskin; it helps him keep his enthusiasm' (p. 161).
6. *The Crayon*, IV, pp. 248, 371.   7. ibid., IV, pp. 329 ff.
8. ibid., IV, pp. 286 ff.   9. ibid., V, pp. 20–2.

next generation, [for it is] a work of merit and genius, second to none in the city'. (Unfortunately the next generation did not agree.) But *The Crayon* did not call it Ruskinian – or, for that matter, Byzantine:

To speak of the style we think it merits the praise of being peculiar to the Unitarian Church of All Souls, designed by J. Wrey Mould, Esq., who, by that effort, has placed himself in the foremost rank of the profession. We may simply add that the building may be classed as Anglo-Italian.

Further extracts from Ruskin's writings were published that year, 1858, and even more the next[1] when the description of *The Oxford Museum*, just published by Sir Henry Acland and Ruskin, was reviewed.[2] The unedifying row between G. G. Scott and Palmerston over the style of the Foreign Office was also reported.[3]

The Crayon was by no means purely Ruskinian in its approach to architecture – Horatio Greenough (1808–52),[4] sometimes considered the grandfather of 'Functionalism', appeared in volumes I and II, and both Henry Van Brunt (1832–1903) and Eidlitz wrote on cast iron in volume VI.[5] However, much of the material its editors presented – and to a sophisticated public very different from the small-town builders who must for the most part have been Wheeler's readers – confirms the evidence of the American publishing history of *The Seven Lamps* as to Ruskin's popularity in these years. This leads me to wonder again if there were not temporary difficulties in the importing, not to say pirating, process which would explain why no American edition of volumes II and III of *The Stones of Venice* was brought out by Wiley in 1853 or before 1860. Yet even the Edinburgh *Lectures* appeared from Wiley, as it were on time, in 1854 as has been noted.

The Ruskinian message had, by that time, reached one young man destined to be an architect who has already been identified as an editor of *The New Path* in the sixties. Peter B. Wight[6] was reading Ruskin's works while still a student at the Free Academy (later the College of the City of New York) before his graduation in 1855. But it would be six years before he designed the unmistakably Ruskinian National Academy in New York (Plate 25). Priority in Ruskinian design has been claimed, therefore, for another architect of Wight's generation, Edward Tuckerman Potter (1831–1904). Potter and his brothers were closely associated with Union College, Schenectady, N.Y., of which their grandfather Eliphalet Nott was president for over sixty years. E. T. Potter graduated from Union in 1853, and his younger brother, William Appleton[7] Potter (1842–1909), a more prolific and successful

---

1. ibid., V, pp. 5, 66, 94, 204; VI, pp. 28, 51, 94, 129, 283.   2. ibid., VI, p. 251.
3. ibid., VI, p. 315.   4. 'A Sketch', ibid., I, p. 243; 'American Architecture', ibid., II, p. 224.
5. ibid., VI, pp. 15, 20.   6. Dickason, op. cit., pp. 98–106.
7. The Witheys (H. F. and E. R.) in their *Biographical Dictionary of American Architects* (*Deceased*) (Los Angeles, 1956) erroneously give 'C' as this brother's middle initial, confusing him evidently with Bishop William Codman Potter. Various other architects mentioned in this article are entirely omitted as the absence of their life-dates here gives evidence.

22. Leopold Eidlitz: Holy Trinity church, New York City, built 1873–4; demolished
(from *New York Sketch-Book*, III)

architect than he in the 1870s and 80s, in 1864. Another brother, Eliphalet Nott Potter (1836–1901), became president-elect in 1871, a trustee in 1872, and was president from 1873 to 1884.[1] The design in question is that of the rotunda, now called Alumni Hall and used as a theatre truly 'in the round', which still dominates the Union College campus (Plate 23).

Union was founded in 1795 and in 1804 Eliphalet Nott became its president. Nine years later he employed J. J. Ramée (1764–1842) to lay out a complete new grouping of college buildings on the edge of a high plateau to the east of Schenectady.[2] Ramée was a French émigré, and I have elsewhere described his plan for the college as 'Ledolcian' from a certain resemblance to Ledoux's town of Arc-Senans. Only the two L-shaped blocks on the west were erected by Nott in 1813–14 before the college's funds gave out. These flanked the broad campus which was to terminate at the east in an exedra. (That feature was finally carried out in a style hardly more Ruskinian than Ledolcian by W. A. Potter during his brother's presidency and has, unhappily, just been demolished.) On the chord of the exedra Ramée proposed to set a tall rotunda.

In the 1850s Nott decided to proceed with the construction of this rotunda, and it is not surprising that he still expected to follow Ramée's design. In 1858, after he laid the cornerstone, foundations were actually begun for the sixteen-sided structure planned by Ramée. Owing to the financial difficulties of the late fifties, followed by the Civil War, no further construction was even considered until 1867 during the brief presidency of Nott's successor, L. P. Hickok, who had been acting president since 1861 in Nott's last years.[3]

In 1858 a model of the rotunda existed. It is evident from a surviving photograph (Plate 24) that this represented Ramée's design of 1813; that the foundations then laid had conformed to the model is equally apparent in a construction photograph of 1872.[4] Nonetheless there was by that time attached to the model a later emendation: Instead of Ramée's pedimented portico, recalling that of the Roman Pantheon, a three-arched porch was proposed, the round arches of which are banded and supported by columns and capitals considerably more medievally Italianate than

1. Most of the information concerning the Potters and Union College comes from A. V. V. Raymond, *Union University*, 3 vols. (New York, 1907).

2. See Christopher Tunnard, 'Minerva's Union', *Architectural Review* (February 1947), pp. 57–62, for more detailed information concerning Ramée and his work at Union, including many relevant illustrations.

3. Raymond, op. cit., I, p. 58: 'For many years this building had appeared in all the college prints'; p. 345: 'Upon July 27, 1867, the Trustees on the motion of Judge Harris, authorized the finance committee to continue and complete the work ... substantially according to the plans'; but no further work was actually carried out until the next decade.

4. These photographs, with much other relevant pictorial material, are preserved in the Schaffer Library at Union, whose authorities kindly had them copied for me.

23. E. T. Potter: Alumni Hall, Union College, Schenectady, N.Y., built 1872–5

Classical. This porch was never executed – in fact no foundations seem to have been provided for it in 1858; yet it may perhaps be accepted as the young E. T. Potter's contribution of this date and even recognized as vaguely Ruskinian.[1]

The rotunda, as finally executed over the years 1872–5 from the later designs of Potter (Plate 23), has nothing in common with the model that the construction of the late fifties was to have followed beyond its plan – for the earlier foundations were utilized – and its dome, which is hardly a Ruskinian feature. The supposition that in 1858 Potter proposed a round structure emulating the Pisa Baptistery and planned to ring it with arcades of pointed and banded arches of a fashion admittedly Ruskinian is therefore quite exaggerated.[2] Dating from the early seventies, Alumni Hall is only one of innumerable examples of the Italianate Victorian Gothic that was at its peak of popularity in the United States in those years.

But the question still arises as to whether Potter's design of 1872 was newly prepared at that time[3] or developed from one worked out on paper, if not in 1858, at least some time in the sixties. In support of the latter thesis, there is Potter's First Dutch Reformed Church in Schenectady, which carries on its front gable the date 1862, for this already has pointed and banded arches, even if it is not otherwise particularly Ruskinian.[4] Against it are the facts that construction of the rotunda proceeded in 1872 only after E. N. Potter became a trustee and that 35,000 dollars towards its cost was given by the president's two architect-brothers, Edward and William. It seems unlikely that a new project was prepared before Nott's death; and the Trustees' motion of 23 July 1867 at least implies that construction was at that time still expected to go forward according to the original design of Ramée.[5]

1. Yet it might as readily derive from Mould's All Souls as from Scott or Street.

2. Informed current opinion concerning Alumni Hall may be indicated by quoting again from Green, op. cit., p. 327: 'The more Italian phase of the Gothic Revival is best represented by a building which had been begun before the Civil War, the Nott Memorial Library [an earlier designation of the rotunda], at Union College, Schenectady, 1858–1876 ... by Edward Tuckerman Potter, inspired by the Romanesque baptistery at Pisa.' In all fairness I must add that this was taken directly from my own *Architecture: Nineteenth and Twentieth Centuries*, 2nd edn (Harmondsworth, 1963), p. 191!

3. In Potter's office ledger, preserved in the Avery Library at Columbia University, the Union commission appears as a new job in 1872. I am most grateful to Adolf Placzek, Avery Librarian, for having relevant entries transcribed for me.

4. The date of E. T. Potter's portfolio, *The Capitals of the Banker Screen in the First Reformed Dutch Church, Schenectady, N.Y....* (New York, photographed by Geo. G. Rockwood, 1864), 7 p., 12 pl., a rather early example of architectural illustration with real photographs, suggests that the church was some two years in construction. St James, Lewiston, Ill., by Potter followed shortly. For other work of his from 1867 on, see the next note.

5. Neither the office ledger nor the cash book in the Avery Library have entries earlier than 1867, but several churches – those I know not dissimilar to that of 1862 in Schenectady – are listed: St John, East Hartford, Conn. (undated but actually built in 1867–9); 1867: Church of the Good Shepherd, Hartford (actually built in 1868–9); St Paul, Staten Island, N.Y.; Baptist Church,

24. J.-J. Ramée: Rotunda, Union College, Schenectady, N.Y., model of project of 1813, with porch by E. T. Potter designed in 1858

That no complete Ruskinian, or generically High Victorian Gothic, project for Union College existed before the early seventies or, just possibly, the late sixties would explain why it is never mentioned in *The Crayon* or *The New Path*.[1] For example, in the first volume of the latter journal Wight, as editor, wrote in 1863[2] on 'What has been done and what can be done', mentioning only Mould's Second Unitarian Church in Brooklyn of 1857–8 and his Parish School for Trinity Church on 25th Street near Broadway of 1861–3[3] as newly erected examples of approved polychromy. For the ensuing years of the sixties he himself was the most important Ruskinian architect, though never very productive.

Wight had had only a year's experience as a draughtsman in the office of T. R. Jackson when he set out for Chicago to begin his own practice in 1858. Since he came back to New York the following year it is unlikely that he then built much in Chicago; in any case, if he did design a modest building or two, they would almost certainly have been destroyed in the Chicago fire of 1871 which preceded his eventual

Philadelphia; 1868: St Andrew, Providence; Diocesan Church, Davenport, Iowa; 1870: St John, Jackson Hill, Florida; 1871: St John, Yonkers, N.Y.; Harvard Church, Brookline, Mass. (original interior reproduced in the *Architectural Sketch Book*, II, 1874, plate XXXVI). Entries for several of these commissions continue to 1872 and the earliest dates recorded evidently represent the commissioning. It seems probable, therefore, that if a new design had been commissioned by Union College in 1867 or any of the years before 1872 it would have been entered in one or another of these office records.

1. In the years at the end of the run of *The Crayon* and before the beginning of that of *The New Path*, the short-lived *Architects' and Mechanics' Journal* published four editorials that refer to Ruskin's ideas about architecture: 'On utility, beauty and truthfulness in architecture', 21 July 1860, p. 151; 'On real and false beauty in architecture', 25 August 1860, p. 201; 'A plea for constructive truth', 22 December 1860, p. 111; 'The source of progress in architecture', 9 February 1861, p. 181. In the last, Ruskin's plea for the acceptance of one universal style in the *Lamps* is criticized. I owe this information again to Mrs Kramer.

2. *The New Path*, I, pp. 52–9, 70–5, 80–4, 130–3. Wight also fails to mention Trinity Church in Marshall, Michigan, then in construction but doubtless not yet completed. Commissioned on 2 July 1860, this High Victorian Gothic edifice by George Lloyd, an English architect newly arrived in America, unlike Mould's New York churches attracted no national attention and its completion was probably delayed by the difficulties of the war years. Lloyd went on to a successful career as a church-builder in Detroit, but was never specifically a follower of Ruskin, as was Wight when he prepared the project for the National Academy in New York in 1861. I am grateful to Mr Van Zanten for calling my attention to the church in Marshall, a small middle-western town, which has been as little noticed nationally later as when it was being built.

3. In the minutes of the vestry of Trinity Church for 12 November 1860 mention is made of a bill for 400 dollars to be paid to Jacob W. Mould and there are records of further payments to him on 10 June and 9 December 1861. Curiously enough, on 11 March 1861 there is also listed a payment to be made to Richard Upjohn & Son 'for plans for school house and porch at Trinity Chapel'; but it was Mould's plans that were used. The school is mentioned in the *Architects' and Mechanics' Journal* (16 March 1861), p. 233, as 'now erecting'. According to other records in the parish office the school was completed in 1863 and cost 37,000 dollars. It was closed in 1912. I am most grateful to Miss Helen Cline, Parish Recorder, for these facts obtained for me by Mrs Kramer.

return there in 1872. During the next three years Wight had some work, reputedly a hospital in Binghamton, N.Y., and definitely a bank in Middletown, N.Y.

The only hospital erected in Binghamton at this time was the United States (later New York) Inebriates' Asylum, begun by Isaac G. Perry (b. 1822)[1] in 1858, very likely the first American institution for the treatment of alcoholics. It is possible that Wight was employed to assist Perry. However that may be, the original building, which was enlarged by Perry in 1875–9 and again in the nineties, is a characteristic Early Victorian Gothic design, more or less 'Collegiate' in character, with no polychromy or other evidence of High Victorian influence.[2]

The Middletown Bank, which was located at 21 North Street in Middletown, opened in 1862.[3] It might, of course, have been designed several years earlier, but the building site was only acquired by the bank in 1861. No trace of the original façade survives since a reconstruction of 1924. A small photograph, reproduced in a brochure of the 1930s commemorating the Golden Jubilee of Middletown, shows that Wight's brownstone façade was of only one storey, though capped with a rather tall gable. Rectangular piers with delicate corner colonnettes carried coved and pointed arches over two windows and a door. A small trilobe window occupied the centre of the gable and there were rather elaborate pointed and cusped machicolations below the raking cornices. This certainly had a considerably more up-to-date flavour than the Binghamton institution, but it is hard to see it as specifically Ruskinian.

In the first year of the Civil War Wight was employed by the United States Sanitary Commission, doubtless because of his previous connexion with the design of the Binghamton hospital. He built the first field hospital in Washington; but when he failed to receive an officer's commission in the Army he returned to New York. There he opened an office in 1862 and took on Russell Sturgis[4] as his partner the

1. Perry is best known for his work on the New York State Capitol in Albany. Appointed Commissioner of the New Capitol in 1883, he took over responsibility for completing the building which had been begun by Fuller & Laver in 1869 and then much modified from the original design by Richardson and Eidlitz from 1875 on. The broad stairs leading up two storeys to the main western entrance and the execution of the great stair-hall on the east side of the building, planned by Richardson just before his death in 1886, are Perry's work. The Capitol was declared finished on 1 January 1899. I must thank Norman S. Rice of the Albany Institute of History and Art for this information.

2. I am most grateful to Donald Schneider of Harpur College, Binghamton, for investigating the rumour concerning Wight's responsibility for the hospital, as also for a reproduction of an early wood engraving of its façade.

3. Mark Boujikian, a student of Donald Schneider and a resident of Middletown, kindly obtained the information given here and provided a photostat of an illustration of the bank. An earlier visit I had made to Middletown had led to a mis-identification of the bank with its commonplace surviving neighbour.

4. Sturgis was born in 1838, the same year as Wight and Richardson, of a Boston family in Baltimore. He was a fellow student with Wight at the Free Academy in New York, from which

following year. Wight's mature career – and undeniable Ruskinian influence on American architecture – began only after he won, in 1861, the competition, in which four other architects[1] were also entered, for the National Academy of Design (Plate 25). Used as we are to the total stoppage of civil construction during twentieth-century wars, it is always surprising to find how much building went on, even if at a reduced pace, during wars a century ago. Doubtless it was the lack of other new buildings of comparable prominence and expense, not to speak of the controversial novelty of the academy's design, that focused, then and later, so much attention on it.

The *Architects' and Mechanics' Journal*, after the competition had been decided in Wight's favour in March 1861, obligingly gave a detailed description of his design. This is of real interest since it evidently differed considerably from that of the building as executed in the years 1863–5.[2] Although in the main Wight and his fellow-competitors were only offered an opportunity to produce *Fassadenarchitektur* – not necessarily an un-Ruskinian procedure! – Wight had occasion in the store-fronts

he graduated in 1856, a year later than the latter. He studied architecture first in New York and then abroad at the Akademie in Munich, returning to New York in 1862: Dickason, op. cit., pp. 106–16. The Wight–Sturgis partnership was as loose as the Nesfield–Shaw partnership of the same years in England and their work was individually, not collaboratively, designed, as seems also to have been true of H. H. Richardson's partnership with Charles D. Gambrill (1832–80), previously a partner of George B. Post (1837–1913), from 1867 to 1874.

1. 'Messrs Hunt [Richard Morris, 1827–95], Eidlitz, Mould and Van Brunt [Henry, later a partner of William Robert Ware and the translator of Viollet-le-Duc's *Entretiens* as *Discourses on Architecture* (vol. I), Boston, 1875] on the 14th inst., handed in designs in competition for the National Academy of Design ...' (*Architects' and Mechanics' Journal*, 19 January 1861, p. 150). 'The interesting competition ... has resulted in the prize being awarded to Mr. P. B. Wight, a young architect...who has recently returned to this city from Chicago. As the Council of the National Academy did not solicit *plans* for the new building it remained only for the architects to submit designs for the two fronts, adapted to the interior arrangement that had previously been determined upon. It was required that five stores fronting on Fourth Avenue should be provided, and that the main entrance to the upper part, from the street, should be at the second storey on Twenty-Third Street ... ': ibid. (23 March 1861), p. 245.

2. The site for the new academy building had been purchased in the autumn of 1860 from William Niblo for 50,000 dollars and, as has been noted, the competition followed within a few months. Shortage of funds – not surprising in wartime – held up the initiation of construction and the corner-stone was not laid until 21 October 1863. This event was celebrated by a lunch at the Century Club and a procession to the site, with a band. Addresses were made by the painter Daniel Huntington, the Academy's president, by the historian – and later Minister to Great Britain – my great great aunt's husband, George Bancroft, by the poet William Cullen Bryant, and by Parke Godwin, part-owner and later editor of the *New York Evening Post* in succession to his father-in-law Bryant. Cards were sent out for the ceremonial opening of the new building on 17 April 1865, but on account of President Lincoln's assassination on 15 April the event was postponed to 27 April. There were as before many speeches by Bryant and others. This information comes from a *précis* prepared for me by Mrs Kramer of the contents of a rare pamphlet: The National Academy of Design, *Ceremonies on the Occasion of Laying the Cornerstone ... and the Inauguration of the Building*...(New York, 1865).

25. P. B. Wight: National Academy of Design, New York City, designed 1861–2, built 1863–5; demolished (from *The Builder*, 12 January 1867)

26. P. B. Wight: Project for Street Hall, Yale University, New Haven, Conn., 1864

of the ground storey along Fourth Avenue to exploit iron structurally, something which Ruskin would have strongly disapproved. This was symptomatic of Wight's later interest in fireproof metal construction. The description, which is very complete, concludes thus:

The style of the architecture is adapted from the Italian Romanesque, the round arch being used throughout, and chromatic effect sought as well as light and shade. The building is estimated to cost when completed about $60,000. No sculpture will be used to adorn the exterior, the purpose of the building being only indicated by the initials 'N.A.' in colored tiles inserted in the spandrils on either side of the entrance.

It is curious to note that at this stage Wight's design, unlike that for the contemporary Middletown Bank, was round-arched and that the style is specifically described as 'adapted from the Italian Romanesque'. Thus it was, in some sense, almost as much a sequel to Mould's churches of the fifties as an application of some of Ruskin's ideas.

Not surprisingly, *The New Path* in its second volume described the exterior at length in June 1864[1] – 'An important Gothic building' – when the construction of the outside walls was nearly completed, and followed this up with another article later in the year[2] on the 'Interior of the New Building'; while in 1866 there appeared a sumptuous publication by Wight, *National Academy of Design: Photographs of the New Building*,[3] after it was finally completed in 1865, that included another very detailed description. The cost of the building was 'about $150,000'.

The rather naive Ruskinism of the National Academy as executed, now provided with pointed instead of round arches and with a top storey echoing even more directly than that originally proposed Ruskin's beloved Doge's Palace, requires little comment. But it is worth mentioning the wood engraving, published in *The Builder* in London two years after the building was finished, both as evidence of the international attention Wight's design received and for the higher quality the perspective view reveals (Plate 25). An old head-on photograph suggests a distinctly two-dimensional sort of façade design and one overpowered by the entrance motif; the wood engraving presents the quieter side façade, with its range of ground-storey stores, and makes evident the plastic interest of the stairs and even of the rather fussy cornice, recalling that of the Middletown Bank, with its cresting intended to mask the skylight behind.

Wight's next important New York building, the Mercantile Library across the East River in Brooklyn, was also illustrated in *The Builder* in 1872, several years after its completion in 1869. Again the wood engraving is more attractive than

1. *New Path*, II, pp. 17–32.
2. ibid., II, pp. 81–5.
3. ...with an introductory essay and description, New York, S. P. Avery, 1866, 10 p., 8 mounted pl. Long ago demolished, the building stood three turnings north of Mould's 'Holy Zebra' which had been completed just ten years earlier.

modern photographs taken before the building was demolished in 1960. But this was a very competent, if hardly original, example of High Victorian Gothic such as might have been built in England at any time in the previous ten years.[1]

Somewhat like Godwin in the 1860s in England, Wight was a competition-winner; but again like Godwin, although he was not quite so unlucky at losing opportunities to execute his winning designs, after a very promising start he had little success in the New York of the boom years. In 1871 he closed his office there and moved to Chicago, where his work, carried out in partnership at first with William H. Drake and later with Drake and Asher Carter, was rarely Victorian Gothic, much less Ruskinian. What is apparently the only surviving work of the firm in Chicago, the Springer Block[2] at 126–146 North State Street of 1872, was extensively remodelled by Adler & Sullivan in 1888, using broad oriels of advanced skyscraper construction such as they had proposed a year or two before for the Auditorium Building, but eventually omitted there in favour of bearing walls of masonry throughout the exterior. In that year and the next Wight also supervised the construction of H. H. Richardson's American Merchants' Union Express Company building in Chicago. This was of equally un-Ruskinian design although not, at that early date, at all characteristically Richardsonian.

But I am getting ahead of the story. At a certain level of doctrinal acceptance the peak of Ruskinian influence came in the mid sixties with the publication of *The New Path*. The Society for the Advancement of TRUTH IN ART (*sic*) was formed, less than two years after the demise of *The Crayon*, in January and February 1863. Among the founders was T. C. Farrer (of English birth), who had studied art with Ruskin and later fought with the Union Army from 1860 to 1863, but there were seven charter members in all, including both Wight and Sturgis though no other architects. Charles Herbert Moore (1840–1930), however, is well known as an architectural historian even if, as was the case with Sturgis, his most important writing, *Development and Character of Gothic Architecture* (London and New York, 1890), appeared relatively late in his life after Moore had become a Professor of Art at Harvard. Of the lot he was the only one who remained a faithful Ruskinian, however.[3]

By May 1863 the new Society had brought out the first number of their journal and it survived for twenty-three more numbers, ceasing publication with that for December 1865.[4] The first number included a letter from Ruskin and the beginning

1. The Mercantile Library of Brooklyn was organized in December 1857, and the building was completed and opened on 18 January 1869, having been some two years in construction (according to information supplied by the Long Island Historical Society). Reputedly there had been a competition, as for the National Academy, which Wight won in 1866 or 1867.

2. J. William Rudd (comp.), *Historic American Buildings Survey, Chicago and Nearby Areas* (Park Forest, Ill., 1966), pp. 30–1, illus.

3. Dickason, op. cit., chapters 7 and 8, *passim*.

4. ibid., p. 72.

of a long article by Sturgis on the aims of the Society, largely a defence of the use of Gothic.[1] The pieces dealing with Wight's National Academy have already been mentioned. But reference should be made to one concerning 'Mr. Street's gift to Yale College'[2] in which it is noted that ground had been broken on 13 August 1864 for the new building on the Yale campus, designed by Wight to house the Yale School of the Fine Arts and the college art collections, which is now known as Street Hall.[3] Street Hall (Plate 26), in fact, was designed three years before the Mercantile Library was begun and a year before the National Academy was completed; yet its design is much less Ruskinian and suggests the new direction in which Wight's ideas were then moving. On the one hand there is very little polychromy, but on the other hand some of the window mullions are of iron. So also, I suspect, is the interior construction, at least in part, although that is no longer evident after several twentieth-century remodellings of the interior.

A major interest of Wight's, initiated in the sixties and maintained throughout his long life, was fireproof construction.[4] Henceforth, he can hardly be considered at all a Ruskinian, since his contributions to architectural development were largely technical and his designing consistently commonplace. It may not be without significance, however, that John Root worked first for Wight and his partners when he came to Chicago. Root's importance as a designer, however, comparable to that of his partner Daniel H. Burnham (1846–1912) as an organizer, did not become apparent much before the Rookery Building of 1885–6. By that time almost all links with the Ruskinian High Victorian Gothic of the 1860s had been severed.

Sturgis seems to have been even less productive than his partner in the sixties. Moreover, he broke off his practice in 1878 when he became Professor of Architecture at the College of the City of New York and then spent the years 1880 to 1885 in Europe. His finest early work, indeed the most distinguished production of his entire career, is, like Street Hall, in New Haven. Farnam Hall (Plate 27) at Yale is as debatably Ruskinian as Street Hall and certainly not comparable to the National Academy or the Brooklyn Commercial Library as an example of direct influence from Ruskin. But it is not anti-Ruskinian either in the way of the critical and historical writings of Sturgis published later in his life. It definitely recalls – and may

1. *New Path*, I, pp. 9–10; 4–9, 18–22, 30–6, 44–8.

2. ibid., II, pp. 146–9.

3. Street Hall housed for half a century the famous James Jackson Jarves Collection, the first important group of early Italian paintings brought to America. In 1871, moreover, Yale College acquired these pictures, the first considerable purchase of works of art by an American institution of learning. Later, for a decade from 1951, Josef Albers taught painting there, and today it houses the University's Department of the History of Art.

4. Wight's developing interest in this subject even in the 1860s, before the disastrous Chicago fire of 1871 focused national attention on the problem, is indicated by his eight-page illustrated pamphlet, *Remarks on Fireproof Construction*, published by the Committee on Library and Publications of the American Institute of Architects (New York, 1869).

echo – that notable dwelling which was designed for the most Ruskinian of younger writers by the subtlest architectural exponent of Ruskin's ideas, William Morris's Red House, built by Philip Webb at Bexley Heath ten years before.

Sturgis's contiguous buildings at Yale, Battell Chapel of 1876 (Plate 28) at the corner of the Old Campus, and Durfee Hall of 1871 at right angles to Farnam, are markedly inferior and even less convincingly Ruskinian, as is also true of his Farmers' and Mechanics' Bank in Albany, N.Y., of 1876. Happily, when he returned from his five-years' stay in Europe and designed Lawrence Hall in 1885 to the south of Farnam, he maintained much of the quality of the latter at the expense of producing a rather retardataire building for that late date.

As the listing of E. T. Potter's churches commissioned in 1867 and 1868 has suggested,[1] by the time Sturgis built Farnam the High Victorian Gothic, usually with what pass (rightly or wrongly) for Ruskinian characteristics, was generally accepted for church architecture by all those denominations, and not the Episcopalians alone, that had aesthetic pretensions. Through the boom years that followed before the financial crash of 1873 and even into the depression years of the mid seventies the sort of Gothic that Wight had initiated in the National Academy during the war years shared the scene with the mode of Second Empire Paris, transmitted more often than not via England, at least for monumental architecture.[2] Already in the early seventies, however, there were several other aspects of current architectural production in the United States that were potentially far more important. Some of these were loosely or ambiguously related to the High Victorian Gothic, some not at all, but they all represented the beginnings of developments that would be more important in the 1880s and 90s.[3]

1. See previous note 5 on p. 186.

2. For a summary view of the two sides of the post-Civil-War picture, see Hitchcock, *Architecture: Nineteenth and Twentieth Centuries*, 2nd edn (Harmondsworth, 1963), pp. 166–70 and 173–95.

3. Although the magazines concerned partly or wholly with architecture in the 1850s and 60s had had short runs – *The Crayon* six years, the *Architects' and Mechanics' Journal* three, and *The New Path* no longer – and the *American Architect and Building News*, the first really comprehensive professional magazine, did not begin publication until 1876, the American architecture of the early seventies was well, if selectively, presented in two handsome periodicals, consisting chiefly of heliogravure plates, some made directly from photographs of executed buildings – Plates 22, 27, 29, and 32 in this article, for example, are drawn from them. The *Architectural Sketch Book*, published in Boston by the Portfolio Club, ran for twenty-four monthly numbers from July 1873 to June 1875, offering 100 plates in all but with minimal text. The *New York Sketch-Book*, published in Boston and New York, ran from 1874 to 1876. According to Jordy in the introduction to Schuyler, op. cit., p. 9, 'Before his removal from New York to Boston in 1874, Richardson served briefly as the initial editor of the *Sketch-Book*, although, as Schuyler later asserted, Richardson deputized practically all of his editorial duties to the young [C. F.] McKim [1847–1900]...'. The editorship of Richardson and McKim explains what was for the period the avant-garde character of much of the material published. (See below, note 3 on p. 198 and note 1 on p. 200.) On the other hand Plates 22, 27, and 32 in this article provide a fair sampling of the High Victorian Gothic material

First, there was the maturing of H. H. Richardson's well-known personal style, which soon became a major influence on other architects.[1] But still more important than the emergence of the 'Richardsonian' in the seventies was the building of the first skyscrapers, the New York Tribune Tower by Richard M. Hunt[2] in 1873–4 and the Western Union Building completed by George B. Post a year later. The project entered by J. Cleveland Cady (1837–1919) in the Tribune competition of 1872 might be called a design for a 'Ruskinian skyscraper' (Plate 29), were that not a

published in the *New York Sketch-Book* in the years 1874 to 1876. Comparable things had appeared somewhat more profusely in the *Architectural Sketch Book*. Conspicuous examples can be found there on plates IV, VII, XI, XII, XXXII, XXXIII, and XXXVI in vol. I (1873), and on plates I, II, XXI, XXIX, XXXVIII, and XLIII in vol. II (1874). These include designs by such architects mentioned in this article as E. T. Potter and Ware & Van Brunt, and also others by C. B. Atwood (1849–95), later D. H. Burnham's designer after Root's death, Sturgis & Brigham, Cummings & Sears, and S. J. F. Thayer. None of the last three were ever of much consequence after this period.

1. Only two designs by Richardson appeared in the *Architectural Sketch Book*, a cut-away section of the crossing of Trinity Church, Boston, vol. I, plate V, in August 1873, at the time the final designs were still in preparation, and an unexecuted project for Trinity Church, Buffalo, N.Y., vol. I, plate XVI, in September 1873, but this had probably been prepared by Richardson in the summer of the previous year. Not surprisingly, there is much more Richardson material in the *New York Sketch-Book*. Plate II in vol. I, 1874, is a perspective of the Hampden County Courthouse as projected in 1871; while plate XXXVIII is from a photograph of the building as completed in 1873. Plate XXXII in vol. I is a sketch perspective, probably by Stanford White, then Richardson's principal assistant, of the final design of the central tower of Trinity Church, based on the lantern of the Old Cathedral of Salamanca. This was a most influential Richardsonian borrowing henceforth, but had only been taken by Richardson as a model in that spring of 1874. Plate XXI in vol. III is from a photograph of the North Congregational Church in Springfield, commissioned in 1868 but re-designed three years or so later and built in 1872–3. In vol. II, plate XXXV is a perspective of the Cheney Block in Hartford, Conn., built in 1875–6, and plate XI an unexecuted project for a 'Village Church'. There are also, all told, designs for six houses (see note 4, p. 198).

2. Hunt's project appears on plate I in vol. I (1874) of the *New York Sketch-Book*. A photograph of the completed building was published on plate XXVI in vol. III (1876). J. C. Cady's project (Plate 29) appeared on plate XXV of vol. I.

As I was completing this article a report in the *New York Times* for 20 May 1966 by Bryon Porterfield brought the unwelcome but not surprising news that Hunt's Tribune Building, completed in 1874 with ten storeys and, in 1905–7, more than doubled in height, is being demolished to make way for new buildings for Pace College. The report included a description of the building taken from 'early guide books', not otherwise identified, as of 'neo-Grec [*sic*] architecture combined with Ruskinian polychromy and certain mediaeval details'. The polychromy, whether or not 'Ruskinian', was never conspicuous any more than the 'mediaeval details'. Yet the rather 'proto-functional' design, with triple windows in each bay and heavy segmental arches, is as remote from the Parisian modes in which Hunt had been trained, when he was the first American to attend the École des Beaux-Arts, as from anything that could possibly be called 'neo-Grec'. But Hunt was extremely eclectic and worked in the 1860s and 70s both in his own version of the Stick Style and in a peculiarly hectic sort of High Victorian Gothic as well as in the manner that he had learned when working under Lefuel on the New Louvre in Paris in the 1850s after he left the École. (See note 1 on p. 200 below.)

27. Russell Sturgis: Farnam Hall, Yale University, New Haven, Conn., built 1869
(from *New York Sketch-Book*, III, there wrongly labelled Durfee)

28. Russell Sturgis: Farnam Hall (*left*), 1869, and Battell Chapel (*right*), 1876,
Yale University, New Haven, Conn. (photo taken before 1885)

contradiction in terms. But the entire development in commercial architecture from this point forward, culminating in the skyscrapers of Sullivan, belongs to a non-Ruskinian world that represented all he hated in the nineteenth century.

Also important in the later decades of the century in the United States were the two successive phases of domestic design that Vincent Scully has identified as the 'Stick Style' and the 'Shingle Style'.[1] The first of these, which flourished in the 1860s and early 70s, had its roots in certain aspects of Downing's version of the Picturesque. Characteristically expressive of American wooden-frame construction, the Stick Style nonetheless affected the verandahs and other external appendages of houses of stone or brick. Thus the house which E. T. Potter built in 1873–4 in Hartford, Conn., for the writer Mark Twain[2] has walls of brick and roofs of slate, both violently patterned in a High Victorian Gothic way. But this, one must feel, is more Butterfieldian or Teulonesque than Ruskinian. The young Ruskin who wrote on the 'Poetry of Architecture' might have appreciated such exaggerated picturesqueness but not the mature Ruskin of the 1850s,[3] much less the soured critic of the seventies.

The Shingle Style, initiated during the seventies and widely popular right up to its employment by the young Frank Lloyd Wright in the early nineties, represented in many respects a reaction against the High Victorian modes of the post-Civil-War decade. Constituent were the influence of Norman Shaw and, to a lesser degree, increasing interest in and respect for the American Colonial.[4]

1. Vincent J. Scully, Jr, *The Shingle Style* (New Haven, 1955).

2. This was published in the *New York Sketch-Book*, I, plate XVI. I owe to Walter K. Schwinn, President of the Mark Twain Memorial, the transcription of many passages concerning Mark Twain's choice of an architect from the book of Edith Colgate Salsbury, *Susy and Mark Twain* (New York, 1965), and from the Mark Twain Memorial Research Files, including many letters of George H. Warner and his wife who had had Potter build their Hartford house in 1872 and encouraged Mark Twain to employ him also. Mr Schwinn also supplied transcriptions of letters by Mark Twain himself and by Potter.

3. The Stick Style was past its prime by the time the *Sketch Books* were being published, especially in the milieu of Richardson and McKim. There are, however, two plates of Stick Style house projects in the *Architectural Sketch Book*, I, plate VII, and II, plate XXXIX, and more remarkably, two for churches that might be called Stick Style, one by the English-born A. J. Bloor (1828–1917) and another by Ware & Van Brunt (plates XXXIII and XI, respectively, in vol. V). Another Stick Style church project by Bloor was published in the *New York Sketch-Book*, II, plate XX.

4. Richardson's Watts Sherman house in Newport, R.I., in the *New York Sketch-Book*, II (1875), plates XVIII, XII, is rather definitely 'Shavian Manorial', while plate XVII presents a sketch of a decorated cove cornice and dormer by A. F. Oakey (?–1916) that is actually Shavian Queen Anne. An earlier house in Dedham, Mass., by Oakey & Jones, published in the *Architectural Sketch Book*, I (1873), plate XLI, was evidently more crudely and generically Shavian. Richardson's Rush Cheney house-project, probably designed in fact by his talented young assistant Stanford White, is much more sophisticated, and is presented in the *New York Sketch-Book*, III (1876), plate XXXVI, with a truly Shavian delicacy of draghtsmanship that is certainly White's.

The other four houses by Richardson and his partner Gambrill are all Shingle Style, or at least

29. J. Cleveland Cady: Project for New York Tribune Building, 1872
(from *New York Sketch-Book*, 1)

The resulting situation as regards the influence of Ruskin in the United States in the eighties is ambiguous. On the one hand, his writings had never been more popular, as the statistics on issues of his architectural writings given earlier in this article make evident. On the other hand, not only were major new developments such as the Shingle Style and the skyscraper in varying degree anti- or at least un-Ruskinian; in monumental architecture the Richardsonian, with its loosely medieval antecedents, was being succeeded by an 'academic revival', so to call it, led by Richardson's former assistants McKim and White.[1] Beginning with their Villard *palazzo* in New York of 1883–5, based on Bramante, what Ruskin had stigmatized so violently as 'the foul torrent of the Renaissance', now undamned and undammed, flooded the eastern seaboard cities and overflowed even into the Middle West with the Chicago World's Fair of 1893.

In dealing with the rivals and successors to the at least partially Ruskinian High Victorian Gothic, I have failed so far to give adequate evidence of its relative dominance and its real achievements in the early seventies. Potter's rotunda at Union College, built in 1872–6, cannot claim the historical priority it would have if designed in 1858, but its quality is not diminished by its actual, so much later, date.

approach the mature mode almost as closely as does McKim's C. G. Francklyn house at Long Branch, N.J., published in the same year in the *New York Sketch-Book*, III, plate XLVII, not to speak of his still earlier Blake house in Newton Lower Falls, Mass. (ibid., II, plate XXV). There is other near-Shingle-Style work by W. R. Mead (1846–1928), shortly to be McKim's partner, and by C. F. Babb but this, like much of McKim's minor work, is of little intrinsic interest.

Remarkable, however, is an interior added to the eighteenth-century Thomas Robinson house in Newport, R.I., in 1872 by McKim, taken from a photograph, that is reproduced in the *New York Sketch-Book*, II (1875), plate XXXVII. This reflects the rising interest in eighteenth-century American Colonial architecture, an interest that is documented in the *Sketch Books* by several plates. In the *Architectural Sketch Book*, I (1873), plate XXXI, there are already measured drawings of two Late Colonial church façades and spires in Boston; in vol. I (1874) of the *New York Sketch-Book*, plate XLV, a very picturesque photograph from the rear of Whitehall, the house Bishop Berkeley built for himself in Middletown, R.I., is reproduced; while plate XXX in vol. II is a measured drawing of the doorway of Washington's Headquarters in Morristown, N.J., and plate XLIII shows another Colonial house in New Jersey. Washington's Headquarters in Newburgh, N.Y., so tumble-down it looks positively medieval, is on plate XV of vol. III.

1. Hitchcock, *Architecture: Nineteenth and Twentieth Centuries*, pp. 227–32. There are already premonitions of the coming academic revival in the material published in the *Sketch Books*. George B. Post's domed Williamsburgh Bank in New York, shown in the *New York Sketch-Book*, I (1874), plate V, is not conventionally Second Empire nor is McKim & Mead's formal project for the Providence City Hall on plate XLI. R. M. Hunt's Lenox Library, vol. III (1876), plate XIII, designed as early as 1868, is very Parisian, though not mansarded, and makes less surprising the publication of the French architect Mangin's New York City Hall, still Louis XVI in style though early-nineteenth-century in date, on plate XXV. Recalling Ware's Beaux-Arts-based instruction at the Massachusetts Institute of Technology, it is less surprising to find the whole May number of vol. II of the *Architectural Sketch Book* (1874) devoted to M.I.T. student projects that are consistently academic, if in a quite unenterprising way.

Though the sixteen-sided shape was determined by the foundations laid in 1858 for Ramée's project (Plate 24), not in emulation of the Pisa Baptistery, the polychromatic 'wall-veil' is a rich example of Italianate Gothic that time has mellowed very happily (Plate 23). A surviving construction photo clearly reveals, however, that the Ruskinism affects only the outer shell. In a Wight-like desire to provide maximum protection against fire, appropriate to a structure then intended for use as a library,[1] the surrounding galleries of the interior and the aisle roof, the drum, and the dome overhead were entirely of iron construction. This is far more frankly revealed internally, moreover, than the iron skeletons of the first skyscrapers that were its contemporaries.

But Edward was neither the more productive nor the more talented of the Potter brothers. Having a rich wife, he could afford to take professional life easily as well as to contribute generously to the construction of this building for his Alma Mater as a memorial to his grandfather. Of W. A. Potter's considerable range of production in the early and mid seventies, however, before he began, even while Richardson's Trinity Church in Boston was still in construction, to move into the Richardsonian orbit, three examples are worth showing rather than the more conspicuous and better known, but less intrinsically distinguished, Memorial Hall at Harvard University, designed in intentionally Ruskinian vein in the late sixties and built by Ware & Van Brunt in 1870–8.[2]

1. It was not actually fully equipped as a library until the late eighties after the end of E. N. Potter's presidency, and then only thanks to a grant from Andrew Carnegie. At first its most conspicuous contents, inappropriately enough, were casts of classical sculpture.

2. Illustrated in the *Architectural Sketch Book*, II (1874), plates I–II, where it is stated that by June of 1874 the 'nave', serving as a University Dining Hall, and the 'transept', called the Memorial Vestibule, were already so far completed that a Commencement Dinner for 1,200 could be served. There is a description of the materials used and the dimensions which need not be quoted here. This most conspicuous of surviving High Victorian Gothic buildings has been shabbily treated of late years by the University. A fire burned off the high slated roof of the tower and it has never been replaced even though it is essential to the silhouette of the building, all too much overhung by a fifteen-storey skyscraper, William James Hall, completed by Minoru Yamasaki (b. 1912) in 1965.

Of the Harvard building Arthur Sedgwick wrote in *The Letters of Charles Eliot Norton* (Boston and New York, 1913), II, pp. 436–7: '. . . very few know that to [Norton] was in great part, if not chiefly, due the existence of Memorial Hall'. It will surprise all those who know anything about Ruskin's relations with Americans that this is the first time the name of C. E. Norton (1827–1908), Ruskin's closest American friend and continual correspondent, has appeared in this article. He had, however, little to do with nineteenth-century Ruskinian architecture in the United States except for his concern with Memorial Hall. He first met Ruskin in 1855 when he was invited to Denmark Hill and not, as Ruskin stated later, on a boat on Lake Geneva the following summer (*Praeterita*, III, pp. 2–3). Evidence for this is Ruskin's note of invitation of October 1855, the first communication included in *The Letters of John Ruskin to Charles Eliot Norton*, 2 vols. (Boston and New York, 1905). The title of Norton's second book, *Notes of Travel and Study in Italy* (Boston, 1860), sounds Ruskinian. Of this a portion had appeared in *The Crayon*, vol. III, in 1856 – or so he stated. I have not found it and presume it was anonymous like his first book, *Considerations on*

The Chancellor Green, or Octagon, Library (Plate 30) at Princeton University in New Jersey, built in 1872–3 to hold 'over 100,000' volumes, continued to serve its original purpose until a new library was built in 1948. In design it has a plastic interest and a consistency of scale lacking in the rather richer Union College building and the polychromy is restricted to banded arches and the boldly patterned slating on the roofs.

In quality, however, W. A. Potter's South Congregational Church (Plate 31) in Springfield, Mass., is a far more notable work. It was built in 1872–3 in tacit rivalry with H. H. Richardson's more conventional, even though round-arched, North Congregational Church.[1] The upward surge of the corner tower is slightly weakened now by the gabled chapel added later at its base; yet its location at a bend in Maple Street still makes it a striking terminus to the view as one descends the hill on which the finest nineteenth-century houses of Springfield are grouped. Equally striking are the enormous rose-window and the bold bulge on the south, no apse in this evangelical edifice but an expansion of one side of the squarish auditorium within. Polychromy there is, but this conduces less to the general Butterfieldian impression than do the curious contrasts of proportion and the coarse assurance of the detailing. There is, of course, nothing Butterfieldian about the non-ritualistic plan or about the compact massing, which somewhat recalls F. T. Pilkington's Presbyterian Barclay Church of 1863 in Edinburgh.

Despite the Houses of Parliament and the Law Courts, it cannot be said that Gothic, much less Ruskinian Gothic, was ever really popular for government buildings in Great Britain. In the United States on the other hand the ranking projects in the two successive competitions for the Connecticut State Capitol of 1871 and 1872 were all Gothic, and Richard M. Upjohn (1828–1905), the winner of the second, eventually erected a curiously eclectic structure, complete with a 'Gothic' dome,[2] while Richardson's far finer design was until lately lost and forgotten.[3] Still

some Recent Social Theories (Boston, 1853). But actually only a short piece on the monuments of Pisa recalls Ruskin, and Norton does not even mention Venice. His interests were at that point far more in political, social, and religious matters. The correspondence between 'My dearest Norton' (1863), later 'My dearest Charles', and 'Ever your affectionate J. Ruskin' (1862) began, as has been noted, in 1855 and continued to 1896.

In 1874 Norton introduced the study of the history of art at Harvard and eventually saw to it that Harvard's Fogg Museum, despite a late start, caught up with Yale's Jarves Collection in the field of early Italian painting. His most considerable book concerned with architecture was *Historical Studies of Church Building in the Middle Ages* (New York, 1880). It was Norton, however, who brought C. H. Moore to Harvard and some traces of Ruskinian instruction still survived when I was a student at Harvard in 1920–7.

1. Published in the *New York Sketch-Book*, I, plate x.

2. See G. L. Hersey, 'Replication Replicated, or Notes on American Bastardy', *Perspecta*, IX/X, pp. 211–48. The final project was published in the *New York Sketch-Book*, II (1875), plate v.

3. See Charles Price, 'Henry Hobson Richardson, Some Unpublished Drawings', *Perspecta*, IX/X, pp. 199–210.

30. W. A. Potter: Chancellor Green Library, Princeton University, Princeton, N.J., built 1872–3
(from *The Princeton Book*, Boston, 1879)

more surprisingly W. A. Potter, as Supervising Architect of the Treasury Department for several years in the mid seventies, was responsible for certain Federal buildings – post offices, court houses, and custom houses, few of which have survived – that recall somewhat the projects of nearly twenty years before entered in the Government Offices competition in London. His Post Office and Court House (Plate 32) at Evansville, Indiana, contrasts sharply with the pompous 'Second Empire' Federal buildings then still rising all over the United States from designs prepared or procured by the preceding Supervising Architect Alfred B. Mullett (1834–90).[1]

Yet, except as a very minor ingredient in the generic medievalism of Richardson's mature style, so soon to be taken up by many other architects, including both the Potters, who had earlier been more or less Ruskinian, the stylistic episode associated with the partial absorption of Ruskin's ideas in the sixties and early seventies was without sequel after 1880. Eventually most American critics were only too ready to damn Ruskin well before Geoffrey Scott came on the scene abroad. Samples may serve to illustrate the vigour of the reaction. In 1891, writing in *Harper's Magazine*[2] on the Chicago architectural scene at what historians have come to consider a crucial moment in the advance of the 'Chicago School', Montgomery Schuyler (1843–1914) had this to say of Richardson's American Express Building which had been completed by Wight, as earlier noted, in 1873:

It is a sober and straight forward performance in a safe monochrome, and it thus lacks the note of that variety that Mr. Ruskin's eloquence stimulated untrained American designers to produce, in whch the restlessness of unstudied forms is still further tormented by the spotty application of color.[3]

Again, in more general terms:

Mr. Ruskin has fallen into deep, and largely deserved, discredit as an architectural critic, by promulgating rhapsodies as dogmas. His intellectual frivolity is even more evident and irritating by reason of the moral earnestness that attends it, recalling that perfervid pulpiteer of whom a like-minded eulogist affirmed that 'he wielded his prurient imagination like a battle-axe in the service of the Lord of Hosts.' All the same, lovers of architecture owe him gratitude for his eloquent inculcation of some of the truths that he arrived at by feeling, however inconclusive is the reasoning by which he endeavours to support them...[4]

There was in Chicago at that date a young man in the employ of Adler & Sullivan of whom Schuyler apparently became fully aware only twenty years later when

1. The Evansville Federal Building and another at Nashville, Tenn., built in 1874, were both published in the *New York Sketch-Book*, II (1875), plate XXXII, and III (1876), plate VIII.
2. 'Glimpses of Western Architecture: Chicago', *Harper's Magazine* (August 1891), pp. 395–406; ibid. (September 1891), pp. 554–70, illus., but more readily accessible in Schuyler, op. cit., pp. 246–91.
3. loc. cit., p. 262.   4. loc. cit., p. 265.

GROUND PLAN

31. W. A. Potter: South Congregational Church, Springfield, Mass., built 1872–3, as originally designed

reviewing for the *Architectural Record*[1] the German publications of this architect's work that were bringing him also at that time to the attention of Europeans. Many have since considered him the one who *really* regenerated American architecture in the opening decade of this century. Frank Lloyd Wright (1867–1959) came of a family of Welsh-born Unitarians who did not disdain 'earnestness' and approved as heartily as Emerson of Ruskin's 'appeal to moral order'. As a student at the University of Wisconsin in the mid eighties Wright read not only Ruskin – he lists[2] *Fors Clavigera*, *Modern Painters*, and *The Stones of Venice*, in that order, as gifts of his school-teacher aunts – but much of Ruskin's own mentor Thomas Carlyle, and also Viollet-le-Duc's *Dictionnaire*. Thus humanistic reading balanced the instruction that he obtained from Professor Conover and the engineer Storm Bull and the practical experience of construction that came to him from assisting on a new building going up at the University.

How much, and what, Wright learned from reading Ruskin is not readily determinable. But much later he urged his sons to read Ruskin if they intended to become architects. In somewhat the same way as Henry Van de Velde in the nineties in Belgium or Walter Gropius a decade later, Wright found generic inspiration in Ruskin's works and, if not a style of architecture, the basis of his own prophetic style of writing.

The overt Ruskinian wave of the 1850s, 60s, and early 70s was a confined episode, more destructive of inherited American architectural traditions in its effect than a foundation for the new developments that followed generally in the later seventies and eighties. But all the reading of Ruskin in the eighties that the American publishing history of his works in the period implies, even though it came at a time when American architecture was becoming aggressively un-Ruskinian, was not without result. Not only did Wright read Ruskin – and, of course, eventually Morris too – but so also did those who would be his clients in the early phase of his career over the years from 1893, when he began his independent practice after leaving Adler & Sullivan, to 1909, when he left his family behind to go to Europe. Once Ruskin was read by Americans with no thought of following literally the medieval models he held up for emulation – in the naive way the young architects of the sixties and early seventies had mostly set out to do – his ideas could set free instead of binding. For the second Ruskin-reading generation, that of Wright and his Middle Western clients, Ruskin's influence could prove regenerative, as it certainly had not been in Emerson's day, in architecture or, for that matter, in painting.

1. 'An Architectural Pioneer: Review of the Portfolios containing the Works of Frank Lloyd Wright', *Architectural Record* (April 1912), pp. 427–35.
2. Frank Lloyd Wright, *An Autobiography* (London, New York, Toronto, 1932), p. 58.

32. W. A. Potter: Post Office and Court House, Evansville, Indiana, *c.* 1875
(from *New York Sketch-Book*, II)

While this article was in the press there appeared *John Ruskin and Aesthetic Thought in America, 1840–1900*, by Roger B. Stein (Cambridge, Mass., Harvard University Press, 1967). This is a far broader treatment of the subject than I attempted, but does not add much as regards the specific issue of Ruskin's influence on American building production.

Street's Yorkshire Churches and Contemporary Criticism

NOTES ON CONTEMPORARY CRITICISM BY BASIL F. L. CLARKE
WITH PHOTOGRAPHS BY JOHN PIPER

THE contributors to the *Ecclesiologist*, from 1841 to 1868, kept an eye on the churches that were being restored, and on the new ones that were being built, and they reported on what they saw, and commented on it. They did not all agree in detail, but all shared the same general point of view.

In the 1840s their ideal church was Middle-Pointed, and they expected a new church to be in that style – honestly constructed of 'real' materials, with a high-pitched roof and a well-developed chancel; and correctly arranged, with low seats, a screen, stalls, and a properly vested altar. Some churches were built which realized their ideal: nothing could be better, in this kind, than the churches of R. C. Carpenter. But they did not believe that they would be confined for ever to Middle-Pointed: they hoped that it would be possible to advance from there – the highest point which Gothic had so far reached – avoiding the mistakes that had led the medieval builders to Perpendicular and to ultimate debasement, and developing a Gothic which would be as suitable to the nineteenth century as Middle-Pointed had been to the fourteenth.

A way forward was suggested in the early 1850s by G. E. Street, the most enterprising of the young architects who belonged to the Ecclesiological Society. Street believed that architects must not merely copy: they must understand the principles on which their art was founded, and work them out for themselves. There would be no progress if they were always thinking about precedent: what was needed was the strengthening of our style by a grafting in of new elements. He suggested, as one of the most important, the borrowing of features from Continental Gothic, and even something from the Classical style – at any rate, the horizontal line of the cornice. The horizontal line was needed to balance the upward tendency; and, since all construction is necessarily horizontal, this should be emphasized by courses of differently coloured stones, which would provide what was needed to harmonize and perfect the Pointed work.

Butterfield had shown how bricks could be used for constructional colour. Tiles had hardly been used hitherto, but could be useful. And England provided plenty of coloured stones and marbles.

Apsidal ends were of great beauty, and should be used. The admission of light should be carefully regulated, and concentrated on particular points, so as to produce alternations of light and shade. And there should be a new outlook in the matter of glass. It had been assumed that it ought to be pictorial, whereas it ought to be only decorative. There should be a return to a more simple and humble system, such as would enhance the beauties of the architecture: wall painting would give the opportunity of developing the painter's art which stained glass could never hope to afford.

The architectural part of this programme might have resulted in a hotch-potch: French thirteenth-century capitals, Italian striped walls, cornices such as occur in some Romanesque churches – and so on. But nothing like this happened. Street did not mean to copy from abroad, any more than from at home. Critics could say, from time to time, that some element had not been properly assimilated: and it is true that, as Goodhart-Rendel puts it, there were at first some lumps that had not been stirred out. But obvious borrowings are very few: the various influences were assimilated by Street's own mind, and they fused into something that was personal, and as English – and Anglican – as he was. He did not mean to make things more complicated; indeed, he aimed at simplification. He believed in building 'a good wall', and he could design a village church, or school, that was almost as straightforward as a barn. His plain chamfered arches, square abaci, and plate-traceried windows were an escape from the mouldings and tracery which the earlier revivalists had copied so laboriously. Eastlake commented that Pugin and his followers had decorated their churches with carved panels, tracery, pinnacles, and niches, which made a showy building: but if they were removed, the churches would cut a sorry figure. Street, even if he were limited to four walls, a roof, a couple of windows, and a chimneyshaft, could make them picturesque. The ecclesiologists were not very fond of the word 'picturesque'; they would have agreed with Eastlake, but would probably have preferred the word 'real': if a thing was done honestly and straightforwardly, it would look right. Street could, of course, design elaborate ornament, and he enjoyed it: but it was not the purposeless adornment of something that would be nothing without the ornament.

After a time he came back to English models, and his later churches are smoother: he could design without apparent effort, and the Vigour and Go are not so obvious. It is the churches of the 1850s and 60s that are the most characteristic: and it was during that time that the *Ecclesiologist*, which knew perfectly well what he was trying to do and was in full agreement with it, described his work, criticized it, and encouraged him. The ecclesiologists were sure that what they hoped for had come to pass: the Gothic Revival was no longer antiquarian or romantic: Gothic had come to life.

After some years, the younger men would naturally come to look on Street as old-fashioned: they had their own ideas about development, and regarded him as one who clothed buildings in unnecessary Gothic fancy dress. Some doubted whether the talk about grafting into English architecture meant anything: was there anything to graft into? But in the 1860s it really did seem, for a time – at any rate to some – that a new English Gothic style had been born, and architects such as Pearson, White, Bodley, and Buckeridge expressed themselves in it.

Many of the churches that were built at this time were in villages. The Church Building Commissioners, first appointed in 1818, had provided churches for the towns; and in the 1850s they were still making grants, though the actual building of the churches was now entirely the business of voluntary agencies. The towns continued to grow, and more churches were constantly demanded – but, though it might be difficult to raise the money, it never seemed to be impossible: if an appeal was made to provide a church for 5,000 or 10,000 people in a town, someone would always respond to it, and, with the help of a grant from I.C.B.S. and the local diocesan association, the church, or part of it, was built.

But the country was different: no one could make an appeal on the grounds that the population was excessive. But there were churchless hamlets, a long way from their parish churches, where life was primitive and uncivilized; and there were villages which had a church of some kind, but it had been allowed to fall into a state of such degradation that it was impossible to worship with decency. Wales had many of these: little damp shacks, of uncertain date, almost without furnishing. The few that remain ought, no doubt, to be kept in that state: but in the nineteenth century there were far too many of them, and they were a real hindrance to Church life. There would have to be new churches to take their place, and new churches, or school chapels, for the churchless hamlets. And, since general appeals were not likely to be of much use, most of the money had to come from the local gentry, clergy and land-owners. There were many of these who had been influenced by the Church revival, and who had a sense of responsibility: they were ready to do what was necessary; and Street, or one of the other younger architects who thought as he did, was just the man that they needed to carry out their wishes. So this kind of commission came to them very often, and they must have found it very congenial. There was no tiresome committee to deal with: the benefactor agreed with the architect in matters of ecclesiology, and the church could be planned to the satisfaction of both.

A village church designed and executed under these conditions is simple in plan, with solid walls and a high-pitched roof. The font is large and massive, the seats are low, and the pulpit – usually of stone, and not too high – is placed in the north-east or south-east corner of the nave. The chancel is raised higher than was usual in the Middle Ages, or in the earlier years of the Revival, and is separated from the nave by a low wall, with either ironwork, or an open screen of metal or wood on the top.

211

The stalls are low, but with more elaboration than the seats in the nave. The organ is in a chamber at the side. As the east is approached, there is a crescendo of colour: the patterns in the tiles of the floor are more complex, and the roof of the sanctuary – sometimes of the whole chancel – may be painted. The sanctuary rises by further steps, and the altar stands in front of a reredos of marble or alabaster panels, either with carved scenes, or, perhaps more often, with emblems: a marble cross in the middle, and alpha and omega, or the instruments of the Passion, or the symbols of the Evangelists, at the sides. The reredos gave plenty of opportunity for constructional coloration: marble shafts, marble inlay, or mosaics. The walls at the sides are usually adorned with tiles. The east window is placed well up in the wall, and often has glass by Clayton & Bell, whose colours always fit well into the ensemble.

It is the ideal setting for Anglican worship as it had evolved under the guidance of the ecclesiologists.

*

Street's most generous patron was Sir Tatton Sykes, who was born in 1826, and succeeded his father at Sledmere in the East Riding in 1863.

The elder Sir Tatton was a character – a sportsman, who enjoyed boxing, and riding in races. He owned racehorses from 1803, and was one of the largest breeders of bloodstock in the country. He was present at the St Leger for seventy-four consecutive years. But he also reclaimed a great deal of land on the Wolds, and went in for sheep-farming: his fifty-eighth sale of sheep was held in 1861.

Sir Tatton the younger continued his father's good work, and was also a church builder on an extraordinary scale. His father had restored one or two churches on the estate, but most of them were dilapidated. He adorned the church at Sledmere, an eighteenth-century building; and then, in 1897–8, replaced it by a splendid new church designed by Temple Moore. He also built, rebuilt, or restored the churches of Wansford, Thixendale, Fimber, Garton on the Wolds, Kirkburn, Weaverthorpe, Luttons Ambo, Helperthorpe, Kirby Grindalythe, Bishop Wilton, East Heslerton, Langtoft, Fridaythorpe, Wetwang, North Frodingham and Sherburn, and left funds to keep them in repair. Parsonages and schools were also built: altogether, he is said to have spent about a million pounds on the Church. He died in 1913.

For his earlier work he employed Street. He was one of those patrons of whom Street once wrote, whose influence could

secure invariably in the churches which they build such arrangements of the interior as would make it difficult, if not impossible, for people long to ignore those truths which the building is intended to teach...The architect who connects religion with architecture dreams to himself of church doors open day after day and all day, of altars properly and reverently decked, etc.

In these churches, his dream could come true. They are all variations of the same type, but they never become monotonous, because each is different; and they are all so complete that nothing needs to be added to them, and nothing could be taken away without spoiling them.

The first of the churches, Wansford, was consecrated in 1868, the year in which the *Ecclesiologist* was discontinued. Nothing really took its place. There were far more Church journals than there are now: but most of them ceased to exist a long time ago, and copies are not easy to find. By this time, anyhow, there was not very much to say. When the ecclesiologists were fighting the battle for correct style, honest construction, and suitable arrangement, new churches had to be carefully watched, and any deviation had to be pointed out. But by 1870 the battle had been so decisively won that almost everyone, including Evangelical and Broad Churchmen, accepted a point of view that in 1840 had been peculiar to the pioneers. Churches which would, at one time, have earned several pages of enthusiastic praise, had become so common that they were scarcely noticed. The *Church Times* mentioned with approval churches that had vested altars with proper ornaments, and liked to describe consecrations; but it seems to have missed the Tatton Sykes churches. The *Guardian* mentioned one or two, and paid tribute to Sir Tatton in an obituary. All his churches were 'carried out in the most costly and elaborate manner by first-class architects and in exquisite taste . . . There can be few districts in England that can vie with the Wolds in respect of its splendid churches; all completely furnished and richly appointed'.

There was, in fact, not much else to say: in churches like these, the ecclesiological movement reached its full development.

Sir Tatton did not parade his generosity: but each of the churches possesses a small bust, simply inscribed 'Tatton'.

WHITWELL ON THE HILL

There was a plan in 1858 for rebuilding the parish church of Crambe on a different site, but this was given up: Crambe was left, and a new church was built at Whitwell by Sir E. A. H. and Lady Lechmere, of Hanley Castle, Worcestershire. Lechmere was one of the admirable country gentlemen who were also keen ecclesiologists: he was an F.S.A., and secretary of the Worcester Diocesan Architectural Society. In 1858 he had employed Street to restore the church at Hanley Castle, and in the 1870s he gave the site for the new church at Hanley Swan, which he helped to furnish. Whitwell was consecrated on 21 August 1860.

The *Ecclesiologist*[1] was enthusiastic:

This is an excellent design . . . The material is Whitby stone; the style a rich Geometrical Middle-pointed . . . We admire the arrangement of the strings and buttresses exceedingly.

1. no. CXXX (February 1859), pp. 65–6.

213

The tower is a good feature and well managed. The belfry windows are of two lights with a geometrically pierced circle of plate tracery above. We do not much like, however, the depression of the shaft of the monial to a lower level than the shafts of the jambs. Why this irregularity?

The stone broach spire was very good, but was the transverse gabling of the sacristy to be recommended? The chimney in the north chancel wall, a banded column, was very effective. So was the chancel arch, with its corbelled shafts of coloured marble.

The eastern wall is of ashlar, banded with coloured tiles; and the reredos is a composition of tesserae, with shafts on each side supporting a rich cornice, and an ornate cross in the middle . . . The woodwork is all carefully designed.

The description ends, 'This is a very complete design throughout.' So it is. There is glass by Clayton & Bell, and a west window by Wailes. The glass in the nave is later, and inferior, but, apart from this, nothing has been done to disturb the completeness.

HOWSHAM

The church in this pretty estate village was built in 1859–60 at the cost of Hannah Cholmley.

Eastlake remarks that there is no better test of an architect's originality than when he has to design a small village church. How can such a building be made to express its purpose, to look interesting, and to avoid conventionality? Street, he says, has shown us how this can be done, at Howsham. 'The effect of the whole is charming. Nothing better could have been devised. It is simplicity itself, but simplicity with meaning and effect.'

The reporter of the *Ecclesiologist* saw the church in 1859, while it was being built, but it must have been almost finished, as he describes the furniture.

The plan comprises a chancel with a round-ended apsidal sanctuary, a vestry at the north-west angle, a nave with a narthex-like porch at the west end, and a tower engaged at the north side of the narthex. This is an admirable and novel plan, and admits of great internal comfort in the nave, and of much good architectural combination externally. The arrangement is excellent, the chancel-levels being well contrived . . . The altar stands at the extreme east of the apse. We should have liked better to have seen it advanced. Externally the treatment is very good. The masonry of white stone is relieved by bands of red. The window-tracery, of geometrical Middle-Pointed design, is good, and the string-courses – as always in Mr. Street's designs – are well managed. The narthex is roofed with a lean-to, and is sustained by massive columns, with horizontal architraves. Surely arches would have been far better, though, or because, less novel. The small engaged tower is

33. Whitwell on the Hill, church and parsonage. 'A very complete design throughout'
(*Ecclesiologist*)

34. Howsham, from the west. A Street silhouette

35. Wansford. Very French, obviously thought of in relation to its flat-country setting

36. Thixendale. Its gables and roofscapes are suited to its valley setting

37. Fimber. A hillside setting

38. Garton on the Wolds. The elaborate roof, a part of the general almost
Byzantine richness of this interior

39. Kirby Grindalythe. Street details and mouldings at close quarters

40. Luttons Ambo. A careful design for the centre of a village

41. East Heslerton. An elaborate composition, here seen from the south-east

square, cleverly splayed into an octagonal open lantern, formed of columns, with a pyramidal capping. A circular west window, above the lean-to of the narthex, is a good feature. Internally the chancel arch, which is continuous at the impost, is cinq-foliated. The roof is of the circular-cradle form. The apse windows are combined with a foliated arcade of hood-mouldings, sustained on detached shafts; and a reredos is formed constructionally by stilting the middle ones. The apse roof is boarded. The woodwork is simple and good; and coloured marbles are introduced, though sparingly, in the font and pulpit.[1]

The glass is by Clayton & Bell. The west window has a Majestas: in the nave, the saints on the south are in clear quarries. The glass in the chancel and apse is very good – very bright in colour: their reds and blues soon became deeper. The best window – the Works of Mercy – is on the south.

WANSFORD

Begun in 1867, and consecrated on 4 February 1868, 'in the place of one of which all vestiges had disappeared with the exception of a desecrated font, now restored to its pristine use' (*Guardian*). Sir Tatton gave £2,000 for its endowment. It is in flat marshy country, very French in its feeling: a flèched gable in a level landscape. *Murray's Handbook* (1882) says:

This church is remarkable for its stained glass, painted roofs, and very beautiful marble rood-screen and pulpit. The turret at the W. end is carried on arches from the floor. There are also a ch-yd. cross, lych-gate, and a new parsonage.

THIXENDALE

This church, and Fimber, were consecrated on the same day – 13 April 1871. The contractors were Simpson and Malone of Hull.

Thixendale is a small village in a deep valley. The church stands by the roadside: it is of the simplest outline, with a bellcote at the east end of the nave, and exactly suits its position.

Nave with north porch and south aisle, and a tiny apsidal baptistery: and a well raised chancel with south organ chamber.

The style is that of the Law Courts, rather than of St James the Less, Westminster – with the lumps stirred out. But it has what it takes to make a good church. The chancel is, of course, the important thing: a screen, modest stalls, and a stone reredos of arcading, with a tile and alabaster facing to the walls at the side of the altar.

The east window, and one other, are by Burlison & Grylls, and others by Clayton & Bell.

1. ibid., no. cxxxi (April 1859), p. 135.

FIMBER

The old church was small and dim, with eighteenth-century windows, and much overgrown: there is nothing of it left.

The new church, which stands on a hillside, cost £3,500. Here, as at Thixendale, there is an attractive stone lychgate.

It has a small tower with a cap, nave with very low seats, and a raised chancel, at the west of which is a brass screen on a stone wall. Alabaster reredos with diaper and a large central cross: stone arcading at the sides. The pointed barrel roof of the chancel is painted: there are four red compartments and two green, with gold stars. The glass is by Clayton & Bell.

GARTON ON THE WOLDS

This church was first restored by the elder Sir Tatton. Pearson's plans were shown to the Ecclesiological Society on 7 December 1859, and the restoration was mentioned in 1860.[1] The chancel was being rebuilt in Romanesque style: 'We doubt whether enough remains to justify this course in preference to the choice of Middle-Pointed for the additions.' The nave was also largely rebuilt.

There was another restoration, by Street, in 1871, and the church was decorated in 1872–80.

This is a wonderful ensemble: reredos, screen, mosaic floors and painted roofs. All the glass is by Clayton & Bell, and the walls are covered with paintings by the same. South of the chancel, Adoration of the Magi; north, the Last Judgement. North of the nave, the Creation, Adam and Eve, etc.; above, the stories of Noah and Joseph. South side: above, the story of David; below, the months of the year. (The cartoons are under the tower.)

The total effect is most impressive – a kind of Byzantine richness.

KIRBY GRINDALYTHE

Restored by Street in 1872: the nave, 'a barn-like structure of brick', was taken down and 'restored on its probable original lines'; and the Norman chancel was carefully rebuilt. It is of ashlar, inside and out: a richly moulded arcade to the aisle on the north, and a clerestory of single lights above the piers.

Screen by Rattee & Kett, and a white marble and alabaster reredos by William Redfern. The glass is by Clayton & Bell. A mosaic of the Ascension on the west wall.

1. ibid., no. CXXXVI, p. 52.

LUTTONS AMBO

East and West Lutton: the church is in West. There was an old chapel here, of which one fragment remains – the outer moulding of a Norman doorway, now built into the west wall of the vestry. The new church was consecrated in 1875.

It was very expensive – £13,125 – and everything is of the best. Nave and narrow aisles, and a Surrey-looking belfry with shingled spire supported on balusters – like that with which, a little earlier, Street crowned the tower of Beachampton, Buckinghamshire. Vaulted south porch, and a fine vaulted chancel of two bays, with a circular east window. Here, again, are painted roofs and carefully designed pavements. The screen, by Potter, is of brass, with a little iron. Painted triptych by Burlison & Grylls.

The glass was originally by Hardman, but Sykes had it taken out, and glass by Burlison & Grylls put in its place. Hardman would probably seem preferable to us, but Burlison & Grylls were more to the taste of the later nineteenth century. The best of their glass is the four-light window at the west – a tree of Jesse.

EAST HESLERTON

1877 in place of an old church: vaulted chancel, north tower and spire. Here are Redfern's figures of the four Latin Doctors, which were made for the north porch of Bristol Cathedral, but were objected to as being Popish.

The glass is by Clayton & Bell.

The Writings of William White

BY PAUL THOMPSON

Of all the leading architects of the mid-Victorian Gothic school, William White[1] came nearest to complete oblivion. He wrote no books, and although a frequent letter writer and speaker almost to the end of his life, by middle age he was regarded in some circles as an intellectual fossil of no contemporary relevance: 'one of those amiable romanticists who command respect because of their guileless confidence in the irresistible force of obsolete systems of argument'.[2]

His buildings did not keep him in the public eye. They were country churches, houses, and schools; apart from two Cornish banks and two colonial cathedrals, he designed no prominent public buildings – no English cathedral, no town hall, railway station, or government office. The *Builder* declared in its obituary that he designed 'no building of the first importance'.[3] When the reassessment of Victorian Gothic began between the wars, he received no mention in either Sir Kenneth Clark's *The Gothic Revival* or H. S. Goodhart-Rendel's *English Architecture Since the Regency*, and less than a page in Basil Clarke's *Church Builders of the Nineteenth Century*. As late as 1958 in H.-R. Hitchcock's *Architecture: Nineteenth and Twentieth Centuries* he receives only three sentences; and while his churches were being noticed in both *The Buildings of England* by Nikolaus Pevsner and *Murray's Architectural Guides* by John Betjeman, neither identified his other buildings. Some of these were taken by Betjeman and Hitchcock to be by G. E. Street (e.g. St Michael's House Wantage and Probus church school), and undoubtedly assisted the reviving reputation of that architect at the expense of White himself.

White deserves a reappraisal for three reasons. First, some of his buildings have absolute qualities which are unequalled. No contemporary developed more fully Pugin's recommendation that 'an architect should exhibit his skill by turning the

---

1. The best biographical note on White is in the *R.I.B.A. Journal*, VII (1900), p. 145. I should like to thank Stefan Muthesius for helping me on a number of important points in this account of White's writing.　　2. *Architect*, XXIII (1880), p. 363.　　3. ibid. LXIII (1900), p. 91.

226

difficulties which occur in raising an elevation from *a convenient plan* into so many *picturesque beauties*'.[1] His houses are fascinating exercises in this direction. At the same time he had a rare skill in handling constructional polychromy, both in the simple contrasts of local stones, tiles, and flints, and in the more elaborate and subtle use of coloured brickwork, above all in his two outstanding churches at Aberdeen Park, London, and at Lyndhurst.

Secondly, White gave lectures and wrote on an unusually wide range of subjects. As a result we can understand his attitude to his profession, to the problems of design, and to Victorian society, and relate these attitudes to his practical work. It is rare to see these connexions so candidly explained.

Thirdly, White's opinions and designs were, especially in the 1850s, an important influence on his contemporaries. He was given very considerable publicity in the *Ecclesiologist*. Street in particular was heavily dependent upon him, both in ideas and in architectural style. He was also a pioneer in church furniture design, for his solid rough benches at Gerrans (1849), fixed by prominent carpenter's pegs, are one of the earliest examples of the 'Pre-Raphaelite' style. Later he was one of the first patrons of the Morris firm – and the standard of his glass design remained high. And although by the 1860s he had made his chief contribution, his numerous papers and interventions in discussion at both the Architectural Association and the R.I.B.A. helped to sustain those of his contemporaries (by no means the least) who remained at heart High Victorians.

William White's life falls into the pattern of early brilliance followed by tedious maturity which was the fate of many Gothic Revival architects, and which may be an inevitable aspect of an age of romanticism. He was born in 1825 into a cultured clerical family. His great-uncle was Gilbert White of Selborne, and his father was curate of Blakesley and private chaplain to Sir Henry Dryden of Canon's Ashby. It is hard to imagine a more beautiful setting in which to grow up: the well-wooded, swelling Northamptonshire farmland; the villages of thatch and golden ironstone; and occasional visits with his father to Canon's Ashby itself, where the medieval fragment of the priory church stood beside a rambling patchwork brick and stone house.

The whole place has a delightful air of antiquity about it; whether in the paved court...or on the long straight paths of the garden, chequered by the shadow of great cedars; on the curved and moss-grown steps, bending hither and thither over the roots of other ancient trees, which guard them on either side; . . . or up in the green court, between the high lichen-covered walls.[2]

With this fortunate beginning White was less handicapped than he might have been by the narrowly practical character of his training under Squirhill of Leamington, to whom he was apprenticed in 1840. He was taken to sites and builders'

1. *True Principles* (1841), p. 63.
2. J. A. Gotch, *Architecture of the Renaissance in England* (1894), II, p. 17.

workshops, 'taught some of the principles of construction, of quantities, and of the supervision of work, but little in the way of design and drawings'; this he largely taught himself through sketching old examples.[1] From Leamington in about 1845 he moved to London to become an assistant to Gilbert Scott, whose father had been a friend of the family. In Scott's office he met G. E. Street and G. F. Bodley, both of whom were fellow assistants. They must have greatly stimulated his development. He was, however, the first of the three to leave, probably because he had the greater financial resources; he set up his own practice in Truro in 1847.

White worked for five years in Truro before returning to London. Street followed him to Cornwall in 1848 to start his own independent career and until Street's move to Wantage in 1850 the two were constant companions. Their common stock of ideas appears clearly in three papers of this period, which present a two-pronged attack upon the steep-roofed, low-aisled, ecclesiological model church, as being incongruously timid and inevitably dark in the town, while in the countryside it was extravagantly assertive.[2] Street's dependence upon White is especially marked in his paper of 1853 'On the Revival of the Ancient Style of Domestic Architecture',[3] which draws directly from White's 'Upon Some of the Causes and Points of Failure in Modern Design' of two years earlier.[4]

White's influence on Street is also clearly revealed in a comparison between their Cornish buildings. Once again most of the original points spring from White. By 1850–1 White's early style was fully formed; it can be found in the parsonages at St Columb (1849–50) and Ruan Lanihorne (1850), the parish school at Probus (1849), in the unexecuted designs for Baldhu and Mithian,[5] and in the sketches with which he illustrated his lectures. Moreover, after his adoption of constructional polychromy in 1853, the principles of design which he used throughout his life were complete. Street, however, having learnt all by 1853 that White had to give him, was to develop continually under the influence of his Continental discoveries and later of his own pupils, while White remained an exponent of the principles of 1849–53. This meant that White had produced his finest works by the age of thirty-five, and scarcely designed a significant building in his last thirty years. Nevertheless his consistency allowed both his ideas and his architecture to reach a complete maturity which is rare in the mid-Victorian period.

Possibly White's secure background made him less restlessly eager to push on than many of his contemporaries. He was a devout churchman, but without any hint

1. *Builder*, XLIX (1885), p. 623.

2. Street, 'On the Proper Characteristics of a Town Church', *Ecclesiologist*, XI (1850), pp. 227–33; White, ibid., XII (1851), pp. 305–13, and 'On Some Principles of Design in Churches', *Transactions of the Exeter Diocesan Architectural Society*, IV, p. 176.

3. *Ecclesiologist*, XIV (1853), pp. 71–80.

4. ibid., XII (1851), pp. 305–13.   5. ibid., X (1849), p. 262; XII (1851), p. 296.

of fanaticism. He enjoyed an argument, even throwing himself into the Bacon–Shakespeare controversy. Neither his clumsy manner nor his unimportant practice deterred him from frequent speeches at both the Architectural Association and the R.I.B.A. He was clearly happy in his work: 'to him everything connected with his art was a delight'.[1] His opinions were apparently honoured at home: readers of the *British Architect*, to which he contributed regularly as a 'Friend in Council', learnt that his whole family had taken up his enthusiasm for Laing's Swedish gymnastics,[2] and that his wife was acting as secretary to his effort to provide residential clubs for clerks and students in preference to 'the usual solitary, comfortless lodging, removed from the supervision or sympathy of friends'.[3] One comes from his writing with the impression of a man of conviction and enthusiasm, with genuine personal warmth and kindness.

It is not perhaps very surprising to find one who had known William Morris campaigning against the unhealthiness and ugliness of wasp waists, tight bodices, and tight shoes.

Anyone walking for a short distance behind the outpourings of a suburban train may see how frightful is the following which folly and fashion obtain in these respects ... Whether we are to be allowed or not to express our opinion as lovers, husbands, wives, parents, teachers or guardians,

White asserts that it is the duty of a professional to protest. But it is characteristic that a reflection provoked by visual irritation leads to a deeper social observation. He sits at a ceremony watching young women (perhaps his own daughter?) climbing the platform 'to receive their well-earned prizes and their University certificate'. They flounder helplessly, their knees tied tightly together, their heels tottering, reaching an arm for assistance which can hardly stretch fully because the sleeves are so closely fitted. How can one defend higher education for women, he asks, when it leaves them so pathetically unfree?[4]

In the same way his social insight led him to different attitudes to craftsmanship from those of Ruskin and Morris. He shared their fundamental belief in a balance between intellectual and physical work.[5] He was as aware as they were that it was contemporary workmanship which made it impossible to recapture the beauty of medieval work. When restoring an old church, imitation of old work was bound to be a 'lifeless body'; 'workmen cannot comprehend the value of a grey surface; or of an ancient profile-moulding left intact; or of that absence of precision which at

1. *R.I.B.A. Journal*, VII (1900), p. 145.
2. loc. cit., XVI (1881), p. 363. His enthusiasm for exercise is also indicated by a booklet, *The Tourist's Knapsack and its Contents* (1875).
3. ibid., XIX (1883), p. 269.
4. ibid., XVI (1881), p. 363.
5. ibid., XIX (1883), p. 162.

times imparts a pleasing tone'.[1] Modern ironwork suffered in the same way: it was 'so intensely tame and shoppy in its finish ... The indiscriminate use of the file, indeed, has given rise to a false taste in metal work very much akin to that of scraping the stonework of the noble minster fronts of Lincoln and Winchester'. Division of labour was the fault: 'the system so largely adopted of imitating forged work on a large scale by the bending, gauging, cutting, screwing together by hands which move as mechanically as machinery does'. One needed to see 'the power of the workman's hand', hammer marks in wrought iron, chisel marks in sculpture; and this required the revival of the 'art workman'.[2]

White was also deeply concerned at the condition of the working classes as a whole. He was well-known as a sanitarian. Much of his interest was technical, as in his booklet on *Domestic Plumbing and Water Service* (1880), but he was a strong supporter of tough legislation against slum landlords – tougher than anything that has even yet been introduced.

Let it be penal to expose for letting an unfit habitation . . . All houses ought to be condemned which have not due provision for pure water supply, proper drainage, thorough ventilation, sufficient light, decent tenantable repair, and enough spaciousness in approach and court-ledges for the admission of external air ... Then the proprietors of cottages will bestir themselves.

He believed that housing for the very poor must be subsidized, perhaps by profits from artisan dwellings. Nor could he accept the degraded tastes and habits of the lowest classes as innate. He rejected the idea of single-room cottages for the very poor; from personal knowledge 'I am convinced that it is not from desire, but from real or imaginary compulsion, if in any case, the poor prefer a single room to two'.[3] He noticed the gaiety of the street grinders' music and 'the exuberant, though genuine, delight expressed by the uneducated at the poorest colouring' as signs of responsiveness to art, and he argued that public buildings such as hospitals, schools, even workhouses and prisons, should be made more humane and cheerful. The starkness of solitary confinement was likely to induce hopeless, desponding madness; perhaps a little warm colouring might bring out the criminals' humanity.[4]

For their date these were advanced views. It is therefore interesting to find that he completely rejected any utopian vision based on the Ruskinian ideal of the independent craftsman. Hand craftsmanship should survive in specialized art work; although even here 'he did not want a man who would think in his own way, regardless of the thoughts of him by whom he was employed; but he wanted a man to learn and take in *his* way of thinking instead of his own'. (This was a frank statement of the method of all the best High Victorian designers, including William Morris.) But art

1. *R.I.B.A. Transactions* (1863–4), pp. 29–42. 2. ibid. (1865–6), pp. 15–30.
3. ibid. (1866–7), pp. 68–70. 4. *Building News*, VII (1861), pp. 50–5.

work apart, machinery was 'an untold blessing to poor as well as to rich, a vast population must have vast supplies at a reasonable cost'. He recognized that the change to machinery caused social disruption, but denied that it made work a drudgery –

the weary round of one unchanging operation which tends to limit the machinist's mental growth...The case is really quite the contrary. There is no drudgery so great, no degradation so low, as in those branches of manufacture requiring large reproductions of one form, or vast repetition of one process, to which as yet machinery has not been extended...The converting of a man into a human machine, which has been tauntingly attributed to machinery, is more truly and more universally attributable to the lack of it.

Nor could art suffer from the mechanization of mass-produced goods, for these required a distinctive treatment of their own.

It is very easy for others again to say, then let us adopt simpler forms and do without machinery; but neither will this do; as I have just said, we want wares for the million: and, in manufacturing for the million, we do not want the highest class of art, or a cheap and nasty reproduction of, or substitute for, that which ought to be costly...We want the best of its kind in everything ... If iron or pewter spoons are wanted for our cottages or for our kitchens, we do not require them to aim at the more ornate patterns employed in spoons of silver, or gold. ... We want a handle for holding. It must not bristle with ornament ... Simplicity is wedded for ever to utility ...We would have them appear useful.[1]

There can be no denying the force of these objections to what Ruskin had said and Morris was to say; and one wonders whether White might have been provoked by his encounters with Morris at this date.

White, although a gothicist, was a rationalist. He believed architecture to be as much a science as an art, and that 'design is not a mere matter of taste. I say it is capable of analysis'.[2] 'More and more scientific research must be made into the nature and causes of beauty'.[3] He regarded most of his lectures as contributions to a rational system of design. Many of them are strictly technical, dealing with questions of fireproof construction,[4] lighting, sanitation, acoustics, and contracting.[5] His descriptions of his own buildings are all of this kind – notably those of his experiments in cheap church building and in the use of brick and concrete walling,[6] and of his house at Humewood in Ireland.[7] It was typical that he should issue a public statement on the failure of the brick pillars at Lyndhurst church.[8]

His papers on historical buildings are plainly descriptive for the same reasons.[9]

1. *R.I.B.A. Transactions* (1865–6), pp. 15–30.   2. ibid. (1880–1), p. 189.
3. *Ecclesiologist*, XIV (1853), pp. 313–30.
4. e.g. *R.I.B.A. Transactions* (1884–5), pp. 65–72.
5. e.g. *British Architect*, XIX (1883), p. 49.   6. *Builder*, XXXIII (1875), p. 48.
7. *R.I.B.A. Transactions* (1868–9), pp. 78–88.   8. ibid. (1866–7), pp. 187–90.
9. ibid. (1885–6), pp. 66–88, Gotland; ibid. (1888–9), pp. 141–64, the Durham Galilee; *British Architect*, XXV (1886), pp. 266, 295, 322, leaning towers of Bologna.

He found restoration work, if unremunerative, absorbing: 'the whole building is full of interest from the bottom to the top'. He was deeply sensitive to the texture of old buildings, and the need to record all the particulars of restoration work, but he believed that old buildings must be used or sooner or later they would be destroyed; thus he rejected Morris's doctrine that they should be repaired, but not adapted to suit contemporary use. 'If old buildings were thus to become mere museums of anti-quarianism, or of curiosity, all affection for them ... would very quickly die away.'[1] Nor, in his careful descriptions of buildings, is White concerned with picking out interesting motives for use elsewhere. His concern is with essential principles. He examines their construction, watches for hints of the medieval methods of building organization, measures their proportions, but only to develop his own system of design.

His own style, it is true, was grounded in English Gothic; but although he was an inveterate traveller, and toured northern France as early as 1850,[2] it is remarkable how rare directly borrowed motives are in his work. (The tower of All Saints Notting Hill of 1852, apparently derived from Ghent, is an exception.) White in fact strongly denied that his design principles applied only to Gothic. The Picturesque, for example, was equally the right principle in classical architecture.[3]

Shall I then decline to treat a quasi-Classic house or church because a Gothic treatment of it would be incongruous and unsuitable, and my own predilections are Gothic? Certainly not ... Style, as such, must be thrown to the winds as a mere piece of eclecticism ... Much more depends upon the mode of treatment.[4]

Design 'should not start from any single style which had a defined expression, so much as from those principles of construction and truth which were enunciated by the requirements of the age we live in'.[5]

The basis of good design was a convenient plan. White believed that an architect should seek as much information on the uses of the building as possible, but should always insist on his liberty to devise its plan.'Ordinary persons who may have an undefined knowledge of what they want can rarely put it into such a form as really to meet their requirements.'[6] There should be no attempt to fit the internal arrange-ment to a preconceived exterior. The elevations should 'be subservient to, and ex-pressive of, the general internal arrangement of a building'.[7] The plan should also be modified to make the best use of the site. White recognized that uniformity and

1. *R.I.B.A. Transactions* (1863–4), pp. 29–42, 'Notes on Newland Church, Gloucestershire, with Remarks on Church Restoration and Arrangements'; *Builder*, XXXVI (1878), p. 115, 'Restoration versus Conservation'.

2. *British Architect*, XXXIII (1890), p. 39.   3. *Builder*, XVIII (1860), p. 278.

4. *British Architect*, XXI (1884), p. 145.   5. *R.I.B.A. Transactions* (1866–7), p. 154.

6. *British Architect*, XXVII (1887), p. 224, 'Plans and Elevations'.

7. *Ecclesiologist*, XIV (1853), pp. 313–30.

simplicity were fundamental aesthetic qualities. Nevertheless, blank windows for the sake of symmetry indicated a failure of design, just as much as striking variety among windows whose function was identical.

In all design it is of far greater consequence that the laws of fitness should be followed than that a rigid uniformity should be observed. The ends of nature and of necessity must be first served, and then the ends of art.[1]

The principle of picturesque planning was thus 'fitting irregularity'. The elevations should express the plan by 'providing an external clue to structural arrangement' (Plate 42). This expression was an aesthetic, not a functional necessity; indeed a feature might need to be 'even humoured or exaggerated in order to make it appear natural'.[2] In general, more important rooms should be emphasized by more prominent roofs. Thus the Houses of Parliament suffered from 'the want of distinctive features'; it was impossible to see where Lords or Commons were. On a small scale the ordinary house failed because it was an undifferentiated box. The L plan would usually be more convenient, and inferior rooms, such as pantries, closets, and passages, should be under separate lower roofs of their own. Instead of horizontal eaves, or the '*needless* multiplicity' of a row of gables, the miniature gables of the smaller rooms made an attractive foil to the main high roof. Cottages should be plainer still. A restless outline 'laden with chimneyshafts' was wrong. 'A cottage will seldom bear more than a single ridged roof, with perhaps a shed at the back or one end, and a dormered window, if *necessary*, and *where* it is really wanted, and a low porch.' In school design the building's purpose should be expressed by emphasizing the school room in contrast to the master's house.[3]

The design of details should proceed in the same manner. White's paper 'On Windows'[4] is a complex discussion of the manifold functions of the window – internal lighting, external prospect, ventilation, insulation – leading to the suggestion of different forms for rooms of different purpose. It is characteristic of the age that he does not advise bright light in a study; 'freshness of thought' is best induced by moderate light, while 'twilight is the most favourable to deep and close intellectual contemplation'. It is again revealing that he argued that houses should be designed for winter comfort rather than for 'a few bright months, when the greater part of the year is comparatively stormy and cold, or at the best changeable and uncertain'. Thus an essentially romantic preference finds a rational justification.

White also wished to rationalize other aesthetic preferences of the period. If he found the cube an 'excruciating proportion',[5] he could not accept that this might be an instinctive reaction to its classical associations. He argued that medieval pro-

---

1. *Building News*, VI (1860), pp. 132–4, 'Architectural Uniformity and its Claims'.
2. ibid. 3. *Ecclesiologist*, XIV (1853), pp. 313–30.
4. ibid., XVII (1856), pp. 319–32. 5. *British Architect*, XXXIII (1890), p. 4.

portions had been based upon plane trigonometry, and in the best periods upon the equilateral triangle.[1] He found systematic proportions one explanation of the attractiveness of the Crystal Palace,[2] and believed that such systems were related to acoustic needs.[3] He also called for a scientific study of symbolism, 'as essential to architecture as poetry to literature...the only means of conveying abstract religious truth in a form comprehensible by man'.[4]

Again, he wished to analyse 'his own intense delight in colour'[5] by the study of chromatic laws. A systematic colour code should be established and taught to common house-painters. The psychological effects of colour should be investigated. It was apparent that responsiveness to colour was a fundamental human quality. Colour delighted children, and could give interest to the blank life of a bedridden invalid; and for this reason he attacked the absence of colour in public institutions. Florence Nightingale had much to answer for in the sanitary obsession with glazed white tiles. It was significant that the renunciation of worldly pleasures by monastic orders included the wearing of black or white habits. Colour was 'a luxury upon which the eye can feast'. Yet different colours had different effects: the nerves were 'excited by the presence of red, soothed by the presence of green, and deadened or benumbed by the presence of blue'. William White was not one of those High Victorian enthusiasts for polychromy who sought the strange pleasures of aesthetic discordance. Colour was wanted as a respite from the whirl of business.

I am not pleading for the indiscriminate, inharmonious, strongly contrasted and fantastic colouring which earnest advocates for polychromy are sometimes supposed to delight in, but for the deep, full, rich, harmonious luxuriance which has the power of exhilarating whilst it soothes.[6]

The consistency of White's thinking is particularly interesting when he turns to the two crucial problems of nineteenth-century architectural theory, to which new solutions were to open the way for the twentieth-century style. First, the problem of ornament. Ornament, he believed, with Pugin, must be related to a rational structure; but from Ruskin he took the idea that ornament was in principle useless, a luxury super-added. 'In all nature the most beautiful objects, as he thought he had learnt from Mr. Ruskin's writings, were those which apparently were least to be regarded as utilitarian.' It followed that since ornament was a luxury, it was inappropriate to cheap mass-produced goods. Mechanized ornament was a sham, which revealed an underlying social disease. 'Each one vies with his fellow to keep up appearances and to follow in this especial respect those above him in the social

1. *Ecclesiologist*, XIV (1853), pp. 313–30.   2. ibid., XVI (1855), pp. 162–3.
3. *R.I.B.A. Transactions* (1894–5), pp. 372–3.   4. *Builder*, XVIII (1860), p. 203.
5. *R.I.B.A. Transactions* (1865–6), p. 42.
6. *Building News*, VII (1861), pp. 50–5, 'A Plea for Polychromy'; *Builder*, XLVII (1884), p. 99, 'The Hygienic Value of Colour in the Dwelling'.

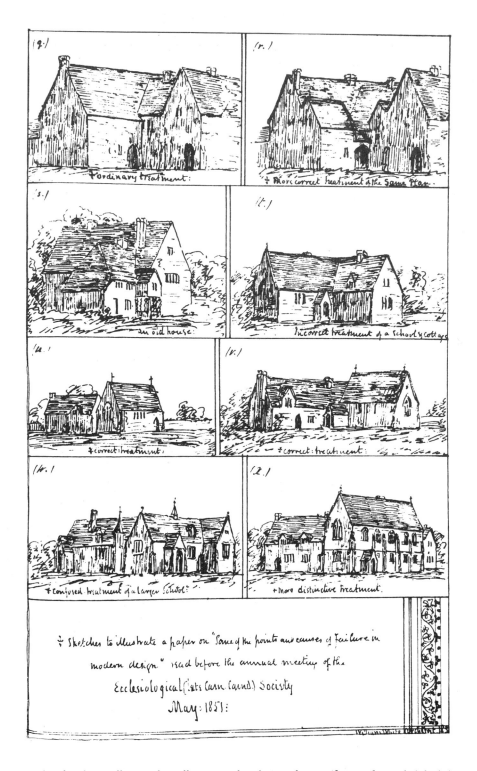

42. Sketches by William White illustrating his design theory (from *The Ecclesiologist*)

scale. . .by catching at some external sign or shadow.' Ornament should be restricted to work where it could be done properly, by hand.[1] White's practical solution has to a large extent come about in modern architectural practice, although he reached it from the assumption that ornamental work was, by definition, the best form of design.

This did not mean that White was uninterested in the second problem – the role of new forms of cheap construction and new materials. He regarded cheap building as 'in one sense a school of art. It teaches the best, the most natural, the most simple modes of construction'. He was prepared to experiment in timber framing, brick, brick and concrete, and iron construction; and his two Hampshire churches at Smannell and Hatherden were planning variants intended for direct comparison. But these experiments confirmed his preference for traditional materials. 'After an animated discussion upon this subject, in the galleries of the Architectural Exhibition' he obtained an estimate for an iron-built chapel for comparison with brick and stone: 'the iron building, in its very simplest form, would have amounted to between twice and three times as much as the other'. The margin of difference had narrowed to about 25 per cent by 1880, but White never found it economic to use iron.[2] In the same way his aesthetic preference for local materials could be justified economically, while it was true in his lifetime that thick walls afforded 'comfort both in appearance and reality'.[3] Thus the massiveness of architecture was both sensible and pleasing.

The consequence was that, for the present at any rate, the development of iron and steel construction was of little relevance to architecture. It was too expensive for small, cheap structures. Apart from wrought iron, it was not a very suitable ornamental material. Where cost was less relevant, it had no special aesthetic virtues to contribute to a system of design based on free planning and solid walls. Its intrinsic quality was its airiness and elegance; 'to give iron a real and apparent massiveness, they at once destroyed its character and ostensible use'. The mass production of parts in a large planning grid made any modification of outline or irregularity of plan almost impossible. 'Where was the massiveness so essential to architecture – the bulk – above everything else, the shadow? How could there be architecture without shadow?'[4]

The only role of iron was therefore in large-scale utilitarian constructions where it was demonstrably swift and cheap: Crystal Palaces, railway stations, bridges, and market halls. White was well aware of the beauty of such structures. He found the Crystal Palace itself 'a noble as well as successful work', 'truly wonderful', reminding him 'of those magnificent palaces described in fairy tales'. He recognized that it succeeded because, apart from its proportions and outline, it did not seek conven-

1. *R.I.B.A. Transactions* (1864–5), p. 152; (1865–6), pp. 15–30; *Building News*, X (1863), p. 391.
2. *Building News*, XL (1881), pp. 258–60, 'Cheap Churches'; ibid., X (1863), p. 391.
3. *Ecclesiologist*, XII (1851), pp. 305–13.
4. *R.I.B.A. Transactions* (1865–6), pp. 15–30, 'Ironwork: Its Legitimate Uses and Proper Treatment'; *Architect*, XXIII (1880), pp. 363, 370.

tional architectural qualities; 'and, indeed, wherever architectural detail has been the most aimed at, there is the greatest amount of failure'.[1] He also saw that a time might come when iron or steel were much more widely applicable, and that a new architecture would then be reached. With the use of iron, 'purity of outline, with almost total absence of ornament, might gradually be made to pervade everything from our buildings to our teaspoons'. But this was utopian; and he was content, until that time, to leave iron constructions in other hands.

For at this point the damaging effects of his views on the hierarchy of ornament become clear. Such utilitarian structures are of an inherently lower order, just as lithography or photography are to painting. White is therefore content to leave their design to the (implicitly) inferior hands of engineers. Engineering and architecture are distinctive professions, 'the one consisting in the science and art of construction – the other in the science and art of composition and design'. He adds lamely, 'it would be well if each knew a little more of the other's branch', as if aware that here was a broken link in his rationalism.[2] One wishes that White's romantic rebellion could have been pushed to its rational conclusion. He had used the calculations of Telford the engineer in constructing Lyndhurst; he could recognize successful design in the Crystal Palace; what logic could there be in the gulf between the two professions?

1. *Ecclesiologist*, XVI (1855), pp. 162–3.   2. *R.I.B.A. Transactions* (1865–6), pp. 15–30.

Architectural Touring with the Little Guides

BY ALEC CLIFTON-TAYLOR

'I AM AFRAID', said my companion with a sigh, 'that this is yet another of the Little Guides' swans which turns out to be a goose.' The church in question was indeed ideally equipped for the evocation of Little Guide raptures. It had a hagioscope, a freak-size aumbry, a low-side window of course, a blocked recess the original purpose of which was obscure (and therefore a talking point), a tomb with a defaced effigy which might, or alternatively might not, have represented a knight who lived locally in the early part of the fourteenth century (another signpost for learned speculation), a gawky old font which had lately been rescued from a near-by hedge, a sanctus bell-turret, a banner-stave locker, a 'serpent' in a glass case to recall the days before so many village churches became encumbered with ugly organs, and some fragments of early heraldic glass in the tracery lights of nave windows otherwise completely reglazed by the Victorians.

It is safe to say that for the architectural tourist, as each new and eagerly awaited volume of The Buildings of England makes its appearance, another Little Guide moves to the back of the shelf. Some of these guides, it is true, have been appearing in revised editions printed in a more up-to-date format; but the revisions, although an improvement, have in my experience never been drastic enough to keep pace with a new taste in architecture which may find the Victorianized parish church to be among the least interesting and enjoyable of a town's buildings. And indeed the gradual supplanting of the Little Guides ante-dates Dr Pevsner by a few years; I have not used W. A. Dutt's books for church visiting in Suffolk or Norfolk since the publication of the late Munro Cautley's two memorable volumes in 1937 and 1949, and for those in a very robust condition of health or rich enough to afford a book-caddie there has been, since 1947, Raymond Richards's weighty tome, *Old Cheshire Churches*.

Shortly after these came other books which are my constant companions. Three counties (alas, so far only three) have been covered in a stimulating and brilliant

238

fashion by Murray's New Architectural Guides: *Buckinghamshire* (1948) and *Berkshire* (1949), both by John Betjeman and John Piper, and *Lancashire* (1955), an invaluable work by Peter Fleetwood-Hesketh. A. K. Wickham's *The Churches of Somerset* (1952) is also a valuable book, but unhappily he did not live to undertake the projected gazetteer. Among the many other topographical books which have been appearing during the past thirty years or so, some, like the Shell Guides, make delightful reading but are too brief for detailed use on the spot, while others are too gossipy or long-winded to satisfy the dedicated architectural tourist.

But suppose that one began looking at England's buildings, as I did, in the early 1920s: what books were there to help one? There were Kelly's Directories on the shelves of the public library, valuable for reference, but somewhat daunting to a schoolboy. For a few counties the library would also produce Royal Commission volumes (but they were only concerned with buildings up to 1714), and for others it was worth browsing in the Victoria County Histories. The parish churches, but no other buildings, in about ten counties had also been covered by a useful set of handbooks bound in green, the County Churches series, which unhappily became a war casualty in 1914. Murray's original Handbooks for Travellers could sometimes be found on the bookshelves of elderly friends, but one seldom seemed to be able to pick up a copy of the county one wanted in a bookshop, perhaps because, understandably enough, no owner of a set of Murrays could ever bear to part with them. Nevertheless, despite their wonderful Introductions, by the twenties these famous red books were no longer really adequate. Their quality, needless to say, varies. The king, I believe, is generally considered to be *Lincolnshire*, by the Rev. G. E. Jeans, which was first published in 1888; *Durham and Northumberland* (3rd edition, 1890) is another which still makes absorbing reading. Yet in the field of domestic buildings Murray is seldom at his best on the purely architectural side, and is likely to devote much more space to the painting and sculpture in a country house than to the house itself. At Saltram, for example, there is two-thirds of a page on the pictures and *objets d'art* but not a word about Adam, while at Wilton the paintings and the marbles receive over two closely packed pages whereas neither Inigo Jones nor Webb is so much as mentioned. The account of Raby Castle, to take one more example, runs to almost three pages, but nearly two-thirds of this description turns out to be a family history of the Nevilles and the Vanes.

It was accordingly the Little Guides which were our perpetual standbys. They seemed indispensable, and in truth for certain counties, *faute de mieux*, they still are. Even today I should not think of visiting, say, Monmouthshire, or Dorset, or Staffordshire, or the East Riding of Yorkshire, without the appropriate little red book in my left-hand jacket pocket.

The first few volumes were the work of distinguished men, but they did not deal with specific counties. Joseph Wells, the author of *Oxford and its Colleges* (1897), spent most of his life as a don at Wadham, of which he was Warden from 1913 to 1927; he also wrote the college history. The companion volume on *Cambridge and its Colleges*, which appeared a year later, was by no less a scholar than the future Professor Hamilton Thompson, whose first book it was: he was then twenty-five. The next two were *Shakespeare's Country* and *Westminster Abbey*, the former, like *The Malvern Country* (1901), contributed by Professor Sir Bertram Windle, F.R.S., President of University College, Cork, who was known primarily as an anatomist and ethnologist. A hint of his qualifications for Little Guide writing, 1900 style, is, however, contained in the recreations he listed for *Who's Who*: cycling and flint-hunting. Here already is the pattern of this authorship in its early phase; academic, antiquarian, and indefatigably bicycle-riding.

The county volumes proper began with the appearance in 1900 of *Sussex* by F. G. Brabant, also a resident of Oxford, and were completed twenty-two years later with the publication of F.T.S. Houghton's *Worcestershire*, by which time most of the earlier volumes had been several times reprinted and at least once revised. There was a book apiece for every county except six; as with The Buildings of England, Leicestershire and Rutland, Cumberland and Westmorland, and Beds and Hunts had to join forces. But Yorkshire was allotted no less than four volumes, for in addition to one for each Riding, York had a book to itself, the last of the whole series, published in 1924.

Contrary to the general belief, the authors of the Little Guides were not for the most part parsons. A biographical survey reveals that several – including Charles Masefield (*Staffordshire*), a young Wolverhampton solicitor who was killed in France in 1917 – were lawyers, while a number of others were journalists. The latter include John B. Firth (*Middlesex*, 1906), with firsts in Mods and Greats, William A. Dutt (*Norfolk*, 1902, and *Suffolk*, 1904), who worked in the Press Gallery of the House of Commons until a breakdown in health sent him back to his native East Anglia, and that strange man Walter M. Gallichan, who proudly described himself as a pioneer of sex education in England and whose books, nearly sixty strong, included 'Sexual Apathy in Women', 'Youthful Old Age', and 'The Poison of Prudery'. In such company it is not surprising to find his Little Guide to *Cheshire* (1905) too insignificant to be listed at all among his publications. It is, incidentally, about the weakest of the whole set.

Among the many other laymen there was George Clinch (1860–1921), for many years Librarian to the Society of Antiquaries, who did the original *Kent* (1903), which was later replaced, *The Isle of Wight* (1904), *St Paul's Cathedral* (1906), and finally *London* (1912). There was also J. E. Hodgkin (1875–1953), a wealthy and genial Quaker industrialist (telegraphic address: Energy Darlington). He was an enormous man in every sense: the boys at Leighton Park School, of which he was Vice-Chairman, knew him as 'Fat Edward', but although in later life he weighed at least eighteen stone his height, which was 6 ft 3 or 6 ft 4 inches, was in proportion. Hodgkin was an enthusiastic amateur archaeologist, and, I am told, he would sometimes toss off a watercolour or two in the train between Darlington and King's Cross, on the way to Friends' House or a meeting of one or other of the twenty-odd companies of which he was chairman. He was also a pioneer motorist (he owned a car in 1901), a Rotarian, and of course a Justice of the Peace for his Little Guide county, *Durham* (1913).

Of the seven or eight clerical writers, Herbert W. Macklin is chiefly known not for his *Bedfordshire and Huntingdonshire* (1917) but as the author of what is still the standard work on English monumental brasses. The Wade brothers did four Little Guides together: *Somerset* (1907), *Monmouthshire* (1909), *South Wales* (1913), and *Herefordshire* (1917). Seven years later J. H. Wade did one more on his own: *Cathedral Cities of England and Wales*. They were a very clerical family: both brothers followed their father into the Church. The elder, Dr G. W. Wade, was Professor of Latin at St David's College, Lampeter, and wrote a number of theological books.

Sabine Baring-Gould, the 'squarson' of Lew Trenchard, Devon ('owns 3000 acres'), was a far more famous character than any of these: indeed, the only one of the Little Guide authors to be accorded a place in the Dictionary of National Biography. Born in 1834 and surviving almost until his ninetieth birthday, this fecund High Churchman – fecund in every sense, for he was the father of five sons and nine daughters – poured forth an endless stream of books, 159 to be precise, ranging from 'Curious Myths of the Middle Ages' and 'The Book of Were-Wolves' to the lives of the Saints (in sixteen volumes) and a biography of Parson Hawker of Morwenstow, which had a great success in its day despite numerous inaccuracies. Every Continental holiday was followed by a travel book; every batch of sermons found its way into print; there was also a quota of popular novels. The author of 'Onward, Christian Soldiers' was by no means a profound writer, and his Little Guide to *Devon* (1907) is as full both of factual errors and entertaining anecdotes as are many of his other books, but lively and picturesque he certainly was.

Dr J. Charles Cox (1843–1919) was only a little less prolific, both in paternity – seven sons and three daughters – and in published works, but for the architectural tourist he was a far more important figure. Cox was a man of multifarious interests, writing also about forestry, sports and pastimes, rambles, parish registers, numismatics, monasteries, and 'The Gardens of Scripture'. But topography, and especially parish churches, was always his foremost concern, and *The English Parish Church*, which first appeared in 1914, was long regarded as the best general handbook on this subject, as perhaps in some respects it still is. In the early years of this century there was probably nobody in England, unless it were Francis Bond, who knew the parish churches so well as Dr Cox; and for his prodigious industry he vies with Dr Pevsner himself. He was the author of seven of the Little Guides, starting with

241

Derbyshire in 1903 and *Hampshire* in 1904. His other five, *Essex*, *Warwickshire*, *Gloucestershire*, *Cambridgeshire*, and *Lincolnshire*, were all published between 1909 and 1916, that is to say between his sixty-sixth and seventy-third years. But they were far from all. In those seven years he also completely rewrote two others, *Surrey* and *Kent*, and produced six volumes (on five more counties) in the County Churches series referred to above, as well as his classic, *The English Parish Church*.

Exactly how this vast undertaking was accomplished has not been easy to discover. In earlier editions of a well-known book of reference, Nikolaus Pevsner used to list as his sole recreation 'road walks of 12 miles and over', and it seems probable that Dr Cox might well have done likewise.

The county [of Warwickshire] did not become known to me at large until 1902–03 [i.e. in his sixtieth year], when I tramped it fairly thoroughly from end to end, and across its entire width, in search of information for the story of the Religious Houses of Warwickshire, and in connection with the second volume of the Victoria County History of this shire.

To the V.C.H. of Derbyshire Cox was also a substantial contributor, and this, the county of his first Little Guide, was evidently one which he knew very well indeed; in fact, as early as 1875–9 he had published four fat volumes on the churches of Derbyshire. Later came Surrey, in which 'I have left no parish nor corner unvisited'. Elsewhere the standard was not quite as rigorous as this: in Essex, despite many visits, 'a small minority of the less interesting and more remote parishes are yet unknown to me'; in Hampshire, his Little Guide contains

my original observation of the buildings of about four-fifths of the whole number of villages; as for the remainder, which are for the most part of minor importance, I have to thank clergy and others who have kindly answered my questions, and I am indebted to the books named in the bibliography.

Whether in the end Dr Cox allowed himself the use of a motor car is a teasing subject for speculation, since the Introduction to *Lincolnshire*, his last and largest Little Guide, published when he was seventy-three, is on this point distinctly ambiguous.

It is a county [he wrote] with many delightfully wide and extensive views ... But this will not be revealed save to those who make use of walking, riding, driving or cycling. There is also, of course, motoring for the wealthy tourist, but for one who uses such a mode of locomotion sensibly, there are a score who are tempted to whirl on at breathless speed, unobservant of surroundings. To study the picturesque from a motor-car is next-door to an impossibility; the impression gained is at best visionary.

The impression gained from Dr Cox's Little Guides is anything but visionary, and if he did steel himself in the end to the use of this new mode of locomotion we can be quite sure that he would have been one of the few who used it sensibly. What is equally certain is that he would have encountered, off the main roads, dusty lanes, shying horses, constant punctures, and not infrequently more serious mechanical mishaps. Which renders his achievement all the more daunting.

With so many authors involved, one must be wary of too easy generalizations. Five Little Guides by one author in particular are notably different from the usual contributions to the series. Joseph E. Morris (who died as recently as 1954) was responsible for all the four *Yorkshire* volumes (the fourth being, as mentioned earlier, the *City of York*) and for *Northumberland*. He also wrote the book on *Surrey* in the County Churches series. His writing is leisurely, discursive, and at times long-winded; he was a very 'viewy' man, highly subjective in his approach. But partly for this very reason, partly because he was really interested in, and capable of, aesthetic criticism, partly also because he had a wide knowledge of Western European as well as of British architecture and the allied arts, and believed, as he wrote, that 'comparison is comprehension', Morris's books can be read with considerable enjoyment *at home* as none of the others can. He had in fact more in common with Francis Bond than with most of his fellow-authors of the Little Guides, and in some ways, including his punctilio in always giving references to sources, he seems to presage John Harvey.

In the course of his long account of York Minster – which he compares very unfavourably (and in my view on the whole rightly so) with Beverley – we are treated to little disquisitions on west fronts with twin towers, on the varying relationship of the central to the west towers at a number of our cathedrals, on the comparative qualities of the three great Flowing Decorated windows at York, Carlisle, and Selby, and on English rose (or wheel) windows, of which for major churches a complete list is provided. At Beverley the second pair of transepts prompts another digression, with as usual a list (in this instance for once not quite complete). At Hexham he can be relied upon for a passage on the function of the pulpitum as distinct from the rood screen, while the distinctive 'open crown' of St Nicholas (the cathedral) at Newcastle-on-Tyne provides the cue for a little critical survey of all the other examples. Such subjects having always interested me, I find these circumambulations endearing, but to others I suppose that this kind of approach could be a trifle irritating. The present chairman of Methuen's has described to me how, as a young man, it fell to him to deal with the revised editions of Joseph Morris's Little Guides, and with what distress this courteous old gentleman – who by the 1930s was a Chestertonian figure of impressive girth – greeted any hint of the need for a contraction or a cut, on the ground that his books, two of which are still easily the longest in the entire series, were just not commercial propositions.

Morris was also more open-minded than some of his fellow-authors. Here, for example, he is discussing Fountains Abbey:

Mr. St. John Hope says (xv. Y.A.J. 282): 'The ashlar work was merely lime-washed, and then the whole wall surface was "masoned" with broad red or white lines.' Not everything mediaeval was admirable! How hideous was this 'masoning' may be seen in the grand abbey church of St. Georges, at St. Martin Boscherville, in Normandy, where the noble interior is quite spoilt by it!

Yes indeed: Saint-Georges-de-Boscherville *is* greatly marred by this trivial painting of straight red lines all over the whitewashed surface of the stone, and so are a number of other French churches, Saint-Pierre at Chauvigny for instance. But 'not everything mediaeval was admirable!' That was a tremendous admission from the author of a Little Guide. Morris was also sensitive to the appeal of Seaton Delaval, which despite its 'curiously forlorn and neglected appearance, is probably the best work of its poet-architect, and unquestionably the finest of its class in Northumberland'. Then again, at Kirkleatham in the North Riding we find him greatly preferring Georgian to Victorian. 'The church was rebuilt *c.* 1763. The style, of course, is quasi-classical, but far superior to the wretched designs that disfigure most of Cleveland.' This is refreshing after the usual description of a Georgian church as 'a most unecclesiastical-looking structure' (Stoke Edith: Rev. G. W. and Rev. J. H. Wade, *Herefordshire*).

There are then, among the Little Guides, considerable differences in quality, and to a lesser extent one may also detect differences of approach. Nevertheless, as indicated in my opening paragraph, there *is* a characteristically Little Guide ambiance, a community of feeling, of taste, and above all of interest, which can be identified and discussed. For these authors were after all near contemporaries. With the exception of Baring-Gould, who was born in 1834, they were all children of the Victorian era: Charles Masefield, the youngest, was born in 1882.

Their leading characteristic, it scarcely needs to be said, was a conviction that the medieval churches are of far greater interest than any other buildings we possess. So strongly was this view held that Victorian 'restorations' would sometimes be glossed over as making (or so it was implied) very little difference. The bias, as we should expect, is towards the earlier styles; some of these authors are inclined to be rather patronizing about Perp, whereas the smallest evidences of Saxon masonry are greeted with almost audible whoops of joy, and a doorway with a chevron moulding, even if blocked up or completely recut, never fails to receive a pat on the head. Many of these entries, it must be admitted, are almost unreadably boring.

The church is of mixed architecture, mainly Dec. and Perp. with two E.E. doorways, and a N. aisle and chapel, but only a porch on the S. side. Clerestory windows are, however, placed on the S. wall as well as the N. Note (1) the Dec. piscina on the S. side of the chancel, with an E.E. lancet window next to it: (2) a low-side window with traces of an internal shutter: (3) a 13th cent. slab in the N. chapel with French marginal inscription, and a stone coffin-lid near it: and more especially (4) the font, which is of doubtful date, but has an interesting French inscription carved round the base, asking prayer for the donor's soul [Keysoe, Bedfordshire].

Passages like this occur in the Little Guides almost *ad infinitum*. What conclusion is to be drawn from them? Primarily, perhaps, this: that in most of these authors, for all their learning, there was a visual deficiency. They seem to be more concerned to discover something old than something fine. Largely, as we know, this was due to a defect in nineteenth-century education, which has not been entirely corrected even today. They were taught to learn but not to look, which may be all very well in some subjects, but will not do for the arts. Hence, within their Middle-Ages-orientated blinkers, we see them recording, analysing, and attempting (sometimes with a good deal of fuss) to date. When they venture upon an aesthetic assessment, Joseph Morris apart, they are not nearly so trustworthy. Often, in fact, they give no real indication whether a church is worth seeing, still less whether – to quote Dr Johnson's nice distinction – it is worth going to see. (But in fairness it must be added that this complaint can also be lodged against Dr Pevsner, who occasionally seems not to be able to see the church for the double-chamfered arches.)

Yet apart from their Introductions, which, although not the equal of Murray's, are generally wide-ranging and useful, there can be no doubt that it is in their church descriptions that the principal value of the Little Guides resides. If some are wearisome, others are really well done, and may be surprisingly detailed; there are, for instance, thirty-two pages on Fountains Abbey, and thirty-nine altogether on Beverley, in both cases with a plan (and incidentally the plan of Beverley is a little work of art in itself). In addition to architecture, in which the non-specialist's attention will be directed to a good deal which he might otherwise have overlooked, these books are often very informative where the interest may be more historical than aesthetic, as with brasses and heraldry. The history and genealogy of the leading local families may be set down in some detail; the subjects of small carvings, whether in stone or wood (e.g. misericords), are quite often elucidated; old fonts, screens, pulpits and medieval monuments scarcely ever go unrecorded. In short, on medieval churches these books are often a great help.

When they leave the Middle Ages, our authors seem to grow increasingly ill at ease. In the seventeenth century it is as usual J. E. Morris who, in his leisurely, over-punctuated way, is among the most open-minded. Here he is on the delightful interior of St John, Leeds (1631–4):

Altogether the general effect of the interior of the church is one of remarkable richness; though its gothic is impure, it still bears important witness to an architecture which, how-ever degraded, was still, in a sense, a living art; and it is scarcely credible, and not at all creditable, that it was actually possible, not many years ago, to propose to pull the church down. That fate, at least, is now impossible.

Leighton Bromswold is also well described (by Herbert Macklin: *Beds and Hunts*): its association with George Herbert almost guaranteed a welcome for this church.

But Staunton Harold, Leicestershire, is no more than 'a very fair reproduction of the Perp. style of 200 years earlier', and its remarkable furnishings (a whole page in Pevsner) are dismissed by Alfred Harvey in a sentence. Ingestre, Staffordshire, 'was rebuilt in an Italian style in 1676'; no other comment is offered upon the architecture of what Marcus Whiffen has rightly described as 'incomparably the most elaborate country church of its time'.

It is, however, when the Georgian period is reached that today's users of the Little Guides can enjoy some really rollicking fun. To begin with, there is that (as it must now seem) startling factual ignorance about eighteenth-century architecture, a subject to which I will recur. Even Dr Cox could describe St Philip at Birmingham (the cathedral) as 'a Palladian building, good of its kind; the architect was Thomas Arden, a pupil of Vanbrugh', and commit the vulgar error of referring to Adam as Adams. Critical comments are even more startling. For John Betjeman and John Piper Gayhurst church in Buckinghamshire, a rather stylish building of 1728 by an unknown local man, is 'one of the classical style treasures of the county', and Marcus Whiffen calls it fascinating; but all E. B. Roscoe in the Little Guide can say is that it is 'a wretched building, showing much 18th century rubbish'. The same author finds Hartwell 'a church of no interest, built at the end of the 18th century'. In fact it was built in 1753–5 by that very presentable architect Henry Keene, and is, as Nikolaus Pevsner observes, 'one of the most important churches of the Early Gothic Revival' – a fact which makes its present semi-ruinous condition a matter of the most bitter reproach, for Hartwell had, amongst its other attractions, a charming plaster fan-vault.

Nuneham Courtenay in Oxfordshire has a rather plain domed church for which Athenian Stuart was consulted, although the actual designer, Colvin tells us, was the Earl of Harcourt himself; to Brabant this was 'only remarkable as an illustration of the depraved taste of the eighteenth century'. As for Shobdon in Herefordshire, the gem of our 'Rococo Gothick' – marred only by the Norman font from the earlier church, a fine old piece which is yet quite out of place, and a dreadful east window of 1907 – here is the view of the brothers Wade: 'The present church was erected (it is said) in 1753, and looks like it'! The elegant, although at present shabby and cluttered, church which John Carr ('of York') presented to his native village of Horbury, near Wakefield, does not get so much as a mention in Morris's *West Riding*, nor does William Halfpenny's Holy Trinity, Leeds, stately but at present in even greater need of redecoration. Robert Adam's twin towers at Mistley in Essex are likewise ignored by Cox, who nevertheless spares space for the run-of-the-mill Victorian church of 1870–1, 'a fine modern building of Kentish rag, of 14th century style'. Many more examples could be cited, but only at the risk of becoming tedious.

For the same reason I do not propose to linger over the reactions of the Little Guides to eighteenth-century monuments. Today there may be a tendency to enthuse about these too indiscriminately, for the fact is, surely, that a good many of them are as works of art decidedly pedestrian; but even to find themselves in the presence of such pagan-looking, self-satisfied productions was sufficient to cast some of our authors into paroxysms of rage and despair. Let a single, egregious example suffice. That fine Queen Anne monument to Sir Robert Clayton, Lord Mayor of London, and his Lady at Bletchingley is now generally agreed to be, for England, a work of very high quality: 'the most important early-eighteenth-century monument in England', said Rupert Gunnis; 'one of the most splendid early c18 monuments in the country', says Ian Nairn; 'one of the most entirely satisfying works of art in the whole kingdom' is the view of Sacheverell Sitwell. But the *Surrey* Little Guide, after cavilling at the 'blatant inscription', prefers to quote a description of it by one Louis Jennings as 'this fearful nightmare of a monument'.

It is evident, then, that for post-Reformation, or at any rate post-Laudian, church art the Little Guides are not very useful. What of the secular and domestic side? Our authors are usually helpful in setting their towns and villages in time and place: there will be a few lines at least on the history, and the local topography, and perhaps industries, will be commented upon. On the other hand, apart from some of the Morris entries ('Alnwick, though a somewhat hard-featured and cold-looking little town, is inevitably one of the most interesting in Northumberland': an excellent opening sentence), we look in vain for analysis of the more subtle aspects of a town's appeal, such as Nikolaus Pevsner or Ian Nairn or John Piper can do so admirably. At Wisbech, for instance, Cox makes no mention at all of what today would be regarded as the town's finest feature, the Brinks.

Nor do these authors seem to have been much put out by what many people now would regard as Victorian excrescences. Here for example is Cox on one of my particular *bêtes noires*, the huge water tower at Colchester (rightly termed by Pevsner a 'painfully assertive composition'):

No notice of modern Colchester, however brief, would be complete without reference to the great water tower, which . . . is beyond doubt the most prominent erection in the town as viewed from a distance. It is not beautiful, and has been nicknamed 'Jumbo' by the townsfolk; but it is eminently utilitarian and has the distinction [*sic*] of being the second largest water tower in England. The cost of its erection in 1881 exceeded £10000.

Turning now to the big country houses, it is important not to overlook the state of scholarship at the time that the Little Guides were being written. By this time there were some very good books on English church art, but the domestic field, particularly after the middle of the seventeenth century, had been far less thoroughly explored. The debt which I personally owe to a number of my contemporaries, including several of the contributors to this volume (and not forgetting the dedicatee), is sufficient to prompt me to make very considerable allowances for the authors of the Little Guides. On scarcely any post-Restoration architect was there an authoritative monograph; attributions were current which we now know to be at least wrong, and occasionally ludicrous (e.g. from Roscoe's *Buckinghamshire*: 'Claydon House was almost entirely rebuilt in 1752 from designs by the brothers Adam'). And in addition to the difficulties of transport already alluded to, 'very few of the many private residences mentioned are open to the public' and it is 'the needs of the ordinary tourist that we have sought to supply' (quotations from Prefaces). Thus the inadequate treatment of individual houses, including many of importance, was to some extent the outcome of deliberate editorial policy. 'The house and grounds are not open to the public but may be seen by special permission.' That is the complete entry on West Wycombe Park. It was apparently regarded as sufficient justification for giving no particulars at all about the building, the contents, or the grounds. Claremont gets a dozen lines on the ownership but nothing on the house. Burton Constable is 'the finest old house in the East Riding' but is not described at all. Among many other large houses, about ten of which are now open to the public, none of the following receives more than a bare mention: Aston Hall, Attingham, Badminton, Berrington, Clandon, Compton Verney ('a fine 13th-cent. house'!), Condover, Cound, Dodington, Duncombe, Dyrham ('built from designs by Sir John Vanbrugh'), Easton Neston, Foremark, Hagley, Harewood, Heaton, Heveningham, Peper Harow ('large and unattractive'), Quenby, Southill, and Wentworth Woodhouse. The case of Harewood is curious, for the entry (Morris) runs to no less than twelve pages; there are long descriptions of the monuments in the church and of the now amorphous and unenjoyable castle, with a page and half on the manorial records for good measure. Nostell is equally frustrating: a whole page on the non-existent Augustinian priory but not a word about the grand Paine–Adam house that carries on the name. Arbury, Beningbrough, Frampton Court, Hatchlands, Kings Weston, and Woodhall Park are among other houses which do not qualify even for a mention.

Medieval, Tudor, and Jacobean houses are of course much more likely to be described than Restoration and Georgian. Half-timbering is the darling material, and a timber-framed farmhouse will stand a better chance of a mention than a Queen Anne house in fine brick. There is a revealing remark in Heath's description of Wilton, in which we are told that 'the central portion of the east front is 17th-cent. work in mullioned style, but Inigo Jones and his son-in-law Webb *curiously enough* [my italics] abandoned the Jacobean style, and gave an Italian facade to the S. front'. To prefer order and reticence to the picturesque was not a common sentiment in the early years of the present century.

A few classical houses – Chatsworth, for example, which was open to the public – are accorded somewhat fuller, albeit very inadequate, descriptions, and usually with disproportionate emphasis on earlier houses no longer in existence. But our authors would surely have been quite incredulous, could they have known that the eighteenth century is now widely regarded as the greatest age of English domestic architecture. The typical Little Guide reaction is summed up in this comment on Blenheim: 'To judge it fairly one should clear one's mind of the prejudice naturally created by the date of its erection.' Neither Brabant at Blenheim nor even Morris at Castle Howard could resist quoting that threadbare little tag on Vanbrugh: 'Lie heavy on him, earth...'. Most of these writers seem to have felt a particular antipathy towards any building which made use of the Classical orders: could it be, one wonders, because of their pagan associations? Here is Baring-Gould on Silverton Park, a house a few miles from Exeter designed in a severe Grecian style, and now in decay if not already demolished. 'The house was built by the third Earl of Egremont, who died in 1845, and the date is sufficient to let anyone know what to expect.' Killerton, near by, has no orders, but is 'a creation of a period of ugliness in architecture' (1788). At Hurstbourne in Hampshire 'a disastrous fire in 1879 destroyed Hurstbourne House and many of its art treasures; but the house only dated from 1785, and its successor in brick and stone, after a Jacobean style, is much superior'[1] (Cox). The garden architects come off no better. At Shugborough 'a Chinese temple and another strange building' – this presumably refers to the 'Lanthorn of Demosthenes', Stuart's copy of the Choragic Monument of Lysicrates – 'seem to have been built for no reason at all'. Herbert Tompkins's comment on Brocket Hall is about as far as our authors will normally go in commendation of Georgian: 'The drawing room and grand staircase have always been admired, but as a whole, the house is large and stately rather than beautiful.'

On the Victorian period, judgements vary – as no doubt they should. Now and again we meet a decidedly complacent comment, such as that from Dr Cox on the Colchester water tower quoted above. Sometimes, on the other hand, one comes upon a glorious piece of lambasting, like Morris's at Hexham. The work done at Hexham Abbey in 1858–60 had already been described in Murray's Handbook as 'a barbarous and lamentable restoration', but Morris did not stop at that. 'In 1858', he wrote, 'the church was subjected to one of the most foolish and disastrous restorations that have ever disfigured the history of English iconoclasm.' In his Introduction to *Northumberland*, he speaks of

the 19th century curse of excessive restoration. In churches like Rothbury, Alwinton and Ford the sense of antiquity has been nearly obliterated; whilst cheap deal roofs, and cheap, varnished deal pews, are everywhere disastrously common. This county suffered unusually severely...

That comment on the Northumberland churches is indeed fully justified; but one cannot feel confident that all these authors would have made it.

1. Insufficiently superior, however, to prevent it from being pulled down in 1965.

The use of the word 'modern' in the Little Guides may sometimes send one's eyebrows up to the top of one's forehead. Instances which I have noted of its application to Georgian buildings are too numerous to be worth recording. Moving backwards in time we have, in the West Riding, 'the imposing modern red-brick house of Ribstone Hall, said to have been built in 1674', and at Chilham Castle in Kent the twelfth-century keep is 'close to the modern mansion', built in 1616. But the prize-winner in this particular event is undoubtedly Newcastle-under-Lyme, which is described (by Masefield) as 'a comparatively modern town, not being in existence at the time of the Domesday survey, for the royal castle to which it owes its name and origin was built either by William II or Henry I'.

Dr Pevsner, in reviewing the relevant books at the end of the Introduction to his *Berkshire*, remarks that 'the Little Guide ... has just that much of historical enrichment as is missing in my pages'. This is true – and sometimes the historical information is welcome. Here is a recent experience of my own. Driving around in west Somerset, we passed close to the village of Combe Florey. The name rang in the memory; it was associated, I was sure, with somebody whom I cherished, but who? Pevsner gave no clue. But the Little Guide told me at once: it was Sydney Smith. He was rector here for sixteen years, and the glass in the east window (very tolerable, fortunately) is in memory of him. I was grateful for this; and it is certainly worth while having the Little Guides as well as The Buildings of England at hand in the car. Yet if one is primarily an architectural tourist, it has also to be said that these historical flights can prove tiresome. Boscobel House provides a good instance of what I have in mind. Here we find our dear professor in no mood to be trifled with.

With its associations Boscobel House is sure to have its crowds of visitors. Architecturally it is of little interest either externally or internally. Panelling and a little plaster of the early c17 is all there is, unless one considers hiding-holes architecture. The house was built *c.* 1600 by John Giffard, a Catholic, as a 'place of concealment'.

That is the complete entry, and it may be added that now the house is of even less interest externally, as it has lately been cement-rendered. But J. E. Auden, in the Little Guide to *Shropshire*, spins out his account – with an interpolation about White Ladies – to nearly three pages, including a longish quotation from the *Iter Carolinum* describing Charles's day-to-day movements following his defeat at Worcester on 3 September 1651. The Civil War and its aftermath, and earlier the Wars of the Roses, seem to have held a special appeal for some of the Little Guide authors.

On the other hand it must be conceded that the anecdotes and reminiscences which, particularly in Baring-Gould's *Devon*, often serve as substitutes for factual information can provide delightful reading, so long as one has Pevsner as well and is not relying solely on the Little Guide for architectural enlightenment. Baring-Gould's two-page description of the church at Colyton is in many ways a model of how not to do it: it is opinionated, incomplete, and inaccurate. Yet one would not willingly sacrifice the passage on the 'recumbent female figure, popularly supposed to be that of "Little Chokebone"', nor the story of the portly churchwarden who, 'some years ago, at a parish meeting, whilst delivering an address, suddenly disappeared, having sunk unexpectedly into the badly arched vault of the Yonge mausoleum'. At Nymet Rowland the church is not mentioned at all, although it is of some interest, as it has a Perpendicular arcade of oak cut in precise imitation of stone. But Baring-Gould's entry is entirely devoted to the 'N. Devon savages, . . . the last of whom, an old man, lived in a barrel in an outhouse to the farm, but set his straw on fire and was burnt'. At Bradninch we are regaled with the enchanting story of a mayor – the town was once of some importance – who was found one day reading his newspaper upside down. 'When this was commented on, he replied haughtily, "And what if I do? The Mayor of Bradninch may read the paper any way he pleases"!'

Dr Cox evidently enjoyed listing the relics preserved in 1445 at St Mary, Warwick. These included portions of the hair and milk of the Blessed Virgin, the frying-pan of St Brandon, a piece of Moses's burning bush, part of the seat (*cathedra*, to avoid misunderstanding) of the patriarch Abraham, and some of the oil in which fire came down from heaven at Pentecost. But, a more sedate character than Baring-Gould, he evidently felt that jokes to which the exuberant Devonian would have given pride of place should more properly be relegated to footnotes. Here, to end, is one which would not, I fear, have got into Pevsner. At Irby-in-the-Marsh, the very name of which fixes it in Lincolnshire, there is a very small font; 'if old, it must formerly have merely served as a holy-water stoup'. (And here comes the footnote.) 'When visiting the church in 1910, I remarked on its small dimensions to the old dame who was cleaning the church. She replied: "Well, the babies in these parts are mostly small".'

Yes, after all it would clearly be impossible to sustain the view that Dr Pevsner has rendered the Little Guides entirely redundant.

Architectural Criticism in the Nineteen-Thirties

BY J. M. RICHARDS

It might almost be said of architectural criticism in England in the nineteen-thirties that there was none – none, at least, in the sense of regular appraisals of new buildings as they were put up. Why not? There were, I think, two main reasons. The first was that architecture had come to be regarded as a professional mystery, and so much emphasis was put on new planning and building techniques and new aesthetic allegiances that only those within the movement – only in fact architects – were thought to be qualified to act as critics, and most architects were inhibited by the professional man's reluctance to infringe etiquette by criticizing his fellow practitioners.

The other, perhaps more fundamental, obstacle to the regular practice of architectural criticism was the importance attached at this time to principle rather than example. The qualified writers were concerned with polemical arguments about modernism. They were dedicated to a cause, and not only did they regard the kind of building that did not adhere to the cause they believed in to be unworthy of serious criticism – or only worthy of being dismissed as wrong-headed rather than discussed in relation to its own terms of reference – but also they could not allow themselves to approach at all critically the buildings that did adhere to their cause for fear of weakening or betraying it.

Architects and architecture, throughout the nineteen-thirties in particular, were either for the modern movement or against it, and there was little incentive until the main battle had been won for those who were for it – the majority of the more objective writers about architecture – to discriminate between good and bad quality in modern buildings. Whatever obeyed the theory had to be supported in practice, and the apologists of the modern movement, aware though they must have been of defects existing in modern buildings like white concrete walls that stained in a damp climate, parapets without copings that let rain run down their face, flat roofs that leaked, and windows too fashionably large to retain internal warmth, loyally defended

252

them – by refraining from criticism if not by actual praise – because what they were defending was not any individual buildings but the white-walled, flat-roofed, wide-windowed, geometrically pure work of architecure in the abstract, which had become the visual symbol of the twentieth-century revolution.

The fact that Britain became involved in the revolution a full dozen years after it had been launched on the Continent only resulted in a greater inflexibility of attitude, the instinct being to follow a pattern which the pioneers of a generation before had already moulded, and the obsession with this pattern – or set of visual images – meant that from the start British architectural criticism, such as it was, was set in the direction of purely stylistic analysis which has bedevilled it ever since.

The same apologists of the modern movement were confirmed in their rejection of self-criticism by the need to close their ranks in the face of attacks by the self-styled traditionalists, which took the form of sweeping denunciations of everything that discarded the ornamental vocabulary of tradition whether it was capable or not of passing the modernists' test of functionalism or fitness for purpose. The anti-modernists attacked revolutionary modernism and modernistic styling indiscriminately, and the ranks were closed further when local authorities and local advisory panels began rejecting modern designs on grounds of stylistic taste – again identifying modern architecture with certain images like flat roofs and removing architectural polemics still further from aesthetic and functional realities.

On both sides therefore polemics took the place of criticism. When Sir Reginald Blomfield published his book *Modernismus* in 1934 he damaged his own case by exaggeration and by ignorantly endowing the modernists with beliefs they did not hold; and when Professor A. E. Richardson attacked everything that seemed to him a departure from his own narrow definition of architecture as it ought to be (ignoring the fact, which he would never allow himself to accept, that the best modern architecture had more in common with his revered Georgian age than nearly all the work of his fellow Academicians), they brought about a false confrontation which again rested on blind repetitions of dogma rather than on the critical appraisal of buildings.

It is interesting to note in this connexion that when, at various times during the nineteen-thirties, old buildings in which the English architectural traditions were embodied were threatened with demolition, it was the modern architects rather than the so-called traditionalists who rallied to their defence. Carlton House Terrace was saved from the depredations of Sir Reginald Blomfield himself by a campaign supported by the leading modern architects, led by the *Architectural Review*, the magazine that had become the advocate and mouthpiece of the modern architectural movement.

In campaigns of this sort the modern architects were joined by the literary intellectuals – Robert Byron produced, in 1936, a celebrated pamphlet (which had previously appeared as an article in the *Architectural Review*) entitled *How We Celebrate the Coronation* which was a scathing indictment of the irresponsibility of the Church, the landlords, and the Government in allowing valuable old buildings to be destroyed in the interest of expediency and short-term profitability, or through inertia. But in a wider sense the influence of the intellectuals was against modern architecture; and this was another inhibiting factor, again throwing its practitioners on the defensive and preventing intelligent and constructive criticism.

Periodicals like the *New Statesman*, which could have served as a forum in which modern ideas were objectively discussed and the buildings that arose from them criticized (and which did fulfil just this role in relation to drama, literature, and the other arts), paid very little attention to architecture and when it did so was generally reactionary or traditionalist. When the Bloomsbury intellectuals (Raymond Mortimer, say, or Peter Quennell or Christopher Hobhouse) expressed their interest in architecture, they seemed as much concerned with safeguarding the old – especially, in the nineteen-thirties, the Georgian – as with welcoming the new, and encouraged themselves and others in the belief that no new building could ever be expected to be an improvement on what it replaced.

This absence of courage and initiative as regards modern developments in architecture was no doubt due to the literary bias of the English educational system, whereby training of the mind is hardly ever linked with training of the eye and things are valued for their associations more than for themselves. Writers and educators – for example, in the older universities – who prided themselves on being well informed about the newest developments in poetry and music, science and the cinema, thought it no shame to be ignorant of, and antipathetic to, equivalent developments in architecture. Without the support of the intelligentsia, and with no leadership offered by Government or civic officials – leadership of the kind that was helping to promote progressive policies in architecture in the Scandinavian countries – modern architects in Britain had to fight their battles alone. The architectural world became increasingly turned in on itself.

The pages of the *Architectural Review* carried a large part of what criticism and discussion did appear in print, the most important contributions at the beginning being the frequent articles of P. Morton Shand, who was the earliest link between Britain and the new developments on the Continent, besides being one of the first writers, along with John Betjeman and Nikolaus Pevsner (who first wrote for the *Review* in April 1936, when he began a series of articles on industrial design), to expound the significance of late-nineteenth-century architects like Voysey and Mackintosh in relation to the architectural revolution of the twentieth century.

In the *Review*, as in the other architectural periodicals, criticism of buildings was implied rather than direct. It was expressed in the choice of the buildings editors took seriously enough to think worth illustrating, rather than in adverse comment on the buildings they did not. Throughout the nineteen-thirties the *Review* paid increasing attention to buildings of the modern school in Britain and abroad. The February

1931 issue, for example, showed both Etchells's building for Crawfords in Holborn and the first work of Wells Coates. Modern buildings abroad were shown in photographs contributed by Morton Shand, which were published over captions written by him containing critical comparisons with buildings serving the same purpose in Britain. Important landmarks of this period were a special issue, introduced by Morton Shand, devoted to the Stockholm exhibition of 1930 – where modern architecture was first seen as an environment rather than in terms of isolated buildings – and another special issue (November 1932), again largely the work of Morton Shand, devoted to iron and steel and establishing the connexion between modern architecture and new structural techniques. In 1932 F. R. S. Yorke began to write in the *Review* on technical matters. Once again his articles were not strictly criticism but, like the editorial choice and description of buildings and the material brought forward by Morton Shand, his articles were founded upon a sense of values that clearly indicated their and their author's allegiance to the principles associated with the modern movement, implying the irrelevance of the traditionalists' outlook. At the same time, historic and vernacular buildings were being studied by the modern architects and their apologists with a critical instead of an antiquarian eye, making them, too, play their part in the reformulation of principles towards which the energies of the new generation of architectural writers were directed.

More overtly critical, though in a more satirical style, were Osbert Lancaster's drawings, which first appeared in the *Architectural Review* in a series launched in November 1934, entitled 'Progress at Pelvis Bay', and the word Criticism itself appeared as the general title of a series of articles by C. H. Reilly, starting in March 1935. These took the form of a subjectively written commentary on recent examples of different types of building – town halls, shops, churches, and so on – which, while making no very consistent contribution to architectural criticism, was at least a departure from the predominant journalistic practice of accepting the work of eminent architects at their own valuation. Finally, in the late nineteen-thirties the *Review* did at last publish regular – though not very substantial – articles critically appraising contemporary architecture over the signature of James MacQuedy.

So much for the role of the architectural magazines in asserting new principles and questioning established values. The only newspaper writing that made some effort in this direction was that of Charles Marriot, art critic of *The Times*, who introduced architectural subjects into his articles with remarkable pertinacity considering the public and editorial apathy he had to contend with. Other writing that was critical even in intention was meagre in quantity and orthodox in ideas. Writers like Trystan Edwards and Howard Robertson, whose influence in any case belongs to the nineteen-twenties rather than the nineteen-thirties, were more concerned with aesthetics applied to buildings than with buildings as a total experience – functional and environmental as well as aesthetic; and they again accepted more than they questioned. There were no successors to, say, W. R. Lethaby and Geoffrey Scott of the generation before. There was an element of fresh thinking in John Betjeman's *Ghastly Good Taste* (1933) and in a few recondite publications of the nineteen-thirties like the symposium *Circle* (1937) edited by Leslie Martin, Ben Nicholson, and Naum Gabo; but most of the architectural writing that influenced British architects and helped define the dogma of the new movement was projected from abroad. It occurred in books like Lewis Mumford's *Technics and Civilization* (published in England in 1934), Sigfried Giedion's *Space, Time and Architecture* (originally the Charles Eliot Norton lectures, given in 1938–9), and especially in the successive volumes devoted to Le Corbusier's buildings, writings, and projects, which were enthusiastically devoured by English architects and students as they came out. In 1937 there appeared, with an only mildly critical text, Henry-Russell Hitchcock's slender volume on *Modern Architecture in England* (originally the catalogue of an exhibition of that title held at the Museum of Modern Art in New York). Pevsner's *Pioneers of the Modern Movement* had come out in 1936.

Those are some of the writings that now seem most significant in relation to the architectural thought of their time. In a revolutionary situation – such as architecture found itself in in the nineteen-thirties – critics, as I have already observed, are bound to concern themselves with basic intentions and the restatement of principles. But the obligation to ally oneself with one side or another, the prior commitment to one or other loyalty, are the negation of true criticism, and as the period progressed there were signs of greater willingness on the part of critics to look at buildings through other than partisan eyes and to write in other terms than those of the rigid confrontations between the Modern Architectural Research Group on the one hand and the traditionalists of the Royal Academy on the other. This rather unproductive confrontation was however prolonged right up to the end of the decade as a result of the closing of the ranks of both parties that took place following the influx of architectural refugees from Central Europe.

Some of these refugees were highly distinguished architects: some indeed – like Walter Gropius (whose book, *The New Architecture and the Bauhaus*, had appeared in English, translated by P. Morton Shand, in 1935) – were leaders of the movement that was already exercising so strong an influence on English architecture, and their sojourn in England (most of them soon moved on to America) was wholly beneficial. But it resulted in a close identification of modern architecture with the political left (in spite of the developments in Russia, where the revolutionary Constructivism of the nineteen-twenties had given way to a bourgeois hankering after historical and regional stylization). There had always been some correspondence between modern architectural ideas and left-wing political principles because the stress that was newly placed by the former on architecture's social responsibilities, and on the building as an element in a larger picture, naturally linked architectural aspirations with socialist

256

planning; but the arrival of refugees from right-wing countries as reinforcements for the architectural left gave the traditionalists cause for fresh confusion between political and artistic revolution, encouraged the historically meaningless use of the term Bolshevist as an opprobrious description of modern art, and gave a moral as well as an aesthetic tone to the running conflict between old and new.

This however was a short-lived phase. The unconstructiveness of such a conflict was shown up by the war and by the practical realities that architecture now had to face, including the discipline of economics and shortages of material. The battle of the styles, if such it can be called, of the nineteen-thirties (or, as some would term it, the battle between style and logic) became irrelevant, not through the efforts of the critics – or indeed of the architects – but because the world that was to emerge at the end of the war had other values and other priorities.

On Architectural Journalism

BY HUGH CASSON

Few people like architects. Fewer still perhaps like journalists. Both, in the public eye, share to an equal degree the faults of incompetence and vanity. It might therefore be thought that the architectural journalist would by his profession suffer a double odium. This, however unjust, might be true if he were more often encountered or more widely read. The truth is that he is a rare bird, and the layman normally takes only a superficial interest – if any at all – in what he writes. Architectural journalism is still written largely for architects, and the battles, however ruthless, and the games, however childish, are mostly domestic ones. This does not mean that they are not serious or important to the participants.

It must be remembered that the main object of the architectural press – small a, small p – is the same as that of any other human organization or individual, whether it be a steel plant or a poet. It is to stay in business. Not of course at any price. No journal as pusillanimous or catchpenny as that would deserve to survive. But clearly if it is to inform, influence, or inspire it must continue to exist. Architectural journalists (who deceive themselves no more nor less often than anyone else) know this. They may speak of higher aims, they may sincerely believe in them, or in their luckier moments even act upon them or attain them, but they know that economic facts are as inexorable and unavoidable as press-day. This means that imperfection and incompleteness (the lot, says Cyril Connolly, of all creative writers) will be their lot too, but in an even greater and more frustrating proportion, since the pressures are so regular and unrelenting. What then drives them to do what they do, so often with such skill and insight and enthusiasm? Certainly not a love of architects. Architectural journalists – and the feeling is frequently reciprocated – do not much like architects. They find them ignorant, vain, fussy, quick to grumble, ungrateful, and ungenerous, 'puffing', said John Betjeman, 'out the opinions of the Daily Express'. From this it is sometimes inferred that architectural journalists must grow to hate the art they write about. The reverse is probably true. Like drama or music critics, they must spend most of their lives evaluating reinterpretations of well-worn themes, and a passion – the love of architecture – that can demand and survive such ceaseless consummation is and must be strong indeed. There may of course be other chains that bind them to their wheel; a fascination perhaps for the building process and all its complex technicalities, a desire maybe to get ideas across, or to ride 'hobby-horses', or no more than the urge for self-expression found by chance in one type of paper more easily than another.

Perhaps it is best not to inquire into motives. The driving force behind creativity, however modestly expressed, may, or may not, be admirable. What matters is the end-product – the ideas expressed, the fact or event truthfully recorded, the technicality lucidly explained. None of this is as easy to do as it looks, and considering that many architectural journalists receive training neither in architecture nor in journalism, it is a tribute to their skill and persistence that the standard achieved is so high.

It may be argued that all those who write in specialist papers for specialists to read have no real need, other than that of personal pride, to arrest the attention or to polish their style. The readers after all – whether they be pigeon-fanciers or architects, motorcyclists, anglers, milliners, or engineers – are with them from the start. There is no necessity to allure or to dazzle. The readers need make no effort to understand the language, to catch the allusions, to recognize the personalities. To them the appearance of their magazine or a critical column is like another instalment of a TV serial, compulsive because unsurprising. They are as familiar with the act as they are with the make-up. Goodness knows how often they have heard the jokes. Repeatedly, readers of architectural journals will tell you how empty of interest, how boringly repetitive, how consistently unimaginative in presentation is the material set before them. The leader written by the fatigued hack who can express an opinion on any subject in 600 words flat – but no more and no less; the multi-authored notes and comments, facetious or portentous, the querulous correspondence, the technical sections filed but never read, the illustrated jobs by rival (therefore enemy) designers ... the ads, the ads, the ads. Yet, if pressed, every architect would probably admit in private that each time he pries open the latest issue, a sense of excitement or at least of heightened anticipation still hastens his fingers, and he will not settle to his work until he has at least glanced through the contents.

What does he expect, and as a rule receive? Three things. First, a record as full and accurate as possible of important or interesting new buildings, domestic and foreign, as they are built. This provides the raw material of architectural history. Secondly, technical information for the use of all those working in the building industry. This is a reference book of data, which is constantly brought up to date. Thirdly, some space allotted for criticism, discussed elsewhere in this book, 'belles-lettres', history, travel, and discussion around the allied arts including interior, industrial, and landscape design.

The comparative space allotted under these headings obviously varies according to the type of journal and its readership, to the frequency with which it appears, and to editorial policy; but with something like 250 periodicals (excluding student squibs and house-magazines) regularly published in this country which deal with building, nobody in that industry could claim that if he was ill-informed it was the fault of the magazines. Too often this does not prevent him from regarding technical journalism as a parasite upon the industry it serves. If indeed this be his opinion, then he is wrong. For apart from the three services listed above there is a fourth, because less easy to define or to evaluate often the less recognized – the contribution made to architecture by the guiding of opinion and the initiating of thought. It is true that leadership in architectural thinking comes in its truest form from practising architects, and is best expressed in their work. But such people are rare and their buildings as a rule few in number, and it is equally true to say that in the nineteenth century the world of architecture was as much dominated by the writings of Pugin, Ruskin, William Morris, as it was by the buildings of Barry, Scott, Waterhouse, or Norman Shaw. Which in fact are the milestones? The *True Principles* – 'the thunder of which', wrote Gilbert Scott, 'roused me from my slumber' – or the Palace of Westminster, the silver tongue of Ruskin or the Oxford Museum? The *Ecclesiologist* or All Saints, Margaret Street? or (to jump the years) the manifestos of Sant' Elia or the Einstein tower? The question may be unanswerable but it is not too ludicrous to put. The history of architectural journalism, although barely 150 years old, is, in fact, a proud one and worth a quick glance – necessarily brief since the early phases are described elsewhere in this book by Mr Jenkins.

Apart from the pattern books, the first genuine architectural magazine that one researcher, Ian McCallum, was able to discover was published in Berlin in 1829. This was followed in 1834 by J. C. Loudon's *Architectural Magazine*, and a few years later (1842) by *The Builder*. This was edited by Joseph Hansom, the first of a great series of architect-editors (Godwin, Statham, H. V. Lanchester) who ruled that paper for seventy-five years until 1917, when the first professional journalist, Mr W. T. Plume, took over. For thirty years *The Builder* had the field largely to itself. Public health and railway construction were regularly dealt with, Mr Godwin wrote the sparky editorials, and the wood engravers, Mr Laing and, later, Mr Hodgkin – the Kidder-Smiths of the 1840s – provided most of the illustrations: as rigid, precise, and hardedged as the subjects they recorded. By 1870 Mr Hodgkin had handed over his engraver's tools to Mr Heaviside, but the style remained competent, impersonally unchanged, although challenged by the two-colour lithography of a new rival – *The Architect* (founded 1869). The real spokesman for the new movement away from Christianity and towards cosiness was *The Building News*, edited and illustrated by Maurice B. Adams, a Bedford Park resident, noted for his grisly competence in current stylistic mannerisms of the period. By 1900 *The Builder* and

The Building News were virtually indistinguishable from each other, though the text of the former was perhaps the livelier and the illustrations in the latter, many by Raffles Davidson and C. E. Mallows, of better quality. The spokesman for the avant-garde had by now become *The Studio*, which every month illustrated examples of architecture and applied art in the new manner from Berlin, Vienna, and Brussels, as well as examples by the home team of Mackmurdo, Smith & Brewer, Voysey, and Baillie Scott. Here you will find C. L. Cowper's Palace Gate House, Kensington, furniture by Walter Cave, interiors by G. M. Elmwood. Drawings by Beardsley and Pennell were interspersed with articles on the design of gasoliers or Japanese sand gardens, and some photographs by Baron Corvo of naked Sicilian boys provoked a lively controversy on 'The Camera – Friend or Foe?' ('No doubt beneficial', said Millais: 'of the greatest use', said Alma Tadema: 'a fatal blow', said Frith.) Whether friend or foe, it certainly conquered, and until the outbreak of the Great War it recorded only too faithfully the weedy Baroque of the Edwardian era. After 1920 Howard Robertson and F. R. Yerbury began to whip *The Architect and Building News* into the lead with their regular reports from Northern Europe – the Scandinavian expressionism that swept the drawing boards of the twenties was virtually the work of *The Architect and Building News*. In 1927 came Frederick Etchells's translation of *Towards a New Architecture*, followed quickly by Silver End, Finella, Crawfords, and the first works of Wells Coates, Emberton, and Fry. In 1934 Morton Shand could already write a history of the movement, which by 1935 was in full swing. By now Queen Anne's Gate was in charge – publicizing, battling (remember Ruislip, Amersham, and Chipperfield?) – the dogged unquestioning champion until the Second World War of Modern Architecture.

The last twenty years are too near and too familiar to be analysed, but certain conclusions may perhaps be drawn from this superficial survey. Here are some of them.

First, the architectural periodicals can reasonably be proud of their contribution to the development of architecture. Few architects have done as much either at H.Q. or in the field.

Secondly, while many of the ideas that they fostered and disseminated were not outstandingly original (some of them indeed continued to reappear at intervals in almost identical language), basic truths can always afford restatement and, as Lethaby remarked, it is the prophet's aim 'to be abolished in absorption'.

Thirdly, the humbler services rendered to architecture and building by the magazines, e.g. campaigns for higher office efficiency, have been carried out faithfully, even sometimes perhaps at the risk of boring, antagonizing, or losing readers.

Lastly, such is the rivalry and variety of editorial attitude between the many periodicals that virtually every point of view somewhere gets heard. There seems to be no evidence, in the last hundred years at least, that any worthy cause was refused support, any articulate spokesman refused a hearing, any outstanding piece of design overlooked. Judgements may, in retrospect and out of context, seem misguided and absurd, but at least the case was heard.

This is a record to be proud of. Where have they failed us, other than in the normal faults, endemic to journalism, of inaccuracy, mischief, log-rolling, failing to check sources, and the temptation to flippancy and generalizing? Increasingly perhaps in two ways – cowardice in the face of currently sacred cows (Godwin would never have pulled his punches as some editors do today)[1] and the lack of adventurousness in presentation. Magazine design has changed enormously in the last ten years, but architectural magazines have looked much the same for thirty years (just look at typical issues of any magazines for 1936, 1946, and 1956 and see what, if any, changes you can spot). Challenging this particular charge, some editors would probably reply that this conservatism is due to the bottomless vanity of their architect readers, who will complain instantly, and at length, if their buildings are not always illustrated in the most conventional, flattering, and unrealistic light – dramatically posed, empty of people (how significant is this!), as trimmed and touched-up as a society portrait or a dog-food ad. This may explain: it does not excuse. The charge still stands. There are other complaints that can legitimately be laid at some editorial doors – equally perhaps at the architects' door? They are the cult of personalities rather than of ideas, resulting in the sins of king-making and court intrigue; blind worship (rather than proper respect) for facts, leading to an over-reverence for those who claim to understand problems rather than for those who try to solve them; the pursuit of novelty for its own sake, thus encouraging the peacock that never lies far concealed within the architect; scarcity of scholarship (for an allegedly learned profession, we seem to be satisfied with too much light-programme level in our reading); and, saddest of all, perhaps, since it seems today inevitable and incurable, the virtual disappearance from the editorial chair of the practising architect – or, as the modern editor would probably and rightly call him, the amateur journalist. For him – opinionated, involved, individualistic, as happy with the typewriter as with the T-square – the modern self-effacing, highly efficient professional editor is no substitute. But perhaps this paragon of the past never existed. Few architects who are good at their own job seem to be able to speak or to write clearly about it. The roll-call of those who could may be impressive, ranging as it does from Godwin, Viollet-le-Duc, and T. G. Jackson to Goodhart-Rendel and Le Corbusier, but it is lamentably short. Nevertheless, it is always to such articulate practitioners who know by training and experience how architecture is actually

1. Has any critic yet dared to complain in public of the dogmatic inhumanity of Le Corbusier's windowless hospital now building in Venice? Only the June 1965 issue of *Domus* admitted that the absence of windows 'might cause some concern', but concluded in the end there was no need to worry with such a masterly hand at the wheel. The true genius has no need of the sycophant.

262

produced that the architect will in the end prefer to turn for understanding and perceptive comment. This is not to say, of course, that those who have never 'done' can never 'understand'. This would be as ludicrous as it is false. The illumination shed by the outsider can, by its rigorous and ranging brilliance, often bring into vivid relief areas conveniently or lazily left obscured by the more professionally involved critic. Nevertheless most architects perhaps instinctively feel that no scholarship or brilliant turn of phrase can substitute for this basic knowledge acquired – however briefly or inexpertly – upon the drawing board.

Luckily perhaps for us a high proportion of those who write for architectural magazines in this country have, in fact, received, and profited from, such training, and the contrast between their work and what appears, for instance, in some American magazines is noticeable. The latter may, at its best, be livelier, or at its worst more theatrical, but, too often, it lacks the bone of a discipline once learned. This inner knowledge of the architectural process is not so vital for those who write for the lay press – where the reader will respond at once to qualities of perception, visual sensitivity, scholarship, and above all enthusiasm, and will take professional know-how for granted or as irrelevant. Such extra-mural journalism, as it were, is a comparatively recent feature of the lay press. But now no weekly or Sunday-posh is without its regular architectural correspondent, and even the dailies find space for the occasional discussion of architecture outside the real-estate columns. This is wholly to be welcomed, inaccurate, frivolous, or uncomprehending as such comment may sometimes appear to be. Architecture is now considered almost as seriously as ballet or TV, and architects, although almost universally loathed in the flesh, rank high, it is said, in the popularity polls as heroes of magazine-fiction. Again this is all to the good. The view, favoured by many architects, that architecture is an art practised in private by consenting adults is not one that does much good for architecture and serves only to exacerbate the latent hostility which lurks within all architect–public relations and occasionally shows itself in unnervingly venomous forms. The serious and sympathetic architectural journalist can be of great help here, but there is much yet to do before the bridges of understanding are secure. Scientists often complain – with some justification – that whereas those moving in educated society are expected to know the names and work of a dozen or so second-rate writers or artists, they are normally hard put to it to think up the name of more than one top scientist. Architects, perhaps less justifiably, but with equal irritation, will find that even the most sophisticated of critics – happy to discourse with equal ease and at equal length upon the merits of a picture, a poem, or an opera – are when faced with the assessment of a building instantly adrift, groping miserably for any aid from another art that may float into view and carry them once more into their depth. The truth is unfortunately that architecture, although the most commonly encountered of the arts, is at the same time the most difficult fully to comprehend, and most difficult to explain. All the more credit to those who struggle in this field – their greatest value perhaps being in the way that they drag the art of architecture out of the temple in which the priests and professional scribes would be only too happy to keep it immured.

Too many scribes in the temple: too much 'in-talk': too much writing with a nudge or wink to the knowing – these contemporary diseases common to all the arts are ultimately degrading and rightly rejected by the public. The artist should be the true outsider, not the 'inside-outsider', locking himself up in the prefects' room with his fags. It is above all the architectural journalist's job to open the windows and clear the air a bit. It's not easy to do this, for as we have already seen, journalism is a suspect profession and the magazine a tainted weapon. 'All magazines', said Tennyson, 'demoralise literature.' 'People who write for the Press', said Somerset Maugham, 'lose the facility of seeing for themselves.' 'Journalism', wrote Cyril Connolly, 'is the deadliest of weeds that benefits only the amateur or the slothful in search of quick returns.' The gods thunder and even mortals squeak the same tale. To the world at large, Fleet Street is still Grub Street. 'Hack' is the kindest of the adjectives applied to those who work there. The image of the furtive, whisky-sodden reporter and the ruthless, power-drunk editor remains as bright as it was fifty years ago. Many journalists would perhaps prefer it to remain so, for it acts as a useful and brightly coloured cloak beneath which they can get on undisturbed with their job. This is understandable but dangerous. It implies where it does not actually signify contempt for the reader; and this in any writer is the ultimate and unforgivable sin. Carelessness and clichés can be forgiven in work that is not, or should not be, intended for immortality. The true professional always knows his place and is proud of it. 'I am a journalist,' cried H. G. Wells, 'I refuse to play the artist ... and if sometimes I am an artist it is a freak of the Gods. What I write goes *now* ... and will probably die.' Hear, hear to that. A sense of urgency of what 'goes now', an enthusiasm for his subject, a background of knowledge, and a respect for his reader – these, when allied to the more modest virtues of competence, punctuality, and a quick turn of phrase, are the qualities that an editor looks for in his professional staff. Such qualities are rarely combined in one man, but when found, and given space to move around in, then architecture will be truly served, in a way that every practising architect should recognize and respect. Another window will have been opened, another tiny, but vital, victory scored against apathy and ignorance. Two cheers then (to borrow Mr E. M. Forster's formula) for the architectural journalist. Reserve the third until he fully deserves it.

Revenge of the Picturesque:
English Architectural Polemics, 1945-1965

BY REYNER BANHAM

Those of my generation who interrupted their architectural training in order to fight a war to make the world safe for the Modern Movement, tended to resume their studies after demobilization with sentiments of betrayal and abandonment. Two of the leading oracles of Modern Architecture appeared to have thrown principle to the wind and espoused the most debased English habits of compromise and sentimentality.

J. M. Richards, author of the highly persuasive *Introduction to Modern Architecture*[1] at the beginning of the war, celebrated its end with *The Castles on the Ground*,[2] an apotheosis of English suburbia for which some have never forgiven him. Similarly, Nikolaus Pevsner, whose *Pioneers of the Modern Movement*[3] had given modern architecture a comfortingly secure historical ancestry, was now publishing (either as author, or as editor of the *Architectural Review*) articles giving equally secure historical justifications for a revival of the Picturesque.[4]

While he was not, in fact, being at all inconsistent in doing so, as a re-reading of *Pioneers* would have made fairly clear, the Picturesque was seen – correctly – as one of the historically contributing causes to the visual disorders of suburbia, and thus fell under the same anathema. So combat was joined between a barely middle-aged architectural 'Establishment' armed with a major magazine, and a generation of battle-hardened and unusually mature students.

1. Harmondsworth, 1940. 2. London, 1946.
3. London, 1936.
4. In sequence, the key Pevsner articles are: 'Heritage of Compromise', *Architectural Review* (February 1942); 'Genesis of the Picturesque', ibid. (November 1944); 'Humphry Repton – a Florilegium', ibid. (February 1948); and (with S. Lang) 'Sir William Temple and Sharawaggi', ibid. (December 1949). To these should be added: H. F. Clark, 'Lord Burlington's Bijou, or Sharawaggi at Chiswick', ibid. (May 1944); and *idem*, 'Eighteenth-Century Elysiums', *Journal of the Warburg and Courtauld Institutes*, VI (1943). 'Sharawaggi' became a favourite term of abuse among the anti-Picturesque faction, and also passed into American usage.

265

But the student generation were without much means of public expression (until Theo Crosby joined *Architectural Design* in October 1953) and little of the polemic is visible in print. Furthermore, the lines of battle were confused by a major political diversion – the adoption by English Marxist architects of William Morris as a patron-figure. This, however irrelevant to the problems of the post-war epoch, had a certain Marxist logic to it. But the mass adoption of the rest of mid-Victorian and late Victorian architecture along with Morris makes less obvious sense. Their interest in the welfare-state architecture of Sweden, however, does make sense; but the *Architectural Review* had also adopted Swedish architecture to exemplify its 'New Empiricism'.[1]

Thus, the younger generation found an apparent solidarity between their intellectual mentors in Queen Anne's Gate, their instructors at the Architectural Association, and their superiors when they qualified and went to work for largely Socialist-dominated local government bodies like the London County Council. Most of them could only sympathize with James Stirling's exasperated, inaccurate, but cathartic epigram 'William Morris was a Swede!'[2] Though the 'Establishment' was not truly as solid and homogeneous as they supposed, many incidents combined to confirm their worst suspicions: thus, when Colin St John Wilson managed to persuade the editors of the *Observer* to publish a short article against compromise and picturesque planning, the response included not only an exercise in conventionally avuncular deflationary mockery by Sir Hugh Casson (numbered by then with Richards and Pevsner among the editors of the *Architectural Review*) but also the appointment of Casson as one of the *Observer*'s two regular architectural critics, the other being Robert Furneaux Jordan, the most substantial exponent of the Ruskinian Left, and former principal of the Architectural Association school.[3]

Yet, in spite of the almost annual deputations of students demanding that the *Architectural Review* should mend its ways[4] and satirical gifts of drain-covers and cobblestones from Lyme Regis,[5] the younger generation found it difficult to maintain

1. On the New Empiricism see *Architectural Review* (January 1948).

2. First uttered at a discussion at the Institute of Contemporary Arts, London, in December 1952.

3. These events of the summer of 1952 were of some consequence, since the *Observer*'s commitment to regular weekly criticism was one of the first signs of increasing architectural awareness in the daily and weekly press. Unfortunately, no talent capable of exploiting the opportunity offered has so far appeared, and the *Observer*'s experience with its architectural correspondents has been as unsatisfactory as those correspondents' performance, from Jordan's ill-judged 'Guide to the Isms of Modern Architecture' to Ian Nairn's equally unfortunate attempts to influence local politics over planning decisions.

4. Led in 1952 and 1953 by Thomas Stevens, later director of historical studies at the Architectural Association.

5. See the 'Astragal' column in *Architects' Journal*, 10 April 1952. The caption accompanying the illustration is a shade too ingenuous, since the gift was organized by members of Sir Hugh Casson's office, their wives and girl-friends, and 'Astragal' at this time was Sir Hugh himself.

consistent hostility to the *Review* – its liberal policy (in spite of propaganda for 'an English visual philosophy founded on the true rock of Sir Uvedale Price',[1] otherwise known as 'Townscape') enabled it to print key articles by such idols of the committed young as Colin Rowe, James Stirling, and the Smithsons.

Nevertheless, the basic issue – for or against Picturesque – was explicitly if ineffectively joined on two occasions. The first was when Pevsner, in order to refute an attempt by Basil Taylor[2] to drive a wedge between Modern Design and the Picturesque, drew attention to Picturesque elements in the work of Gropius and Le Corbusier and observed that 'the Modern revolution of the early twentieth century and the Picturesque revolution of a hundred years before had all their fundamentals in common'.[3]

Had Pevsner deliberately set out to infuriate the young, he could hardly have done better. His words occasioned deep offence, and the letter of rebuttal which appeared over the signature of Alan Colquhoun[4] was the outcome of considerable discussion among the offended parties. For it was to Continental modern architecture and, above all, the work of Le Corbusier, that they looked for exemplars of a sane and rational design method (as they saw it) to set against the empiricism and compromises of the Picturesque.

Le Corbusier, even more than Mies van der Rohe, was seen as the great living exponent of a European classical tradition. That the origins of this tradition were seen to lie in the Renaissance, rather than Greece or Rome, is a tribute, above all, to Professor Wittkower's *Architectural Principles in the Age of Humanism*[5] – said *Principles* being supposititiously related to the present day by Le Corbusier's *Modulor*[6] – and the associated essays on Italian and Anglo-Palladian architecture[7] in various journals. The effect of such massive methodology applied to topics that had hitherto

1. See the article introducing Townscape in the *Architectural Review* for December 1949. Its pseudonymous author, 'I. de Wolfe', is, as one may reveal, now that John Betjeman has breached the long-standing conspiracy of silence (on Independent Television, 29 July 1967), H. de Cronin Hastings, the remaining member of the *Architectural Review*'s four-man editorial board.

2. In a series of radio talks that have not been reprinted.

3. In *Architectural Review* (April 1954).

4. ibid. (July 1954).

5. First published as *Studies of the Warburg Institute*, XIX (London, 1949); republished by Tiranti (London, 1952). It is indicative of the temper of the age that the Tiranti edition treats the words *Architectural Principles* alone as the title, and adds 'in the Age of Humanism' as a kind of sub-title, both on the title-page and the dust-jacket.

6. English translation by Peter de Francia and Anna Bostock (London, 1951).

7. The series runs from: 'Alberti's Approach to Antiquity in Architecture', in *Journal of the Warburg and Courtauld Institutes*, V (1940–1), to 'The Perspective of Piero della Francesca's Flagellation', in ibid., XVI (1953). Important also are: 'Lord Burlington and William Kent', *Archaeological Journal*, CII (1945); 'The Influence of Palladio's Villas', *Country Life*, CXV (25 February 1954); and 'Inigo Jones, Architect and Man of Letters', *R.I.B.A. Journal*, series 3, LX (1953).

been reserved for the amateur attentions of professors at the Bartlett School,[1] or the compilers of country-house profiles in *Country Life*, was galvanic.

On the one hand, it helped to trigger a general revival of studies in English classical architecture from Inigo Jones to Lutyens – though with splendid irony the most appreciative review of Hussey and Butler's work on Lutyens[2] came from Pevsner in the *Architectural Review*,[3] and the most distinguished contributions to both scholarship (outside Wittkower's studies) and popularization came from a historian normally associated with the 'Establishment': John Summerson, with his crucial paper on John Thorpe,[4] and his two short monographs on Soane[5] and Wren.[6]

But on the other hand, it also lent weight to the idealizing concept of an intellectually coherent English classical tradition in architecture, which had guarded against the debilitating effects of the Picturesque. With this opinion Pevsner came into direct collision when he delivered his Reith Lectures on 'The Englishness of English Art' for the BBC.[7] This protracted encomium-cum-psychoanalysis of 'the most compromising, the most adaptable, the most practical of all nations'[8] was clearly understood in some quarters as an attack on English Classicism, and Pevsner was hailed in a satirical letter in the *Listener*[9] for 'proving that the ideals of such architects as Thorpe, Webb, Wren, Inigo Jones, Gibbs, Holland, Chambers, Adam, etc., are un-English...'.

These same Reith lectures also sparked the second assault on Pevsner by the younger anti-Picturesque faction. The lack of any obvious link between themselves and the classical content of Modern Architecture (their own immediate predecessors

1. Professor Sir Albert Richardson's book, *Robert Mylne, Architect and Engineer*, finally appeared in 1955 (Batsford, London).

2. It is common practice to take Christopher Hussey's *Life of Sir Edwin Lutyens* and the three volumes of A. S. G. Butler's *Architecture of Sir Edwin Lutyens* together as a single work since they were published simultaneously (Country Life, London, 1950).

3. 'Building with Wit', *Architectural Review* (April 1951).

4. ibid. (November 1949).　　　　5. *Sir John Soane* (London, 1952).

6. *Sir Christopher Wren* (Collins's Brief Lives) (London, 1953).

7. The lectures were broadcast in October and November 1955 and published in book form, revised, as *The Englishness of English Art* (London, 1956).

8. This phrase is not taken from the Reith Lectures, but from Pevsner's earliest printed animadversions on the English and their Picturesque design philosophy: 'Heritage of Compromise', *Architectural Review* (February 1942).

9. This letter from Bertram Hume, printed in the *Listener* for 8 December 1955, is notable also as one of the rare occasions when native xenophobic distaste for foreign experts on Englishness was made explicit: 'Determined attempts used to be made to prove that England was Mitteleuropa; for example, the Germans exerted themselves to show that Shakespeare was a German. Now we know beyond any reasonable shadow of doubt that the opposite is the case, namely, that Mitteleuropa is really England.' Professional English eccentrics, who might also be expected to show explicit hostility, were more circumspect at this time, and contented themselves with unsigned parodies in *Punch*.

in England, like Frederick Gibberd and Maxwell Fry, being too deeply compromised with the *Architectural Review*) had led them to put a very high valuation on Wells Coates – who had virtually ceased to practise in England – and, above all, the long-dissolved partnership of Connell, Ward & Lucas. To these last, the *Architectural Association Journal* was persuaded to devote virtually a complete issue[1] adorned with an article by Professor Henry-Russell Hitchcock[2] and another by Thomas Stevens which concluded: '. . . the work of Connell, Ward and Lucas is patently free of the two main English vices, picturesque muddle-headedness in planning, combined with a casual formal confusion'.

Even more explicit in its hostility, however, was a letter from Colin Rowe which appeared in a subsequent issue of the *Journal*,[3] praising the publication of the Connell, Ward & Lucas houses and concluding: '. . . after the insufferable tedium of Town-scape, the dreary accumulation of public-house chi-chi[4] . . . it is the most extreme relief to be allowed to recognise that English architecture is not necessarily degraded nor essentially corrupt. The Connell, Ward and Lucas houses are so authentic and so English and yet rise so far above that provincial quality of "Englishness" lately so much valued, that they have still, after all these years, the invigorating qualities of a manifesto.'

But, by the time Rowe wrote these words, the classicizing party represented a lost cause; not for any lack of intelligence or erudition, nor because Pevsner or the *Architectural Review* had come forward with any knock-down arguments. The trouble lay in the lack of internal coherence in the body of ideas assembled by the anti-Picturesque party, the revelation of an inner contradiction, and their inapplic-ability in real life. At the head of his justly celebrated essay linking Palladio and Le Corbusier, 'The Mathematics of the Ideal Villa',[5] Colin Rowe had quoted Wren's well-known dictum: 'There are two kinds of beauty – natural and customary. Natural is from geometry consisting in uniformity, that is equality and proportion.' This appeal to mathematics, backed by a quotation from Matila Ghyka towards the end of the article,[6] would be understood as an appeal to reason and thus to 'science' – not that Rowe would be so naive as to intend any such thing explicitly.

1. November 1956.

2. Professor Hitchcock was much cultivated by the younger generation at this time, partly as an 'antidote' to Pevsnerian influence. His frequent and continued presence in England was assured by the preparations for his contribution to the (Pevsner-edited) Pelican History of Art, *Architecture: Nineteenth and Twentieth Centuries*. When this finally appeared in 1958, it was greeted with almost universal disappointment by his younger supporters.   3. January 1957.

4. The traditional style of public-house interiors was such a preoccupation of the *Architectural Review* at this time that the *Punch* parodists made much of 'the extreme horizontality of the tradi-tional English bar, or *lokal*'.   5. In *Architectural Review* (March 1947).

6. Ghyka's book, *The Geometry of Art and Life*, was quite an important piece of underground cult-literature at this time, its 'discoverer' being reputedly H. S. Scorer, who had come across a copy during flying training in the U.S. during the War.

But much had happened to destroy the congruities of geometrical beauty and science since Sir Christopher's day, and members of the anti-Picturesque connexion who were interested in such topics were already making free with concepts such as Heisenberg's Uncertainty Principle, were growing suspicious of 'one-to-one' relationships and the concept of 'uniqueness', were beginning to talk of topology rather than geometry, and if they did not yet dispose of the concept 'open-ended', were certainly reading Professor Karl Popper's *The Open Society* [1] as implying the downfall of all closed and determinate systems such as Plato's politics – or classical architecture based on elementary [2] geometry.

The break had begun as early as 1953, when the Smithsons – the bell-wethers of the young throughout the middle fifties – declared their rejection of proportion and symmetry [3] and embarked on a period of very equivocal relationship with such previously admired classical imagery as Poussin's architectural backgrounds [4] or the planning of Greek sacred sites, which Peter Smithson finally decided [5] were organized by function and circulation, and not by any mathematical system.

There can be little doubt that convulsions in the style of Le Corbusier's architecture in the mid fifties helped to break up the geometry-obsessed school of thought that had been fathered on him – long and frustrating hours were spent trying to apply the Modulor dimensions to the plan of Notre Dame du Haut at Ronchamp, to no avail. More intellectually nonchalant members of the younger generation, including some from Colin Rowe's former circle at the Liverpool School of Architecture, were able to follow their father-figure's stylistic acrobatics without undue difficulty – James Stirling's articles on the Jaoul houses and Ronchamp [6] being the outstanding examples of this.

Stirling adapted himself to the new Corbu with modest erudition; others merely followed fashion. But the change in fashion rapidly acquired respectable scholarly

1. It is regretted that Popper is the only hard-cover reference that can be given here; most of the other concepts came up by way of magazines as diverse as *Discovery* and *Astounding Science Fiction*, or were picked up from lectures on the Third Programme or at the Institute of Contemporary Arts. Readers wishing to sample the intellectual tone of the period might do worse than read, *cum grano salis*, the present author's article 'The New Brutalism', in *Architectural Review* (December 1955).

2. Conversationally, it was customary to equate classical architecture with Euclidian space, and thus to find it unacceptable in an intellectual climate in which non-Euclidian geometries had greater prestige. The irrelevance of non-Euclidian geometries to the business of architecure, on the other hand, was not a popular topic.

3. In a discussion at the Architectural Association in December 1953.

4. See 'Cluster City' in *Architectural Review* (November 1957).

5. In a lecture given at the Architectural Association in November 1958 and reprinted in the *Architectural Association Journal* for February 1959.

6. 'Garches to Jaoul', *Architectural Review* (September 1955); 'Ronchamp', ibid. (March 1956).

underpinnings, with the revival of scholarly interest in Gaudí,[1] Futurism,[2] and the Berlin Expressionists.[3] Pevsner himself contributed to this re-appraisal of the Modern Movement's disorderly ancestors, but late,[4] and only after giving due warning against the revival of their styles.[5]

Fear of revivalism was prevalent at that time, and it is ironical that Pevsner should have made an issue of it, since he had identified proneness to revivalism as an English characteristic in his Reith Lectures. But England produced nothing to rival the bathos of Neo-Liberty in Italy,[6] and this seems largely due to a difference between English and Italian views of the cultural basis of architecture. Whereas Italians prefer to stand entirely within the traditional trivia (and quadrivia) of humane learning, and are thus prone to over-persuasion by historical and philological arguments, British architects seem to rely much more heavily on the intellectual (as well as practical) support of technology and the sciences.

Thus it was British architects above all others who, in the post-war years, threw themselves into the 'industrialization of building', and by their enthusiasm carried the process further than architects had ever done before.[7] Yet the apostolic succession that runs from the pre-fabricated station-buildings for the L.M.S. before the war, through the Hertfordshire schools to CLASP and beyond, has failed to produce any major intellects of the sort one would expect such a rationalizing and analytical enterprise to need. It produced excellent organizers and good architects, it produced its own historian in the person of Guy Oddie,[8] but it produced no general theory.

The nearest approach to a major theoretical concept to emerge was the idea of

1. George R. Collins's small monograph, *Antonio Gaudí* (New York and London, 1960), was probably most influential, partly because of its modest price, more because of its readable, but impeccably scholarly tone.

2. See the present author's paper, 'Futurism and Modern Architecture', *R.I.B.A. Journal* (February 1957).

3. A prime source of information here was Conrads and Sperlich, *Phantastische Architektur* (Stuttgart, 1960); English translation with expanded notes and other revisions by George R. Collins and Christiane Crasemann Collins (London and New York, 1962).

4. His first contribution, 'Finsterlin', appeared in *Architectural Review* (November 1962). Pevsner also regards himself, with chronological jutsification, as a pioneer Gaudí-revivalist, with his radio talk, *The Strange Architecture of Antonio Gaudí* (reprinted in *The Listener*, 7 August 1952). Though this earned him a prize from the 'Amigos de Gaudí' in 1953, it was forgotten in subsequent discussion, except by Collins (see above, note 1).

5. 'Modern Architecture and the Historian, or: the Return of Historicism', in *R.I.B.A. Journal* (April 1961).

6. The first use of the term 'Neoliberty' appears to have been by the Italian historian of Piedmontese Baroque architecture, Paolo Portoghesi, in *Communità* (Milan, December 1958). See also *Architectural Review* (April 1959 and December 1959).

7. It remains true, however, that financial pressure in the U.S. home-building industry has driven the industrialization of building far beyond the British achievement, without benefit of either architects or general theories.

8. See 'The New English Humanism', in *Architectural Review* (September 1963).

endlessness, advanced as early as 1950 by John Weeks and (Lord) Richard Llewelyn-Davies, as an aesthetic interpretation of the façade composition of Mies van der Rohe's immediately post-war work.[1] This was probably the first break against the finite and closed aesthetics of the classicists to come from the 'scientific' side, and the breach was ignored, both the authors of the 'Endless' theory remaining *persona grata* with the classicists, and Llewelyn-Davies clearly regarding himself as an exponent of some sort of classicism still.[2] But when he returned to the theory of endlessness as applied to Mies in 1955, he was attacked on Wittkowerian grounds by Alan Colquhoun (for instance), who insisted on the closed, axial symmetry of these façades at Illinois Institute of Technology.[3]

Ten years later, when John Weeks presented a much richer and more complex version of the same propositions, in a paper on 'Indeterminacy' in the design of hospitals, the idea had gained such acceptance that he was virtually preaching to the converted.[4] Such 'scientific' concepts as open-endedness, the promulgation of growth and change as qualities to be incorporated in building-designs,[5] the acceptance of expendability and impermanence, all combined to bring on a kind of architecture, and architectural philosophy, that must have looked reassuringly familiar to the editors of the *Architectural Review*.

When applied to particular sites, that is. Those who had so often professed themselves disinterested in the *Review*'s repeated injunctions to follow the advice of Alexander Pope and 'Consult the genius of the place in all'[6] proved themselves adepts both in the theory and the practice of topographical consultation of this sort. The Smithsons had already paved the way for this in the Cluster City article,[7] and demonstrated the *praxis* in their design for the *Economist* buildings in St James's Street. James Stirling and James Gowan had resolved the almost impossible problems of the site of their Engineering Laboratories at Leicester University, in an asymmetrical composition of towers and low buildings that fully deserves the name of Picturesque,[8] as does Harvey Court in Cambridge, by Sir Leslie Martin and Colin St John Wilson (the father of Modern-Movement rationalism in England and his

1. 'Endless Architecture', in *Architectural Association Journal* (November 1951).

2. See his letter in *Architects' Journal* (3 November 1955), invoking Mondriaan, Mies, and the classical tradition back to Palladio.

3. In a discussion at the Institute of Contemporary Arts, May 1955.

4. 'Indeterminate Architecture', in *Transactions of the Bartlett Society*, II (1963–4).

5. The first systematic study of this topic will be found in Peter Cowan and Jill Nicholson, 'Growth and Change in Hospitals', ibid., III (1964–5), but the topic had been of growing interest for some years before, and many collegiate and university plans, for instance, had made real or token provision for growth, if not for change.

6. Epistle IV; to Richard Boyle, Earl of Burlington.   7. See note 4 on p. 270 above.

8. Pevsner has now, however, re-opened the quarrel of the factions by singling out the Engineering Laboratories at Leicester for attack in his radio talk *The Anti-Pioneers* (reprinted in *The Listener*, 29 December 1966 and 5 January 1967). The grounds of the quarrel have nothing to do with

most able follower), while the *Times* buildings by Llewelyn-Davies and Weeks are picturesque not only in the best intellectual sense in their ingenious adaptation to the site, but almost in the popular sense in the 'unfinished' gable-walls that proclaim the design's endlessness.

Such designs should best be regarded as the products of classical rationalism modified by the demands of the site – and thus, perhaps, more aptly compared to the work of Schinkel than to his English Picturesque contemporaries. For, if the Picturesque has triumphed once again as a pragmatic technique of site planning, it is still unacceptable to most thinking British architects as an aesthetic discipline, and the battles of the early nineteen-fifties are still being fought.

Thus, *The Times Literary Supplement* has recently reviewed[1] the Warwickshire volume of *The Buildings of England*.[2] After paying the inevitable and proper tribute to Pevsner's achievement in this series – for *The Buildings of England* is probably the most sustainedly distinguished feat of architectural writing in England in this century – the *T.L.S.* then turns on him and devotes fifteen column-inches to a denunciation of his defence of Sir Basil Spence's picturesque (in the picture-postcard sense) Coventry Cathedral. Not only is the language strong enough to include phraseology of the order of '*trahison du clerc*', and the required citation of Peter Hammond's *Liturgy and Architecture*,[3] which might yet prove to be the most influential English book on architecture of the sixties, but the argument is clinched by '...there was surely some duty not to pass over in silence the one really "uncompromising" entry – the not surprisingly unpremiated design of Alison and Peter Smithson'.

Not only was the Smithsons' entry in the Coventry Cathedral competition 'uncompromising' and anti-picturesque (it declined to make anything of the remains of the old bombed cathedral and proposed to sweep away all the ruins except the tower), but it was also laid out on a strict, quasi-Wittkowerian geometrical platt with a centralized, quasi-Renaissance plan. It was the last formal and geometrical project which the Smithsons produced, and this design of 1951 is still almost the last secure point in history on which the opponents of Picturesque compromise can rely, so total has been the triumph of the unacknowledged Picturesqueness of the Picturesque's avowed enemies.

the Picturesque ostensibly, but concern the architects' alleged return to Expressionism, against Pevsner's historical preference for the International Style.

1. 18 August 1966.   2. Harmondsworth, 1966.

3. London, 1960. Its influence still pervades all discussion of church design in England, has perverted the design of some important churches (e.g. Liverpool Metropolitan Cathedral) against its author's wishes, and has galvanized the design of others into a clarity and purposefulness rare in English church-building of the years immediately before its publication. Not even the Ministry of Education Bulletins have had quite so direct an effect – and this is a fair comparison, since Hammond himself invites it by recommending MoE pamphlet no. 33, as an 'admirable Lent book for bishops, archdeacons and ecclesiastical architects'.

A Select Bibliography of the Publications of Nikolaus Pevsner

BY JOHN BARR

T HIS select bibliography includes all Professor Pevsner's major scholarly publications up to the end of 1967; it lists each separately published book, and a selection of his many articles and reviews made according to their length, importance, or interest.

In order to trace the outline of his career as a scholar and the spread of his influence, the material has been arranged not by subject but by year of publication: the complete books of each year precede contributions to books, which are in turn followed by articles in journals, then book reviews. Within these sections, however, works are set out alphabetically by title, not chronologically. For convenience and conciseness, translations and later editions of a work are listed in one place below the original or first edition. The separate volumes of *The Buildings of England* have also been listed together under the year 1951.

Pagination is given as printed in each book or journal; the number of plates is stated only when the plates are numbered separately from the main pagination.

Certain early articles and reviews in periodicals have been recorded in brief collective entries only. Professor Pevsner's editorial work, especially as the editor of the *Pelican History of Art*, and as an editor of the *Architectural Review*, has not been mentioned.

A selection of Professor Pevsner's articles and essays will be re-issued in a volume to be published in 1968 by Thames & Hudson Ltd, London; texts originally in a foreign language will be translated into English. All these articles and essays are included in this bibliography, marked with an asterisk.

ABBREVIATIONS

AR	Architectural Review
Burl. Mag.	Burlington Magazine
RIBA	Royal Institute of British Architects
ZfbK	Zeitschrift für bildende Kunst

1925-28

[Reviews, including 14 articles on the International Art Exhibition, Dresden, 1926.] *Dresdner Anzeiger*, 1925–8.

[Reviews and notices.] *Cronache d'arte*, vols. 3–5, 1926–8.

1925

Gegenreformation und Manierismus.* *Repertorium für Kunstwissenschaft*, Bd. 46, 1925, pp. 243–62.

Die Gemälde des Giovanni Battista Crespi genannt Cerano. *Jahrbuch der preussischen Kunstsammlungen*, Bd. 46, 1925, pp. 259–85. Illus. See also Bd. 49, 1928.

1927

Catalogue of painters and draughtsmen represented in the library of reproductions of pictures and drawings formed by Sir Robert and Lady Witt (with supplement), London, 1920, 1925. *ZfbK*, Jahrg. 60, 1926–7: Beilage *Kunstchronik und Kunstliteratur*, February 1927, pp. 130–1.

1928

With Otto Grautoff: *Barockmalerei in den romanischen Ländern. Teil 1. Die italienische Malerei vom Ende der Renaissance bis zum ausgehenden Rokoko.* Von Dr Nikolaus Pevsner. 214 pp. *Teil 2. Die Malerei im Barockzeitalter in Frankreich und Spanien.* Von Dr Otto Grautoff. Akademische Verlagsgesellschaft Athenaion: Wildpark-Potsdam, 1928. 333 pp. 20 pl. Illus. (Handbuch der Kunstwissenschaft.)

Leipziger Barock. Die Baukunst der Barockzeit in Leipzig. Wolfgang Jess: Dresden, 1928. 208 pp. 102 pl. Plans.

Beiträge zur Stilgeschichte des Früh- und Hochbarock.* *Repertorium für Kunstwissenschaft*, Bd. 49, 1928, pp. 225–46.

Nachtrag zu Giovanni Battista Crespi genannt Cerano. *Jahrbuch der preussischen Kunstsammlungen*, Bd. 49, 1928, pp. 48–9. Illus. See also Bd. 46, 1925.

Eine Revision der Caravaggio-Daten. *ZfbK*, Jahrg. 61, 1927–8, pp. 386–92.

1929

Magnasco, Alessandro; Magnasco, Stefano. Ulrich Thieme and Felix Becker: *Allgemeines Lexikon der bildenden Künstler*, hrsg. von Hans Vollmer. E. A. Seeman: Leipzig, 1907–50. Bd. 23, 1929, pp. 560–1.

Das Altstädter Rathaus in Dresden und die Frage nach dem Schöpfer des Wiener Reichskanzleitraktes. *Zeitschrift für Denkmalpflege*, Jahrg. 3, 1929, pp. 125–8. Illus. Plan.

Giulio Cesare Procaccini. *Rivista d'arte*, anno 11 (Ser. 2, anno 1), luglio–settembre 1929, pp. 321–54. Illus.

Die Lehrjahre des Caravaggio. *ZfbK*, Jahrg. 62, 1928–9, pp. 278–88. Illus.

Die Rokoko-Ausstellung in Venedig. *ZfbK*, Jahrg. 63, 1929–30: Beilage *Kunstchronik und Kunstliteratur*, Oktober 1929, pp. 73–9. Illus.

Gino Damerini: *I pittori veneziani del Settecento*, Bologna, 1928. *Göttingische gelehrte Anzeigen*. Bd. 191, nr. 10, Oktober 1929, pp. 417–39. Illus. Bibliog.

1930

Ein Altargemälde von Gentileschi in Turin. *ZfbK*, Jahrg. 63, 1929–30, pp. 272–5. Illus.

Giorgio Nicodemi: *Pier Francesco Mazzucchelli detto il Morazzone*, Varese, 1927. *Repertorium für Kunstwissenschaft*, Bd. 51, 1930, pp. 260–3.

1931

Gemeinschaftsideale unter den bildenden Künstlern des 19. Jahrhunderts. *Deutsche Vierteljahrsschrift für Literaturwissenschaft und Geistesgeschichte*, Jahrg. 9, 1931, pp. 125–54.

Le Corbusier und Jeanneret. Ihr gesamtes Werk von 1910 bis 1929. Zürich, 1930. *Göttingische gelehrte Anzeigen*, Jahrg. 193, August 1931, pp. 303–12.

1932

Die Wandlung um 1650 in der italienischen Malerei.* *Wiener Jahrbuch für Kunstgeschichte*, Bd. 8 (22), 1932, pp. 69–92. Illus.

1933

Die Bautätigkeit des Heiligen Godehard am Hildesheimer Dom. *Die Denkmalpflege: Zeitschrift für Denkmalpflege und Heimatschutz*, 1933, pp. 210–14. Illus. Plan.

An unknown early work of the School of Caravaggio. *Art in America*, vol. 22, December 1933, pp. 16–17. Plate.

Ernst Michalski: *Die Bedeutung der ästhetischen Grenze für die Methode der Kunstgeschichte*. Berlin, 1932. (Kunstwissenschaftliche Studien Bd. 11.) *Zeitschrift für Kunstgeschichte*, Bd. 2, 1933, pp. 40–4.

Rationelle Bebauungsweisen. Ergebnisse des 3. Internationalen Kongresses für neues Bauen (Brussels, 1930), Frankfurt am Main, 1931. *Zeitschrift für Ästhetik und allgemeine Kunstwissenschaft*, Bd. 27, 1933, pp. 86–9.

Aby Warburg: *Gesammelte Schriften*, Leipzig, 1932. *Theologische Literaturzeitung*, Jahrg. 58, 23 Dezember 1933, col. 465–70.

1934

Das Englische in der englischen Kunst. Die retrospektive Ausstellung britischer Kunst in der Londoner Akademie. *Deutsche Zukunft: Wochenzeitung für Politik Wirtschaft und Kultur*, Jahrg. 2, 4 Februar 1934, p. 15.

Zur Kunst der Goethezeit. Übersicht über das Schrifttum des letzten Jahrzehntes. *Deutsche Vierteljahrsschrift für Literaturwissenschaft und Geistesgeschichte*, Jahrg. 12, 1934, pp. 306–27.

1936

Pioneers of the Modern Movement from William Morris to Walter Gropius. Faber & Faber: London, 1936. 240 pp. Illus.

Published in the U.S.A. by Frederick A. Stokes Co.: New York, 1936. Reprinted 1937.

Pioneers of modern design from William Morris to Walter Gropius. Second edition [of *Pioneers of the Modern Movement*]. Museum of Modern Art: New York, 1949. 151 pp. Illus. Reprinted 1957.

Revised and partly rewritten edition. Penguin Books: Harmondsworth, 1960. 253 pp. Illus. (A 497.)

[Corrected, with a bibliography of new literature.] 1964. 255 pp. Illus. Reprinted 1966.

TRANSLATIONS:

I pionieri del movimento moderno da William Morris a Walter Gropius. Traduzione di Giuliana Baracco. Rosa e Ballo: Milan, 1945. viii, 130 pp. 8 pl.

I pionieri dell'architettura moderna. Tradotta da Enrica Labò. Edizioni Calderini: Bologna, (1963). xiv, 215 pp. (Città nuova 2.)

Modan dezain no tenkai. [i.e. The development of modern design.] Translated by Hirozō Shiraishi. Misuzu Shobō: Tokyo, 1957. 167 pp. 33 pl.

Wegbereiter moderner Formgebung von Morris bis Gropius. Übersetzung von Elisabeth Knauth. Rowohlt: Hamburg, 1957. 142 pp. Plates. Bibliog. (Rowohlts deutsche Enzyklopädie 33.)

Os pioneiros do desenho moderno. Tradução de João Paulo Monteiro. Editora Ulisseia: Lisbon, 1964. 190 pp. Illus. (Colecção Livros Pelicano AM8.)

The designer in industry. *AR*, vol. 79, 1936: April, pp. 185–90; June, pp. 291–6; vol. 80, 1936: July, pp. 45–8; August, pp. 87–90; September, pp. 127–9; October, pp. 179–82; November, pp. 227–30. Illus.

Post-War tendencies in German art-schools. *Journal of the Royal Society of Arts*, vol. 84, 17 January 1936, pp. 248–62.

Some notes on Abraham Janssens. *Burl. Mag.*, vol. 69, September 1936, pp. 120–30. Plates.

William Morris, C. R. Ashbee und das zwanzigste Jahrhundert. *Deutsche Vierteljahrsschrift für Literaturwissenschaft und Geistesgeschichte*, Jahrg. 14, 1936, pp. 536–62.

ENGLISH TRANSLATION 1956: William Morris, C. R. Ashbee and the twentieth century. *Manchester Review*, vol. 7, Winter 1956, pp. 437–58. Illus. Bibliog.

1937

An enquiry into industrial art in England. University Press: Cambridge, 1937. xi, 234 pp. 24 pl.

Clarendon Palace, eine Pfalz der englischen Könige. *Der Burgwart: Jahrbuch der Vereinigung zur Erhaltung deutscher Burgen für 1937*, Jahrg. 38, pp. 48–52. Illus. Plan.

Minor masters of the XIXth century. IX. Christopher Dresser, industrial designer. *AR*, vol. 82, April 1937, pp. 183–6. Illus.

1938

With Sacheverell Sitwell: *German Baroque sculpture.* With 48 photographs by Anthony Ayscough and descriptive notes by Nikolaus Pevsner. Duckworth: London, 1938. pp. 49–84. 48 pl. Bibliog.

English and German art, and their interrelations. *German Life & Letters*, O.S. vol. 2, July 1938, pp. 251–9. Bibliog.

Fifty years of Arts and Crafts. A review by Nikolaus Pevsner and an early commentary by Bernard Shaw [on the Arts and Crafts exhibition, 1888, published in *The World*, 3 October 1888]. *The Studio*, vol. 116, November 1938, pp. 225–30. Illus.

The first plywood furniture. *AR*, vol. 84, August 1938, pp. 75–6. Illus.

Harlech und Beaumaris, der Höhepunkt britischer Burgenarchitektur. *Der Burgwart: Jahrbuch der Vereinigung zur Erhaltung deutscher Burgen für 1938*, Jahrg. 39, pp. 32–8. Illus. Plans.

A pioneer designer: Arthur H. Mackmurdo.* *AR*, vol. 83, March 1938, pp. 141–3. Illus.

1939

George Walton, his life and work.* *Journal of the RIBA*, 3rd Ser., vol. 46, 3 April 1939, pp. 537–48. Illus.

The history of plywood up to 1914. *AR*, vol. 86, September 1939, pp. 129–30. Illus.

1940

Academies of art past and present. University Press: Cambridge, 1940. xiv, 323 pp. Plates. Bibliog.

Published in the U.S.A. by Macmillan: New York, 1940.

Charles F. Annesley Voysey.* *Elsevier's Maandschrift.* Jaarg. 50, Mei 1940, pp. 343–55. Illus. Plans.

1941

Criticism. By Peter F. R. Donner [i.e. Nikolaus Pevsner]. *AR*, vol. 90, August–December 1941. Illus.

Omega. [On Roger Fry and the Omega Workshops.] *AR*, vol. 90, August 1941, pp. 45–8. Illus.

Whistler's Valparaiso Harbour at the Tate Gallery. *Burl. Mag.*, vol. 79, October 1941, pp. 115–21. Plate.

Richard Norman Shaw, 1831–1912. Sir Reginald Blomfield: *Richard Norman Shaw. R.A., architect 1831–1912*, London, 1940. *AR*, vol. 89, March 1941, pp. 41–6. Illus.

Reprinted 1963: *Victorian architecture.* Edited by P. Ferriday. pp. 235–46.

1942

An outline of European architecture. Penguin Books: Harmondsworth; New York. 1942. 159 pp. 32 pl. Plans. Bibliog. (A 109.)

Revised and enlarged edition. 1945. 237 pp. 48 pl.

New and enlarged edition. John Murray: London, 1948. xxi, 238 pp. Plates. Illus. Plans. Bibliog.

First American edition. Charles Scribner's Sons: New York, 1948.

Second revised [i.e. third] edition. Penguin Books: Harmondsworth, 1951. 301 pp. 64 pl. Bibliog.

Fourth edition, revised and enlarged. 1953. 317 pp. 64 pl. Bibliog.

Fifth edition, revised and enlarged. 1957. 328 pp. 64 pl. Bibliog. Reprinted 1958, 1959, 1961.

Sixth, jubilee edition. 1960. 740 pp. Illus. Plans. Bibliog. Reprinted 1961.

Seventh edition. 1963. 496 pp. Illus. Plans. Bibliog.

TRANSLATIONS:

Geschiedenis van de bouwkunst in Europa. Nederlandse vertaling van E. Kossmann. Ad. Donker: Rotterdam, 1949. xiv, 273 pp. Illus. Reprinted 1960, 1965 (Donker-pockets 32).

Yōroppa kenchiku josetsu [i.e. An introducto European architecture. Translated by Bunji Kobayashi.] Shōkokusha Publishing Co.: Tokyo, 1953. xiv, 292 pp. Plates. Plans. Bibliog. Reprinted 1963.

Europäische Architektur von den Anfängen bis zur Gegenwart. Übersetzt von Kurd Windels, Prestel Verlag: Munich, 1957. 740 pp. Illus. Plans. Bibliog.

[Later German edition.] 1963. 547 pp. Studienausgabe.

Esquema de la arquitectura europea. Versión castellana corregida y ampliada de René Taylor. Revisión de Emilio Orozco Díaz. Ediciónes Infinito: Buenos Aires, 1957. 351 pp. Plates. Plans. Bibliog. (Biblioteca de arquitectura vol. 2.)

Storia dell'architettura europea. Traduzione di Enrica Labò. Laterza: Bari, 1959. xi, 407 pp. Plates. Plans. Bibliog. (Biblioteca di cultura moderna vol. 535.)

Seconda edizione. 1963. 418 pp.

[Later edition.] 1966. 427 pp. (Universale Laterza 42.)

[Another Italian edition.] Il Saggiatore: Milan, 1966.

Perspectiva da arquitectura europeia. Tradução de Ernesto de Sousa. Ulisseia: Lisbon, [1964?] 420 pp. Plates. (Livros pelicano AM 15.)

Génie de l'architecture européenne. Traduction Renée Plouin. Tallandier: Paris, 1965. 430 pp. Illus. Plans. Bibliog.

A bronze statuette by Peter Vischer the elder. *Burl. Mag.,* April 1942, pp. 90–3. Plates.

The evolution of the easy chair. *AR*, vol. 91, March 1942, pp. 59–62. Illus.

Nine swallows – no summer. [On certain early twentieth century buildings in Britain.] *AR*, vol. 91, May 1942, pp. 109–12. Illus.

Patient progress: the life work of Frank Pick.* *AR*, vol. 92, August 1942, pp. 31–48. Illus.

The term 'architect' in the Middle Ages. *Speculum*, vol. 17, October 1942, pp. 549–62.

Terms of architectural planning in the Middle Ages. *Journal of the Warburg and Courtauld Institutes*, vol. 5, 1942, pp. 232–7.

Treasure hunt. Critical notes [on nineteenth century buildings] by Peter F. R. Donner [i.e. Nikolaus Pevsner]. *AR*, vols. 91–2, January–December 1942.

1943

The end of the pattern books. By Peter F. R. Donner [i.e. Nikolaus Pevsner]. *AR*, March 1943, pp. 75–9. Illus. Plan.

A Harris florilegium. By Peter F. R. Donner [i.e. Nikolaus Pevsner. On Thomas Harris: *Victorian architecture*, 1860]. *AR*, vol. 93, February 1943, pp. 51–2.

Model houses for the labouring classes. Compiled by Nikolaus Pevsner.* *AR*, vol. 93, May 1943, pp. 119–28. Illus. Plans.

A short Pugin florilegium. Compiled by N. Pevsner. *AR*, vol. 94, August 1943, pp. 31–4. Illus.

1944

The genesis of the Picturesque.* *AR*, vol. 96, November 1944, pp. 139–46. Illus.

Price on picturesque planning.* [A summary of Sir Uvedale Price: *An essay on the Picturesque*, 1810, compiled by Nikolaus Pevsner.] *AR*, vol. 95, February 1944, pp. 47–50.

1945

The leaves of Southwell. Photographs by F. L. Attenborough. Penguin Books: London & New York, 1945. 71 pp. 32 pl. Illus. Plan. (K17).

With Geoffrey Grigson: The *Architectural Review* Gothic number: Act 2: Romantic Gothic: Scene 1: Goethe and Strassburg. [A translation, with marginal commentary by Nikolaus Pevsner.] *AR*, vol. 98, December 1945, pp. 156–9. Illus.

Thoughts on Henry Moore. *Burl. Mag.*, vol. 86, February 1945, pp. 47–9.

1946

The architecture of Mannerism. *The Mint*. A miscellany of literature, art and criticism. Edited by Geoffrey Grigson. Routledge & Sons: London, 1946. pp. 116–37. Plates. Bibliog.

Rococo to Romanticism. Sidney Fiske Kimball: *The creation of Rococo*, Philadelphia Museum of Art, 1943. *Times Literary Supplement*, 23 March 1946, pp. 133–4.

1947

The other Chambers [i.e. Sir William Chambers]. *AR*, vol. 101, June 1947, pp. 195–8. Illus.

The Picturesque in architecture. Read before the Royal Institute of British Architects, 25 November 1947. *Journal of the RIBA*, Ser. 3, vol. 55, December 1947, pp. 55–61. Illus.

The English sculptor. Katharine A. Esdaile: *English church monuments, 1510 to 1840*, London, 1947. *Times Literary Supplement*, 9 August 1947, pp. 397–8.

1948

With S. Lang: Apollo or baboon.* [On the Greek Doric revival.] *AR*, vol. 104, December 1948, pp. 271–9. Illus.

Design in relation to industry through the ages.* Cobb Lecture, 24 November 1948. *Journal of the Royal Society of Arts*, vol. 97, 31 December 1948, pp. 90–100.

Humphry Repton: a florilegium. *AR*, vol. 103, February 1948, pp. 53–9. Illus. Plans.

Monsù Desiderio, a little-known precursor of Rococo and Gothick. [On François de Nomé, called Francisco Desiderio.] *AR*, vol. 104, September 1948, p. 149. Bibliog.

1949

Helmut Gernsheim: *Focus on architecture and sculpture*. An original approach to the photography of architecture and sculpture. With a foreword by Nikolaus Pevsner. Fountain Press: London, 1949. Foreword: pp. 9–13.

Early iron: 2. Curvilinear hothouses. *AR*, vol. 106, September 1949, pp. 188–9. Plans.

Judges VI, 34. On Lewis Mumford and Sigfried Giedion. [With special reference to Sigfried Giedion: *Mechanization takes command, a contribution to anonymous history*. New York, 1948.] *AR*, vol. 106, August 1949, pp. 77–9.

Richard Payne Knight.* *The Art Bulletin*, vol. 31, no. 4, December 1949, pp. 293–320.

With S. Lang: Sir William Temple and Sharawaggi. *AR*, vol. 106, December 1949, pp. 391–3. Illus. Bibliog.

1950

Charles R. Mackintosh.* Traduzione di Cornelia Tamborini. Il Balcone: Milan, 1950. 151 pp. Illus. Bibliog. (Architetti del movimento moderno no. 8.)

Matthew Digby Wyatt. The first Cambridge Slade Professor of Fine Art.* An inaugural lecture. University Press: Cambridge, 1950. 44 pp. 6 pl. Bibliog.

Double profile: a reconsideration of the Elizabethan style as seen at Wollaton. *AR*, vol. 107, March 1950, pp. 147–53. Illus. Plans.

Good King James's Gothic.* *AR*, vol. 107, February 1950, pp. 117–22. Illus. Plans.

SELECT PEVSNER BIBLIOGRAPHY

1951

The Buildings of England. Penguin Books: Harmondsworth, 1951– . Plates. Illus. Plans. Maps. Bibliog. [The imprint varies.]

    Cornwall. 1951. 251 pp. 64 pl. (BE 1.)

    Nottinghamshire. 1951. 248 pp. 64 pl. (BE 2.)

    Middlesex. 1951. 204 pp. 64 pl. (BE 3.)

    North Devon. 1952. 200 pp. 48 pl. (BE 4.)

    South Devon. 1952. 351 pp. 80 pl. (BE 5.)

    London, except the Cities of London and West-minster. 1952. 496 pp. 64 pl. (BE 6.)

    Hertfordshire. 1953. 313 pp. 64 pl. (BE 7.)

    Derbyshire. 1953. 282 pp. 64 pl. (BE 8.)

    County Durham. 1953. 279 pp. 64 pl. (BE 9.)

    Cambridgeshire. 1954. 453 pp. 72 pl. (BE 10.)

    Essex. 1954. 440 pp. 64 pl. (BE 11.)

        Second edition. Revised by Enid Radcliffe. 1965. 482 pp. 64 pl.

    London. I. The Cities of London and West-minster. 1957. 631 pp. 96 pl. (BE 12.)

        Second edition. 1962. 696 pp. 96 pl.

    Northumberland. With notes on the Roman antiquities by Ian A. Richmond. 1957. 362 pp. 64 pl. (BE 15.)

    North Somerset and Bristol. 1958. 510 pp. 72 pl. (BE 13.)

    South and West Somerset. 1958. 394 pp. 56 pl. (BE 14.)

    Shropshire. 1958. 368 pp. 64 pl. (BE 16.)

    Yorkshire. The West Riding. 1959. 603 pp. 72 pl. (BE 17.)

    Leicestershire and Rutland. 1960. 373 pp. 64 pl. (BE 18.)

    Buckinghamshire. 1960. 340 pp. 64 pl. (BE 19.)

    Suffolk. 1961. 516 pp. 64 pl. (BE 20.)

    Northamptonshire. 1961. 510 pp. 64 pl. (BE 22.)

    With Ian Nairn: *Surrey.* 1962. 501 pp. 64 pl. (BE 21.)

    North-East Norfolk and Norwich. 1962. 390 pp. 64 pl. (BE 23.)

    North-West and South Norfolk. 1962. 438 pp. 64 pl. (BE 24.)

    Herefordshire. 1963. 364 pp. 64 pl. (BE 25.)

    Wiltshire. With notes on the prehistoric and Roman antiquities by Derek Simpson. 1963. 578 pp. 64 pl. (BE 26.)

    With John Harris: *Lincolnshire.* 1964. 768 pp. 64 pl. (BE 27.)

    With Ian Nairn: *Sussex.* 1965. 692 pp. 64 pl. (BE 28.)

    Yorkshire. The North Riding. 1966. 454 pp. 64 pl. (BE 29.)

    Berkshire. 1966. 355 pp. 64 pl. (BE 30.)

    With Alexandra Wedgwood: *Warwickshire.* 1966. 529 pp. 64 pl. (BE 31.)

    With David Lloyd: *Hampshire and the Isle of Wight.* 1967. 832 pp. Plates. (BE 32.)

    Cumberland and Westmorland. 1967. 339 pp. Plates. (BE 33.)

Building with wit. The architecture of Sir Edwin Lutyens. *AR*, vol. 109, April 1951, pp. 217–25. Illus.

COID: Progress report. Industrial design: 1951. [An examination of the exhibits chosen by the Council of Industrial Design for the South Bank exhibition.] *AR*, vol. 110, December 1951, pp. 353–9. Illus.

Canons of criticism. [A discussion of Coventry Cathedral, and of certain letters to *The Times*.] *AR*, vol. 109, January 1951, pp. 3–6.

    SPANISH TRANSLATION: Cánones de la crítica. [A translation by Raul Gonzalez Capdevila.] Faculdad de Arquitec tura y Urbanismo, Universidad de Buenos Aires; Ministerio de Educación: Buenos Aires, 1954.

Il Festival di Londra. *Comunità*, 12 ottobre 1951, pp. 48–51.

Goethe e l'architettura.* *Palladio: rivista di storia dell'architettura*, N.S. anno I, ottobre–dicembre 1951, pp. 174–9.

High Victorian design. A study of the exhibits of 1851. Architectural Press: London, 1951. 162 pp. Illus.

SELECT PEVSNER BIBLIOGRAPHY

1952

Art furniture of the eighteen-seventies.* *AR*, vol. 111, January 1952, pp. 43–50. Illus.

Schinkel.* Paper read before the RIBA, 11 December 1951. *Journal of the RIBA*, 3rd Ser., vol. 59, January 1952, pp. 89–96. Illus.

The strange architecture of Antonio Gaudí. *The Listener*, 7 August 1952, pp. 213–14. Illus.

Thoughts on Coventry Cathederal. *The Listener*, 17 January 1952, pp. 94–6.

Tintoretto and Mannerism. *AR*, vol. 111, June 1952, pp. 361–5. Illus.

1953

A note on the art of the Exeter carvers. C. J. P. Cave: *Mediaeval carvings in Exeter cathedral.* Penguin Books: Harmondsworth, 1953. pp. 25–32. 64 pl. (K41.)

Bristol, Troyes, Gloucester. The character of the early fourteenth century in architecture. *AR*, vol. 113, February 1953, pp. 88–98. Illus. Plan.

British Museum: some unsolved problems of its architectural history. *AR*, vol 113, March 1953, pp. 179–82. Illus. Plan.

Colonel Gillum and the Pre-Raphaelites. *Burl. Mag.*, vol. 95, March 1953, pp. 78–81. Plates.

Johannesburg: the development of a contemporary vernacular in the Transvaal. *AR*, vol. 113, June 1953, pp. 361–82. Illus. Plans.

1954

Arts, manufactures and commerce 1754–1954. The three Bicentenary Lectures: I. The Arts. By Nikolaus Pevsner, 23 March 1954. *Journal of the Royal Society of Arts*, vol. 102, Bicentenary issue II, 16 April 1954, pp. 392–405.

Old Somerset House. *AR*, vol. 116, September 1954, pp. 163–7. Illus. Plans.

Sir Christopher Wren. (Paper read 19 March 1954.) *Proceedings of the Royal Institution of Great Britain*, vol. 35, no. 161, 1954, pp. 734–9. Plans.

Twentieth century Picturesque: an answer to Basil Taylor's broadcast. [On English art and the Picturesque, published in *The Listener*, 1954.] *AR*, vol. 115, April 1954, pp. 227–9. Illus.

1955

Michael Farr: *Design in British industry. A mid-century survey.* With a foreword and postscript by Nikolaus Pevsner. University Press: Cambridge, 1955. Foreword: pp. xxvii–xxviii. Postscript: pp. 310–20.

Hill Hall [Essex]. *AR*, vol. 117, May 1955, pp. 307–9. Illus.

1956

The Englishness of English art. An expanded and annotated version of the Reith Lectures broadcast in October and November 1955. Architectural Press: London, 1956. 208 pp. Illus. Plans.

> Published in the U.S.A. by Praeger: New York, 1956.

> Originally published in *The Listener*, 20 October–1 December 1955.

> Later edition. Penguin Books: Harmondsworth, 1964. 229 pp. Illus. Plans. (Y35.)

Palladio and Europe. *Venezia e l'Europa.* Atti del XVIII Congresso Internazionale di Storia dell'Arte, Venezia, 12–18 settembre 1955. Arte Veneta: Venice, 1956. pp. 81–94.

With S. Lang: The Egyptian Revival.* *AR*, vol. 119, May 1956, pp. 242–54. Illus.

Fischer von Erlach, 1656–1723. *AR*, vol. 120, October 1956, pp. 215–17. Illus.

1957

Architecture and William Morris.* Read at the RIBA on 19 February. *Journal of the RIBA*, Ser. 3, vol. 44, March 1957, pp. 172–7.

Bohemian Hawksmoor. [On Giovanni Santini Aichel.] *AR*, vol. 121, February 1957, pp. 112–14. Illus.

An Italian miscellany: Pedrocchino and some allied problems. *AR*, vol. 122, August 1957, pp. 112–15. Illus. Bibliog.

Universities: 1. Yesterday. *AR*, vol. 122, October 1957, pp. 234–9. Illus.

1958

Christopher Wren, 1632–1725. Traduzione di Enrica Labò. Electa: Milan, 1958. 64 pl. Plans. Bibliog. (Astra–Arengarium. Serie architetti no. 45.)

With Michael Meier: *Grünewald.* Thames & Hudson: London, 1958. 44 pp. 117 + 26 pl. An introduction to Grünewald's art: pp. 9–19.

Georgian sculptors: Victor Alexander Sederbach. *AR*, vol. 123, May 1958, pp. 332–4. Illus.

The three dimensional arch from the sixteenth to the eighteenth century. *Journal of the Society of Architectural Historians*, vol. 17, no. 4, Winter 1958, pp. 22–4. Illus. Plan.

1959

Commonwealth I. [On modern architecture in Canada, South Africa, Australia, New Zealand.] *AR*, vol. 126, October 1959, pp. 149–217. Illus.

Roehampton: LCC housing and the picturesque tradition. *AR*, vol. 126, July 1959, pp. 21–35. Illus.

Time and Le Corbusier. [A plea for the preservation of Le Corbusier's early works.] *AR*, vol. 125, March 1959, pp. 159–65. Illus.

   GERMAN TRANSLATION: Die Zeit und Le Corbusier. *Deutsche Bauzeitung*, vol. 65, Juli 1960, pp. 367–72. Illus.

1960

Architecture and the applied arts. *The sources of the XXth century. The arts in Europe from 1884 to 1914.* [Catalogue of the Council of Europe exhibition, Paris, 4 November 1960–23 January 1961.] Musée National d'Art Moderne: Paris, 1960, 61. pp. 41–55. Plates.

Art and architecture. *New Cambridge modern history.* vol. 10: 1830–70. University Press: Cambridge, 1960, Ch. 6, pp. 134–55.

Architecture after 1960: propositions. *AR*, vol. 127, June 1960, pp. 381–6.

The east end of Winchester Cathedral. *Winchester Cathedral Record*, 1960, pp. 7–10. Plates.

The planning of the Elizabethan country house. An inaugural lecture delivered at Birkbeck College 23 May 1960. Birkbeck College: London, 1961. 24 pp. 4 pl. Plans.

1961

With Jean Cassou and Émile Langui: *Les sources du vingtième siècle.* Éditions des Deux-Mondes: Paris, 1961. 363 pp. Plates. Illus. (L'art et la culture.) L'architecture et les arts appliqués par Nikolaus Pevsner: pp. 229–60.

   BELGIAN EDITION: Éditions de la Connaissance: Brussels, 1961. (Collection 'Le Conseil de l'Europe' 2.)

   ENGLISH EDITION: *The sources of modern art.* Translated by Katherine M. Delavenay and H. Leigh Farnell. Thames and Hudson: London, 1962.

   AMERICAN EDITION: *Gateway to the twentieth century; art and culture in a changing world.* McGraw-Hill: New York, 1962.

   GERMAN EDITION: *Durchbruch zum 20. Jahrhundert. Kunst und Kultur der Jahrhundertwende.* Die Übersetzungen besorgten Eleanore Seitz [and others]. Georg D. W. Callwey: Munich, 1962.

   ITALIAN EDITION: *Le origini dell'arte moderna.* Traduzione: Enrica Labò [and others]. Electa: Milan, 1962.

   SPANISH EDITION: *Génesis del siglo XX.* Salvat: Barcelona, 1963.

John Bodt in England. *AR*, vol. 130, July 1961, pp. 29–34. Illus.

Lethaby's last. [On W. R. Lethaby's church at Brockhampton, Herefordshire.] *AR*, vol. 130, November 1961, pp. 354–7. Illus.

Libraries: nutrimentum spiritus. *AR*, vol. 131, October 1961, pp. 240–4. Illus. Plan.

Modern architecture and the historian, or the return of historicism.* [A lecture.] Given at the RIBA on 10 January. *Journal of the RIBA*, 3rd Ser., vol. 68, April 1961, pp. 230–40. Illus.

BROADCAST VERSION: The return of historicism in architecture. *The Listener*, 16 February 1961, pp. 299–301.

GERMAN TRANSLATION: Moderne Architektur und der Historiker oder, die Wiederkehr des Historismus. *Deutsche Bauzeitung*, Jahrg. 66, Oktober 1961, pp. 757–64.

EXTRACT: *Historismus und bildende Kunst*, 1965, pp. 116–17.

1962

Art and architecture. *New Cambridge modern history*. vol. 11: 1870–98. University Press: Cambridge, 1962. Ch. 6, pp. 154–76.

Faith and feasibility. Nikolaus Pevsner analyses the architecture of Coventry Cathedral. *The Guardian*, 25 May 1962, p. 6. Illus. Plan.

Finsterlin and some others. [On Hermann Finsterlin.] *AR*, vol. 132, November 1962, pp. 353–7. Illus.

Gordon Russell and twentieth century furniture.* *AR*, vol. 132, December 1962, pp. 421–8. Illus.

1963

The choir of Lincoln Cathedral. An interpretation, Oxford University Press: London, New York, 1963. 15 pp. Plates. Plans. (Charlton Lectures on Art delivered at King's College in the University of Durham, Newcastle upon Tyne.)

Victorian prolegomena. pp. 21–36. Richard Norman Shaw. pp. 235–46. Illus. Plates. *Victorian architecture*. Edited by P. Ferriday. Jonathan Cape: London, 1963.

Visión de la arquitectura en 1963. *Arquitectura 63*. Publicación de la Escuela Tecnica Superior de Arquitectura de Barcelona: Barcelona, [1963]. pp. 9–12. Illus.

ITALIAN TRANSLATION: Un allarme di Nikolaus Pevsner. Si ritorna all'architettura di facciata? *L'Architettura*, anno 9, ottobre 1963, pp. 482–3.

Gropius and Van de Velde. [With special reference to Henry Van de Velde: *Geschichte meines Lebens*, Munich, 1962.] *AR*, vol. 133, March 1963, pp. 165–8. Illus.

Rede zur Eröffnung des Gebäudes der Kunst- und Architekturabteilung der Universität Yale, New Haven. Address at the inauguration of the Building of the Fine Arts and Architecture Department of Yale University, New Haven.* *Deutsche Bauzeitung*, vol. 68, 1963, pp. 432–4. Illus. Plans.

1964

History of the DIA [Design and Industries Association].* *DIA Yearbook*, 1964: Fiftieth anniversary issue, pp. 34–52. Illus.

With Enid Radcliffe: Randall Wells. *AR*, vol. 136, November 1964, pp. 366–8. Illus.

1965

With M. Besset, H. G. Evers, and L. Grote: *Historismus und bildende Kunst. Vorträge und Diskussion im Oktober 1963 in München und Schloss Anif.* Prestel Verlag: Munich, 1965. (Forschungsunternehmen der Fritz Thyssen Stiftung. Arbeitskreis Kunstgeschichte: Studien zur Kunst des neunzehnten Jahrhunderts Bd. 1.) Möglichkeiten und Aspekte des Historismus. Versuch einer Frühgeschichte und Typologie des Historismus: pp. 13–24; Diskussion unter Leitung von Nikolaus Pevsner. pp. 73–106; Nachwort: pp. 107–13; Anhang: Die Wiederkehr des Historismus: pp. 116–17.

Goodhart-Rendel's roll-call. [A transcript of a conversation between H. S. Goodhart-Rendel and Nikolaus Pevsner in July 1946.] *AR*, vol. 138, October 1965, pp. 259–64. Illus.

1966

With John Fleming and Hugh Honour: *The Penguin dictionary of architecture*. Penguin Books: Harmondsworth, 1966. 248 pp. Illus. Plans. (R13.)

Ludwig Münz and Gustav Künstler: *Adolf Loos: pioneer of modern architecture*. With an introduction by Nikolaus Pevsner and an appreciation by Oskar Kokoschka. Translated from the German [*Der Architekt Adolf Loos*] by Harold Meek. Thames & Hudson: London, 1966. Introduction: pp. 13–22.

Edoardo Persico: *Tutte le opere*, 1923–35. Milan, 1964. *AR*, vol. 139, February 1966, pp. 97–8.

1967

Eric Mendelsohn: letters of an architect. Edited by Oskar Beyer. Translated by Geoffrey Strachan with an introduction by Nikolaus Pevsner. Abelard-Schuman: London, New York, Toronto. 1967. Introduction pp. 13–20.

Nikolaus Pevsner, 1967 Gold Medallist. [The RIBA Gold Medal address.] *Journal of the RIBA*, 3rd Ser., vol. 74, August 1967, pp. 316–18. Illus.

Quarr and Bellot. [On Quarr Abbey, Isle of Wight, designed by Dom Paul Bellot.] *AR*, vol. 141, April 1967, pp. 307–10. Illus.

Sara Losh's church. [At Wreay, Cumberland.] *AR*, vol. 142, July 1967, pp. 65–7. Illus.

Index

Note references are given in the form 51³, which indicates page 51, note 3. Material in the Notes is referenced only where there is no direct reference to the subject in the text. Names in parentheses after book titles refer to the author of the work; after places and buildings to commentators upon them. Topographical works are indexed under the name of the town or county which is the subject of the work, biographies under the name of their subject.

INDEX

INDEX

INDEX

INDEX

INDEX

Note on the Illustrations

The following photographs were obtained by the courtesy of the sources indicated, to whom we wish to express our gratitude: Plates 8 and 9, Collection Destailleur, Bibliothèque Nationale, Paris; Plate 10, Drummond Young, Edinburgh; Plate 12, Giraudon, Paris; Plate 16, British Museum, London; Plate 21, The New-York Historical Society; Plates 23 and 24, The Shaffer Library, Union College, Schenectady; Plate 26, George Hersey; Plate 28, the late Carroll L. V. Meeks.